CW00458510

G.E.M. SKUES

Books by the same author

F.M. Halford and the Dry-Fly Revolution

ISBN 978-0-7198-1058-9
ISBN 978-0-7198-1371-9 (Collectors' Edition)

Robert Hale Limited
Clerkenwell House
Clerkenwell Green
London EC1R 0HT

www.halebooks.com

A catalogue record for this book is available from the British Library

2 4 6 8 10 9 7 5 3 1

Typeset by e-type, Liverpool
Printed in Great Britain by Berforts Information Press

G.E.M. SKUES

THE MAN OF THE NYMPH

TONY HAYTER

Robert Hale · London

Contents

For

Acknowledgements

Iowe a considerable debt of gratitude to many people who have been uncomplainingly helpful to me in many different ways while I was assembling the material for this book.

The following people kindly allowed me access to useful material: John Austin, Simon Ball, Marie Hélène Barbotin and Annick Barbotin, David Beazley, Brian Clarke, Mark Cope, William Daniel, John and Judith Head, John Knott, Dr Jean and Mme Françoise Niaussat, Janet Robson and Malcolm Thorne.

In my researches in the Flyfishers' Club I have been guided by John Morgan, who has the care of the unique stock of manuscripts and memorabilia, and by David Beazley, who looks after one of the great angling libraries of the world. I am also grateful for the help of the former Secretary of the Club Tim Boycott and his successor Paul Varney.

John Mundt, former President of the Anglers' Club of New York, discovered several interesting items for me and was a welcoming host during my visit to the Club. My time doing research at the Rare Books and Special Collections section of the great library at Princeton University was made much more pleasant and fruitful by the help and kindness of Charles Greene, AnnaLee Pauls and the staff.

I am grateful for the professional attention of staff at the Bodleian Library, the British LiΦbrary and the Salisbury Public Library. Suzanne Forster guided me in the hunt for records of Skues' schooldays at the Winchester College Archive, Raya McGeorge helped me to unearth valuable finds in the library of the Fishmongers' Company and Christine Fletcher and Anne Harrison of the Victoria College at Jersey provided me with information about Skues' final year of schooling

I am indebted to Roy Darlington and Stewart Newell for allowing me to explore the fishery at Abbots Barton for photo (and fishing) opportunities. For access to the two fisheries frequented by Skues at the latter end of his life I have to thank Chris Rolfe of the Wilton Estate Office and David Nickol, who piloted me around the meadows. Photography of

Skues' paraphernalia at the Flyfishers' Club has been expertly dealt with by my son-in-law Simon Turtle.

I would like to thank Mr T. Chaytor Norris for granting permission to reproduce an image of G.E.M. Skues fishing on the Itchen in Winchester, the National Portrait Gallery for leave to use the Howard Coster image of Skues, the Princeton University Library for allowing me to deploy quotations from the papers of Louis Bouglé and Robert Austin, *The Times* (NI Syndication) for permission to quote from the correspondence columns of March 1935, the Anglers' Club of New York for permission to quote from the letters of Theodore Gordon and Edward Boies, and the Flyfishers' Club for permission to quote from material in their possession.

I have also appreciated the support and help of a number of people, which has shown itself in hints, discussions, a free and friendly exchange of information and simply a general helpfulness. In this category come Timothy Benn, Frederick Buller, Sir Peter Cresswell, John Drewett, Tom Fort, Dr Allan Frake, Neil Freeman, James Gilman, John Goddard, Professor John Gooch, Morten Harangen, Peter Hayes, Angela van der Horst, Hugh Kitchin, Philippa Kitchin, Jim Krul and Jerry Girard of the Catskill Fly Fishing Center and Museum, Geoff Lee, Gordon Mackie, Andy Martin of the Environment Agency, Philippa Napier, Neil Patterson, Dr Christopher Prior, Ken Robson, Raymond Rocher, Professor Valerie Sanders, Chris Sandford and Keith Skues.

My warm thanks are due to Gill Jackson, Nicola Edwards, Nick Chaytor and their colleagues at Robert Hale. A special mention must also be made of Martin Kendall who, although now retired from Robert Hale, has maintained a watching brief, with much priceless advice and support.

Finally I should mention the never-failing support of my wife Philippa, who has also taken some of the photographs in the book, and in the latter stage of the project has come to the rescue of a battle-fatigued author with her more advanced computer skills.

Introduction

IN 1910 THERE appeared one of the truly great angling books: *Minor Tactics of the Chalk Stream and Kindred Studies*, by G.E.M. Skues, already well known for his thoughtful articles in *The Field* and *The Fishing Gazette*.

Angling books are legion; most fade and die, and only a few can be called seminal or ground-breaking. These terms can, however, be applied without reserve to *Minor Tactics*, for this book began to change the way in which anglers thought and set about altering the rules of engagement on the river.

1910 was perhaps a significant time for something radically new. Years later Virginia Woolf was to suggest that aesthetic perceptions altered so much that human character changed in that year. The Edwardian era is sometimes thought of as one of golden calm before the shock of the Great War, ushering in a period of accelerating change and violence which was to extend into our own uneasy age. There is a tempting tendency to cherish an image of tranquillity, of long summers and croquet on the vicarage lawn. In fact the years before 1914 witnessed a good deal of tumult in British society, with embittered labour relations, skirmishes between police and suffragettes, a great constitutional struggle culminating in the Parliament Act of 1911, and always in the background the sense that a European conflict was inevitable. New ideas emerged in art, literature and the study of human psychology, and all of these involved a questioning of traditional ideas and values. We do not know if Skues had any notions about Viennese psychoanalysis, or votes for women, or the new modernist movement in literature and the arts. Did he admire Picasso, Stravinsky, Diaghilev? Did he go to the extraordinary Post-Impressionist Exhibition in 1910? His unpublished memoir is a cautious and not very revealing document, and much of his life will always be a mystery. But he must have been aware that he was living in an age of intellectual questioning and reassessment. If he was not responding – even unconsciously – to the spirit of the age he would have been very unusual. *Minor Tactics*, although written in measured and polite prose, was in fact revolutionary, though the effects only built up slowly to the explosion of the late 1930s. Even today the shrapnel is still flying.

Three more books followed in the next thirty years. These, together with a great flood of articles in several journals, continued to put the revolutionary ideas of Skues before the angling public. This book is an attempt to examine his part in developing and making acceptable these ideas and in promoting the acceptance of the use of the nymph on the chalk streams. It also investigates the difficulties that confronted him in this work. Some of these problems lay in the very strength of the purist culture that derived from the teachings of Halford, while others, in part, arose from the nature of his own personality.

The energy of Skues was phenomenal: when he was not fishing he was thinking about it or writing about it. But this is not just a fishing book. It is a biography of a man as well as an angler, and surveys areas of his life away from the river, the Flyfishers' Club and the fly-tying bench. By telling the story of Skues' life from the beginning I hope to throw light on the slow but sure process of change, and also to celebrate the achievement of the man who, in the words of John Goddard, 'was the greatest thinking fly fisher ever to put pen to paper'.

1

Childhood

GEORGE EDWARD MACKENZIE SKUES, the man who was to breach the walls of the fortress of dry-fly purism by extending and liberalizing fly-fishing methods, was born at St Johns, Newfoundland on 13 August 1858, two years after the end of the Crimean War, and died in 1949, in the atomic age and four years after a much more dangerous and destructive war. In that time the world around him was changed in an enormous variety of ways, and in his own way, for the benefit of a relatively small body of people, he made his contribution.

The most part of what we can know about Skues' early life is to be found in a long memoir which he began to write in the 1930s and finished when he withdrew from London to Wiltshire. He called it 'Trivialities of a Long Life by a Person of No Importance' (hereinafter cited as 'Trivialities'). In it he wrote: 'I was the first-born, and it is said that the first-born is always an amateurish effort.' His father, William Mackenzie Skues (born 1828), had been Assistant Surgeon to the Forces since 1853. In 1855 he was appointed Surgeon to the Newfoundland Companies. He was the son of an earlier George Skues, a lieutenant in the Royal Marine Light Infantry, and of Mary Gibbs Mackenzie, a sister of Lord Seaforth. William's wife was Margaret Ayre (born 1836), daughter of Christopher Ayre, Secretary to the Governor and Clerk to the Newfoundland Parliament, the existence of which only dated from 1836.

The Skues family, like many members of the less fortunate section of the middle class, were inclined to dwell upon the more impressive areas of their ancestry. Victorians were fond of doing this sort of thing. If there was a coronet somewhere, even if the connection was tenuous, this would be a source of comfort and satisfaction. William's mother's family, being derived from the Mackenzies of Seaforth, could trace their lineage through the royal families of Scotland and England as far back as the eleventh century. The honorific-sounding name of Mackenzie was added to the names of young George and of every one of his seven siblings.

William's descent was less glamorous but nevertheless interesting. The Skues family was of Cornish origin. One of his forebears had reputedly been part of the secretariat of Cardinal Wolsey and therefore permitted to wear his hat in the presence of the king. At least, so the family believed. It may have been the same ancestor who was made Receiver of the Dues of the local tin mines, a privilege which lasted for three hundred years up to the eighteenth century. He must have been a person of some local consequence in Cornwall, and therefore useful to government, to have been given this interesting office of profit in perpetuity.

In the sixteenth century the family name had been spelt Skewys in documents. In modern times this probably more correct pronunciation has been kept by some of the more remote descendants in Cornwall. Skues' great-nephew Keith Skues has settled for a one-syllable rendering.

Mary was born a year after the appearance of George. After the birth of Mary children appeared fairly regularly, punctuated by some gaps when William was away on some foreign station: the children of the servants of Empire in Victorian times tended to arrive in separate salvoes. Eventually there were eight Skues children, not a particularly large number for those times.

Newfoundland nowadays has many attractions to tourists, but in the middle of the nineteenth century it must have seemed one of the less desirable postings for an Englishman overseas. It was a place about which no European country with imperialist ambitions would have bothered itself, had it not been for the enormous value of the cod fishing. These marine riches were interesting enough to provoke quarrelling between European powers over control of the area. The population was largely composed of fishermen, with a leaven of outlaws, deserters from the armed forces and other runaways who had made their countries too hot to hold them. In 1892, some years after the Skues family had quitted St Johns (no doubt with relief) the entire town burnt down in a catastrophic fire and had to be rebuilt.

The upbringing and nurture of many thousands of the children of parents in the colonies was inevitably going to be less than satisfactory. George and his brothers and sisters were a fairly typical sample of the category. It became the usual practice to settle the growing family back in Britain with relatives or even paid child-minders, while fathers and sometimes mothers continued in the service of Empire overseas.

Historians have been interested in such children, and have wondered what effect such a rackety and generally dysfunctional life might have had upon them. For many there would have been a distressing sense of loss as parents disappeared from their lives, often for years on end. Their place would be taken by other people, sometimes familiar, at other times strangers. The trials and sorrows of some of them have been well documented. Kipling wrote at length of being abandoned to the care of a pair of professional minders of scarcely believable unpleasantness. Relatives were sometimes only a little more satisfactory. Aunts, frequently irritable and short-tempered, often appear in other memoirs of the time. H.H. Munro, whose short stories were published in Edwardian times under the pseudonym of 'Saki', wrote on the subject with a pen dipped in acid. He and his siblings were parked with tyrannical aunts in Devon while their father was in Burma. Munro was writing fiction, but clearly some of it was derived from real-life experience. Aunts do not come out well in his tales, being outmanoeuvred by their young charges, and in one or two cases are killed by wild animals.

It must, in fairness, be said that misery was not universal in this class of young people. But there is a good deal of evidence of many who were emotionally stunted and scarred. There was a much larger number whose life stories have never been told. To be separated from parents for long periods was a common enough experience to have been regarded as normal. One must learn to be tough and not to complain: one was, after all, being constantly reminded that father was 'serving the Empire', a role which, in the latter part of the nineteenth century, was assuming an almost religious significance. Compared to the high ideals of serving Crown and Country, the fact that thousands of children were marked for life by their early conditioning was part of the price that had to be paid.

In 1861 William and his wife came back to Britain with George and Mary. In after years George was to have much contact with American anglers but, unless they visited England, mainly by letter. He was never to cross the Atlantic again. The family settled for a short time with Margaret's parents in Aberdeen. Here was born another child, Margaret Caroline Mackenzie and, in 1862, both parents left their offspring in Aberdeen and sailed away to India, where William had been appointed Brigade Surgeon in Karachi. However, the birth of a third daughter, Gertrude Eliza Mackenzie, meant that his wife had to come back to Britain. Babies and small children were unlikely to survive for long in India. For several years the parents were living in separate hemispheres, and the steady stream of new babies ceased. But it did mean that, for a while, George and his sisters had a mother with them.

At some time in the 1860s (probably 1863) the children, with their mother and the Aberdeen grandparents, moved south to Langford, a village in Somerset. Soon afterwards they moved to Wrington in the same county. Nearby was a tiny tributary of the River Yeo, which some years later was impounded further upstream to make the reservoir at Blagdon. It was here, at the age of five, that George's interest in fish life was kindled. A small paddock adjoined his grandfather's garden, where he kept a pony, several goats and 'some aggressive geese'. Shoals of minnows inhabited the tributary on the edge of the paddock, and there also one day was an unmistakeable trout. He never forgot this first sighting of what was no doubt a very diminutive fish.

At a date which is not specified in 'Trivialities' there was another heart-wrenching parting when George's mother left to rejoin his father in India, and when he was seven years old plans were made to put him into a boarding school. To most people in the twenty-first century this might seem a painfully premature stage of one's life to be sent away from home and pitched among strangers, but the accepted wisdom of the age (and for long afterwards) was that a child could hardly begin too early to be toughened for the struggles of life by a little dose of adversity. The decision might also have been an indication that his ageing grandparents were beginning to find him a rather a trial, and wanted some peace in the house. In 1865 therefore he boarded for a year at a school near Bristol, an experience about which in his memoir he maintained a silence which may have been eloquent. At the end of that time his father and mother came back from the East, and another period of wandering from one place to another commenced.

After a short sojourn in Portsmouth and Southsea the family moved to London, perhaps with an eye to better schooling. They settled first in Upper Holloway and then in neighbouring Hornsey. Soon afterwards William Skues left once more for India.

This restless style of life must have been a less than ideal scheme for child-rearing, but at least the children had got their mother back again. George was established for the next two years in a dame school in Hornsey Rise. He seems to have got on well enough at this school, and probably aroused some interest by attending wearing the kilt and sporran of the Mackenzies. But the disappearance of his father seems to have brought about a deterioration in his behaviour. His mother was therefore astonished when he was awarded the Good Conduct Prize at school, and enquired why his conduct was not more acceptable at home. He answered that there were no marks for good conduct at home: his mother's rejoinder was that if his father were available he would soon be receiving marks of a different sort.

The change in his nature towards bumptiousness, arising perhaps from feelings of insecurity in an unsatisfactory and threatening world, may have dated from this time. It lasted with him until well into his twenties. It was about this period of his life that he began a number of surreptitious experiments with smoking, using whatever materials came to hand, such as oak leaves and blotting paper. He wrote that he never succeeded then or subsequently in discovering any charm in smoking, and remained firmly against it all his life, forbidding it in his own house. He was also inclined to confront people smoking on railway journeys, at which times, according to his friend Dr Barton, 'he was worth hearing'. Thursday nights in the Flyfishers' Club, in the days when no social occasion could take place without a pall of smoke in the room, must have been difficult for him.

He soon found other ways to entertain himself in the district as his interest in the natural world increased. Hornsey had not yet been swallowed up by the expansion of Greater London, and rural opportunities were to hand. Beginning by fishing for newts in neighbouring ponds, he then became fascinated by the nearby New River, an artificial channel cut in the seventeenth century to bring fresh water into the capital. Here he watched the local anglers fishing for roach and perch, and longed to emulate them. He got as far as providing himself with a wooden winder with line, float, hook to gut and some split shot, and was wondering how to obtain some sort of rod when he was sent off to another boarding school, this time at Stokes Bay near Gosport.

In 1867 George acquired his first brother, when Frederick William Mackenzie was born. In later life Frederick worked as an engineer in South Africa, and for a time served in the local defence force on the borders of Rhodesia. He would occasionally come home on leave, and on one long furlough early in 1914 he busied himself with some research into the Skues family, discovering the details of their forebears already referred to above. He was remembered for his generosity with presents to the young members of the next generation, but for many years at a time he was far from England. He never married and seems to have been a somewhat mysterious, almost invisible member of the family. He did not return home from Africa until the late 1930s.

In 1870 the Skues children were yet again bereft of proper parenting when their father returned from India and took their mother away to Malta, where another post awaited him. They were not to see her again for five years, although two more children were born in Malta: Minnie Mackenzie in 1870 and Elsie Mackenzie in 1872.

In 1875 the birth of Charles Ayre Mackenzie completed the tally of the Skues children. In course of time he became an architect and also an extremely effective Secretary of the Flyfishers' Club. Although Charles was seventeen years younger than George the brothers had a great regard and need for each other throughout their joint lives. Two of the sisters died young from tuberculosis – Margaret in 1888 and Gertrude in 1905.

In 'Trivialities' George insisted that both Minnie and Charles had far more natural abilities than he, but added 'none of us had any bump of acquisitiveness, and all remained poor'.

From the age of eleven George's life became more eventful. An acquaintance of William, a retired major in the Marines and an object of some respect, having been with General Gordon in China, recommended a preparatory school at Alverstoke, not far from George's previous school near Gosport. The major may not have been more than a chance acquaintance of William's, dating from their short stay in the Portsmouth area, but this somewhat slender chance took George into what turned out to be an efficient school. Discipline was harsh, but in that age there was nothing unusual in that. Prep schools were becoming more competitive at this date, and George became well-grounded in useful material which was soon going to change his life.

At first he came home at the end of terms, but from 1871 at the age of thirteen he was boarded out in the holidays as a paying guest in the household of Dr Kealy of Ashley House, Gosport. The rest of the children remained with their grandparents. This arrangement, no doubt set up by his parents before leaving for Malta, might appear to have been rather heartless, but it seems to have worked well. The doctor was a cheery, helpful sort of man who encouraged George's interests. These included fishing in the brackish waters of the various tidal inlets in the area, where school bass, mullet, small perch and eels could be caught. And it was the doctor who organized his first serious expedition, under the guidance of one of his patients who was a keen angler. This historic event took place on the nearby River Meon. It would be pleasant to be able to record a youthful triumph with the trout of Hampshire, but it was not going to be that sort of day. The Meon is an excellent small stream with a good population of trout in its middle and upper reaches, but the venue for the visit was a slow, deep stretch at Titchfield near the estuary, where coarse fish abounded. The roach could be seen lying in shoals and were easy to catch. In five hours they caught 108 roach weighing 70lb, and three trout. George's share had been twenty roach for 16lb.

'Trivialities' contains several alarming examples from this period of rough and tumble boyhood life. George consorted for a while with a gang of other young ruffians in the district and suffered from a campaign of bullying from another boy of about fourteen or fifteen, when George was a somewhat undersized 12-year-old. One day the older boy hit him on the forehead, causing extra damage because he was wearing a ring decorated with stones. Enraged by this George retired a few paces and fashioned a makeshift sling from his handkerchief. He then hurled a large pebble with all his strength at his tormentor. Conflicting emotions surged through him – momentary triumph at the success of his tactic, succeeded by terror as, like Goliath the Philistine, the boy fell senseless to the ground, and finally relief as he came to after a few minutes. 'I thought I had killed him', he remembered in 'Trivialities'. However, the account finished thus: 'He left me alone after that.' About the same time there developed a long-running enmity between George and another boy, which ended in a duel between them with bows and arrows. He came out of this encounter with a wounded arm which left a permanent scar.

In 1869 the school arranged for George and three other promising boys to travel to Southampton to take the Oxford and Cambridge Local Examination. The boys regarded this trip as a holiday spree: 'We had a great time there, pea-shooting, catapulting windows, tying door-knockers of a row of houses together so that as each door was opened to a knock it operated the next door knocker, and generally made ourselves unmitigated young nuisances.' In spite of his behaviour out of hours in Southampton he learned soon afterwards that he had passed in all subjects except (intriguingly perhaps) the principles of faith and religion. Securing a prize in the competition involved the awesome business of a public presentation at the hands of Bishop Wilberforce at the Hartley Institute in Southampton. Wilberforce, son of the more famous father who led the anti-slavery movement, is remembered today for his notorious clash over Darwin's theory with Thomas Henry Huxley at the meeting of the British Association at Oxford in 1860. The bishop was much in favour as a platform speaker, although some people considered his manner too unctuous on such occasions, and had long ago fastened upon him the nickname of 'Soapy Sam'. When George stepped up to receive his prize – Dean Stanley's *Memorials of Westminster Abbey* – Wilberforce said: 'May I express the hope that you will come to lie there?' George responded: 'I hope not yet, Your Grace', causing some merriment among 'the black-coated gentry on the platform'. The bishop's response was not recorded.

In the summer of 1872, when George was approaching his fourteenth birthday, the question arose of more advanced schooling. This was the period in Britain when the rising middle class were eager to get their sons into public schools, and there was a corresponding expansion of school places. There was an interesting dualism in the process of turning public school boys into men. On the one hand it would convert the high-fliers into an élite group of politicians and administrators to run country and Empire. At another less ambitious level it would provide recruits for the professions of law, medicine and the armed forces. In this way the hereditary ruling class would be joined by the brighter members of the middle class aspiring to be gentlemen.

Many new public schools were founded at this time, and others were formed by the elevation of some small ancient foundation, often an Elizabethan grammar school, under the leadership of a powerful and ambitious headmaster. There was a much longer list of schools for the Skues parents to look over than there would have been a generation earlier. Their attempt to get him into Winchester, one of the most prestigious schools in Britain, might have seemed a forlorn hope, for the process of getting a place was a daunting one. In fact his parents did not really imagine that their son could be successful in such a harshly competitive situation, and only arranged through his preparatory school for him to be entered because it would serve as a practice run for a later entrance examination to another public school of lesser fame.

There were two categories at Winchester of boys, or 'men' as they were traditionally called. In the fourteenth century the original intention of the founder, William of Wykeham, had been to provide education for seventy poor boys, in order to train recruits for the priesthood, which at that time had been severely reduced by the Black Death. By the latter part of the nineteenth century things had changed a good deal. Over the years boys had been admitted in addition to the original roll of the Scholars or Foundationers. These were known as the Commoners. The Scholars lived in the old school buildings, while the Commoners, who had to pay fees, were accommodated separately. By 1867 the combined roll of both categories of boys was 285. Scholars now also had to pay fees – twenty guineas a year – but the parents of Commoners would have had to pay much more. William Skues would not have been able to contemplate paying at the Commoners' rate.

The competitive examination was a comparatively recent innovation at Winchester. In earlier times, boys applying to share in the charity of the Founder got in by more informal routes, in which nomination through influence played the major part. If one could claim acquaintance with one of the Fellows, or better still could take advantage of a useful clause in the will of William of Wykeham and claim 'Founder's kin', entry could soon be arranged. Frank Buckland, the well-known naturalist and fisheries expert, was an example of this brazen nepotism. He was elected a Scholar in 1839 because his father, Dean Buckland of Christ Church, Oxford, had a quiet word with his colleague Dr Shuttleworth, the Warden of New College, Oxford. New College had been founded by William of Wykeham at the same time as Winchester and as part of the same project, in order to provide scholars to carry on to a higher level their education for the priesthood, and many old Wykehamists down the centuries have moved on to Oxford by this route. But the old days of patronage were doomed. Mid-Victorian Britain was in an age of reform and many areas of privilege and antique inefficiency were coming under scrutiny, including the senior rank of public schools. In 1857 the Oxford University Commissioners ruled that the old system of entry must be replaced by something more efficient and less susceptible to corruption, and a rather ferocious cycle of examinations, written and oral, was established.

In July 1872 George Skues was brought to Winchester along with 150 other boys, accompanied by anxious parents or schoolmasters, all needing accommodation in or near the city. Only fifteen places were offered: nine candidates in ten were going to be disappointed. A great deal of frantic work in marking papers must have taken place each evening, and each morning a success list was posted in the window of Wells' bookshop in College Street. To his mounting astonishment George survived the massacre of the first two days. On the second day the list recorded the survival of forty of the original aspirants, and a doleful exodus of the unsuccessful from the city would have followed. By the third day only twenty survivors were left. The final round was perhaps the most alarming of all, for each of the remaining candidates had to appear in the imposing Election Chamber before a board made up of the Headmaster, the Warden of the sister foundation of New College (the famous Dr Spooner), one or two ancient clergymen who were Fellows of Winchester (whose role, having lasted for many centuries, was about to be abolished by Parliament), and two 'Posers', the prime movers in the encounter, whose task it was to ask most of the questions. George records that he did not enjoy the prospect of the third day: 'I felt that I was certainly done, for I never shine in viva voce.'

One by one the boys came in to be grilled; the whole procedure was over by the end of the morning, and in the afternoon the final list was published. The name of George Skues appeared as number fourteen. How had he done it? His own view was that he owed his place to his prowess in mathematics, particularly geometry, or Euclid as it was then called. There is perhaps a little more to it. He had clearly kept his head in the exam room and worked out which were the most difficult questions and therefore carrying the most marks. The geometry paper contained eighteen problems. Twelve of these were from the first four books of Euclid, the rest were riders, or problems arising from the main propositions. Skues explained his strategy thus:

> It occurred to me that the marks for the twelve propositions would be relatively small and, being full of impudence, I tackled first the last of the riders and soon worked it out. In the end I sent up only six selections, namely the riders in reverse order – and I appear to have got them right.

It is a pity that we do not have any record of the surprised reaction of the man who marked a paper in which the candidate had begun at the end and worked backwards. Perhaps he was won over by this unexpected evidence of originality. If so, it decided the future direction of the life of that candidate. Certainly to have had such a good grasp of exam tactics at such an early age was a remarkable gift.

Of the 1872 Winchester intake, apart from Skues, only one name is really remembered nowadays: Charles Oman, who came first in the exam, became afterwards a distinguished military historian and received a knighthood for his work in Whitehall during the First World War. Two other successful candidates, David Samuel Margoliouth the orientalist, and Cuthbert Hamilton Turner, the ecclesiastical historian, had distinguished academic careers but are not familiar names today. However, all four men made it into the pages of the pantheon of the great British dead, *The Oxford Dictionary of National Biography*.

George's parents must have been elated. He might easily have gone to a minor public school of the third rank, or to a private school, or even to one of the many grammar schools, which in that hierarchical age were regarded by the alumni of public schools as existing in outer darkness. However, following his success he was now entitled to join Winchester in the following term and to wear the gown of a Foundation Scholar in what was properly called the College of St Mary the Virgin at Winton. His success produced 'a small harvest of tips', and he immediately spent the money on fishing tackle – a wooden rod costing 1s 6d, a hank of twisted silk line and other items.

But serious fishing was still some way off.

2

Winchester College 1872–1877

O N 20 SEPTEMBER 1872 George Skues passed under the arch of Outer Gate in College Street, Winchester. Above his head, there looked down from her niche the benign image of the crowned Virgin and Child. Ahead was Outer Court and the second impressive entrance of Middle Gate. Above this gate was more sculpture fashioned five centuries earlier, depicting the Virgin uncrowned with the Archangel Gabriel. At her feet was the image of the Founder, William of Wykeham, kneeling to offer up the gift of a new school. Beyond was Chamber Court, the very centre of this ancient school, where the Foundation Scholars lodged: it was to be Skues' dwelling in term time for the next five years.

The place was very like a college of Oxford or Cambridge, over which, in the words of the poet, one might imagine the whispering of the last enchantments of the Middle Ages. All around him were walls and buttresses of great age, formed from the flint stones derived from the local chalk beds, from the famous greenstone of the Isle of Wight and, in some special parts of buildings, from the much-prized limestone imported from Caen in Normandy. Beneath his feet were the flint stones put down to replace the cobbles torn up as ammunition in the schoolboy rebellion of 1818, a revolt which had required the intervention of soldiers with fixed bayonets.

Little or nothing of this could have been known on that first day to young Skues. He was concerned with the rather alarming here and now. He had successfully surmounted a great hurdle in getting access, not merely to a public school, but to one of the oldest and greatest of them all. It was an extraordinary achievement, and one which was to make an enormous change in his young life. As he picked his way through the unfamiliar surroundings he must have felt a sense of pride, but there was probably also a certain amount of apprehension. If he had known what was in store for him he might have been even more frightened.

What sort of a school was it anyway? The nineteenth-century public schools have given rise to an extensive literature, which falls into two main categories. The older books, particularly those commissioned by individual schools, tend to be laudatory and sometimes a little smug. More recent work, analysing the schools rather as sociological phenomena, have been less than complimentary, and have emphasized many deficiencies and abuses in organization as well as individual miseries in the lives of the boys – in short, the gap between the rhetoric and the reality of school life.

There is no doubt that, in earlier times, schools were wild places where the law of the jungle prevailed, and vice and disease flourished. Staff and boys were often at loggerheads and savage physical discipline was thought to be the only way to contain disorder. The rebellion of 1818 was not the only one in Winchester's history. Many parents would not have dreamt of sending a young boy into such a dangerous situation, and preferred to hire tutors to educate boys at home.

By the 1870s public schools had altered in some ways for the better, but there was plenty of room for improvement, and there were still pockets and corners of appalling barbarism, from which Winchester was not free. The example of Thomas Arnold of Rugby and his followers had helped towards taming and liberalizing the public schools, but there remained much about them that would strike a modern eye as bizarre. However, by the time William Skues had started to look around for a berth for young George he was only one of a growing number of parents who had begun to be interested in the reformed schools and were clamouring for places.

How did parents perceive these schools? What would strike them as the advantages?

The first and most obvious advantage was that the school would take over the life of a boy whose parent or parents were compelled to be abroad and therefore had little option in the matter. But there was much more to it than just convenience. There was no doubt that many were impressed by the main idea of Dr Arnold (which was taken up generally by headmasters), that the development of character was the most important aim of a school. Arnold had famously said that religious and moral principles came first, followed by gentlemanly conduct, with intellectual ability in third place. Character was often identified as 'manliness', a term not much used today. It meant a growing maturity and responsibility, a sense of the seriousness of life, and this would mainly derive from moral guidance. Organized games held little appeal for Arnold: in his scheme of things the main encouragement to the development of character or manliness would come from religion. In the years after Arnold's premature death in 1842 the ethos in most public schools began to alter. Chapel and the sermon were still regarded as important, but character was increasingly seen as a matter of a physical rather than a moral quality and likely to be encouraged by hard and plucky activity on the games field. Many parents seem to have found this reassuring.

There was also the notion that living a communal existence away from home was a good thing. If life was a little rough at times, it might for that reason be a good preparation for adult life in a fiercely competitive world, where the soft and the spoilt would fall behind and be submerged in life's race. By the 1870s the ideas of Charles Darwin were beginning to spread, and to be applied to human society as well as to the natural world, often with considerable approval. The notion of struggle in society and of the survival of the fittest suited the spirit of the age. The traditional attributes of self-reliance, toughness and of course a trusting and unthinking patriotism would all be useful to future officers of the Army or Navy, or to imperial administrators. To be able to endure discomfort, poor food and from time to time acute physical pain could be an advantage. The ideal of 'plain living and high thinking' was often extolled, although in most schools of the time the boys were more likely to experience the first than the second.

The boarding preparatory school was regarded as a necessary first stage for the public school. If a boy were to be separated from home life for the greater part of the year one could hardly begin too early, and many boys were sent away from home at the age of 7 or 8. To have a diminished sense of family might, after all, be useful if one were later to be posted to faraway places abroad. One would be separated from one's own family anyway. If one married and created another family one was not going to see much of it. Some men posted to India or Africa never married, or at least delayed marrying for years.

But most of all, a boy's father – particularly if by luck or hard work he had only recently arrived at middle-class status – would have been attracted by the idea of his son joining what was really an exclusive club. The percentage of English boys at public schools in 1870 was still minute. The boy would make contact with others who could be exemplars at school and useful connections in later life. Whatever Papa may have been, his son would, at the end of his schooling, emerge a gentleman – or so it was hoped.

Behind this encouraging version of affairs lurked several worrying disadvantages. It had often been recognized, even in earlier times, that there were boys who should not be sent away to school at all. Some were simply delicate and would not prosper in such a harsh environment. Thomas Arnold himself had been aware of this drawback. The boarding school, he thought, to a considerable extent, took the place of family, and the boy would drift away from his parents. In his words 'it loosened the affections'. He was uneasy about the extent to which he had unwillingly become a surrogate father to boys distressed by loneliness and homesickness. More subtly, there were boys who were temperamentally unfitted for a boy-society that placed so much value on conformity and enforced it by fairly heavy methods. A rebel at Winchester (or at any of the public schools of that era) was going to have a thin time of it: the day of the progressive school was still far off. Skues, as it turned out, was just such a boy: with him the habit of thinking for himself started early.

The programme of study in the 1870s also left much to be desired. It had begun to change, but not nearly as much as some reformers would have liked. The policy, sanctified by hundreds of years of custom, was to subject the boys to a heavy diet of Greek and Latin, with mathematics, divinity and a smattering of history. Modern languages were not much attended to. There was little or no treatment of current affairs or of economic, political and commercial matters, at a time when the country was on a steep upward curve of expansion and wealth. When the Parliamentary Commission under Lord Clarendon in 1861–2 investigated the nine ancient public schools they were unable to find much enthusiasm for the teaching of science. The result of these deficiencies was that most boys would leave one or other of the great schools with little knowledge of the world outside.

If he knew anything about these drawbacks the average father did not pay them much heed. The boy was on the right ladder.

Skues' own account of his time at Winchester, written decades later in 'Trivialities', is interesting as far as it goes, but it is, in the main, a recital of facts and is lacking in real insight. The reader does not feel a sense of being taken back to the Winchester of those days. In later life Skues was good at recreating in his writing a day on the river, where his ideas and discoveries would be given a running test, but he was much less good at describing people. His reticence and restraint, and also his notion of privacy and good form, prevented him from telling us about his own deeper feelings and those of others.

Fortunately we have a valuable addition (and in some ways a corrective) to his version in the form of a longer and much more lively and
analytical account written by his exact contemporary and friend, Charles
Oman, who had come first in the Winchester entrance exam. Oman later
became a Member of Parliament, the Chichele Professor of Modern
History at Oxford and a Fellow of All Souls College, Oxford. His reminiscences, published as *Memories of Victorian Oxford* in 1941, do much to
bring Winchester in the 1870s to life and make a real appeal to the
reader's imagination.

The Headmaster of Winchester at this date was the remarkable
George Ridding, one of the great men of Winchester's history. He did a
great deal to alter and improve the school, drained and laid out New
Field, embarked on an ambitious programme of building and greatly
increased the number of boarding houses. He even made some halting
steps in the direction of science, instituting a Natural History Society
and providing a scientific lecture room with apparatus and a botanical
garden. His predecessor Dr Moberly had declared the creation of a new
sports field to be impossible, and had been dismissive of the value of
science in education.

Some of Ridding's improvements did not receive the approval of the
Warden and Fellows, and in order to achieve them, he was forced to dig
deeply into his own purse. But gradually those who had been frightened
by and had scoffed at his energetic reforms came to realize the greatness
of his achievements. Some years later, in 1887, Dr James Sewell, Warden
of the sister foundation of New College, Oxford, admitted that twenty
years earlier he had thought Ridding was going to ruin the school, but
'now I say he is our Second Founder'.

Not everything Ridding achieved was ideal. The selection of William
Butterfield as architect was not a happy choice. The eighteen new
classrooms were not much admired by those who had a feeling for good
design, and what he did to the chapel was never forgiven by many old
Wykehamists of the nineteenth century. It is true that the original medieval
layout of the chapel had become inadequate for the growing number of
boys, but the removal of the fine seventeenth-century panelling which,
having cost £1,100 in the seventeenth century, was sold off for £60, was
tragic. The carved screen also disappeared, along with other priceless
items. The whole destruction and refurbishment was described by Oman
as 'an aesthetic crime'. But for Ridding and Butterfield efficiency was
more important than aesthetic design, and they were quite happy with

what they had achieved. In 1936 the legendary Winchester schoolmaster 'Budge' Firth (J.D'E. Firth) wrote in his book on the school: 'It was as if a Tamerlane had been commissioned by a Genghis Khan.' But some leaders can be allowed a mistake or two, and Firth had no doubt of Ridding's greatness, writing of him: 'He found us medieval; he left us modern.'

Meanwhile young Skues, all unaware of these great issues, picked his way around his own humble allotted sphere in the College, and went through the somewhat alarming process of induction. He was first fitted out with the distinctive uniform of a Scholar, a gown of antique design reaching down almost to the ground, adorned with the badge of the School. He kept the badge for the rest of his life: it now forms part of the collection of Skuesiana in the library of the University of Princeton. He and the other new Foundationers were installed in their quarters in Chamber Court (which were quite separate from those of the Commoners), and their difficulties began.

Any newcomer into a public school in any era would remember the alarm and unhappiness of the settling-period, the need to pilot oneself through a minefield of taboos and prohibitions, the frequent mistakes (quickly identified by one's superiors), and the agonies of agitation that would result. There would have been little sweetness or light in the first days and weeks. Much of this was inevitable anyway. But there was an additional factor which was unfair and oppressive, and had nothing to do with the work in the schoolroom. There were two areas of life at Winchester, and they were separate and governed by different individuals and by different customs. In the classroom, Skues and his fourteen fellows were introduced to an intensive programme of work. After hours, masters and boys had little contact, and another world took over, a sort of boy republic, almost an underworld, where authority and discipline were in the hands of the prefects. The new boys were speedily made to understand that they were lowly creatures in the scheme of things and that their main role was to be hard-working servants. Each boy was given a mentor or 'pater' from the next group or 'roll' above him, to instruct him in fagging duties and other school mysteries. Fourteen days of grace were allowed in which to learn all the manifold duties of their place, which included preparing the portable baths for the prefects early in the morning and getting supper and hot drinks for them in the evening. In recreation hours the juniors had 'kicking in' duty, which meant retrieving balls kicked outside the canvas screens during sessions of Winchester football, a game peculiar to the school and incomprehensible to the outside world. Oman wrote: 'This watching out was hard work in December, when the rain or sleet was intermittent.' In the summer fags and indeed older boys could be requisitioned to spend hours fielding for the prefects at cricket practice, a privilege that was much resented as it deprived the boys of a large part of their half-holiday afternoons.

But for a 'new man' the most mysterious and alarming part of his Winchester life was the pressure put upon him to master the curious Winchester language, or 'Notions'. No one could tell how far back Notions went: some words were said to date back to the time of William of Wykeham in the fourteenth century. By the mid-nineteenth century the vocabulary had become enormous. In 1840 there were about 350 nouns and verbs in the list: by 1900 there were about a thousand. Some of these words can be found in Edward Grey's book *Fly Fishing* (1899), but the list changed confusingly from one generation of boys to another. 'Brum' meant to be short of money (a common problem with the young), a 'brock' was a misfortune (plenty of them, no doubt), 'to thoke' meant to be idle, 'jig' meant clever or talented (Grey was described as jig), a 'remedy' was a holiday – hence 'half rem' was a half-holiday. There were also a number of curious contractions, such as 'examina' for examination, 'mathema', 'steeplecha' and many others. Skues, to his sorrow, quickly became aware of the word 'spree'. To be 'spree' was to be bumptious, cheeky, above oneself. This was exactly what a new man was not supposed to be. The usual treatment for him was to put him in his place and to knock any self-love out of him. Skues was soon identified as one of the spree, and harsh punishment swiftly followed.

The problems and miseries of the new intake of boys in 1872 could be paralleled more or less in many schools at that time. But at Winchester there was an extra factor that was oppressive and intolerable, even by the harsh standards of the age – the excessive and capricious employment of corporal punishment by the prefects.

To us in the twenty-first century it is a distasteful subject, but it needs to be examined to get an understanding of the predicament of young Skues and his companions. The flogging of boys is as old as human history and, until comparatively modern times, objections to it were fairly rare. Most pedagogues and indeed many parents were supporters of the hearty English tradition of savage flogging. Children were student adults, full of original sin which had to be beaten out of them. But at this particular date at Winchester the system had got seriously out of hand,

and had become one of pure sadism. (Public school history contains examples of other outbreaks of this sort: there was a similar period of cruelty at Harrow in the 1850s.) The Winchester prefects had long possessed these rights; their conduct out of school hours was unsupervised and no one in authority seems to have been at all inquisitive about it. These appalling beatings were inflicted with the ground ash, a 6ft sapling, supplies of which were regularly collected from particular thickets nearby. The slightest infringement of rules, or indeed any small fault, such as an unsatisfactory performance on the part of a boy told to build a fire or run an errand, was enough. It was clear that the prefects were looking for excuses to exercise their power. On one occasion Skues overheard a conversation between two prefects, from which he learned (probably without surprise) that one of them had laid a bet with the other that he would succeed in making young Skues break down in tears. He lost his bet. In his first eight weeks at Winchester Skues was flogged ten times with the ground ash and once with the handle of a racket, the bruises from which remained for weeks. He later believed that it might have affected his growth. In 'Trivialities' he adopted the conventional line of making light of it, having come from a fairly rough prep school ('I soon acquired a prompt contempt for ground ash lickings'). Charles Oman, a rather more sensitive boy who had probably never been treated unfairly in his life, wrote graphically: 'I must confess that my first month at Winchester was a time of pure misery.... In a very few days I realized that I had chanced into the middle of a perfect nightmare of thoughtless cruelty.'

Oman recorded that, out of school hours, some boys simply hid away in remote corners, aware that any chance meeting with a prefect would quickly result in a flogging upon some trivial excuse. One new scholar in the 1872 roll, David Margoliouth, was clever in the classroom – he afterwards became a professor of Arabic studies at Oxford – but maladroit at his fagging duties and therefore always in trouble. Oman wrote: 'I happened once to be sent on an errand into the chamber where he was billeted, on the night when he was having his regulation hot bath. His body showed a really dreadful criss-cross of blue and black weals.'

Oman's letters to his parents filled them with concern. They left their house in Cheltenham for a time and came down to Winchester, where they established themselves in lodgings in Eastgate Street, so that at least he could visit them on Sunday afternoons. For a time his father was thinking of taking him away from Winchester, so enraged was he at hearing the unpleasant details of school life. Oman records that several other fathers were having similar thoughts.

Although Victorian public schools could be rough places, the reign of terror was something quite different; in fact it ran counter to the Arnoldian spirit of chivalry that was supposed to guide public school prefects. The ideal was that those in advantaged positions ought to be forbearing and compassionate to the lesser fry of the school. In particular, part of their role was to protect the young from being bullied. In this case it was the prefects who were the bullies. Oman shows in his memoir that he knew well enough the real motive behind the conduct of the prefects – it was, he wrote, a mixture of megalomania and sadism.

It was bad luck for Skues to have arrived at Winchester when things were in this state. But help was at hand, and it came in a remarkable form – in fact it was one of the most dramatic events in the school's history. At the beginning of Skues' first term the reign of terror was a private and secret system: halfway through the term it became a matter of public discussion outside the school in the country at large, and eventually all over the British Empire. It is worth looking in some detail at the extraordinary events of the second half of the Autumn Term of 1872 at Winchester College, for the result was to save Skues, Oman and their young colleagues from a great deal of persecution.

The original cause arose over the matter of Notions and it concerned, at first anyway, the Commoners, not the Scholars in College. The Commoners' prefects had decided that not enough serious respect was being shown towards the school language, and set up a system of oral exams for all their boys up to the rank of prefect – mistakes of course to be punished with the ground ash. However, a hero, one Macpherson, stepped forward and quickly became the central figure in what became known in Winchester annals as the 'Great Tunding Row' – a 'tunding' is Notion-speak for a flogging. William Macpherson, endowed with a rare sense of legality and precedent, and an example of the fact that some Winchester boys in those days were capable of thinking for themselves, refused to co-operate in this exercise. He was seventeen and due to become a prefect in the following year. The basis of his objection was that people of his seniority had never been examined in the Winchester vocabulary before. The senior prefect in Commoners, J.D. Whyte, repeated the summons, and Macpherson appeared before the meeting of Commoner prefects and again stated the grounds for his exemption. Whyte demanded an apology for this insubordinate conduct, which

Macpherson refused, and then subjected him to a tremendous flogging. Thirty strokes were administered, and five ground ashes were broken in the process.

Macpherson included a version of this event in his Sunday letter home. His father, Allan Macpherson of Blairgowrie, was angered by this act of tyranny and wrote to Dr Ridding, receiving from him a reply which he considered less than satisfactory. He took counsel with a friend, Charles Wordsworth, the Bishop of St Andrews, who had formerly been Second Master at Winchester. The Bishop lost no time in writing to the Headmaster, warning him that this tough, independent-minded Scotsman was likely to go to law or to make everything public. Ridding, already embarrassed, became seriously alarmed. Oman says in his account that the brutality of the regime was a shock to the Head. The Second Master, the Revd W. Awdrey, who lodged much closer to the scene, had no idea of it either – or at least said he did not.

Shortly afterwards the whole affair became public knowledge and a storm of abuse descended upon both Headmaster and school, and continued from the last week of October 1872 until the Christmas season. The first letter to *The Times* came from an Old Wykehamist, R. Maude. He was a friend of William Macpherson's father, and had probably been persuaded by him to write this letter. Eventually over a hundred letters appeared in *The Times*, the *Telegraph and Courier*, the *Globe*, *Pall Mall Gazette* and several others, and the original victim acquired the name of 'Tunded Macpherson'. Meanwhile, to add to the acute embarrassment of Headmaster, Warden and Fellows, reporters began to appear, sent down from London to prowl about and obtain some local colour.

The letters make interesting reading. As one might expect in that period, there were examples of the customary 'never-did-me-any-harm-made-me-the-man-I-am' sort of response. But the majority were heartily and at times savagely critical. It was suggested that Whyte should be expelled (which Ridding rejected). One correspondent, a county magistrate, wrote that such beatings were 'puerile practices. They are simply assaults, and ought to be dealt with as such' (that is, in a court of law). A journalist wrote: 'Parents, if they are wise, will not send their children there.'

It would be difficult to exaggerate the electric effect upon the College of this unwished-for matter. Public schools in the Victorian era (and for long after) were secretive about their culture and their day-to-day arrangements – although there would be the occasional nod in the direction of candour and openness when great achievements needed to be given a public airing. But to be lampooned in the public prints, and to have scandalous shortcomings as reading matter for the breakfast tables of the nation, was deeply humiliating. The embarrassment of the masters and the terror of the prefects were in notable contrast to the muted delight of the small boys. Ridding, normally a confident handler of events, began to flail around in a manner akin to panic and to add to the list of his errors of judgement. He intervened more than once in the newspaper correspondence, and on each occasion made things worse. In trying to defend the action of J.D. Whyte, he referred to him as 'a good and gentle boy'. This was a splendid gift for the journalists, who proceeded gleefully to put it to satirical use. However, Ridding took a firm line within the school, summoned the prefects, made Whyte apologize to Macpherson, and called for an exact list of the number of floggings, both in Commoners and in College, since the beginning of term. According to Oman the prefects were terrified when their reports were aggregated and the total became clear. And at a meeting of the governing body Macpherson was vindicated, the enforced examinations in Notions were condemned and, most importantly, the use of the ground ash was limited to 'grave moral offences'.

And so, for some weeks, Skues and his fellow slaves of the lamp were gleeful spectators of a great drama, which had the effect of humbling their tormentors, after which they could breathe more freely. The Second Master shortly withdrew to a convenient canonry away from Winchester and eventually became Bishop of South Tokyo. He was replaced by the much more effective and popular George Richardson, whose wife, according to Oman, 'became a sort of second mother to us all'.

It is possible that Skues may have regarded Macpherson as a hero. Being himself a square peg in a round hole, a troublesome rebel might have been an object of interest. Besides, Macpherson was an accomplished angler, with no doubt better opportunities than Skues of acquiring good equipment.

The Great Tunding Row marked a watershed at the time. It would not be quite true to say that a new dawn of sunlit happiness shone upon Skues and his friends but, as Oman wrote tersely: 'life ceased to be absolutely unbearable', and his parents decided that it was now safe to leave him at Winchester. The endless indoor routine of fagdom – 'chamber sweat', as it was called – continued unabated, as also did the wearisome 'kicking-in' duty at football. In the summer there would be hours of fielding at cricket practice, although Skues tells us that he was usually to be found in the outfield staring at the river instead of the batsman.

The food continued to vary from the unpalatable to the frankly inedible: Charles Oman recorded an infestation of maggots in the cold beef one day in the summer of 1873. But poor food was the rule at most schools: Kipling records that, at his school, the cuisine would have raised a mutiny in Dartmoor Prison. This meant that a reasonable amount of private funding was important to the boys in making up for lost calories. There was a College pastry-cook, and College servants could be persuaded with a small bribe to get supplies from the town. Oman got the occasional hamper from home, but there is no record of any such thing for Skues. Nor did his parents seem to realize the need for money for extra food at school, or indeed for fishing tackle. He simply had to learn to go without these things. This may account for the fact that, for the rest of his life, he never had much interest in good food, or indeed any of the small luxuries of life.

Skues recorded that he was greatly taken with the river environment at Winchester. Few schools can have been better placed to provide opportunities for the fly-fishing beginner. As we have seen, he had already experienced various forms of bait fishing in both fresh water and the sea. On saints' days (half-holidays) he would prowl disconsolately around the streams nearby, watching with burning eyes the townsfolk and the more fortunate boys casting the somewhat primitive flies of the time over the clear waters. Parallel to the main course of the river was the Itchen Navigation – or Old Barge, as it was locally known – a canalized section made in the seventeenth century to connect Southampton and Winchester. The coming of the railways had brought its usefulness to an end, and by Skues' day the river traffic had ceased, although in 1872 an ancient decaying barge could still be seen stranded on a mudbank near the College. This prime place for fishing was available to anyone who could afford the tackle and the appropriate ticket from John Hammond's well-known shop in The Square, but Skues could not afford either. For a long time there was little for him to do but watch. Lack of pocket money meant that he could not even assemble the basic equipment.

At other times he ranged over the countryside on nature rambles, often accompanied by Charles Oman. Oman's expeditions were of two types. He enjoyed looking at old churches and had a taste for archaeology, in neither of which things Skues had the slightest interest. But

Oman was also, as he expressed it, 'an enthusiastic birds' nester, fisher, entomologist, and I fear that I must add wilful trespasser'. Evading gamekeepers was all part of the sport. Nearly seventy years later golden memories still remained with him: 'On some of these excursions G.E.M. Skues, a junior boy on my own "roll", was a companion. He was primarily a fisherman, but had also a general eye for the countryside.'

Together they travelled far and wide, following through marsh and woodland any reports of rare birds seen. Most of these forays were to the south and west of Winchester. Skues admits that until 1883 he knew little of Abbots Barton, the fishery that was to become his spiritual home, and that he got no nearer to it than the Nuns' Walk. In the meantime watching others at work on the river must have been exciting, for there would have been plenty of action: local anglers who knew the water well made respectable catches, sometimes of several hundred trout in a season. But Skues was not part of that action, and the frustration must have been correspondingly great. As a poor substitute he was also frequently to be found hanging around John Hammond's shop. Hammond was a friendly, easy-going man, well aware that the young boy had no money, and was happy enough to allow him to admire the rods and tackle, and to read the angling books without buying.

Eventually Skues was able to amass enough capital to acquire a fly rod ('an awful bean pole, 11 feet long and of a paralysing stiffness'), and a silk and hair line, much too light to be cast effectively with such a rod. He also got from John Hammond, and no doubt with his advice, a selection of the usual flies for the area, all tied on fine gut: Pale Watery Dun with a white wool body, Blue Dun, Blue Quill, Red Quill and Wickham's Fancy. There were also a dozen Champion Mayflies, a pattern invented by Hammond, although in fact the mayfly was disappearing from the Old Barge at that date.

The dry fly had already made a conquest of the Winchester area, but the construction of these flies still left much to be desired. Skues writes that they had wings sloping backwards and that generally when cast they would fall on their sides. In fact they would have done equally well for wet- or dry-fly work.

Armed with this lamentable outfit Skues set forth to conquer on the Old Barge one windy spring day in March 1874. He records that he had only one level gut cast, so that when it wore out he had to suspend fishing until he could afford another one. He says little about his early humiliations: no doubt they were best forgotten. He was so astonished at the rise of the first trout that he forgot to strike. It was not until July that he caught his first fish. The sum total of much hard work in his first season produced two trout, one of which he admits was probably undersized. His enthusiasm never wavered, but this must have been a hard school of fishing, in which he floundered almost entirely on his own: 'I had no one to teach me anything of the entomology of the river ... and no one explained to me the theory of fly fishing.'

One evening he attended a meeting of the Natural History Society, known colloquially to the boys as the 'Bug and Snail', one of the societies started by Ridding to make life at Winchester more interesting. He says in 'Trivialities' that he listened with little understanding to a talk on river entomology, without making any connection between natural flies and his own attempts on the river. He still had a long way to go.

The reminiscences of Skues about the fishing of his schooldays were necessarily brief, because there was little to write about. They make sad reading. Self-pity was never part of his make-up, but he must have bitterly regretted his lack of funds – *res angustae* as he calls it, a phrase from Juvenal that recurs elsewhere in his writings, and not just about his financial problems at school. Other boys had good tackle and considerable success: a boy called Paull had a 9ft greenheart rod with a lively action, and another, Mitchell, landed a 6lb trout in the Warden's garden: the hero 'Tunded Macpherson' himself, with a useful apprenticeship in Scotland, had a 5lb fish in the Logie stream. Some years later the publication of Edward Grey's *Fly Fishing* must have given Skues a pang. Grey came to Winchester four years after Skues, who had only the vaguest memory of him. Grey's performance was the natural result of a much more advantaged background, so that funds and tackle were no problem. Even so, coming from a downstream wet-fly tradition in Northumberland, Grey made a slow start. However, he soon accustomed himself to chalk-stream ways and his tally of fish increased each season. In 1880 he captured seventy-six trout. Skues must have felt that his own record was, by comparison, regrettably insignificant.

The memoirs of Oman are, again, informative and interesting about the school day. Boys rose at 6.15 a.m. and had a good deal of fagging work to do before early school ('morning lines') at 7 a.m. After breakfast, middle school ran from 9 a.m. until midday, and afternoon school did not end until 6 p.m. Boys who fished could escape to the river for a short time at midday, but had to be back for lunch, described by Grey as 'a compulsory meal for which one might be rather – but not very – late without notice being taken, and the adjustment of this point in one's mind, when fish were rising, was a very distressing business'.

In the classroom Skues and his fellows laboured over a syllabus which had only fairly recently begun to alter under Ridding's reforms. Winchester has always prided itself on its tough programme of study, and its alumni in later life often turn out to be prodigiously hard workers. In 'Trivialities' Skues says little about schoolwork; indeed, it does not appear to have made much impression on him. The younger boys were taken through an enormous amount of textual material in Greek and Latin, but mainly as an exercise in grammar and syntax. There was a good deal of learning by heart or 'standing up', and of translation into English. The most potent torture of all was to render pieces of English poetry into one or other of the dead languages. Woe betide the unskilful young compositor guilty of 'false concords' or 'false quantities'. There was no attempt, at least in the lower forms, to convey the excitement of exploring the literature and history of the world of classical antiquity although, even so, a few boys caught the flavour of it. Charles Oman, who was one such, found that, as he moved up the school, things became much more absorbing, especially when he came to have as teachers the kindly and charismatic W.A. Fearon, and later the volcanic Headmaster himself. Skues, on the other hand, seems to have been an unenthusiastic classicist, and admits in 'Trivialities' that 'I never felt that there was any music in Latin verse'.

For many boys of that era the process of being hauled through several years of ancient texts and grammar served only to provide them with one more ingredient in the gentlemanly veneer at one time so much prized and nowadays long gone. It expressed itself in the ready production of (sometimes) appropriate Latin tags for use in conversation or parliamentary speeches. Skues, at least, did derive two of his numerous *noms de plume* for his later writings – 'Integer Vitae' ('of a life unstained'), a phrase from the Odes of Horace, and 'Simplex Mundishes', a sort of whimsical reference to *simplex munditiis* ('simple in neat attire'), also from the Odes. He seems at least to have had some appreciation of Horace, that witty and succinct poet who was plundered by so many English authors for useful quotes. But overall he gives the impression of being just one more of that great army of boys down the centuries who regarded their years of Classics-grind as a drudgery, to be instantly banished from their minds on leaving school.

Oman, in contrast, began in his fourth year to have a real feeling for classical literature and history. His description of the syllabus is interesting.

The boys had to get through nearly all of Virgil and most of Horace, also large parts of Livy and Cicero, but none of the more racy Roman authors, such as Tacitus and Juvenal. Any hint of sexual impropriety was enough to ban an author. So Catullus was not on the list, and there was no chance of Petronius even being thought of. In Greek the emphasis was mainly on the great dramatists – Sophocles, Aeschylus and Euripides (but not Aristophanes), and the orators, such as Demosthenes, but not the interesting historians such as Herodotus and Thucydides. 'And why not Plutarch?' Oman added regretfully.

Charles Oman was a natural scholar, unlike his ally of the poaching expeditions. He was obviously marked out for an academic career. By contrast the summary of Skues' scholastic progress has survived, and shows him to have been an average middle-of-the-road scholar, whose order in form was not anywhere near the top, and who won none of the coveted prizes. In his final year he was twelfth in his form (Sixth Book, Junior division).

It is instructive to compare his unimpressive entry with that of the other entry on the same page, for one James Parker Smith, who carried off several prizes, was awarded a scholarship to Trinity College Cambridge, was called to the Bar, and became an MP – in other words, a Wykehamist star. However, it would be safe to say that the name of Skues has survived down the years in better shape than that of J.P. Smith.

In 1876 Skues continued his attempts to get on terms with the trout of the Old Barge, with little success. By his own account he must have been over-enthusiastic at striking. One afternoon he lost a good fish and the whole of his gut cast at the same moment, and was rescued by a kindly angler who provided him with another. Skues wondered long afterwards if he might have been Major Carlisle, the Secretary of the Houghton Fly Fishing Club. It was the first time he had ever seen a tapered cast, and he was so innocent that he attached it to his casting line by the fine end. His bad luck continued, however, for he rose another good trout and lost fish and cast once more: 'It was the biggest trout I had ever hooked or even seen hooked. I went back to the college on the verge of tears of disgust and chagrin.'

In the holidays Skues was still living with the family of Dr Kealy at Gosport, and getting some days of saltwater fishing. The productive roach fishing expedition mentioned in Chapter 1 took place about this time. This period of his life in Gosport came to an end when his parents returned from Malta in 1875 and settled in St Helier on Jersey. William

Skues then took up his final post as Principal Officer of Health for the Channel Islands.

The College magazine provides a little more information about Skues in the autumn of 1876. He is recorded as having put on an exhibition of Lepidoptera as part of a meeting of the 'Bug and Snail' with another boy. His partner showed examples from Switzerland, while Skues' specimens came from Jersey. Sixty boys attended this show, and Ridding, who often chaired these meetings, may have been there. Skues was also praised in the magazine for his performance in a game of Winchester football on 26 October. This was the period when he began to enjoy himself a little. Moving up the College year by year meant acquiring small freedoms and privileges, and the earlier miseries and humiliations could be forgotten.

But life became more serious after Christmas, and there was to be no fishing for him at Winchester in 1877. He was working for his leaving examinations and could allow himself little free time. His labours paid off, and in the summer he was recorded as being one of sixteen Wykehamists who had been awarded the Oxford and Cambridge Examining Board's Certificate. Sixteen was a good score: Marlborough was close behind with thirteen successful candidates and Dulwich with twelve. Only Eton, a much larger school, did better, with twenty-five. At the end of the summer term of 1877 he left the College, and the next stage of his life began.

What had he taken away from this school experience? He had first of all acquired certain attributes of the conventional sort, that is to say advantages of which the College would approve. He was not afraid of hard, sustained work and application. Unlike some old boys of the public schools who could look forward to a comfortable existence on their own means, Skues knew that his life would be one of unremitting work. He did not, in fact, retire until he was eighty-two. He had also been toughened by his experiences of austerity and adversity, and had made the useful discovery that the world could be an awkward and unfair place.

The downside of all this, which the College authorities would not have admitted, took several forms. The curriculum, even though it had moved forward under Ridding, did not contain much that would prepare someone for the modern world of the time, although the school societies may have helped a little. Winchester was probably as philistine as any of the other public schools of the day, at least until the advent of a very different kind of leadership, in the person of Monty Rendall in 1911.

There were two rather more subtle influences that were less beneficial.

Winchester, as we have seen, was a place that valued conformity. This might do no harm to many boys – the average, perhaps not very penetrating sort, who can contrive to be happy in most situations. Such pupils derive advantages from their school experiences from simple acceptance. But there have always been a number of disgruntled rebels in the public school system who, in later life, have complained about the pressures to conform. Harold Nicolson was in good company in thinking that the public school system 'standardizes character and suppresses originality'. Skues had a hard task holding on to his own sense of self, and such people flourish as much by rebellion as by acceptance. He wrote in 'Trivialities': 'All through my five years at Winchester I was dimly conscious of a pressure to mould me to a pattern, and though I count these five years as the happiest of my life … my instinct was to resist the pressure and to retain my individuality.'

Finally, for young Skues, the experience of living for several years in a closed single-sex community certainly slowed down his emotional and social development, already damaged by the sketchy arrangements of his home life and by his imperfect and interrupted relationship with his parents. The old public school system has often been charged with sending its alumni out into the world in an emotionally impoverished state, innocent as babes and quite unable to relate to women. Charles Oman admits that, after Winchester, he was a gauche young man at Oxford, avoided all social engagements and was frankly terrified of women. At least after many years of bachelordom he achieved a happy marriage. The experience of Skues in that area was destined to be far less satisfactory.

3

Apprenticeship

IN THE SUMMER of 1877 Skues joined his family in St Helier and enrolled in the Victoria College on the Island of Jersey. There had been some talk at family conferences of his going to Oxford University, but his father probably realized that this might be too expensive, even with a scholarship. About the same time, Skues was offered the chance of articles with a London solicitor who had, on occasion, acted for the family. Having got his School Certificate he would not have to take the Law Society's entrance examination. This move decided the next stage of his life. He says in 'Trivialities' that if he had gone to Oxford he would have turned out to have been an idler. This has an air of sour grapes, but perhaps his instinct was correct, though for quite different reasons: a shy and impecunious young man might not have enjoyed college life much in the 1880s.

His job interview with James Powell of 34 Essex Street got off to an odd start. Powell began, perhaps a little pompously, by saying: 'This is a very old-established firm.' Skues, no doubt a little apprehensive, and compensating by a show of worldly confidence, answered: 'So I inferred from the blotting paper.' Powell responded: 'Damn your impudence.' This must rate fairly high in the annals of bad-start interviews. However, Powell's impression of Skues improved during the interview, although he must have had doubts about having such a pert young man about the office. Skues was therefore offered a two-month trial period to begin in 1878 before being judged fit to be granted articles.

No record survives of the sequence of events here, but it was probably as a result of this interview that Skues was placed at Victoria College, Jersey for the latter part of 1877. The College had a more wide-ranging approach than Winchester and many other traditional English schools. From its beginning in 1852 the intention had been to avoid being too narrowly academic, and there was a modern as well as a classical side.

Commercial subjects such as book-keeping and merchants' accounts were taught, and it may be that Powell knew something of the curriculum at Victoria College and advised Skues to spend some time in catching up on some useful modern subjects before becoming an articled clerk. Accordingly the entry shortly afterwards appeared in the College records as having arrived in the third term of 1877 (there were four terms a year): 'SKUES, George E.M. Son of Dr. W.M. Skues, Clarence Terrace.' His experience there may have been of great value, for the approach complemented that of Winchester. He would also have been able to improve his written and conversational French in the classroom and his colloquial French in leisure time.

In due course Skues returned to London, established himself in a cheap hotel, and began work in Essex Street on the edge of the City of London. Powell soon realized that this hard-working clerk was good value, and the memory of the ill-timed familiarity at their first meeting faded. Skues was taken on for five years, was given a post when he qualified in 1883 and was eventually made a partner in 1895. Skues never moved from Essex Street: he was to stay with the firm until the end of his working life in 1940.

Skues was fortunate in some ways to have entered the profession when he did. The steady increase in commercial activity in late-Victorian Britain had created a need for more lawyers. Moreover, their status was rising. Earlier in the nineteenth century the public tended to look a little askance at solicitors, many of whom had ascended from the ranks of office clerks, and in whom a professional code was often lacking. Charles Dickens' satirical sketch of the sharp but shifty firm of Dodson and Fogg in *The Pickwick Papers* would have been received with widespread recognition in the 1830s. But this had begun to change twenty years later, when the tide of reform of institutions gathered pace. There was a growing feeling that more competence was required from the professions, and in various ways the government decided to administer a wake-up call to the civil service, the medical profession, the forces and also the lawyers. The Law Society believed that public confidence would be increased if every solicitor had the benefit of a liberal education and could be recognized by his clients as a gentleman. This was never going to be easy, but in 1860 the Society took a first step in setting up a preliminary general knowledge test for intending articled clerks. In 1873 all members of the profession became Solicitors of the Supreme Court, and the word attorney officially disappeared, surviving ironically as a shorthand term of disrepute in conversation. In these and other ways the Law Society hoped to attract more people from the public schools and universities into a profession of growing status.

Powell's firm was not one of the prominent and highly successful firms likely to provide good or even sensational copy for the newspapers, such as Freshfields, Paine and Layton (later Linklater and Paine) or Lewis and Lewis. It was solid and dependable rather than showy, specializing in inheritance law, trusts and family settlements, although litigation crept in from time to time. James Powell ran a small outfit. There was a sleeping partner (another of the Powell family), who was rarely seen and who spent most of his time on the Riviera. Years later Douglas Goodbody wrote of Powell's that 'professionally they had a high reputation but not a large business'. Essex Street was just off the Strand and therefore well placed in legal London. Barristers' chambers in the Temple were within a walk of a few minutes, and Lincoln's Inn (a more likely connection for Powell's sort of practice) was only a little further away. Sending out the office boy in buttons to hail a cab would not often have been necessary, except perhaps for a trip to Gray's Inn.

The office of the Victorian solicitor was generally a stuffy, respectable place with a good deal of dark polished wood, in which a deep silence reigned, at least until the advent of the typewriter. In 1879 *The Solicitors' Journal* reported that 'an eminent firm of City solicitors' had installed a telephone, but it was to be some time before such a novel idea became generally accepted. By Skues' day the steel pen had come in, but the quill pen still had its devotees. Apart from the 'necessary woman', the employment of females in offices was almost unknown. In fact, women were not likely to be seen at this end of the town, and less and less so the further one journeyed into the City; indeed, they were at times treated with discourtesy if seen wandering in such a masculine enclave.

Superficially the area still resembled the London of Charles Dickens, but great changes were taking place, particularly on the north side of the Strand opposite the junction with Essex Street. Photographs of the 1860s show a down-at-heel slum ripe for development. A decade later the government resolved to move the courts of law from their inconvenient but centuries-old home in Westminster, and this became the site they had in mind. Within a few short years 400 buildings were swept away, as also were over 4,000 hapless citizens, and in 1874 work began on the construction of a home for the Law Courts. By 1883, when Skues began his time as an articled clerk, the new buildings, designed by the architect G.E.

Street and not destined to be much loved by those using them, were nearing completion a hundred yards from 34 Essex Street, and already absorbing the black smut of the appalling atmosphere of the age.

The relocation of the Law Courts to the Strand was only part of the story. When Skues was starting on his career as a lawyer the legal system had just gone through its most profound change in centuries. Lord Selborne's Judicature Act of 1873 had merged the curious tangle of the older courts, some parts of which went back to the time of Edward I, and had set up the Supreme Court of Judicature in three main divisions. Furthermore the ancient distinction between Common Law and Equity was done away with. There would now be less chance of the endless suits in Chancery, of baffled and despairing litigants voyaging from court to court in pursuit of claims and of similar anomalies, to which the label of 'Dickensian' has generally been applied. Also, the criminal code had been tidied up and consolidated.

These great changes meant that Powell and colleagues of his generation, who had learned their trade under the old system, would have had to learn new tricks. However, new entrants to the profession would have found studying the theory and practice of the law less complicated than had their seniors some years earlier. Skues was to have a more straightforward time than if he had begun articles earlier in the century.

For five years Skues toiled in the gaslight of the Essex Street office, puzzling over abstracts of title, trying his hand at the drafting of wills and trust instruments, following his master to the courts and to chambers in one of the Inns of Court for a consultation with counsel, and observing how clients might be treated. He had to live and dress on the parental allowance of £80 a year and, in his own words, 'a tight squeeze it was'. He lodged in a private hotel in Paddington and walked several miles a day across London to get to work. There could be no question of public transport. Trainee solicitors could expect no wage during their term of articles, and this bohemian style of life must have been hard – *res angustae* again. As he made his way home in the evening it was his habit to buy from a stall a hot baked potato for twopence.

However, in spite of being on short commons he developed physically and, by 1883, he attained the weight of 11st. He admits in his memoir that Winchester had slowed down his growth. When he left school at nineteen he was only 5ft 4in tall but, in the next three years, in spite of his circumstances, he grew to 5ft 8½in. Realizing that life in London was poor training for the fatigues of a long day on the river he developed the habit of running up the stairs of the Law Courts three or four at a time, carrying a heavy bag of documents. One evening he helped in a small crisis at Powell's house in Connaught Square, by carrying the cook three floors up to her bedroom. Her dimensions were not recorded but she was certainly drunk and incapable. In later life his stamina and dogged style were useful for long days at the riverside, especially at Abbots Barton, a tiring fishery which caused much wilting of guests. This useful quality stayed with him well into his eighties.

During these years he acquired a great love of the theatre, although he could only afford the cheapest of all seats in the pit. From there he watched Henry Irving, the Bancrofts and many other giants of the day. He records in 'Trivialities' that one evening an overwrought but unknown young woman in the next seat laid her head upon his shoulder and 'sobbed unrestrainedly' at the performance of Irving as Charles I and Ellen Terry as Henrietta Maria at their last meeting before Charles' execution.

For a time Skues' theatre-going encouraged him in the idea of becoming a playwright, and be admits that he 'perpetrated some appalling trash in pursuit of that ambition'. Some of his synopses and part-scenes have survived, and are enough to confirm his later opinion that the Victorian stage lost nothing by being deprived of his contributions.

Fishing during his years of articles was infrequent and not memorable, consisting mainly of coarse fishing expeditions to the Thames, sea fishing in the Channel Islands and occasional visits to a carp pond on Jersey. In 1879 he acquired from Bowness Ltd in the Strand, a curious and not very practical combination rod of the sort that impresses beginners who lack experience or good advice. This fearsome rod could be converted to various uses by a system of alternative top joints. He kept this rod (for some reason) until 1887. But the delights of shopping for tackle were not for him. He would study the trade catalogues and mark down the shops, so that on Saturday afternoons he could prowl around ogling the unattainable merchandise of Bernard, Farlow, Holroyd and many another.

The really important step forward, which was to settle the course of his fishing life in the channel for which it is known today, came in 1883, the year of his qualifying as a solicitor. Sometime in the late spring or summer of that year he visited the International Fisheries Exhibition at the Royal Horticultural Society's hall in Kensington. It is likely that he went more than once, although the cost of entry of 1s may have discouraged him a little. Shillings were not plentiful for Skues the articled clerk and he would certainly not have made a Wednesday visit since, on that day, the entry cost 2s 6d, a customary tactic with big public exhibitions to raise the tone and discourage the attendance of the lower orders.

Victorians were good at big shows of this sort. The Fisheries Exhibition was the largest of its kind up to that date, and it lasted from 12 May until the end of October, by which time it was able to record 2.7 million visits. There was a bewildering array of stands from home and abroad, and it is a pity not to have an account from Skues, written at the time. Did he seek out the life-saving apparatus, the Marquis of Exeter's whale and the flamingo pond? Did he pass by the otters, the seals and the beavers? Did the Native Guano Company merit a glance? He has, however, told us that his attention – and admiration – was chiefly for the fly-fishing section. Here were Holroyd's double-winged floaters, Little and Co.'s Mayfly with hook at the head instead of the tail (to aid the process of hooking, so it was claimed) and Farlow's Red and Grey Gnats and a fly called Hollock's Peculiar (a midge, apparently). Alfred & Sons of Moorgate Street had 400 patterns on show, all tied on 'Mr Hall's new eyed hooks'. Hardy's flies, described by the editor of *The Fishing Gazette* as better than any others on show, were 9s a dozen, which, he added, 'places them beyond the means of the majority'. By contrast the flies of David Wells of Edinburgh, said to be as good for fishing in the south country as in the north, were 1s 3d a dozen.

Best of all to see were the fly-tiers in action: Mrs Cox of Winchester, Mrs Brocas of Victoria and Miss Horne of Hereford, a comparative newcomer, whose productions included Green Midges, Yellow Duns, Iron Blues and Dotterels. It was intoxicating: Skues says in his memoir that seeing the fine show of split-winged floaters 'fired me with an ambition to be a fly fisher'. It would seem therefore that posterity owes a considerable debt of gratitude to these talented women.

In the same year he at last had the chance of making a start on a trout stream. This arose from an extraordinary piece of random good fortune, rather than any purposeful act on the part of Skues. If he had not joined that particular firm it is unlikely that he would have ever come into contact with the Cox family, to whom he was to owe his introduction to the Abbots Barton fishery.

In 1854 an uncle of James Powell, one Edward William Cox, had taken what might have appeared a risky step in purchasing an ailing sporting paper, *The Field*. In its short life of a little over a year it had not prospered, and might soon have shared the fate of many such ventures.

Cox was, however, a bold and also a capable speculator, and under his guidance its fortunes changed. Soon it became one of the most successful papers of the Victorian publishing scene. Cox went on to build up an impressive magazine business, which included *The Queen, The Law Times, Crockford's Clerical Directory, Yachting Monthly*, and other prints. On the death of Edward Cox in 1879 Powell was appointed solicitor to the trustees of his estate. This meant that he had frequent professional contact with his cousin Irwin Edward Bainbridge Cox, the son of Edward William Cox, who had become part-proprietor and the major shareholder of his father's empire. This was a fortunate professional connection for Powell, for Irwin Cox found him to be a safe pair of hands, and passed over more and more of the legal side of his business interests. The premises of *The Field* were near at hand, and Cox would, of necessity, have been frequently in Powell's office in the period after 1879, and would have become aware of the young clerk who was aiming to qualify. After a while he discovered that he was mad keen to get started on fly-fishing, but was lacking opportunities. Cox was generous with his permissions, and a number of anglers had cause to be grateful to him. In 1883, to his great joy, Skues was able to hold in his hand a day ticket for Cox's water at Abbots Barton on the fabled Itchen above Winchester.

And so in May 1883 began the association of Skues with the fishery that was to become a central part of his life. At first Irwin Cox gave him odd days, and for some years he only had three or four days a season but, he records, 'when he saw how desperately keen I was he got into the habit of sending me a comprehensive ticket which allowed me to go down whenever I liked'. So he owed a great deal to Cox, but the arrangement was perhaps not as one-sided as might appear. Cox was giving a good deal of work to James Powell, and some of the more straightforward matters would no doubt have been placed on the desk of the newly qualified recruit. The relationship may have had a professional element.

Skues' first impressions of Abbots Barton must have been bewildering. The fishery began on the upstream side of Winchester, and was an extensive and rather curious place. It is sad that one has to speak of it in the past tense, for it has undergone a great change. As late as the 1960s, when the Piscatorial Society had the fishing there, its aspect was not greatly different from Skues' time. He would not know it today.

Its character was not much like other Itchen waters. For a considerable distance upstream from Winchester the main river was impounded in order to get a good head of water for the service of a mill. This involved a good deal of embanking, so that the river level was higher than the surrounding meadows. The slow pace of this stretch and the clarity of the water meant that the fish could make a close scrutiny of flies natural and artificial. Also, ascending nymphs would have more difficulty here in piercing the surface envelope of the water, a snag for Skues at the dry-fly stage of his education, but an immense opportunity in the future. Success with the dry fly was more likely to be attained in the carriers to the west of the main water, where the pace was quick and lively. Fly life was everywhere abundant, and the hatches were frequently on such a scale that the fish would only take the occasional natural, a situation guaranteed to drive the angler to distraction. John Goddard has recorded that, in the 1960s, many of the Piscatorial Society found the trout of Abbots Barton too difficult for them and went elsewhere in search of less complicated fishing.

Trout were plentiful in the early days. The size limit was 12in, and there was no bag limit of numbers in the Cox era. There were two-pounders to be had here and there, but they were not numerous: the first that Skues looked upon were three in number, laid out on the floor of the fishing hut by their captor, Francis Francis, another beneficiary of the kindness of Irwin Cox. Skues must have yearned to catch a leash such as this, but success was a long way off for him. Francis was the Angling Editor of *The Field*, and possessed the skill of many years.

Much later, Skues discovered that Francis and George Selwyn Marryat had previously rented the Abbots Barton fishing, from 1879 to 1882 (in other words just prior to the tenancy of Cox), and had put in some stew-bred fish. He wondered if the fish in the hut had been the survivors of this stock. Cox saw no need to stock such a prolific natural fishery. The larger fish were seen less and less at Abbots Barton, and by the middle 1880s the average size of the fish was 13 or 14in. It is something of a shock to learn from Skues' later writings that he did not catch his first two-pounder until 1892. However, it is worth reminding ourselves that, in that era, on both the Itchen and the Test, fish of that size were looked upon with respect. The artificial stocking of chalk streams was already an established practice, and in some places large fish were put in, but many owners, well aware of the average size of the natural progeny of their waters, would only stock with fish of moderate size. In any case, after 1882, no more experiments in stocking took place at Abbots Barton until the early 1920s.

It might have been better for young Skues to have been let loose on a more forgiving piece of fishing, where his tyro efforts could have been rewarded, but nothing else was available and he struggled on for some years with little to show for much hard work. However, he eventually grew to appreciate the challenge, and in his later years had little time for straightforward easy fishing. After the publication of his first book in 1910 he received invitations to well-known fisheries elsewhere, but they often seem to have had little interest for him. Dr Barton took him to his fishing at Leckford on several occasions, but a day with stocked trout was not something that he considered worth an article. He had notable days in Bavaria and Würtemberg, at least as to numbers, but always returned to Winchester 'convinced that this was the real thing'.

In the 1880s Skues made up for the rather meagre allowance of time on the Itchen each season by fishing many other streams. A weekend of fishing at Winchester, as it would be understood today, was not available to him, because the lease to Irwin Cox forbade Sunday fishing. Also, Skues had sometimes to be in the Essex Street office on Saturday mornings. This meant that his progress in chalk-stream technique was painfully slow. Beginners, even those who go on to great things later, still need frequent visits to the river to overcome the early problems of a fishing career: having only the occasional day is more likely to confirm mistakes than to solve them. But by the end of the decade, when he was able to go to Abbots Barton at will, Skues wrote in 'Trivialities' that he felt he was becoming an effective practitioner. In 1890 and 1891 he was able to record a total of thirty days on the Itchen – in his own words 'none of them blank and some days up to five brace'.

If this seems an inordinately slow development at first, there are several other factors that might also account for it. First, he had two fairly important physical disabilities. A bungled operation on his left eye when he was nine years old had left him with very little sight on one side, a serious matter on a chalk stream where sight fishing is so important. An unlucky fall in 1877 while playing football on holiday with his family in Jersey smashed both his wrists: they were never quite the same again. In more modern times an extensive and delicate procedure in a hospital theatre would no doubt have followed, but nothing like that was available to the injured sportsman of 1877. In his memoir he writes, somewhat breezily, that accidents of this sort aroused little interest in those days – the only treatment he was advised to employ was to hold the damaged wrists under a cold water tap. A photograph of Skues taken by his old friend Dr Barton when he was over eighty shows both defects: Barton, the observant medical man, pointed out the distortion and enlargement of the right wrist in particular, and also the drooping upper lid of the partially blind left eye. The heavily-built rods of the early split-cane era must have been torture for him. Casting was no joke anyway on many days at Abbots Barton. It was a bare, open place, where there was very little shelter from the winds that swooped down or across the bare valley. Trees were most likely to be found along the Ducks' Nest Spinney: in most other places accurate casting could become very difficult. It is curious to reflect that the man who has been called the greatest angling mind of the twentieth century began as a disabled angler and continued so throughout his life without any improvement from medical science.

However, there may have been another and more subtle reason for this rather laboured and sluggish start to what became a great angling career. In 1887 Skues began to read Halford's first book *Floating Flies and How to Dress Them*. For him (and many others) this was a revelation, and he soon afterwards began his first experiments in fly-dressing. At the end of the book was a short section on riverside tactics. Here were set forth in condensed form the basic maxims of the craft: keep out of sight as much as possible, find a feeding fish, try to ascertain on what it is feeding and give it the best copy as possible of the natural, and present it carefully to the fish, without drag. In 1889 there appeared *Dry-Fly Fishing in Theory and Practice,* Halford's major study. Much later in his career, even after a coolness and then an antagonism had grown up between them, Skues gave generous acknowledgement to these two books, which had done so much to advance the skills of contemporary anglers. But their effect, though liberating, was at the same time inclined to be oppressive. Halford, perhaps unwittingly, gave the impression that he had provided the reader with a complete and definitive guide. Individual initiative and experiment seemed to be discouraged. This was in direct contrast to the impression created by Skues' writings some years later. Instead of a sort of blueprint of instructions by a man who seemed to have done all the necessary experiments, Skues' writings often took the form of a series of intriguing observations and suggestions, written in undogmatic terms, and frequently encouraging the angler to do his own observing and experimenting. And whereas Halford clearly liked the notion of being regarded as an authority, Skues rejected the title for himself and frequently reproved correspondents for describing or addressing him as such.

But all this lay well in the future. In his early years he was completely in thrall to Halford and regarded his books as the last word. His own shyness and lack of confidence at that stage of his life also contributed. All that was needed, he thought, was to pore over Halford's books, learn all the advice and apply it on the river. Relying on Halford may have been useful at first, but after a year or two it must have slowed him down a great deal. The idea that these sacred texts were insufficient, or could in any way be questioned, would not have occurred to him. Hills said much the same in *My Sporting Life*: writing in 1936 he imagined someone observing his bungling attempts to beguile the trout of the Test at Whitchurch in his days of innocence in 1890 – endlessly false casting to dry the fly, casting underhand, as prescribed by the master's books, in order to cock a too heavily winged pattern, and feverishly changing the fly: 'Had he followed me to the inn, he would have wondered as I restlessly turned over the pages of *Dry-Fly Fishing in Theory and Practice* to discover where I had gone wrong.'

So Halford had cast a heavy shadow, and in his inability to escape from it Skues was only one of a large number. Why busy himself with experimenting if it had all been done for him? Many years later C.A.M. Skues, in the foreword to *Itchen Memories* (1950), alluded delicately to this rather uneventful part of his brother's angling life.

And so between 1883 and 1887 Skues struggled on at Abbots Barton, hampered but not discouraged by these obstacles. The heavy rods he used were at least better than 'the awful pole' of his schooldays, but their performance (and indeed his) was unimpressive – 'owing to my nervous haste I left far too many flies in the noses of indignant trout'. As for flies, he had not yet got hold of any systematic principle. They were not imitations of nature so much as mere instruments to catch fish. For such beginners a fly-box is a collection of lottery tickets: that one pattern should succeed rather than another is a mystery. Many anglers can relate to this familiar groping and stumbling process of learning. Some never really emerge from it. It is not surprising that he wrote almost nothing about his catches in the few years at Abbots Barton. As with his attempts on the Old Barge as a schoolboy, there was very little to tell.

He was, however, making certain advances in fly-fishing theory. His experience at the International Fisheries Exhibition and his reading of *Ogden on Fly Tying* and Halford's *Floating Flies* in 1887 had left him with a fascination for imitative flies that lasted all his life. Before 1887 he had no theory upon which to proceed. Soon after reading Halford's first book he took his first steps in fly-dressing, and he began a systematic survey of artificial flies. To this end he started to visit the Reading Room of the British Museum (the forerunner of the British Library) to gain access to all that had been written and published on the subject down the ages. The earliest library request slip to have survived is dated 14 May 1887. For several years he spent what spare time he could contrive under the great blue and gold Panizzi dome searching through ancient volumes back as far as the *Treatyse* of 1496.

His early contributions to *The Fishing Gazette* are interesting signposts to his progress as a fisherman. They are unremarkable and carry no clue of his later extraordinary development as an angler. His first appearance was in the form of a letter on 27 February 1886, appealing for information about sea fishing in April in the harbours in the south-east of England and on the opposite French coast. Two months later he enquired about flies for catching grey mullet. He made several more rather low-key interventions in the correspondence column. In February 1887 he used for the first time the *nom de plume* 'Val. Conson.'. This became (without the full stops) his usual signature for letters and contributions to *The Fishing Gazette*: 'val conson' is a piece of lawyers' shorthand for 'valuable consideration', i.e. money or money's worth. He wrote later that when he began to write articles he hoped that the editor R.B. Marston would take the hint and that payment might be forthcoming, but it was some time before there was any response from him. For his appearances in *The Field* he called himself Seaforth and Soforth, a whimsical title derived from his schooldays at Winchester. Skues had rather unguardedly revealed that he was descended on the maternal line from the Earls of Seaforth, whereupon one of his contemporaries fastened upon him the nickname of Seaforth and Soforth and the Isles Thereof. We do not know how long this mock title stuck to him, but the name of the witty inventor has survived: he was one Lucas, known as 'Pink' Lucas.

These rather inconsequential letters continue at intervals for some years. Almost none of them give any inkling of the quality of the man who was one day to become a leading and gifted innovator. There is, however, one that is worth noting. On 26 November 1887 he wrote a somewhat ill-tempered letter objecting to the manner and content of articles in *The Fishing Gazette*. There followed a list of commonly appearing details that ought to be discarded, such as tired and misplaced humour, long descriptions of eating, drinking and angling accommodation, railway journeys and descriptions of scenery. The important thing, he insists, is the fishing – all else is unnecessary padding. He set out examples of what is acceptable detail:

Tell us something of your water ... its feeders, the nature of the soil it flows through, its width, depth, pace, volume, colour, its vegetable and insect life, its overhanging bushes and trees and their insect life, the flies or baits that you use and their makers, your rod and its maker, your novel devices, your practical observations, your new patterns, the weather, the colour of the clouds and of the bottom, the state of the wind, the season of the year, and all those thousand and one things germane to the subject.

Thus, early in his career, did Skues set out his plan for his own journalism: fine writing is not wanted – angling deserves to be taken seriously. He stuck to this prescription throughout his life. He had no interest in an angling book that did not tell him something new that would improve his skills. His heroes among the writers of the past were therefore few in number. In his own writing he did not quite keep to a programme of high seriousness, and some years later readers of the newly established *Journal of the Flyfishers' Club* were to find themselves reading many articles of a humorous nature.

Other letters followed, and in the latter part of the 1880s a change can be observed. It becomes clear that the writer is acquiring a wide knowledge of artificial flies. He seems to have begun, as do many beginners, in a search for the killing fly, but he fairly quickly moved on to a systematic historical survey of artificial flies in general. This meant delving into the entirety of angling literature at the British Museum and copying and comparing all the fly patterns ever devised by the wit of man. His first intention was to master the subject as a piece of self-education. After some time he became ambitious to write a book on fly-dressing, distinguishing the schools of practice in different geographical areas and in different periods. However, as his knowledge and his critical sense increased, along with his self-confidence both as an individual and as an angler, he came to realize that there might, after all, be little value in this laborious exercise. Many of the inventions of past ages were illogical, whimsical and unsystematic. In the end he abandoned the research in some disgust, realizing that relying on his own observation and beginning with the natural world was the better plan. Later in life he looked back with relief on his decision not to publish a pattern book. All his later experience convinced him that a prescriptive list would be a bad thing. This was, he believed, Halford's mistake. Anglers ought to have their own ideas and to aim at personal versatility rather than being slaves to authority.

In March 1893 he drew a line under that period of his life in an article in *The Fishing Gazette* titled 'An Ideal Dictionary of Fly-Dressing'. It began: 'It was an idea of the hot wayward youth of my fly-dressing experience, and, in view of it, I expended no small labour in digesting from numerous authorities, and upon a uniform principle, all the dressings of all the flies (except Mayflies) on which I could lay my hands.'

His aim was to restore 'our classification of our British flies to something like intelligibility', and he was prepared to go to a great deal of trouble to achieve this, by obtaining 'from every tackle maker of note in England, and from other authorities lists of flies suitable to their localities'. He then sets out his desiderata for such a project, running into eighteen chapters. It was, he says, 'a beautiful dream', but it foundered on several problems. The historical record revealed numerous patterns that could never be identified against any natural fly. Also, many patterns were simply of no use, and many new ones were being invented and mentioned in the sporting press at a speed which made it impossible to keep up with them. He finishes, tongue rather regretfully in cheek, by writing: 'Wherefore I make a present to whoso will of the scheme of my Ideal Dictionary of Fly-dressing, and may he make it a great success.' No doubt daunted by his rather grim list of chapters to cover the essential areas to be covered, no one came forward for many years to take up the gage he had thrown down, until Courtney Williams produced his *Trout Flies: A Discussion and a Dictionary*, later expanded into *A Dictionary of Trout Flies* in 1949.

So, was this lengthy pursuit of knowledge all wasted? In fact several useful advantages came out of it. By 1893 there can have been few people in Britain who knew more about fly-fishing history than Skues. For him this new knowledge was not mere antiquarianism, but something useful on which to build for the future. A series of his notes survives from this period, examining the contributions of over forty authors, each one in a penny note book. Generally they contain a list of flies, with the recipe for each, but sometimes trenchant comments appear; for example, against the list derived from Richard Brookes, *The Art of Angling* (1781) he wrote: 'This is a plain prig from Chetham of Smedley.' He had no time for copyists, a fairly numerous body of angler-writers over the last 500 years. James Chetham was one of his heroes, together with Cotton, Bowlker, Ronalds and Cutliffe, and of the moderns, Francis Francis, Halford and Robert Austin of Tiverton.

The 1893 article represented a great step forward for Skues. The years of research had not been in vain. They helped him to build up his own store of knowledge, and to have the confidence to move away from meek acceptance of tradition and book learning. And there had been other milestones. His early attempts at fly-dressing had suddenly begun to show results when a few years earlier he had been marooned on a strange river – he does not say which, but it may have been the Teme – with no helper to advise and no tackle shop nearby. Forced to proceed empirically, he had caught examples of hatching flies, had improvised with such materials as he had with him and, as he wrote: 'I had quite enough success to cure me of reverence for a pattern merely because it was described in a book, and I have ever since been an advocate of free trade and free thought in fly-dressing as opposed to tradition.'

And there were several other significant pointers for the future, although he later admitted that he had been slow to learn from them. His experiments with gut-bodied flies in order to achieve a measure of translucency on the Coquet at Weldon Bridge in September 1888, his meeting with Halford in September 1891 and the often-quoted incident of the poorly dressed dry fly which sank all come into this category. In 1939, looking back on his long life, he wrote: 'Such success as I have had has been due to hard thinking and close observation and an intense desire to probe the real reason of things.' The process of thinking for himself began in the early part of the 1890s and by the end of the decade he was becoming a thinker of great originality.

Perhaps one has to have been in a straitjacket in order to make one's escape and to rejoice in freedom.

4

The Other Life

NOT ALL OF Skues' life was to be on a river. If he had been a man of means, as was Halford, he could have and probably would have done little else but fish. But there were other matters apart from fishing calling for his attention after 1883. He had to maintain himself in life and, with the health of his parents failing towards the latter end of the decade, it was becoming clear that he was going to have to look after his brothers and sisters as well. In fact he had already taken on a good deal of the business of running the family for some time before the death of his father in 1892. This threw a considerable physical and mental burden on a young man who was working hard to establish himself in his profession, and who struggled for much of his adult life with feelings of shyness and lack of self-esteem.

Sources for this period of his life are scattered and tantalizing. If he had come from a literary family that had left behind a rich archive of lively correspondence dealing with day-to-day life and the world of men and women, then a biographical investigation would be much more fruitful, and a fair picture of the man could have emerged. But the Skues family was not of that type, and discussions of personality and of the deeper feelings were not going to happen. 'Trivialities' contains some useful clues, but it is in the main an unsatisfactory source, cautious and reticent, which conceals as much as it reveals. There is a good deal of Skues' life about which we will never know anything, and that is how he would have wanted it.

However, one interesting source has survived, which in an oblique manner can tell us a great deal about the real man who was G.E.M. Skues. This is a collection of twelve manuscript notebooks, beginning in 1882 when he was twenty-four and finishing in 1894. On the covers they are entitled 'Notions' – no doubt a Winchester College memory, although they have no connection at all with the local slang of his schooldays.

Inside are 2,366 numbered entries of varying length, some of only a line or two, others of a page or more. These notebooks are in fact commonplace books under another name. Records of this type turn up fairly frequently in the family papers of past ages, but it is doubtful that they are much seen today. Young, socially uneasy people used often to look for and write down material which could be made use of in a social gathering. They seem to have thought that this might enable them to adorn their conversation and advance themselves in the opinion of others, although the results must at times have been a little stilted. If the commonplace books of Skues had amounted to no more than that, they would hold little interest for us today. However, their focus changes after a while, providing a number of useful insights. In particular they throw an oblique but intriguing light on the attempts of Skues to understand and get on terms with women, and to resolve the conflict between libido and inhibition. It does not look as if he was very successful. It was a common enough problem in that age, and the years spent in a single-sex boarding school could have the effect of increasing the feeling of estrangement between the sexes. Women, however delightful, were sometimes seen as baffling, even frightening creatures, as if they belonged to another species altogether. The art and literature of the time were not much help either, deriving many of their ideas from romantic notions of the medieval world. For some men the object of their attraction was seen as a goddess upon a pedestal.

The commonplace books begin in a fairly conventional manner. The entries, as with many other examples of this genre, are of smart and witty sayings and quotable ideas, some from books and newspapers, or from conversations with friends and acquaintances; also a good deal of bad verse. Some appear to have originated in Skues' own head. Epigrams and proverbial sayings also occur from classical authors – Ovid, Martial, Persius and most frequently from Horace, the author whose work seems to have stayed with him from the schoolroom to a greater extent than other writers of the ancient world. There are also a good many appalling puns and jokes deriving from unfortunate mistakes in advertisements and other public prints, mostly too heavy-handed and regrettable to be quoted here. One sample will suffice: 'Piano offered for sale by lady having handsome carved legs.' However, allowance has to be made for the change in humour that has taken place since that time, as anyone will know who has seen the cartoons in Victorian numbers of *Punch*.

But the scope of the entries soon changes to include other and more original subjects. His ambition to be a playwright has already been noted. Sketches for theatrical pieces begin to appear, even whole scenes. He admitted in later life that his attempts in this area were all tosh, but to be fair a good deal of late Victorian dramatic writing was unremarkable. Perhaps he was being a little unkind to himself. In 1889 the stage critic J.T. Green offered a prize for the best one-act play with not more than six characters in it. Skues, who at that time was part of an amateur dramatic group, entered a piece called 'Humble Pie', and was probably astonished to find that he was the winner, defeating forty-eight other contestants. The runner-up, even more surprisingly, was Israel Zangwill. Green tried to get a manager to stage Skues' play, without success. He then did the same with Zangwill's play, with no better success. Neither received the prize.

Halfway through the first notebook the thoughts occasionally become less second-hand and more personal. This process increases, and there are interesting signs that the collection is turning into a sort of alternative diary. Stray references to the younger members of the family creep in. Part of a school essay about Henry I by his 8-year-old brother Charles (C.A.M. Skues 1875–1958) ran thus: 'He had one sone and too dauters his sone and one dauter was drouned at sea.' The love between Skues and his younger brother was strong and lasted all their lives. In a later entry there is an affectionate note about Charles, then aged nine: 'Charles still keeps up his character of a philosopher. He comes out with the most sage remarks when you least expect it. I believe he thinks more than most people.' And a little later it seems that Charles also wishes to become a lawyer, and is accordingly making deep calculations: 'I mean to take George's place when he dies.'

Less happy are the indications of shyness to which I have already referred. They are paralleled and supported by the admissions he made in 'Trivialities'. It may be a fair inference that his problems stemmed from hurtful experiences in the early part of his life. The first term at Winchester College must have left its mark. But even earlier the lack of proper parenting and the sense of emotional deprivation probably went deep. In all his voluminous writings there is almost no mention of his parents, and when he does do so it is only in mundane contexts, and with no trace of affection. He makes a conventional reference only once to his 'admirable mother' (because of her efforts to teach him good manners), and none at all to his father. There is a certain irony in the fact that he saw little of them when he was young, and was not very far into maturity when they died, bequeathing to him the care of six siblings and little besides to maintain them. In 'Trivialities' he writes, with a touch of bitterness, that he was more or less pitched by fate into the unwished-for role of surrogate father and head of a family, with far more responsibilities than he had bargained for.

As time passed the feelings of reticence became modified and smoothed out. Success in his profession gave him a better opinion of himself. In later years the knowledge that he was becoming a figure of note in the world of angling would also have helped. But he was always a very private man, and a certain reticence remained with him. He records having seen George Selwyn Marryat at one of the annual Eton–Winchester cricket matches, but was unable to pluck up courage to go up and introduce himself. He regretted this piece of bashfulness all his life.

This lack of self-assurance had other odd results. Several passages in the 'Notions' commonplace books show that he had, by his early twenties, become convinced that he was ugly, and this became permanently fixed in his mind. There is a disturbing entry that refers to the time when he was articled and living in the cheap hotel in Paddington:

> Ugliness and ungainliness didn't matter to me at 20 for I had the grace of youth to believe in myself and whoso believes in himself can accomplish all things. But at 21 I was given a bedroom with a long pier glass in it and that has so destroyed my confidence in myself that I have long since adopted the conclusion that lady killing is not my vocation.

It may have been about this time that he acquired a morbid horror of being photographed (see Chapter 10).

A man of this sort was obviously suitable for the more sedate side of the legal profession. He was never going to be cut out for the role of barrister. He may well have appeared in the lower courts in small-scale matters, but solicitors could not appear in person in the High Court, and we cannot imagine that Skues would ever have been happy in such an arena. His métier was all for the careful and painstaking work of the office, including the briefing of barristers. He could be effective on paper but not in a verbal encounter. This trait was much later to surface very noticeably in the 1938 debate at the Flyfishers' Club.

The emotional life of Skues, such as it was, has always been a matter of speculation and mystery. Conrad Voss Bark, in an introduction to *The*

Chalk-Stream Angler (1975), muses over this question: 'He was a confirmed bachelor. He lived alone. He was certainly lonely in his age. Was he, like Theodore Gordon, denied a fuller life by inner complexities and inhibitions?' The writer adds, a little delicately, 'We do not know and perhaps it is as well not to know.' And yet Skues seems to have been as subject to the usual stirrings of the heart as any other young man of his age. A number of the earlier entries in 'Notions' are about women, but they are general rather than particular. Several of them are obviously the product of his imagination, being sketches for scenes or part scenes in the days of his ambition to be a playwright. The later entries are intriguing and much more specific. In real life, as far as can be gathered from the surviving sources, his success with women seems to have been painfully limited.

We may not know much, but there are a few clues as to the unsuccessful flounderings of Skues in the areas of love and romance. In the absence of letters, which would be the most revealing of all, the records of his private life at this time are the autobiographical fragment 'Trivialities', certain entries in the 'Notions' commonplace books, an enigmatic writing called 'To Incognita' published in *Sidelines, Sidelights and Reflections* (1932), the typescript of a curious descriptive piece called 'A Mayfly Idyll' about a young woman called Kate (see below and Appendix 1) and his own confession as to the real identity of 'Incognita' made to Dr Barton in the early 1930s.

'Trivialities' we may dismiss at once as a source for affairs of the heart. As mentioned above, its tale of real truths is a meagre one, and the dilemmas and defeats of life are not going to be described. Here and there in the memoir a door opens momentarily and is quickly shut. Enough has been said about Skues' cast of mind to show how unlikely it would ever be that he would breach his own privacy about most things, and even more so about the deep hurt of his life. Such men do not write frank Rousseau-esque confessions.

We might therefore never have known of his hopeless passion had it not been for the 'Incognita' piece and, many years later, his startling admission about it. In this somewhat fanciful essay he addresses an unnamed lady and wishes to walk with her through the water meadows on a summer evening in order for her to witness the most impressive display in the natural world that he can show her. This turns out to be (unsurprisingly) the dance of the spinners, which he compares to the fairy inhabitants of another world. This imitation of a Pre-Raphaelite vision is not first-class literature, but it is undoubtedly the outpouring of an ardent and distressed young man. As a source it presents certain problems. *Sidelines, Sidelights and Reflections* (1932) is an anthology of previously-published pieces by Skues, and each has at the end the place and date of previous publication. 'To Incognita', however, merely has '*Fishing Gazette*. Date missing, about 1890.' There is in fact no sign of it in *The Fishing Gazette*, either in 1890 or at any other time. Most probably it had been submitted to, and rejected by, the editor.

When it was first published, 'To Incognita' must have occasioned some puzzlement. It did not quite look as if it was an effort of imagination. It had all the lineaments of a real-life yearning, and some of the detail looked circumstantial enough – for example, the beginning: 'Dear Lady, Forgive the liberty I take in writing to you. You do not know who I am. You are never likely to know, nor need you care.... If I were rich, if I had anything to offer, I might come to you in other guise.'

And towards the end, another clue: 'And so in silence to your home. And tomorrow, when you sit enthroned in the cathedral, you shall never guess who among the worshippers is he who has opened to you the gates of fairy-land.'

So the inferences would seem to be that Skues is in love and that the object of his regard is to be seen each Sunday in the cathedral. He can therefore only worship the lady from afar, after the manner of a medieval troubadour. As John Keats expressed it, in lines lamenting the unattainable:

> *She cannot fade, though thou hast not thy bliss,*
> *For ever wilt thou love, and she be fair!*

One wonders if Skues came in for some gentle raillery at the Flyfishers' Club when 'To Incognita' was finally published in *Sidelines, Sidelights and Reflections*, but the only person to whom he revealed anything was Dr Barton. It is a testimony to the warmth of this friendship that Skues should have chosen to make him and no one else a confidante about a period of his young life, decades earlier, which had left him with a sense of failure and of loss. Barton learned, no doubt with astonishment, that the lady in the case was Alexandra Kitchin (known to family and friends as Xie, pronounced Ecksy), the daughter of the Dean of Winchester, George William Kitchin. All the detail of her parentage and background tends to show that, in raising his eyes to this paragon, Skues was setting his sights rather high.

Before coming to Winchester, Kitchin had been a tutor at Christ Church, Oxford, the largest college of the university. He was acquainted with the Danish royal family through his wife, who was a friend of the king's daughter Alexandra, shortly to become the wife of the Prince of Wales, later Edward VII. Princess Alexandra consented to be godmother to the Kitchins' first child, born in 1864, and accordingly she was christened Alexandra Rhoda. There survive a number of excellent photographs of Alexandra as a child. Charles Lutwidge Dodgson, better known as 'Lewis Carroll', the creator of *Alice in Wonderland*, was a colleague and close friend of the Kitchins at Christ Church, and a keen amateur photographer. He was particularly fond of photographing young girls, which has given rise to a good deal of unfavourable comment, both at the time and up to the present day. We can never be certain how innocent or otherwise his intentions were towards his young sitters. What is not in doubt is that he was an accomplished photographer at a time when the process needed a great deal of skill and hard work, and that he regarded Alexandra ('my dear little friend Xie') as his best subject. Between 1869 and 1880 he took more photographs of her – nearly fifty in fact – than of any other of his girl subjects. Unfortunately he took no pictures of her in her twenties, when Skues saw her in the full flower of her beauty and at once lost his heart. Dodgson tended to lose interest in small girls as soon as they were well into adolescence.

Kitchin had an impressive career at Oxford, writing many well-regarded books, and steering the new project of taking into the university the first students allowed to lodge outside College. No one could have been surprised when Gladstone arranged his translation as Dean to the diocese of Winchester. Here, his energy showed itself in a number of projects, amongst which may be mentioned co-operating with William Senior, R.B. Marston and Halford to set up in the cathedral the memorial to Francis Francis, and also the Izaak Walton window, in which Halford and Marston were also involved.

Kitchin may not have noticed the new face in his congregation. It seems doubtful that Skues would have been found in the cathedral at all on a promising fishing morning, but for the owner's ban which prevented Sunday fishing. At some point in 1884 he became aware of the beautiful girl in one of the neighbouring pews, and this shy, repressed young man was soon in the grip of a strange and one-sided predicament. We may imagine the unfortunate lovelorn swain, Sunday after Sunday, manoeuvring himself into a good vantage point, perhaps a row or two behind and to one side to secure the best view: she is said by those who knew her to have possessed a classic profile. No doubt Skues paid only a passing attention to her father's sermons.

Some commentators, relying on 'To Incognita', have left matters there – they never met, she was unattainable and perhaps not even aware of an admirer. There are some cryptic indications in the 'Notions' books, but they are not conclusive and seem more likely to have been references to another lady called Kate (see below). If he had contrived, perhaps clandestinely, to meet her, the 'Incognita' piece would have been written in the early 1880s. The unsuccessful attempt to get it published in *The Fishing Gazette* may have been in or around 1890.

No doubt it would have been a great triumph on Skues' part to contrive a meeting, but this would have been virtually impossible. In the Victorian era, in the absence of a formal introduction by someone of her circle, the business of getting to know a lady was fraught with difficulties. The protocol of the matter was a minefield, and was entirely directed towards preserving the good name of a woman, and of steering any attachment in the direction of engagement and marriage. Access to a woman of the middle class or upper class was only allowable under these rules, and flirtation (or, worse, an irregular liaison) might be her ruin. Casual encounters in the street or the public gardens were therefore not encouraged. From childhood onwards a girl's view of the world was carefully formed by parental precept and by the numerous etiquette books of the time. The advice columns of the girls' magazines were full of enquiries about behaviour from young females sheltering under pseudonyms such as Little Judy, Dimpled Dottie, Daddy's Little Pet and Worried Blue Eyes. The advice was severe and invariable: it was as much as your reputation was worth to be seen talking in the street to a stranger of the opposite sex not previously known to your family.

So all the signs are of an unrequited and doomed love, which must have left Skues at first shattered and, on recovery, a different man. Apart from having been badly hurt he must also have felt that, as a lover, he had cut a rather ridiculous figure in his own eyes. Dr Barton wrote in the margin of the 'Incognita' piece in his copy of *Sidelines*: '*Sunt lacrimae rerum*', a tag from Virgil that might loosely be rendered as 'A sad tale'.

The final end to an affair which never began came on 6 April 1890, when *The Times* reported the marriage in Winchester of Alexandra Kitchin to Mr A. Cardew, barrister at law.

Among the surviving fragments of his papers there is another sad soliloquy, composed by Skues in the 1880s (see Appendix 1). Its importance lies in its indications of an attachment to a different woman, which did not prosper either. Whereas 'To Incognita', though rejected at the time by R.B. Marston, was published about forty years later, this second piece was submitted, rejected and never published. Called 'A Mayfly Idyll', it describes an episode in which Skues appears to have made more progress, at least for a time. The manuscript was acquired by the great American collector Otto von Kienbusch when Skues passed over to him a bundle of his papers and books in 1946. Kienbusch loaned it to Alfred Miller, familiar to American anglers as 'Sparse Grey Hackle', who rendered the handwriting into a typescript. It is now part of the collection of the Anglers' Club of New York.

The first part of the piece dwells on the beauty of the riverside meadows, which is contrasted with the author's feelings of depression and youthful angst, and even thoughts of pain, fear and death. The Fitzgerald translation of the *Rubaiyat of Omar Khayyam* also makes an appearance: its themes of the transitory nature of human life and the emphasis on pleasure and the need to make haste made it a best-seller, particularly after Fitzgerald's death in 1883. There follows an account of a walk by the River Kennet with a young woman called Kate Anson (no doubt an invented name), with some smart and edgy dialogue. The ramble ends in a nearby church. Skues certainly knew this area well. In the early days of his time as a newly qualified solicitor a friendly client made him free of his fishery on the Kennet. The reference to a tributary called the 'Elbourne' may refer to the Lambourn or to the Enborne, which would mean that the scene was set near Newbury or Theale.

It would be unfair to reflect too harshly on the style of this odd, over-written piece, composed by the young Skues at a frustrated and unhappy time of his life. Many young people unburden themselves of similar writings in lovelorn prose or sentimental poetry. If they discover them years later in a turning-out of old cupboards the reaction is usually one of slight embarrassment, followed by recourse to the nearest wastepaper basket.

The 'Notions' commonplace books contain several references which specifically mention a lady Skues frequently saw in church. At first this might seem to be a direct reference to Alexandra, but the entries make it clear that these sightings are in a church, not a cathedral. Furthermore a gallery is mentioned, more than once, something which does not exist in Winchester Cathedral. Dates only occur spasmodically in 'Notions', but as far as can be guessed, the date of the first three entries that appear to relate to Skues and a lady was in April 1885: 'You call yourself a pagan. Yet I see you regularly in church.' And a little later: 'She knows not that I love her. I know she does *not* love me', followed by the more practical 'What is the use of thinking of such a thing while I pay the same income tax as a church mouse?'

This last consideration was a real problem. For some years Skues' salary would have been fairly modest. Things would have improved when he became a partner, but this did not happen until 1895. The first direct question of an intended father-in-law: 'Are you able to maintain my daughter in the style to which she is accustomed?' – nowadays a sort of joke – was serious enough in Victorian times. If Skues ever considered presenting himself before a formidable parent he knew he would not have much to offer.

As the entries continue the probability increases that they represent evidence of a deadlock in the mind of this unhappy young man. The distress of a man in love but making no progress is evident in this entry, later in the same year:

> As I lay in bed last night and looked out of the window I saw one solitary star rising from behind a chimney, and for some unexplained reason my thoughts flew to you. I never see anything fair on earth or sky without thinking of you. Perhaps because the last few days seem to have put you as far off from me as that same star – as far above me.

A little later come more forlorn lines on the same theme. Was the lady beginning to amuse herself with him, believing him not to be taken seriously? 'She is very elusive. One day I seem nearer her. She likes me – I know it. The next I am as far off as ever I was.' This sad game may have continued through the summer of 1885, and appears to have ended with rejection and, on his part, with bitterness:

> She looked about often in the direction of the place where I used to sit. Oh you little witch, does it ache? Ah I'd like to make it ache, ache if only one quarter as badly as you have made mine – only one quarter. Not because I want you to suffer pain, but because love transcends pain & transmutes it into pure gold, making the world better and brighter...The happiest time in my life was when

I loved you without hope. With hope came agony and sleepless nights.

There follow several entries about the pain of rejection and the need to face up to renunciation, but later he recovers a little and resolves not to give up hope:

The quickness of her apprehension is marvellous. The moment she entered the church she looked straight to the place in the gallery where I was, though it was quite inconspicuous and I had never sat there before. Again the first time I ever sat in the church I had not taken my seat two minutes before she saw me and that though it was three rows behind & 4 or five persons off.

But if there was any cause for optimism it soon fades:

When I look at her, when I see her in church, and she does not see me then I feel – nay I always feel like a fly upon the inside of a window pane. Clear clear, but impervious a wall of solid air stands between me and the beauty and the sunshine and the freshness of life and I beat my head and wings against the pane and ache for light and liberty but between her and me is a great gulf fixed.

If the references from 'Notions' quoted above are to be relied upon – and we have to remember that the commonplace book is not a straightforward diary – then what looks like a promising beginning to a romantic relationship did not lead anywhere. By the end of 1885 all references to the second lady have ceased. Much later there is a short entry: 'I seem to have got back to some part of my life unhaunted by her.' And as a final tailpiece to a sorry tale, he records some years later a short dialogue with a friend (possibly James Powell):

P. I thought she liked you.
G. She gave me the best reasons to know the contrary.
P. What reasons?
G. Oh, I can't talk about it, please. It is impossible to explain, but it was definite enough. I can't blame her. I was very unfortunate. I made blunder after blunder. Everything I did or didn't do or said or didn't say put me more wrong with her. If I had loved her less, I

should have played the game with more skill & refrained from many of the mistakes I made.

All this evidence, though tantalizingly inconclusive, is that there may have been two women instead of one, as has usually been thought, and that he wished to give the world encrypted accounts of both of them and thus, to some extent, unburden himself. There is no doubt that he attached value to the published version, and indeed to the other pieces included in the last section of *Sidelines,* entitled 'Oddments and Dreams'. Skues evidently thought well enough of 'Incognita' and the other pieces to publish them long after they were written. He was piqued to find that no one seemed to have responded to the 'Incognita' piece (or indeed anything else in the same section), which may indicate that he attached a deep though secret significance to this strange piece of encoding. He wrote to Douglas Goodbody in November 1945: 'Apropos of Sidelines, in the numerous press notices it had, *not one* referred to the final section, and it made me wonder whether its inclusion was a mistake – something inappropriate to an angling book.' Of the letters he received about *Sidelines* only one writer, his American friend Edward Boies, referred to it.

Eventually Skues came to feel that staying single would be a wiser policy in a life that was going to be devoted to the all-embracing and excluding pursuit of angling. As with many confirmed bachelors of the time, his attitude to women became one of amused detachment rather than of downright misogyny, and he certainly admired good-looking women. He referred to his sisters as 'my womenkind', and some of his female acquaintance did not quite know how to take him. One bold young woman proposed to him in writing, ending her letter thus: 'Will you be mine, or would you rather be your own?' which would have been considered a bit 'fast' in the time of Queen Victoria. Arming himself against a possible leg-pull he replied by telegram: 'Why certainly, my own.' She replied in some irritation: 'I suppose you think that funny', so it may have been a purposive approach on the part of the lady. He wrote in 'Trivialities' that Charles Skues' wife did not like him, but after his death Charles wrote in the margin: 'Not so. She liked and admired him, but was rather shy because of his somewhat mordant wit.' She also engaged in some unsuccessful matchmaking on behalf of her brother-in-law, and in later years several local ladies in Croydon, out of well-meant matronly solicitude, tried to fix him up with suitable partners. He recorded in 'Trivialities' that he eluded their attempts. The only clue we have as to his reflections on the single life he had chosen was a brief comment in a letter he wrote to W.H. Lawrie in 1948, in which he referred to marriage and parentage: 'I entertain no doubt that I have missed the best part of a man's life.'

After Skues' death Dr Barton told C.F. Walker that his parents, or at least his mother as the time of her death was approaching, had tried to point out that marriage would interfere with his duty to look after his siblings. There does not seem to be any direct evidence that this happened, but it is quite likely that Skues felt an unspoken moral charge had been laid upon him. Also, it was going to be some time before he would be sufficiently secure financially to entertain the idea of marriage. Even when he had been made a partner of the firm – and evidence does not survive as to the division of the profits – money was still a problem with him.

In time, no doubt, a merciful healing occurred; he resolved that he was not going to put himself in the position of being hurt again, and the carapace of bachelordom closed over him.

The two other areas of Skues' life outside fishing – professional and family – claimed more and more of his attention from 1883 onwards. Perhaps Powell hoped that this capable young man would throw himself into the task of bringing in more clients, but he would soon have found that Skues, although good at his job, was not constituted that way. A cheerful extrovert, skilled at getting alongside people, would have joined several London clubs. Powell introduced him to social life, a useful way of attracting clients, and Skues records being at dinner parties in the company of interesting people, including Oscar Wilde, H.M. Stanley the explorer, Alice Meynell, Harold Speed the artist, the young Ramsay Macdonald and Francis Dicksee the portrait painter. He recorded envying Dicksee for his success with women, but Ramsay Macdonald 'I detested at sight and I avoided making his acquaintance'. But it seems doubtful that this shy young man shone in such company or indeed enjoyed the experience very much. His line in life was not to concentrate on extending the fame of the practice, but rather to get onto the river as often as possible. Powell was, himself, not inclined to run after business, and was quite content with the trade that came through the door, and to have time for his own agreeable social life. It was a far cry from the frantic whirl of the office of the twenty-first century, where might be heard the not infrequent sigh of 'No time for a holiday this year'.

In 'Trivialities' Skues wrote at some length about his early years in the Essex Street practice. In writing of this he is careful to avoid any breach of professional confidences, even though he was writing of events occurring decades earlier. Powell's was an old-fashioned firm, with a particular emphasis on professional propriety. Readers of Skues' books will be familiar with the odd roundabout way in which he acquired his adored Leonard rods. As with many other solicitors of the day he made a rule of refusing all extra gratuities over and above the amount of the final bill for work done, but he would allow himself to accept something else, such as an expensive rod, by way of a personal compliment. Over the next thirty years Skues acquired several Leonard rods, all presents from grateful clients.

Clearly, then, Skues never allowed himself to be tempted to behave in an unprofessional manner over money matters, even in the early days of his professional career, when his salary would have been modest. It was some little time before he felt sufficiently solvent to be able to lunch at The Cock, the well-known hostelry and resort of hungry lawyers in Fleet Street. As far as can be known he kept up his straightforward line of conduct in his profession to the end of his career in 1940, and in course of time he became the type, perhaps more familiar in those days, of family solicitor or 'my man of business', in whom one could place an absolute trust. After his death Dr Barton wrote that he was 'the soul of honour'.

Skues settled well to the law. His mind was well adapted to the knotty intricacies of draughtsmanship and interpretation, and he became proud of his skill. Not one of his wills was ever contested. Powell would every now and then carry him off to a consultation with counsel at one of the Inns of Court, usually Lincoln's Inn, and these experiences did a great deal towards his development, both professional and personal. In 'Trivialities' he wrote: 'Somehow I nearly always felt at my best in conference or consultation with counsel, the more distinguished the better ... the contact with the acute intellects of great counsel seemed to key up my mind and to shake off the shyness from which since my childhood I suffered.'

Powell may have been a little startled one day when the young articled clerk, taken along to a consultation with counsel in the role of observer, broke into his master's conversation with a well-known Chancery barrister, Charles Swinfen Eady, later Master of the Rolls. The discussion was about an accumulation case. In earlier times it had been recognized that to allow capital in a family settlement to be tied up in perpetuity was a detriment in terms of public policy. In 1800 an Act of Parliament was passed in restraint of this, generally known as the Thelusson Act, after the name of the rich testator whose plans for his descendants would eventually have resulted in an accumulation of money amounting to £140 million. Neither Swinfen Eady or Powell thought that the Thelusson Act applied to the problem on the table, at least until Skues broke into the discussion, and began to argue the opposite point of view. Evidently he had been doing some late-night work on the 1800 Act and any subsequent case-law he could find on perpetuities and accumulations. If there had been any feelings of impatience or irritation on the part of the two older lawyers at this interruption they would quickly have changed their minds. The young man clearly had something interesting to say. The discussion continued for two hours, and Skues must have done a good deal of the talking. At length Swinfen Eady said: 'I will think it over and write my opinion.' A few days later the opinion arrived, approving of Skues' thinking, but recommending that the opinion of the court be taken. Eventually the court supported the view of a very junior solicitor.

By this stroke Skues must have improved his employer's view of him, for the case involved a great deal of money. This little anecdote, which he recorded many years later with nostalgia and some pride, tells us something about the development of his mind, and also how one form of research could cross-fertilize another. Edward Gibbon once famously wrote about his military service in the militia, which later helped him to understand the working of the Roman Army: 'The captain of the Hampshire grenadiers ... has not been useless to the historian of the Roman Empire.' In the same way, the facility that Skues developed for getting relevant facts together in the Essex Street office had also shown to advantage in those long sessions in the Reading Room of the British Museum, tabulating all that could be known of 500 years of fly-dressing. At length he became a well-informed historian of fly-fishing as well as an accomplished solicitor.

In another long-running matter Skues recalled nursing the estate of a client who had died in 1879 leaving £180,000. The last life interest did not fall in for many years, and one of the final tasks of his long career was to distribute among some happy relatives a sum which by 1939 had risen to £570,000.

By 1895 James Powell had acquired enough respect and liking for Skues to cut him in as a partner. For many years they ran a reasonably busy but not an overloaded and exhausting practice. Powell was able to get away to his houseboat with his family on the Thames, and Skues would get down to Abbots Barton as often as he could. It was his custom to work at home far into the night, sometimes until 3 a.m., in order to clear off arrears of office work. In this way he could avoid being kept in London at weekends, which he wished to be devoted to fishing. Two years later he had enough leave to be able to sample the opportunities of fishing in Europe.

The firm was respected for its expertise and reliability. Skues wrote that some of the Masters of the Supreme Court before whom he appeared would, in small ways, show a trust in him that they would not extend to all solicitors. One of them said: 'We Masters know whose word we can take and those we can't.' Skues even remembered being, from time to time, asked his own opinion on points of law by Masters in Chancery. Some years later he was asked by the Law Society to be one of the practising conveyancing solicitors to give evidence on behalf of the profession before the Royal Commission chaired by Lord St Aldwyn, which had been given the task of enquiring into the Land Transfer Act.

Skues also became known for the rapidity with which he dispatched business. He discovered that several clients called him 'the lightning solicitor'. Matters were cleared up quickly and letters were usually answered by return of post. He says in his memoir that really this was a 'counsel of caution', because of his defective memory: 'I had to do things at once to be sure of getting them right.' Later, when they came into general use in offices, his manner on the telephone was extremely brisk.

Part of the 1895 agreement was that Skues would take over the firm's litigation practice. He got much satisfaction from researching a case and preparing a brief to counsel, but admitted that he was not much good at appearing in person in small matters in the lower courts. However, he got on well enough before a judge in chambers. There was a certain amount of privacy with the latter and a less daunting atmosphere. He claimed in 'Trivialities' never to have lost a single action or even an interlocutory application in nine years, although there do not seem to have been very many of them: the main business of Powell and Skues was almost entirely in conveyancing and family wills and trusts, and it was never very big in litigation. He lost his first case in 1905, but this was because the client had misled him in an important particular. In his early days at Powell's, divorce cases were almost unknown, but in one year three Admiralty cases came his way. He won them all against a firm specializing in

Admiralty law. Taking pains with preparing a good brief made him the sort of solicitor who will always be popular with barristers.

One startling episode disturbed the even tenor of the partnership. Powell announced that he was applying to be appointed a Master in Chancery, and that he hoped to get a testimonial from Lord Randolph Churchill. Powell had helped Churchill in his parliamentary election and was expecting some return. This was a source of excitement and agitation to Skues, who thought he might succeed to the practice. But the expected testimonial was not forthcoming, Powell remained in place, and little change occurred in the practice until Graham Smith was taken on as a junior partner. Skues did not become head of the firm until Powell's withdrawal in 1925.

Meanwhile, the Skues family was getting into difficulties. His mother and six of his siblings had settled in St Helier in the Channel Islands, where Skues would join them for holidays. The 1881 census shows that they had only one servant for a large household, which suggests that money was a problem. William Skues retired in December 1881 with the rank of Brigade Surgeon, and returned from India to join his family. By this time his health had been shattered by a near-fatal bout of sunstroke. His temper, also, is said not to have been improved. When they came to London towards the end of the 1880s the fortunes of the family had moved even further into decline. They now lodged in a rented property in Linden Grove in Camberwell, with the dreary view beyond the windows of Nunhead Cemetery. Both parents were unwell and prematurely aged by life in the tropics, and a daughter, Margaret Caroline (born 1861) had died in 1888 of tuberculosis. Money was short and the family struggled on with, in the words of the 1891 census, a 'domestic general servant', in other words a grossly overtaxed maid-of-all-work.

The life-experience of the officials of the British Empire has been discussed by historians and explored by novelists such as Somerset Maugham. At home the Empire was a matter of pride and satisfaction, a glittering achievement and something which it was an honour to serve. For the participants the reality was something a little different. To be part of the top rank in the hierarchy and familiar with Government House was a very pleasant thing, but in the lower ranks of colonial society the years of bearing the white man's burden could be troublesome. On arrival back in England the shock of adjustment to new conditions could be painful. In the colonies, domestic help at least was not a problem, and even those in the minor posts felt they had status.

The change from being 'somebody' in India to 'nobody' back in England was hard to take. When ex-colonials met together the main topic of conversation was often about 'the servant problem'. The striking change in the lives of those returning to the mother country would often make them morose and depressed, and with an excessive reliance on the consolations of alcohol. No information survives about this difficult period in Skues' life, but he was more and more drawn into helping to run the family. It was he, not his parents, who arranged the placing of his younger brother Charles at Dulwich College.

By the end of 1889 Skues' mother had not long to live, and she was removed to a nursing home in Christchurch, Hampshire, where she died in January 1890. She was only fifty-four. Later the same year Skues took most of his siblings away for a farmhouse holiday at Harefield, an easy journey into Middlesex. His invalid father was left behind in the care of one of the daughters.

This holiday may have had the effect of improving the health and spirits of the rest of the family, but Skues himself was going downhill physically and mentally. Forty years later he wrote in 'Trivialities': 'In 1890 after the death of my mother I was very worn out with trouble and overwork.' The growing responsibility falling upon him as the eldest son, as well as the work at the office, took their toll. In September 1891 he went away with an angling friend called Ellis from the British Museum to fish the Yorkshire Yore (nowadays called the Ure). He wrote in *Itchen Memories* that, after ten days, 'I was not a little surprised to find that, thanks to the bracing moorland air and the good feeding provided by the good-natured landlady of the inn at which we stayed, I had put on no less than 13lb in weight.' He then moved on to Abbots Barton for more open-air therapy. Skues was entitled to three weeks of holiday a year, but it was not enough to recoup the health of this exhausted man. It was about this time that his tendency to baldness began to increase, much to his distress. He continued in a low state of spirits, was liable to catch any cold going around, and was frequently unwell. He thought that he was drifting into consumption, that ominous but very common disease of those days, which had already killed his sister and his mother. When Halford offered to put him up for the Flyfishers' Club he thanked him but declined, believing that he was a dying man.

In June 1892 William Skues died at the age of 64. Skues mentioned in 'Trivialities' the deaths of his mother and father without regret or comment. He had received little in the way of nurture from them and probably not much in the way of love, and it is likely that the bond between them was not a close one – dutiful on his part without being affectionate. It was hard on a young man to have inherited the unshared burden of head of the family. To add to the problems it turned out, perhaps unsurprisingly, that his father had not left a great deal of money. He had not made a will either, and Skues applied for and was granted letters of administration. The gross value of his father's personal estate amounted to £2,482.

In the autumn of 1892 an epidemic of influenza swept through the population. Skues remembered that it had the effect of sending scores of funeral processions past the house every day on their way to Nunhead Cemetery. In his enfeebled state he soon succumbed and became dangerously ill, and a nurse was brought in to look after him. Double pneumonia developed – frequently a death sentence before the days of antibiotics – and Skues began to feel his life slipping away. In spite of the attentions of doctor and nurse there developed what appeared to be the final crisis. At this point, no doubt at a loss for anything else to do, the nurse gave him a glass of claret, which he was convinced 'had turned the scale'. Later he was told that he had been within half an hour of death. Upon hearing of this unorthodox but apparently miraculous cure, James Powell sent round two cases of claret in half bottles. The doctor, no doubt baffled by the turn of events, advised regarding the gift as two cases of medicine, and Skues, who hitherto had not had much use for alcohol, obediently drank his way through forty-eight half bottles at the rate of one a day. After an anxious fortnight he was able to get up.

This was not quite the end of it. Even after apparent recovery he was still subject to weakness and constant colds. Realizing that something radical was needed he negotiated with Powell for an absence from Essex Street of two months, in order to make a return voyage to South Africa. Somehow he raised the remarkable sum of £120 and booked his passage on the *Dunottar Castle*. Powell wanted him to go only as far as Madeira, 'in case something came up' in the office, but Skues stood firm. On embarking he refused to be vaccinated against smallpox, even though an epidemic was known to be raging in South Africa, because he felt too weak for it. The ship's doctor advised him that the problem was partly one of nutrition and advised substantial feeding. Skues took this very literally, recording in 'Trivialities' that there were eight courses for breakfast, none of which he missed. Lunch was eleven courses, dinner even more. He wrote: 'I did justice to most', and further claimed, rather startlingly, that he was always hungry.

Skues said little in his memoirs about South Africa, although he later published several pieces about fishing in harbours. On his return he arrived home with sixpence in his pocket. He had left England weighing 10st 5lb and returned at 12st 12lb. Doctors nowadays do not prescribe heavy feeding or a daily course of claret, but Skues remained convinced that he had owed his preservation to these simple remedies.

It was another two years before he felt entirely well again and capable of carrying a creel or bag with a strap across his chest. The experience had made him much more health-conscious. He worried about the lack of exercise in his life, apart from the daily walk to the railway. He felt secure enough now to join the Flyfishers' Club, which at that time had premises in the Arundel Hotel on the Thames Embankment, a short walk from Essex Street. Halford, with the help of William Senior, arranged his election in the latter part of 1893. Skues wrote years later: 'I could not say how much pleasure my membership has brought me nor what a number of good friends it has made for me', and in 1921 be dedicated *The Way of a Trout with a Fly* to the Club 'In gratitude for many happy hours and some priceless friendships'. On the other hand, by 1897 Halford must have come to think differently about his intervention, as he realized that he had brought into the Club a man whom he regarded as a friend and disciple, but whom later he came to regard first as an irritant and eventually as an enemy.

Early in 1894 Skues moved his family away from Nunhead and its sad memories and into a substantial rented house called Hyrst View in Campden Road, Croydon. In those days the countryside was near at hand, and his memoir mentions the nightingales and nightjars nearby. Also the fowls in neighbouring farmyards could be inspected for good hackles and a quick bargain could be made with a farmer. Perhaps it was not a coincidence that he had lighted upon a dwelling that was near the River Wandle. This once superlative stream was, in the 1890s, affected but not yet overwhelmed by pollution. Skues was still catching fish in his own neighbourhood in the early years of the twentieth century.

5

Birth of a New Idea

I<small>F</small> S<small>KUES</small> H<small>AD</small> not survived his near-death experience in 1892 he would be an unknown today. At the time he would, for a short season, have been mourned by family and by a few angling friends, and perhaps worth a brief epitaph in conversation in the fishing hut at Abbots Barton: 'Interesting man – knew a lot. Promising, perhaps' might be near the mark. There was no particular sign that he was to become famous as a great innovator, and that his ideas would shake the fly-fishing community for decades.

At the beginning of the 1890s he was a good average performer in the conventional sense, respectful of Halford and operating within the lines laid down by the master's two published books. The teething stage was over and he could move on to solving the more interesting problems on the river and to fishing with more confidence. And in fly-dressing, from halting beginnings in the 1880s, he had quickly become a master, increasingly exploring the subtleties and complexities in which all true fly-dressers delight. In a few short years he was to take his place as one of the leaders in the field, and his journalism would attract a wide audience. But these advances were almost all in the area of the dry fly. With Skues the sunk fly had a long and hesitant gestation.

During this decade he fished with several rods, all more or less unsuitable: a Hardy Houghton, a Hardy 'Test' rod of 11ft and another split-cane rod of 10ft by Ogden and Scotford. The Houghton was a powerful rod but a poor hooker. He once rose twenty-eight trout on the Itchen in the course of one day and landed only eight. A little later on the Kennet the rod broke at the ferrule (perhaps a good thing), and he was surprised to find that his second rod, a 10ft 6in 'Perfection' by Hardy, was far better at hooking and holding. He went on to catch twelve trout and chub during a mayfly riot, from 1lb 12oz to 4lb 2oz. This rod was one of the early examples in the 'Perfection' series (no. 18) and had the lasting qualities for which the House of Hardy has always been known, for he gave it away in 1941 to a friend to use for sea trout. In 1889 he was sufficiently enamoured of his greenheart rod by Farlow, 10ft in length and painted a dull heron grey (the gift of a grateful client), to have it copied, significantly adding another 6in to the length, by Walbran of Leeds, for a friend called Rennie. Walbran thought well enough of the result to begin marketing it, and the 'Rennie' fly rod soon appeared in his catalogue.

These over-heavy rods were all discarded in the new century when Skues made the blessed discovery of the American Leonard rods. Years later Skues had painful memories of the ounce-to-the foot monster rods of the pre-Leonard era. His term for them, often repeated in his writings, was 'wrist-breakers' – no doubt stated with feeling by one whose wrists might be described as half-broken already, which made fly-tying during a fishing weekend difficult. He wrote in 1892: 'After a long day's fishing my wrist (owing to a bad sprain) is not in a condition favourable to winging floaters', which may account for the fact that most of his fly-dressing on campaign was done before breakfast rather than at night.

In spite of this drawback Skues had mastered the basic technique of the chalk stream, and when Irwin Cox gave him standing leave to be at Abbots Barton whenever he liked his education must have advanced considerably. As with Halford at Houghton, it was a tough school and an excellent place for advancing one's skills. When, in 1890, he was let loose for two days on Henry Nicoll's preserved and stocked fishery on the Test at Sutton Scotney, he had no difficulty in catching a large number of fish. On the third day he and Nicoll came over to Abbots Barton and found that the fish 'as almost always, were as pernickety as possible'. In January 1892 he wrote in *The Fishing Gazette* that he had, in the previous two seasons, fished for thirty days on Itchen and Test, none of them blank, and some days with catches up to five brace. He later wrote that, in 1891, he had begun to think that he was at last beginning to understand the game. This was probably in September, after his first encounter with Halford, and well before he became critical of that gentleman's ideas and influence.

The story of their meeting was told more than once by Skues, most vividly in *Itchen Memories*. In September 1891 anglers around Winchester learned that Halford was to stay at the George Hotel for a week, and would be fishing at Abbots Barton. Skues encountered him on the river and in the evening at the hotel, and the results must have seemed to him a little odd. The 'great man' (as he rather ironically called him in this account) laid down the law in conversation and would brook no dissent, and by day was less competent as a practitioner on the river than might have been expected. On the first morning Halford had offered him what Skues afterwards described as an India-rubber Olive, probably the Detached Olive with undyed rubber over a bristle, as described in *Dry-Fly Entomology* (1897), pattern no. 7. Skues, however, stuck to his prescription of a Quill Marryat. There was a hatch of small pale olives and by lunchtime Skues had caught five trout and Halford one. This pattern continued for three more days. By day Skues did better than 'the great master' and in the evening the assembled anglers listened 'with becoming reverence' to yet more doctrine. By the end of the week Skues must have been somewhat thoughtful. He kept the killing fly as a memento of this success, and was still showing it to friends towards the end of his life.

As the years passed Skues, in his writings, looked back to this momentous meeting, musing over it and weaving it into his own mythology. In *Itchen Memories* he wrote that 'it encouraged me to rely on my own observations and not to attach undue importance to authority', and in 1948 he wrote to a correspondent: 'From the way he talked at night to the anglers assembled at the George, I had imagined him infallible. It was a lesson that made an impression on my mind.' These two descriptions of his feelings are only partially accurate. He did not see things in that way at the time. Only retrospectively did the encounter of September 1891 become significant for him as his ideas came together over a period of years. In fact, one of the most notable factors in Skues' path towards independence and eventually to dynamic heterodoxy was its extreme slowness. It was not a brisk, consciously planned journey of enquiry, but rather a long and meandering process, during which the behaviour of the trout provided him with hints and suggestive incidents from which he was rather slow to profit. In 1950 his brother Charles wrote in the foreword to *Itchen Memories*: 'Many writers on angling urge their readers to observe. The trouble is that most of us observe much without learning anything from it. My brother began like that, and it took him many years to develop that keen power of observation that made him such a master.'

It is worth dwelling on the phrase 'many years'. In fact the process of disentangling himself from the influence of Halford and becoming the prophet of the nymph took over twenty years to accomplish. It might even be argued that, in some ways, the process was never quite completed.

Later in life Skues was inclined to be rather hard on himself for having been so slow off the mark to learn about the existence of nymphs and then to explore the imitation of them. And yet there was plenty of information to be picked up from observation on the river and from the reading of books, both ancient and modern. He acquired a copy of Eaton's *Revisional Monograph*, but does not seem to have used it much. He was inclined to blame his uncertain grip of entomology on the lack of any training in science at Winchester College. In his extensive campaign among the books in the British Museum Reading Room had he, for example, not noticed the interesting and oft-quoted passage in John Taverner's book of 1600, *Certaine Experiments Concerning Fishe and Fruite*?

> I have seene a young flie swimme in the water too and fro, and in the end come to the upper crust of the water, and assay to flie up: howbeit not being perfectly ripe or fledge, hath twice or thrice fallen downe againe into the water: howbeit in the end receiving perfection by the heate of the sunne, and the pleasant fat water, hath in the end within some halfe houre after taken her flight, and flied quite awaie into the ayre. And of such young flies before they are able to flie awaie, do fish feede exceedingly.

And down the years that followed many perceptive anglers knew that the up-winged and other sorts of flies appearing on the surface of the stream had begun life beneath. In 1681 James Chetham of Smedley gave instructions about dressing and using an imitation of the caddis larva or, as he called it, the 'Artificial Cod-bait'. Skues had a great admiration for Chetham, and in *Minor Tactics* he mentioned, perhaps a little unwisely, a short-lived experiment with an imitation of 'a caddis or gentle which I once tried, with mad success for a few minutes, and gave up, conscience-stricken'. The diary of Richard Durnford for 22 April 1809 included, at the end of a short description of a fishing day, the remains of a nymph embedded in sealing wax, underneath which is written: 'Taken from the stomach of a trout, they are the nymphae of the gnats ascending through the water before they take wing.' There were many other hints available in *The Fishing Gazette*, of which Skues was an enthusiastic reader from the early 1880s. If he had read the series in seven weekly parts called 'Fly-Fishing for Trout' he would have seen the following suggestive passage in the number for 13 October 1883:

> Occasionally trout which appear to be rising freely refuse a dry fly floated down over them. They are then often taking the larva as it

rises from the bottom before it arrives at the surface, and will sometimes come at an artificial fly if it is allowed to sink a few inches. It may be thrown above them, as in dry fly fishing; or they may be fished for downstream, with a good length of line out, the angler keeping as much out of sight as possible.

In May of the following year *The Fishing Gazette* published a letter from H.S. Hall, admitting to the use of a sunk Wickham for 'bulging' fish and, on occasion, 'when I am tired of rambling aimlessly in search of feeding fish', to using a sunk fly with a lead shot at the head in a hatch hole. In 1887 there was a correspondence in the same journal on the relative merits of dry and wet flies. It was begun by an angler who, after the usual practice of the time (though irritating to posterity), sheltered behind the alias of 'Silver Doctor'. He claimed to use the wet fly on almost all occasions, casting single flies upstream, and mentioned his considerable bags of fish, all caught in chalk streams. What followed was a welcome gift to an editor – a correspondence that lasted for five months. H.S. Hall, a firm advocate of the dry fly, posed a pertinent question in a rather veiled manner: 'Now it would, of course, be unreasonable to ask "Silver Doctor" on what streams he gets such excellent sport as he has described.' 'Silver Doctor' replied casually: 'Through the kindness of friends, the chalk streams I fish in, are the Kennett, the Test, the Itchen, the Lambourne, and the Chess.' He added that a single wet fly made no more disturbance on the surface than a dry fly. This was a direct challenge to the new dry-fly followers, who considered wet-fly practice to be bad for a fishery, although, to be fair to them, they were drawing this criticism from the old style of raking downstream with a fly; sometimes a large fly and frequently with two or more flies.

Whether or not Skues had read the article of 1883 cannot be known, but it is certain that he had followed the correspondence of 1887, because he intervened in it. His letter made it clear that he was a wholehearted supporter of Halford. He attempted to be even-handed to both sides, but he concluded by writing: 'You will have gathered from the foregoing that my predilections are in favour of the dry-fly method.' There was certainly no sign here that he had any notion yet of the great potential for the sunk fly on the chalk stream. And in the same year he recommended Halford's flies to another correspondent in the same journal. At this stage of his life Skues, in common with most anglers in the South, simply could not imagine that Halford could be wrong and that there could be another way of fishing for chalk-stream trout.

The Halford problem may have gone deeper. The origins of Skues' personal diffidence have been discussed in Chapter 2. As we have seen, the experience of a dysfunctional family lacked some of the elements useful for the building up of self-assurance in later life. Having been farmed out with relatives and a paid child-minder he was then placed in the formidable environment of Winchester College, where boys were taught to fall into line, to listen rather than to talk, to respect the older and allegedly wiser, and to admire the heroes of the games field. If one had wished to contrive to knock the self-confidence out of a young person the above programme would have served very well. Emerging from childhood and school thus programmed and predisposed, his years of Halford-worship need not surprise us. His experience of regular parenting having been rather sketchy, perhaps he even needed a father-figure. Only gradually did he come to realize that the heroic Halford had serious defects, and that thinking for oneself might be the better course.

In several of his later articles Skues looked back and identified signposts along the route of his developing education. The first was the discovery of nymphs in the mouth of a freshly-caught trout at Abbots Barton, followed by his suggestion (six months later) to George Holland that perhaps subaqueous larvae could be imitated. These and several other incidents, well known to anglers familiar with Skues' writings, deserve more detailed examination, especially as they have not all been recorded accurately by Skues himself. Unfortunately for posterity, Skues did not keep a diary. He wrote that he had started to do so more than once, but could not keep it up. However, he must, from time to time, have kept notes recording the happenings of fishing days otherwise many of his interesting papers, later gathered into book form, could not have been written in such circumstantial detail.

The first memorable incident happened at Whitsun 1888 at the top end of the Abbots Barton fishery, in the carrier known, because of its swift, brawling nature, as the Highland Burn. Here he hooked and broke in a smallish trout which had taken his Pink Wickham. Two days later he hooked and landed the same fish, identifiable by the original fly in its mouth, and with some of the gut still attached. While he was dislodging the two hooks he found in the mouth 'a number of tiny pea-green creatures, which I later learned were nymphs'. The interesting word here is 'later': after five years on a chalk stream Skues did not know nymphs when he saw them. He was at least frank about it: writing in 1939 he admitted 'this was my first observation of the kind and my first realization that trout did not feed exclusively on the winged fly'.

The incident remained with him although, at the time, he seems to have treated it as a curiosity. Four months later he returned from an expedition to the River Coquet in Northumberland, very fired up with an early piece of success in fly-tying. This involved the use of flat gut selected from some poor samples – his word for it was 'tawsey' gut (a word, I think, unknown to lexicographers) – and dyed a hot orange colour for use as a body material. This fly secured the downfall of thirty-eight trout during a fall of sherry spinner. His holiday companion, whom he had met during his visits to the British Museum, caught only three. On his return south he wrote to George Holland suggesting the idea of imitating nymphs with dyed gut wound around bare hooks. In 1939 he discovered this long-forgotten correspondence and mentioned it in a short letter in the spring number of the *Journal*: 'On 4th October, 1888, I wrote both Currell and Holland suggesting tying of creepers with bodies of flat gut or dubbing and tails with the transparent points clipped off and the upper part of the big hackle cut off thus:–'

The drawing of a nymph to which he refers is a reasonably accurate likeness of the natural creature, and makes it even more puzzling that Skues did not immediately set to work at the fly vice to make a good representation.

Instead he followed an entirely different course with sunk flies, did not mention the idea of a nymph imitation until 1904 and did not actually carry out his own advice to himself until 1908. Perhaps he was discouraged by Holland's response, which was a little dismissive: 'Larvae have been tied years ago by Mr Marryat and myself, though not with gut as you suggest, which might be an improvement. They [i.e. Halford and Marryat] never killed any fish either with larvae or shrimp which I enclose.' Holland was not quite correct here: Halford may not have been successful with larvae and shrimp patterns but Marryat certainly was.

The experiments of Marryat and Halford with nymphal forms had, in fact, given rise to several promising patterns. The best example is numbered 61 in *Floating Flies* – the grannom larva (more correctly a swimming pupa). Marryat also devised a Mayfly nymph which appears in G.A.B. Dewar's *Book of the Dry Fly* (1897). When, after the Great War, Skues examined Marryat's capacious fly book containing many hundreds of patterns he was 'impressed by the enormous predominance of many of the patterns better calculated to fish wet than dry', and by the fact that several of them were 'quite nymphal in type'. There were also one or two interesting pieces of evidence for Marryat's pragmatic approach to be found in the fly book, such as an Alexandra and some split shot.

But in 1888, or indeed 1891, Skues knew nothing of all this. After Holland's letter he did not proceed with the idea. If Marryat and Halford had caught nothing with larval imitations what chance had he? So the events of 1888–9 were a false dawn for Skues, and for a time he abandoned subaqueous thoughts. If trout were tailing or bulging he covered them with a Gold-ribbed Hare's Ear or a Pink Wickham, as recommended in *Dry-Fly Fishing in Theory and Practice* (1889). Skues would have been very familiar with this extraordinary book, which established a rule of procedure on chalk streams that intensified in the years that followed, and which mesmerized anglers for two generations. Hills wrote in 1936: 'No fisherman of this age can realize the effect Halford's books had upon our generation … suddenly the whole of the new art burst upon us full-grown. We drank deep and we were intoxicated.'

The year 1891 was a memorable one for the advancement of Skues' learning. Apart from the meeting with Halford, trout of the Itchen provided more suggestive lessons in fish behaviour. There was, at that date, still a substantial rise of mayfly: later it disappeared altogether from Abbots Barton, and never appeared again in his lifetime.

DRESSING OF NYMPHS

To the Editors of the Journal of the Fly Fishers' Club.

Dear Sir,—I had occasion lately to look over some M.S. notes which I made in 1888 in the early days of my fly-dressing. I find one in the following terms :—

" In September, 1888, I used gut-bodied flies tied with "stained flat gut, and on 4th October, 1888, I wrote both Currell "and Holland suggesting tying of creepers with bodies of flat "gut or dubbing and tails with the transparent points clipped "off and the upper part of the "big hackle cut off thus :—

This shows at what an early stage the idea of nymph fishing had occurred to me.

Yours faithfully,

G. E. M. S.

Skues' first attempt at replicating the nymphal form (in 1888), recollected by him in the *Journal of the Flyfishers' Club* (spring 1939)

DECEMBER 19, 1891.]

SOME JOTTINGS OF AN AMATEUR FLY-DRESSER.

By Val Conson.

THE FRESH-WATER SHRIMP.

I SOMETIMES wonder whether a good many of the soft hackled wet flies are not taken by the trout for the fresh-water shrimp. His shape when in motion in the water is a curve not unlike the outline of a well-dressed hackle fly (Fig. 1).

FIG. 1.　　　　　FIG. 2.

Stick a hook through the middle of him and there you are (Fig. 2). The colour of the shrimp varies from a pale translucent flint pebble colour to a deep olive green. The shades of the Golden Plover hackle very nearly reproduce the darker varieties, the golden tips very effectually reproducing the legs. Some of the partridge and woodcock hackles are not bad imitations of the lighter shades. The opening and closing of the plumes of a hackle fly not unfairly represent the peculiar jerking motions of *Gammarces pulex*. The body—if the colour be kept dim and in harmony with the hackle—is little off-set to the illusion. Thickish dressing is better than spare for the purpose of imitating a shrimp. I made several ingenious and singular efforts at reproducing the shrimp before this brilliant idea occurred to me. They were more ingenious than elegant, and were mostly combinations of partridge and yellow silk. This was the sort of thing (Fig. 3).

FIG. 3.

Early experiment: the shrimp (*The Fishing Gazette*, 1891)

One afternoon he observed a great hatch:

> The drakes came down in incredible swarms, and on each side of the river for a rod's length or so their discarded shucks formed a scum on the surface of the water. It was a wonderful sight. The trout fed frantically, but seldom on the surface. For one trout taken from the surface, they took a hundred larvae below.

Skues did not know yet how to deal with fish behaving in this way, but at least he was becoming a little more nymph-aware. The above passage closely resembles Halford's autopsy descriptions in Chapter 6: 'Studies of Fish Feeding' in his 1889 book.

In 1891 the incident of the accidentally sinking fly (mentioned in several books) provided another broad hint from the obliging trout of the Itchen. And once again Skues did not take it up, at least not for some time. This event was later described several times by him, each time slightly differently, one of many reasons why posterity wishes that he had kept a diary. The passage in *Minor Tactics* described a day in September, with trout taking the numerous black gnats on the surface. With the instructions of Halford in mind, Skues plied them with the recommended patterns: 'Silver Sedge on a 00 hook, Red Quill on a 00 hook, Orange Bumble and Furnace'. By three o'clock, becoming desperate, he observed a single example of a spent dark olive and tied on a Dark Olive Quill from a shop, made with a soft hen hackle. At the second cast the fly sank and was immediately taken by a fish. Skues was so startled that he struck too hard and left the fly with the fish. Mounting another badly made soft fly of the same pattern he caught a trout, the belly of which was full of black gnats. What was a Halford-trained angler to make of that? The fly had sunk and according to the master it should therefore have been of no use, and it was the wrong pattern anyway. He then caught eight more trout by this supposedly improper method. Skues ends his description of this momentous experience with a frank confession: 'It was a lesson which ought to have set me thinking and experimenting, but it didn't. I put by the experience for use on the next September smutting day, and I have never had quite such another.'

These two sentences suggest that Skues was still not drawing any general lessons from experience, except to note that, for some illogical reason or other, trout taking small smut were prepared to take a large sunk olive. For him, that September day was unusual and specific to the strange conditions prevailing. Perhaps he had in mind the well-known passage in

Halford's second book, in which he allows that the sunk fly might on certain days succeed in the chalk stream, 'but in many years' experience such days have not fallen to my lot, and I should be inclined to consider them as *happening ones*, or, in other words, as the rare exceptions which go to prove the rule'. For Skues, at that stage of his mental development, this was enough: if Halford said such things were a fluke, it must be so.

Similar incidents had occurred with Halford. The case of Marryat's sinking Mayfly (whether by accident or design), which resulted in a heavy bag of fish at Newton Stacey in 1883 (see Hayter, *Halford*, p. 85), only served to puzzle the master 'as anything more opposed to the action of the fly could not be imagined'. In the early 1880s Halford was engaged in building up his inflexible system, and incidents which did not fit with it were aberrations that were best ignored. Skues, however, was capable of learning, albeit rather slowly at first.

The above account in *Minor Tactics* is worth comparing with two other accounts: they do not quite agree, and the mystery remains as to whether or not the fly sank by accident or design. The first is to be found in *The Fishing Gazette* for 19 December 1891, showing that the incident cannot have been in 1892 anyway, or later than September 1891:

> The fish were smutting gorgeously. By a fluke that day I dropped onto something that tempted the fish – a big dark Olive, soaked and cast, undried almost onto the nose of a fish. With that I took four and a half brace between one and 3.30 o'clock that day, and there was not a trace of Olive of any sort in their bellies. It was all smut, smut, smut.

Even nearer in time to that interesting afternoon, and therefore perhaps more accurate, was his version as recorded in *The Field* on 10 October. Skues wrote to respond to an interesting article by William Senior called 'A Wet Fly Chalk Stream'. This article was another discussion of proto-nymph fishing, and described the use of wet flies on several chalk streams. Senior referred, without naming him, to a brother angler who 'declares that if Itchen, Test and Kennet trout are treated to the proper flies, the sunken method would be as successful as it was in the old days'. Skues read this piece with interest and proffered his own recent experience. In this version the discrepancy is even more marked:

> I picked out a fish, soaked my fly well, and put it to him without drying. There was no hatch of fly till the next day. I coaxed up the

contents of the stomachs of some of the fish, and found they consisted of nothing but a mass of smuts, not a trace of an olive of any sort ... I never tried a north country hackle fly on a chalk stream, but see no reason why such a fly should not succeed at times when the natural insect is either knocked down by wind or rain, or when the fish are taking larvae.

Well, perhaps the question of which year it may have been does not matter much, but whether the delivery of a sinking fly was accidental or deliberate certainly does. Whichever was the case, Skues has not exactly discovered nymph fishing, although his mention of larvae shows a growing awareness of underwater events. His thinking was beginning to catch up with other anglers who were fishing the sunk fly to bulging trout, the difference being that they knew quite well what the fish were eating. There were quite a number of wet-fly rebels at this time who refused to be dictated to by Halford. William Senior, who never pretended to be a purist, wrote in 1885 of watching trout feeding under the surface on the Test: 'Fly-fishing at such times is hopeless, unless you use the imitation nympha, sunk a few inches.'

At the beginning of September 1892 Skues put an article in *The Fishing Gazette* entitled 'September in Hampshire: a Plan of Campaign'. It was an excellent example of his growing knowledge of natural flies and their artificial counterparts. He included a table of seven different sorts of dun and two spinners, and fourteen artificials to imitate them, all of which are dry flies. The one exception was the black gnat, against which is written 'Hopeless (put up Pink Wickham 0 & 00, Silver Sedge 00, or Large Dark Olive fished wet)'. So, without (it must be said) a great deal of confidence, he is suggesting a principle upon which to proceed, although a rather odd one, i.e. a sunk dun works during a swarming of black gnats on the surface. To the modern observer the education of the future Man of the Nymph seemed to be proceeding by rather a circuitous route.

The week at Abbots Barton followed quite closely the above plan of campaign, with fairly good fortune until the last day. The weather, which had been gusty and rainy, changed entirely to a day of bright sun. The fish fed strongly, and for some time Skues cast many different flies over them, mostly quill-bodied patterns for which he would have little use in later years. At last he changed to a Blue Dun (mole fur body ribbed with yellow silk, wing of snipe), with which he secured a trout. A second fish accepted the same fly when it sank, this time accidentally. In *Minor Tactics* once again he frankly admits that he did not realize that he 'was on the edge of a great adventure'. In fact his diagnosis was once more at fault, for he thought that the important factor had been the dressing of the fly, not the fact that it sank. In his account in *The Fishing Gazette* a few weeks later he wrote: 'But what puzzles me is, *why* was the mole's fur dressing so much in request that day, and *why* were the fish content with Blue Quill on the previous days, with the same series of flies on the water?' Once again the Abbots Barton trout had been helpful, but he had only picked up a part of the message.

It is one of the attractive aspects of Skues' personality that he is so candid and honest about these early perplexities. There was no attempt in his later writings to excuse his failure to draw correct conclusions, and no sign of the self-dramatization or artful tidying up of a graceless jumble of thoughts and experiments so often found in memoirs.

There may have been another and rather odd reason why Skues made such slow progress in his observation of fish feeding patterns. There is a clue in the above-mentioned article in *The Field*, in the mention of 'coaxing up' the stomach contents of trout. This laborious process was not a habit of Skues in the early days, because to do it properly involved a dissection. For some reason this was a procedure for which he had an almost morbid disgust. Years later he made what he considered to be one of his major discoveries – the marrow scoop. This enabled him to examine the recent diet of a caught fish without resorting to a process he found repulsive. It is difficult to understand quite what was so appalling about a little riverside dissection, which many anglers down the ages have practised without complaint, from the *Treatyse* of 1496, where the author urges anglers who have caught a large fish to open the stomach ('undo the mawe'), up to the nineteenth century. Halford and Marryat performed riverside dissections constantly, as did other anglers: many do so today. But there can be no doubt about Skues' attitude. He seemed to have been unable to mention his new discovery without also expressing disgust about the pre-marrow scoop era of his life, with shrill epithets such as 'hateful and messy autopsies', 'nasty mess', 'dilatory and horrid mess'. This is enough to indicate that for him autopsy was a desperate measure, not to be resorted to often. If he had done so he would have become much more nymph-minded much earlier. It might also be added that clearly Skues had never stood at a kitchen sink and cleaned a fish.

In the last decade of the nineteenth century, a pent-up flood of writing began to flow from the pen of Skues, and he emerged as a considerable angling journalist. The articles from this period are virtually unknown now, which might be a pity. However, there exist for us two collections of his journalism not published elsewhere in book form. Donald Overfield provided a useful anthology, *G.E.M. Skues: The Way of a Man with a Trout* (1977), but this only contains contributions from the *Journal of the Flyfishers' Club*, of which publication began in 1911. Skues' own selection, which appeared in 1932 under the title *Sidelines, Sidelights and Reflections*, included pieces from the *Journal*, and also *The Field*, *The Fishing Gazette* and *The Bulletin of the Anglers' Club of New York*. But there were no papers dating back to the nineteenth century in *Sidelines* except the 'Incognita' piece mentioned in Chapter 4 – indeed nothing else at all pre-1914. Perhaps in 1932 he felt that his thinking had moved on, and that advice about tactics and fly-dressing from the 1890s would have lost some of its value. But these articles are not just historical curiosities. They are valuable for anyone interested in the progress of his self-education, and contain much that is interesting and useful today.

The first article under the title 'Some Jottings of an Amateur Fly-Dresser' appeared on 19 December 1891. It was not quite his début. As we have seen, letters from him over the signature 'Val Conson' had been appearing in *The Fishing Gazette* since 1887, at first in the form of enquiries and tentative comments. The first sign of change can be found in a longer letter in March 1889 about fly-tying by the riverside. But the first 'Jottings' article was quite different, with nineteen sections under headings such as 'The Soft Hackle', 'Hooks' and 'Hare's Ears', as well as the first mention of finding the nymphs in the mouth of the trout in 1888. By now his mind was teeming with ideas. One section, headed 'Hampshire Series', was a list (described as 'a short series') of essential flies: Hare's Ear, Olive, Red, Ginger and Blue Quills, Iron Blue, Quill Marryat, Red Spinner, Whitchurch, Wickham's Fancy, Pink Wickham, Alder, Red Ant and Coch-y-bondhu. He added (perhaps unwisely): 'I don't know any others really indispensable.' Some years later he would have abandoned the use of several of these patterns. The Alder he found to be of little use on the Itchen, although, as we shall see, it worked well on the Kennet and the Nadder, and in Germany. The Coch-y-bondhu was soon forgotten. And in the new century he was to move away from quill as a body material. Perhaps we have a clue here as to why he did not republish such articles, which had contained material he later regarded as obsolete.

Readers reeling a little from an article five columns long and densely packed with information and ideas were treated to another thoughtful piece only a week later, on Boxing Day 1891, this time dealing with the fly-tier's feathers and their availability. Over three columns in length, it is a rhapsody on the excitement and romance of collecting materials for flies:

> Then the pleasure of hunting feathers and materials! The joy of ravaging the work-baskets of one's lady friends and carrying off their most delicate silks and wools and crewels. The rapid survey of the poulterer's stock as one passes, and the rapture of picking up an unexpected blue dun or honey dun. I am a Londoner by adoption and necessity, and I have to get my feathers how and when I can. Leadenhall Market is my happy hunting-ground. Here one may buy curlews, woodcock, jay, golden plover, peewit, snipe, coot, moorhen, landrail, waterrail, thrush, blackbird, lark, owls, partridge, pheasant, grouse (black and red), teal, widgeon, etc. One may buy squirrels at times, and hares and rabbits, of course, but not much else in the way of fur…. Starling wings, especially young, are difficult to get in any quantity. Sometimes they are to be had in Leadenhall Market at from one penny to twopence per pair, but frequently they are unobtainable. I then get them at a shop on the south side of New Oxford-Street just by Southampton-Row, called Plumaria, but they are not so good as the fresh article.

On the subject of the Devonshire Blue Upright he becomes lyrical, almost mystical:

> The hackle used for this last fly is a lovely colour, so dark as almost to be undistinguishable from black, till you put it on your black coat, and then on the downy strip down the centre you seem to see the violet reflection of a strip of blue sky, such a colour as one sees once or twice in a lifetime in the eyes of a woman.

The stallholders must have got used to seeing him conducting a minute search for a good neck, and sometimes to being confronted with irritable enquiries about the shortage of cockerels of two years and over. He set himself a high standard for quality in cocks' hackles and kept to it for the rest of his life. In 1891 he acquired some live birds with promising necks, and arranged with a man at Chilworth on the River Tillingbourne to look after them. Whether the nature of the arrangement had not been made clear, or whether the unknown person had simply been unreliable, cannot now be known now, but soon afterwards they were all slaughtered. The fact that they were turned into soup may have been an indication of their advanced age and therefore of the fine quality of their hackles.

In 1892 twelve more articles were published under the 'Jottings' title. They ceased temporarily in 1893: instead twelve more articles appeared under other headings covering various subjects, including one called 'An Ideal Dictionary of Fly-Dressing'. 'Jottings' articles reappeared in 1894 and, by the end of the decade, totalled thirty-two in number, mixed with many others on kindred subjects.

In his articles, Skues returned several times to the question of getting good feathers. In the winter of 1898 he addressed the subject again, releasing another flood of articles on plumage of all sorts. This series, called 'The Fly Dresser's Birds', appeared in every issue of *The Fishing Gazette* for ten weeks and was one of his most ambitious so far. These articles were included in *Silk, Fur and Feather* (1950), a posthumous collection of his fly-tying writings. An interesting feature of these articles was a change from engravings to photogravures, ninety-seven in total, of ideal feathers. In an age untroubled by the concept of protected species, no one would have raised an eyebrow at his list, which began on 22 January with adjutant, blackbird and bittern, and ended on 26 March with woodlark, wren and wryneck.

Many of his articles dealt with hackles; their quality, the ideal shape to aim for, and their lax nomenclature in the published works – what exactly, for example, was ginger, or honey dun? He would have had an appreciative readership, for nineteenth-century anglers were obsessed with this subject, and an article on hackles was always likely to produce letters from readers. In February 1892 a Best Bird competition was held at the Piscatorial Exhibition at the Royal Aquarium, arousing a good deal of interest among amateurs. There were prizes in eleven classes, with the highest awards (£3) for cocks in Blue Dun, Honey Dun and Coch-y-bondhu. The hen classes in these shades only carried prizes of one half the value of the cockerel classes, showing how completely the dry fly had come to the fore by this date.

Some interesting points of detail emerge for the first time in Skues' writings in this period, to reappear later in his life, sometimes in a more refined form. In March 1892 he announced a principle, to which he adhered for the remainder of his life, that the colour of the silk is just as important as the dubbing in an imitation of a dun, and should imitate that of the spinner: 'The sub-imago of every dun is simply the spinner in a thin, delicate envelope, and the dresser aims by his dubbing to simulate the envelope, and by the silk underneath to represent the hidden spinner.'

Other details appearing for the first time in the writings of the 1890s include the Pope's Green Nondescript, E.M. Tod's double hooks and, most important of all, his discovery of the Orange Quill.

The Nondescript came to the notice of a wider public as a result of another learned article by Skues in November 1896. He was attempting to identify the correct dressing for the Apple Green Dun, a popular pattern in late Victorian times, and the subject of much variation at the hands of different fly-dressers, and in different parts of Britain. At the end of this article Skues wrote: 'Bye the bye, what is the Green Nondescript? Is it another variant of the Apple Green Dun?' A week later W.H. Pope wrote that he believed it was. He claimed no originality in the design: he was only the popularizer of the fly, which was an invention of George Holland. Pope had been seeking a fly that would cope with the smutting fish of the River Frome. In the season of 1896 he caught 269 trout, of which the Nondescript had accounted for 106. Holland then admitted that the pattern had been devised by Mrs Holland. Skues adopted this pattern with enthusiasm and used it for years, but more for tailing than for smutting trout.

In the same year he began to use E.M. Tod's midge double hooks, particularly the Greenwell's Glory: 'They are certainly marvellous at holding, and I think somewhat better at hooking than flies dressed on single hooks.' They were to become even more useful to him as he developed wet-fly and nymph techniques.

Like many chalk-stream anglers, Skues had discovered how baffling a hatch of blue-winged olives could be. He was sufficiently proud of his discovery of the effectiveness of the Orange Quill during such hatches to include it in his list of 'Firsts' for posthumous publication in the *Journal of the Flyfishers' Club*. He had prepared this list towards the end of his life, and had asked Dr Barton to publish it after his death. It was intended to be a sort of testamentary reminder to the angling world of his achievements. The search for consistency, mentioned above, of the Apple Green Dun and its close relation the Throstle Wing Dun produced several suggestions from readers, including W.H. Foster of the well-known angling business in Ashbourne. But all the variations were attempts, generally not very successful, to get on terms with the natural blue-winged olive. The artificial, Skues wrote in another 'Jottings' in 1896, was not a killing fly in Hampshire, because no one seems to have discovered the dressing which truly represents the natural fly. Mr. H.S. Hall says of it, that no satisfactory dressing has been devised. It is rather a large fly, and when it has been on I have never done much, until one occasion, when I put up a big Red Quill, dyed in Crashaw's Red Spinner. That brought them up grandly. [But he adds acutely] I suspect they took it for the change of the Blue Winged Olive, known among Hampshire anglers as the Sherry Spinner.

A month later he returned to the subject. He had learned all about the sherry spinner from the Winchester tackle dealer George Currell, who was always worth listening to. Currell used to dress a useful pattern, virtually a Red Quill, with a dyed orange body and a 'grannom' tail, presumably a tag of green wool. Currell was perhaps a little ahead of the game here, although other anglers, including Francis Francis, had noticed the striking blue-green ball of eggs carried by the spinner. Skues admitted:

I had not previously observed the natural insect. Since then I have found that when it is on, a big bright Orange Quill kills well of an August or September evening at sundown, just as the sun gets off the water. Then it will often account for a brace or leash of good fish before dark. [With a fresh burst of candour, he adds] It will be observed that in 'Floating Flies' Mr Halford, writing of the Red Quill, says: 'A larger size dressed on a No.2 hook is found very killing after dark'.

So it would appear that the credit for discovering good medicine for turning failure into success on a B.W.O. evening ought to be shared between Skues, Currell and Halford.

Apart from these many points of detail, of which only a part can be considered here, there were other and more profound ideas, introduced artlessly but which nevertheless expressed his overall point of view about angling problems. Readers of Skues' writings published between the wars will be familiar with them, but to a great extent they were fully formed in the 1890s. He more than once urged amateur fly-tiers not to be too narrow in their approach, but rather to base their work on direct observation of the natural world. In December 1891, towards the end of an article filled with many original ideas, appeared something very like a manifesto:

I think that the above instances go to show that it does not matter very much about taking books with you, or learning patterns by heart. The important thing is to acquire such a mastery of material and method, and such a facility of expedient as will enable you to successfully imitate any fly you come across.

His own book-learning, acquired from those sessions in the Reading Room of the British Museum, had, in the long run, liberated rather than congealed his approach. Other readers might have been swamped by the vast corpus of traditional patterns, many of them based on nothing but guesswork or mere fantasy, and would have relapsed into a sort of antiquarianism. For Skues the research had become a dynamic springboard for his own more original work. Skues believed that all art was rooted in the past, as W.H. Lawrie commented years later. In April 1892 Skues wrote: 'I do not see much to be gained by stereotyping patterns by a royal academy of anglers' and, in December of the same year: 'If, instead of bewildering oneself with the selection of the best of the myriad patterns made, one can catch and imitate the natural fly with reasonable accuracy, one is spared alike the agonies and helplessness of the man who merely flogs.'

These intriguing and subtle articles were enough to make the name of 'Val Conson' well known in the fly-fishing world. In 1895, only two years after joining the Flyfishers' Club, he became a member of a small committee chaired by R.B. Marston, formed to create a collection of fly-dressing materials. Members of the Club were urged to contribute to this, with a preference for quality over quantity, by communicating with the committee through Skues, who was to act as Secretary. He took a leading part himself in amassing materials. His *Fishing Gazette* articles had put him in touch with many professional and amateur poultry breeders, and soon an impressive collection developed, with specimens of the best hackles mounted between glass sheets in order to display their colour and sparkle. He wrote in 'Trivialities': 'I do not think it would be possible nowadays to get together such a priceless collection.'

It may have been about this time that Marston began to pay him for his articles. At this period of his life Skues was acquiring a certain status. To have been invited, when still a comparatively new member of the Flyfishers' Club, to join this committee was a singular mark of regard. His fellows on the committee – Marston, F.J. Ohlson and Hedley Norris – were all members of long standing. A year later another mark of esteem came from the acknowledged leader in the field. For Skues it must have seemed the crowning achievement to have been asked by Halford to write a section of his forthcoming book *Dry-Fly Entomology* (see below). Skues had found an arena in which he could shine. As he approached his fortieth year the cautious and diffident young man was growing into a more confident and happy person.

In June 1895 there appeared in *The Fishing Gazette* a stimulating piece on fly-tying by H.G. McClelland, writing under the name of 'Athenian'. Readers now had two authors on the same subject on whom to base their own efforts. Skues was very far from feeling crowded by a new competitor; in fact he gave a generous welcome to the article, hoping that it would be the first of a series. For several years contributions arrived from McClelland, which were eventually gathered together in book form under the title of *The Trout Fly-Dressers' Cabinet of Devices*. At times, a learned conversation in print developed between the two men in the pages of *The Fishing Gazette*. It was inevitable that a certain difference of view would emerge between them, but their arguments were carried on with respect and good humour, and Skues was astonished at the reach and grasp of the thinking of someone only a few years out of school. Seldom can a fly-fishing readership have had access to such a rewarding double act. But it was not to last. Tuberculosis, for many generations the great scourge, was increasing its hold on the young man. Skues was shocked and grieved to learn of his death in July 1898, and paid him a generous tribute, calling him 'the most prolific, ingenious, and inventive intellect of the century' (see Appendix 2).

It is a curious point about the development of Skues, both as an angler and as a man, that he began to break loose and slip away from the all-embracing influence of Halford just when he had been awarded by Halford what many would have regarded as the ultimate compliment, in the form of the invitation to contribute to the book of 1897. Signs of a growing independence of mind, and of a suspicion that the leader was not after all infallible, had been appearing in Skues' writings for some time. They were in no way connected with sunk-fly experiments, which had scarcely begun in the early 1890s. Skues was at first confining his criticisms to Halford's pet subject – the floating fly and its construction. From the beginning of the decade there was an undercurrent of disagreement with the pronouncements of the master. It began gently enough, and at first there was nothing calculated to irritate. In the third 'Jottings' (January 1892) Skues refers to Halford's method of winging a dry fly, as set forth in his first book, with four turns of silk to tie down the wings:

In my first article the two illustrations of winging are shown, as in Mr Halford's book, with four turns of silk tying down the feathers. As a matter of fact, I *prefer* to dress double-dressed floaters even with only two turns (Holland, of Salisbury, can tie them with one, but he is an exception).

Perhaps by way of tempering this piece of *lèse-majesté*, he added later in the same piece: 'I desire to record my own deep indebtedness to Mr Halford for his epoch-making work "Floating Flies and How to Dress Them".' The soothing effect of this last comment may have lost some of its impact when he wrote the following week in the same journal that although he admired Halford's 'great book ... it came out some years back, and things may have moved since then, and fresh methods been invented'. Later in the same year he objected to Halford's method of constructing detached-bodied flies, adding for good measure that he himself had little time for detached bodies anyway. This may have slightly nettled a writer who had adopted the pen-name of 'Detached Badger'.

In April 1894 Skues returned with a more damaging attack on the subject of winging:

Mr Halford's book recommends the fixing of the wing in the first instance on the middle of the shank of the eyed hook, and then sliding it up to the eye after cutting off the waste ends. The result is often disastrous, and many promising wings are ruined in the forward pull.

He then goes on to describe two better methods. Halford rarely made any attempt to justify himself in print, but on this occasion he responded the following week to point out that this was the earlier known method of winging on eyed hooks, and that further on in his book 'the modern plan now generally adopted is described as "An Improved Method of Winging Upright Duns"'. He added, as a small piece of gentle reproof, that Skues had, 'no doubt unintentionally', conveyed a wrong message to readers. Skues apologized the following week, but still managed to leave the impression that he had been in the right. Reading it today, it certainly seems puzzling for Halford to have described at such length in his book an obsolete method, followed twenty pages later by a better one. Skues, with his legal training, could be a tricky opponent when it came to the precise meaning of words. He pointed out that Halford had written (rather misleadingly) at the beginning of the chapter in question: 'The methods herein described and figured are such only as have been thoroughly tried by the author, and in many instances exhaustively threshed out by comparing notes copiously with other amateurs.' There may have been some wincing on the part of that author.

All the same, these incidents were mere pinpricks compared with the storm that was to develop and to destroy their friendship in the next decade. Halford was capable of being urbane and magnanimous about small differences of opinion, and relations between them at this time remained cordial. In 1894 or 1895 – writing about it many years later Skues could not remember which – he was invited for a weekend at the Ramsbury fishery rented by Halford and his three colleagues, a mark of favour eagerly sought after by many at the Flyfishers' Club.

In 1896 Halford and Skues collaborated to put together a two-page article on fly-dressing in *The Field*, Halford dealing with dry flies and Skues with wet flies; and a little later, as mentioned above, Halford invited Skues to contribute to his cumbersome and somewhat costive work, *Dry-Fly Entomology*. The fly-dressing section was divided between Skues, who used a vice, and W.H. Brougham, a master of the older method of using the fingers only. This two-man section was arguably the most distinguished part of an otherwise not very valuable work. Modern publishers venturing on republishing Halford's books have justifiably ignored this work, but at the time it increased the reputation of Skues.

There was a curious prequel to the publication of *Dry-Fly Entomology*. The first review of it appeared in *The Fishing Gazette* in two parts in June 1897. It was written by the editor, and was descriptive and cheerfully supportive rather than analytical. But Skues had already published a review in *The Fishing Gazette* of a part of the book, the 'Hundred Best Patterns', which had been published separately in *Baily's Magazine* a year earlier. Halford must have been taken aback to find that a man he had hitherto regarded as a protégé was reviewing what was in fact an advanced copy of part of his book, in another part of which the work of that protégé was to appear. He must have been even more affronted at the minute and critical line taken in Skues' review. We cannot be quite sure if Skues had already been approached to be a contributor for the 1897 book (and had even done his piece) when he wrote the 1896 review, but it seems likely. Otherwise, Halford would not have allowed him to participate at all.

In this review, which ran to three and a half columns, Skues brought to bear all his accumulated knowledge. Halford must have read it with mounting alarm and irritation. Skues began with a swipe at *Floating Flies and How to Dress Them*, the book he had once so much admired, noting in it the lack of entomology. Entomological considerations had, it was true, entered into the classification of the artificials, but they had not been applied systematically. Now, he said, 'at an interval of ten years, Mr Halford has broken out in a new place', language which the High Priest of the dry fly may have found a little too breezy and lacking in proper deference. Next, Skues took issue with the idea of gallina for whisks, rather than cock's hackles, rejected by Mr Halford as being too brittle. Gallina fibres, thought Skues, were not appreciably stronger, and in any case were far too thick to have a good resemblance to the setae of the natural fly. The move away from winged to hackle flies also met his disapproval. Halford's aim had been to make flies lighter so as to fall upon the water with less disturbance. He had often observed highly educated trout melting away in panic at the too-obvious fall of an artificial fly, especially on bright, calm days. Under Halford's new scheme the new flies dispensed with wings as such, but acquired a third soft hen hackle in front of the two cock's hackles. But Skues pointed out that Halford's reasoning applied mainly to sedge flies: 'It is not quite obvious why the same principles are applied by Mr Halford to numerous duns and spinners.' He added that trying to cram three hackles onto a size 000 hook would be too difficult. Having spent much time trying to instruct his readers how to master the art of winging, Skues was not likely to care much for the appearance of these new hackle patterns. He could not resist a quiet gibe: 'it is safe to say that they strike a bad blow at the "precise imitation theory"'.

This critical dismembering of Halford's famous list continued: 'I must protest against No. 1 Whitchurch being included among fancy flies.' The omissions were called 'interesting' – he mentioned thirteen flies that should have been included; for dubbed flies the reader should be told the colour of the silk; and 'the wisdom of such whole-hearted devotion to quills' was doubted – dubbings and floss for dry flies were the way for the future.

The 1896 review marked a turning point. The relationship was never going to be quite the same again. Perhaps a drifting apart was inevitable. There was no bitterness yet – that came later. In 1897 Halford and Skues, as committee members of the Flyfishers' Club, were frequently in each other's company. There may have been a feeling of wariness on both sides, but appearances were kept up. As late as 1904 Halford, in a speech at the annual dinner of the Flyfishers' Club, praised the work of Skues and his colleague Ohlson on the fly-dressing sub-committee. But the days of discipleship were over. Skues had come of age.

The performance of Skues on the river improved greatly in the last years of the nineteenth century. He was still fishing with a selection of heavy rods, with short hooks in sizes 0, 00 and only rarely 000 at this date. He was fastidious about gut, generally using Holland's cobweb gut. The combination of this and the long, heavy rods must have required some careful management, but he was seldom broken, whereas in his first few years on the Itchen he frequently broke at the strike. His method was to avoid alarming the hooked fish, to take charge quickly, to confuse it and to keep out of sight during the playing of it. The netting was often a sudden ambushing performance. Major Carlisle, in a letter to *The Fishing Gazette* in 1892, wondered how he managed it: it would certainly not do on his home pitch at Houghton. Skues agreed that it would be unwise for fish over 2lb, a rare occurrence at Abbots Barton at that date, where the size limit was 12in, and the average was about 1lb 4oz. Skues was badly caught out when he came to Ramsbury as a result of the invitation mentioned earlier. His name does not figure in the Ramsbury record book, for the simple reason that he caught nothing. In his later reminiscences he said little about this visit, the memory of which may have been painful, merely remarking that he found his Itchen points over-fine for the strong, ungovernable Kennet fish, 'for they smashed me again and again'.

To what extent he was experimenting with sunk flies at this period it is difficult to say. At some point he must have moved away from the Halfordian teaching that success with such tactics would only be a sort of random fluke, and began to use sunk flies more systematically. It is a pity that he has not told us exactly when he began to use what, in *Itchen Memories*, he called 'some weird looking nymphs', made with a single strand of macaw feather (yellow, with a dark-blue rib) and with whisks of the same material. Drifting them underwater close to the edge of rafts of cut weed, he began to catch trout that were feeding below the surface. At all events, enough success with sunk flies had come about, even if not recorded, during the latter part of the 1890s for him to pen the well-known harbinger letter in *The Field* in 1899 (for the full text see Appendix 3). In it he describes the familiar and frequently occurring situation for the angler on a fishery populated by trout everywhere taking nymphal food below the surface:

What is the moral for the dry-fly man? What but this: when your fish are bulging, give it to them wet … In years gone by, anglers used to get good baskets on Itchen and Test with the wet-fly. They will have to come back to it again. Some day they will learn to combine a judicious admixture of wet-fly science and dry-fly art, and then – Then will be the time for some new development. In the meanwhile, why not?

He adds at the end, tongue in cheek: 'I speak as a dry-fly man.'

It was the prelude to what he later called 'the great adventure'. The 'new development' took a further decade and a period of more solid research to accomplish, but by 1912 the nymph revolution was becoming a reality.

6

The Light Rod Argument

D URING HIS CAREER as a journalist Skues engaged in several controversies in the angling press. Most of these were small-scale skirmishes, quickly dispatched after a brisk exchange of fire. There were, however, two major battles. The more serious of the two was undoubtedly the 1938 debate about the acceptability of the artificial nymph on the chalk stream. The other great confrontation blew up in the first decade of the twentieth century over the effectiveness of the light American fly rods that were beginning to appear in the British market. The controversy over the nymph was upsetting for Skues. By 1938 he was an old man facing a radical criticism of his life's work. By contrast in 1902 he entered the fray on behalf of the light rod with the zest and enjoyment of a man in his prime. In time, for it occupied several years, he became one of the leaders of the new movement. The British tackle trade fought back savagely, but in the end the logic of the light rod prevailed, largely because it had been carefully explained by Skues in a series of brilliantly persuasive letters. The manufacture of the heavy 'wrist-breakers' began to decline and a major change took place in rod-building. In his later writings Skues occasionally mentioned that he had 'thrown himself into the controversy', but with his usual modesty neglected to add that he played a major part.

The campaign was mainly conducted in the columns of *The Fishing Gazette*, in letters sometimes of enormous length. Skues had three effective allies, two of whom were personal friends: W. D. Coggeshall, an American living mainly in England, and Louis Bouglé, a leading light in French angling circles. Coggeshall was an ideal ally to have in the controversy; a civil engineer who, in his earlier years, had been a railroad pioneer in South America. He had a good understanding of many scientific and technical subjects of which Skues lacked real knowledge, and had developed a method of dressing lines which resulted in a product far in advance of the examples found in the shops. Unfortunately the process was too time-consuming and uneconomic to be taken up by the trade. When Coggeshall died in 1923 his widow discovered among his effects eight completed lines and dispatched them to Skues' office. To Skues' great regret this valuable package somehow disappeared en route. It is sad to think that the finder probably had no sense of the value of the lines and that they may have ended their existence as string for securing parcels. Coggeshall's lines, which he gave away generously, were much sought after at the Flyfishers' Club, of which he was a popular member for twenty years and of which he became President in 1918. He was also Vice-President of the Casting Club de France, founded by the Prince d'Aremberg, and a member of the American Tuna Club of Catalina Island.

Skues' correspondence with Coggeshall seems not to have survived, but the collection of 300 letters of Louis Bouglé provides a rich source of information about the light rod argument. Bouglé was one of the leaders in French angling circles a century ago and also deserves a place in British angling history. He was born in Orleans in 1864, the son of a provincial doctor. He was educated in Orleans and Paris, and spent a year at St Augustine's College at Ramsgate. After doing his compulsory military service at Blois he studied law for three years and practised with a notary for a year, during which time he became more and more involved in commercial projects. By the time he got to know Skues through correspondence he was a *commanditaire* (sleeping partner) in several commercial undertakings, mainly in printing.

The third actor in this drawn-out drama was a contributor calling himself Viator, who wrote almost more than anyone else. His letters were pungent and effective, but his identity was not revealed. It is very likely that Coggeshall was sheltering behind this alias.

When the controversy began in 1902 most fly-fishermen in Britain were using rods of considerable strength, length and weight. If they were wet-fly fishermen in the north and west of Britain their rods were usually more limber in action. In the chalk country rods were powerful and stiff, designed for driving a heavy line into the wind. The influence of Halford ensured that split cane reigned supreme in the south, and the rods had plenty of cane in them. Single-handed weapons of 10 and 11ft, weighing at least an ounce to the foot, and sometimes more – so that a rod might weigh as much as 14 or 15oz – were used almost universally. Plying these heavy weapons might have been a pleasure for anglers with the steely wrists of Marryat, but for men of more average physique casting could be exhausting. And for Skues, with permanently damaged wrists, casting throughout the angling day could become torture. It is not surprising that he welcomed the new movement for lighter rods.

The first warning shot came appropriately from America, in the form of an article entitled 'Scientific Tackle' by Edward G. Taylor in *American Field*. It caught the attention of Marston, who reprinted it in *The Fishing Gazette* of 17 May 1902. In this article, which deserves to be seen as a piece of history for its part in triggering a great change, Taylor referred to the lightness and convenience of the latest American rods, and praised the virtues of his own equipment for dealing with the strong, active rainbow trout of the Au Sable river in Michigan: 'My choice is a 4½oz split bamboo rod, hand-made, 9 feet in length. A rod of this length and weight, if properly made and handled, will tire out and kill a 5lb rainbow trout.' He added that a 6oz rod and a size H line was 'as heavy tackle as any angler should use in taking trout'. This last parting shot must have raised various reactions from British readers: amusement or irritation at such a bizarre and impossible idea and deep unease amongst the tackle makers, especially John James Hardy. If he had been able to divine what the future might bring he would have been much more alarmed.

A week later *The Fishing Gazette* carried a letter of enquiry over the signature of Viator:

> Where can I get a 4½ oz fly rod such as is described by Mr Taylor? … Personally, I have always found the characteristic difficulty with all English rod-makers is that they apparently cannot make a rod both strong and light. Indeed, the average make of English rods in comparison with those manufactured by Americans is clumsy and heavy in the extreme. I refer, of course, to the leading American firms, not to those who send us over split-cane rods which are retailed at something like six shillings.

Coggeshall was a fervent believer in the virtues of the Leonard rods and the style of the letter fits with what we can know of him. The name of 'Viator', no doubt suggested by Charles Cotton's collaboration with Walton and its Latin meaning of 'traveller', might identify it as belonging to an expatriate American. Skues left the odd clue, which may have been deliberate, as to Coggeshall's part in the campaign. He more than once referred to 'Coggeshall's battle', and in writing his obituary in 1925 wrote: 'He took but a slight overt part in the press controversy of 1902.'

This might have been an encoded way of indicating a real, though disguised, contribution which was not slight at all but extremely vigorous and effective. But we cannot be certain. In *The Fishing Gazette* Viator gave his address as Chelsea, whereas Coggeshall lived in Upper Phillimore Gardens in Kensington. Whoever he was, Viator was successful in getting a good discussion going.

In the next three years the subject was seldom absent from the columns of *The Fishing Gazette*. Eventually a record was created for the number of responses. The eagerness and deep interest shown by the angling public were a godsend to an editor eager to fill his columns. At no time did Marston feel tempted to write 'This correspondence must now cease', although in the early stage of the argument he was slow to admit the value of the American rods. He wrote: 'Mr Whitley, fishing tackle maker, Basnett Street, Liverpool is agent for the celebrated "Leonard" split-cane rods. There is practically no demand in this country for 4½oz fly rods, except possibly for ladies and girls; no doubt they could be made if they were wanted.'

Marston may have regretted writing this, for by the end of the controversy he was a firm supporter of Skues and an admirer of the American rods. He was a conservative in many things: in the 1880s he had been slow to admit the usefulness of the eyed hook, but he could be convinced by evidence.

The fabulous Leonard rods were not unknown in Britain. A few individuals had discovered their worth, one of whom was Marston's father, who had written several books of reminiscence, using the pseudonym 'Amateur Angler'. But their main support was in America, particularly in the streams of the Catskill. There were other producers of light rods: Bouglé at first considered that the work of Payne was equally good.

Hiram Lewis Leonard, the founder of the business, had begun to make rods from the native timber of the woodlands before moving on to bamboo, at first the cane of Calcutta. The discovery of the superior qualities of the Chinese cane, *Arundinaria amabilis*, supplied the essential ingredient. Called Tonkin cane (inaccurately, in fact, but the name stuck), the fibres of this steely wonder timber made it powerful and durable. It was to make a great difference to the split-cane rod of the future. Leonard and his craftsmen were soon making examples of what some connoisseurs still call the perfect rod. But they ran into the problem familiar to all makers of the best rods, then and now. There is an unfortunate gulf between creating works of art, which takes much love and time, and running a commercial operation. As George Black put it in his book *Casting a Spell*, it was 'perfectionism versus economics'. Leonard was bound to run into difficulties. By the time the controversy arose in Britain he had been taken over by William Mills and Sons, who were, however, wise enough to press on with marketing rods carrying the name of H.L. Leonard.

In England the opposing teams lined up quickly in the late spring of 1902. Foremost among the scoffers was the firm of Hardy Bros., with Farlow and Allcock in support. Hardy's had, in fact, been expecting a threat to their supremacy since the 1880s, and for some time had been conducting a covert campaign of espionage, borrowing American rods to test them, and in several extreme cases purchasing rods through intermediaries and dismantling them by steaming them so as to examine the build in detail and perhaps identify some magic ingredient. At the Hardy workshop this information, which would have been a threat to their reputation, was kept strictly secret, although it was known to Louis Bouglé.

Hardy Bros responded smartly in *The Fishing Gazette* the following week, referring to Viator's letter: 'We hope he does not include us in his sweeping condemnation of English rod makers, who, he says, "cannot make a rod both light and strong". If he is in any difficulty about this we will be pleased to make him a rod which we will guarantee as light and strong as any American.'

Viator ignored the offer contained in this salvo, and continued in his letters to show a minute knowledge of the American market, which is enough to show that his first letter was not really an innocent search for help by a beginner. He had written to a number of anglers in America, and now revealed his results. They must have increased the feeling of alarm at Hardy Bros. One correspondent wrote that he had used a rod of 10½ feet and 5¾oz. With this and another rod of 6oz he had landed many heavy fish up to 7½lb. An American firm (unnamed, but no doubt Wm Mills & Son of New York) wrote to announce that they had already sold a number of 2oz rods in 1902, also models of 9ft weighing 3oz and another weighing from 3½oz to 3¾oz: 'The latter is quite powerful enough for any ordinary trout fishing.' With this promising beginning Viator mounted a major attack on the technical skills and commercial methods of the British tackle trade. The average weight of a British rod was 12 to 14oz, 'although a leading London manufacturer is trying to bring out one of 7½oz'. If, as Hardy Bros had suggested, there was no demand in Britain for light and powerful rods

> this is due to want of knowledge, and still more to the lack of enterprise and initiative which is so marked a characteristic of our people in the present day in comparison with the go-ahead methods of certain other nations, notably the Americans. Were our rod makers willing to put on one side their time-worn methods, and to discard many of their obtuse insular prejudices against change, they could easily compete successfully with their foreign rivals.

This wide-ranging attack marked the real beginning of the controversy, for it went much deeper than matters of quality in the manufacture of fishing rods and brought into the discussion issues of commercial and technical habits in a much wider context in Britain. In the last years of the nineteenth century Victorian optimism had begun to falter. The country which had been responsible for the world's first industrial revolution was aware that their lead was being lost to American and German competition, and some observers were pointing to complacency in long-established businesses and a lack of interest in new techniques.

Hardy Bros responded on 14 June with a more measured and reasonable letter, but there was an ill-tempered and sarcastic undercurrent which henceforth was seldom absent from their correspondence. The writer, most probably John James Hardy, wrote that if Viator had consulted his firm or even looked at a catalogue he would have noticed the 'Gem' range of rods of weights between 6oz and 8oz, also the 'Featherweight Perfection' rod of 8½ft and 4½oz. As for rods of 2oz: 'No man in his senses would believe that such a toy could be of any use either to cast a fly against a wind or to hold a fish out of weeds.' He pointed out that Hardy rods enjoyed a constant sale across the Atlantic, and that this was enough to show that not all Americans approved of light rods, and were prepared to buy from Hardy Bros, even though they had to pay an added import duty of 45 per cent. As for their own stronger rods, the weight was mainly in the fittings, not the cane.

A week later seven letters on the subject appeared in *The Fishing Gazette*, including contributions from E.M. Tod and Fosters of Ashbourne. Marston now knew that he was presiding over that gift to editors, a worthwhile controversy. These letters were long and detailed and ran to four columns. Viator reappeared, congratulating Hardy Bros with much irony. Of twenty rods in their catalogue they made one equal in weight to the American rods: the rest simply had far too much timber in them. The Redditch firm of Allcock joined in for the first time, insisting that they were 'perfectly acquainted' with rods from the USA, having handled 'thousands', and proceeded rudely and irrelevantly to discuss the cheapest types on the market:

> The very light rods made in America, which, by the way, vary from 5oz upwards, are made with nearly the whole of the centre of the cane left out of the butt, leaving simply a thin shell or outer bark. The ferrules and fitting are made of very thin brass, nickel plated, in fact so thin that an indentation can be made with the thumb and finger.

Having set up such an obvious straw target, the writer of this foolish letter was ill-advised to have added an ungracious reference to what he termed 'American puff and Yankee bunkum'.

In his next letter (which was over a thousand words in length) Viator dealt roughly with Allcocks for bringing into the discussion American rods of a grade which he had specifically rejected in his letter, adding witheringly: 'It is a most extraordinary spectacle to find educated British businessmen apparently unable to read the meaning of a short English sentence.' He then revealed some of the interesting material he had derived from the current catalogue of William Mills, for example, the H.L. Leonard 'Fairy' Catskill rod of 8ft 2in: a three-piece and costing $40. Although a very light rod, it could lay out a line of 72ft. Another three-piece rod of 9ft weighed only 3½–3¾oz. A more powerful model, in lengths varying from 9 to 10ft and weights varying from 4½oz to 7oz sold for $35. These were high prices for that date – 40 dollars was then the equivalent of £8.

Marston added a note at the end of this ground-breaking letter which must have caused J.J. Hardy some sleepless nights: 'Viator has certainly done good service by calling attention to the fact that rod makers in this country do often make rods which are quite *unnecessarily* heavy ... I can back up his statement as to a really good "Leonard" being equal to any rod made.' From this note one can see that Marston was moving towards the point of view of the light rod enthusiasts, and was therefore beginning to look like a threat to Hardy Bros. By the early part of July he had himself made trial of a Leonard rod.

In the second week of August Skues came back from a fishing trip to Norway and immediately plunged into the battle. He soon emerged as an arbiter of the conflict, insisting on precision and clarity in the use of terms, and pointing out that the main point had so far been missed in the previous correspondence. The assumption that American rods lacked strength was quite wrong. Having handled several American rods he was impressed by their 'extraordinary courage and temper ... quite equal to hustling heavy fish on South country rivers.... I for one am tired of the hand paralysers which our first-class makers turn out for dry fly fishing, and I heartily thank Viator for his spirited effort to induce them to mend their ways.'

The traditionalists fought back stubbornly for several months. For these anglers, light rods belonged in a cabinet of curiosities rather than on the river. In September the energy of the dispute seemed to die. If the feeling at Hardy Bros was one of relief it was not to last for long. Five weeks later the fight broke out again, provoked by the reprinting in *The Fishing Gazette* of a coat-trailing article originally in *Forest and Stream* by E. Hough of Chicago. It included another shrewd hit at the English character and its effects in the world of commerce: 'There is a cock-sureness about our English cousins which is sometimes a trifle amusing', and quoted some of the ill-tempered remarks in print of Hardy's and Allcock's. He praised the Catskill rods, where all the weight went into the essential parts, and not into spears, balls or metal butt caps. If, as J.J. Hardy alleged, much of the weight in British rods was in the fittings, why make the latter so heavy?

Encouraged by this, Viator again made an appearance in a piece which more resembled a lengthy article than a letter. It must surely be now widely accepted, he wrote, that the light and powerful rods of America were far superior to 'the heavy and clumsy ones manufactured in this country'. To call them whippy or invertebrate and only fit for ladies and children was simply not true. He had received many letters from home and abroad praising the qualities of the Leonard and Payne rods. His instinct was correct: already acceptance was growing. Some British tackle dealers had already begun to show an interest in lightness in their advertisements for rods, and Hardy Bros were about to produce one of 9½ft weighing 5oz and costing one third less than a Leonard. They insisted that they had always been able to make light rods and had produced a 9ft rod of 4½oz in three pieces for the International Fisheries Exhibition of 1883. The argument of insufficient demand was, of course, a circular one. If Hardy Bros and the other major producers filled their catalogues with heavy rods the angling public would take this as the informed choice of the tackle trade and would accept that this was how rods should be.

In November 1902 Skues intervened in his self-appointed capacity as occasional arbiter in the dispute. This was in the form of another of his 'Jottings' articles. He had followed the lead of Viator by obtaining a catalogue from Wm Mills. He urged anglers to cease their attempts to discredit the light American rods, 'if only in the interests of international good feeling'. The 2oz and 3oz rods on which they concentrated their scorn performed well on the river: one angler had cast 72ft with a 2oz rod, and another had, with the same model, caught 200 Long Island trout in four days. And he went on to include a lengthy list of rods by H.L. Leonard from 4¼oz upwards. He also noted with satisfaction the recent conversion of 'John Bickerdyke' (C.H. Cook of *The Field*) to the progressive party and quoted his remark that British rods were generally 50 per cent too heavy. The combined effect of a change in the attitude of the editor of *The Fishing Gazette* and the angling editor of *The Field* must have increased the despondency of the traditionalists, both producers and consumers. Skues ended with an appeal, clearly aimed at Hardy Bros and the trade in general: 'The change to lighter rods has got to come, why not accept it in a spirit of fairness and strive to be first in the field with the new article?'

By the end of 1902 this interesting and at times bitter controversy had produced thirty-seven published letters. Many more had been kept back by Marston, as being irrelevant or even offensive. In late November the entry of Louis Bouglé into the controversy had transformed it for Skues. Bouglé had been following it with great interest in *The Fishing Gazette*, but had been careful not to appear directly in it. He believed that foreign critics of English manufacturers were not likely to be well received, and controversies could anyway become ill-tempered and rude. But most importantly he was working at the time with Hardy Bros towards the manufacture of the Bouglé fly reel and could not afford to offend them publicly, although in fact Hardy knew all about his views on rods.

His letters show that he knew far more than Skues about rods, reels and tackle in general, but he deferred to Skues' much deeper knowledge about fly-dressing and patterns, and was eager to learn from him. This symbiotic relationship was useful and indeed personally agreeable to both of them, and lasted for three decades. In all the letters there is evidence of a determined search for excellence and for the best information about the latest discoveries and ideas. In his letter of 25 November 1902, Bouglé attributed the American success in rod-building to their use of the Tonkin cane, the resilient and close-grained variety found in a comparatively small area of East Asia. He believed that English rod-builders were ill-advised to stick to Calcutta cane. By corresponding directly with Hardy Bros, Bouglé had acquired a great deal of information which he was prepared to share with Skues under pledge of secrecy. He was trying to help Hardy's and had gone to the trouble of getting some samples of Tonkin cane from C.G. Levinson, a well-known angler and a judge in casting tournaments in America. He had then passed them on to J.J. Hardy. Earlier in the year Hardy had asked to see Bouglé's Leonard rods, but as the trout season was just beginning he sent one in April and two more in October. He considered it 'bizarre' that J.J. Hardy would need to borrow American rods from a French fisherman in order to examine them, but the real reason must have been that it was important for Hardy not to give any public impression of losing confidence in the products of his own firm.

Bouglé then described his own experience of Hardy Bros. Some years earlier he made the error ('*j'ai commis la sottise*') of ordering two standard Hardy rods: a 10ft 'Houghton' of 10½oz, which he could only use for an hour, and a Halford 'Priceless', which he could only use for half an hour. He added: 'My wrist is normal and my strength average.' Six months later he sold them both at a loss of 30 per cent. He then asked Hardy Bros for a lighter rod of 9½ft, which lacked power ('*sans aucune puissance*') and which he could not use with any precision. The ferrules were not good either. It was after these discouraging attempts that he turned to the Leonards, which were a revelation for him, and eventually he became a frequent and successful competitor in French competitions. His letter is full of praise for William Mills and for Payne, the maker of the Kosmic rod, and he referred to the extraordinary achievements in distance casting in the United States. He made particular mention of Walter D. Mansfield, President of the San Francisco Casting Club, who had thrown a line of 129½ft with a rod of 10ft weighing 5½oz in a tournament in San Francisco in October 1901.

Skues must have read this important letter with delight as well as interest. To have the inner secrets of Hardy's revealed, including more evidence of their mounting panic, would tell him that the battle for the light rod was being won. He at once began to put information from

Bouglé's two letters to use. Continuing to defend the American rod-builders, he wrote: 'I have certainly been struck by the steeliness and tensile strength of the cane in the best American rods.' He also turned irritably on the contributors, chiefly J.J. Hardy, who accused him of unpatriotic behaviour in urging anglers in Britain to buy American rods instead of British: 'It is the business of the patriotic Englishman to point out where the American excels and to encourage the Englishman to excel the American in that respect.'

1902 had been a worrying year for J.J. Hardy. At the Christmas party given for his employees at the Alnwick works he held forth in a rallying speech, insisting that he was always willing to learn new ideas from expert anglers. 'If there was anything that was new; if there was anything that was any improvement in that direction the firm of Hardy Bros were first in the field ("Hear, Hear").' The foreman of the rod-building section followed with a loyal speech, saying that light rods 'might be all right in theory, but in practice they were a long way out'. (No doubt there was another wave of applause.)

In January 1903 there was no slackening in the battle, and Skues was once again active. In the previous year he had several times been irritated by the letters of the barrister William Baden-Powell, an immovably rigid traditionalist. Baden-Powell had demanded to know why English rod-makers should be 'spurred up to give us extremely light rods'. Skues reminded him and other readers that the real question at issue was that English rod-makers insisted on providing extremely heavy and clumsy weapons. At the end of this letter Marston added a note in an attempt to reprove him, always a risky line to adopt with Skues: '"Val Conson" is hardly correct in saying that our rod makers have insisted on giving us extremely heavy and clumsy weapons; they have done their best to give what angling authorities like "Ephemera", Francis Francis, Stewart, Marryat, Halford and others have demanded.'

Skues replied a week later to offer a sharper definition. Marston was quite used to being corrected by Skues and never stood on his dignity. In this case he may have been impressed by the following piece of logic:

> I do not think the rod makers are entitled to shift responsibility onto the shoulders of Mr Halford and the others you name. These gentlemen demanded the power, they never stipulated for the weight; they were told the power could not be got without it, and the power was essential. Who but the rod makers should find out

that the power could be got without the weight? The American rod makers did; why did not the English know?

He then administered another reproof to Marston, who had written that if the American makers could produce a rod capable of the same results in casting and playing fish and weighing a quarter of a pound less than an English rod 'then, manifestly, we shall all want the American rod'. Somewhat wearily Skues wrote: 'I must have expressed myself very badly if I have not made it clear to every unprejudiced reader that this is just what the American rods can do.' Later that year he replied to a letter written by an evidently slow-witted correspondent who had written of the possible usefulness of the light rod 'time will tell'. Skues retorted irritably: 'Well, time has done it in America.'

If Marston felt at all bruised at receiving two rebukes in the same letter it made no difference to his sense of fairness. Perhaps he was impressed by this further injection of unanswerable logic by Skues into the discussion. Later he reported that:

I am glad to say many of our best makers have taken the matter up seriously, and the result will be a great benefit to the art of fly fishing generally. The heavy rod and heavy line have been overdone, as well as the idea that the chief art of fly fishing is to force a fly against a gale of wind.

In January and February of 1903 it was clear that a sort of watershed had been reached. Fosters of Ashbourne had succeeded in producing an 8ft rod weighing 3½oz. A satisfied customer wrote of receiving a rod of 9ft and 5oz specially made for him by Allcock: 'I cannot see where any rod maker could improve on this rod.' On 15 and 22 January there were informal discussions at the Flyfishers' Club and a number of light rods by Leonard, Hardy Bros, Ogden & Scotford, Wyers Frères of Paris and Redditch and Milward were examined by members, including men who had been active in the correspondence. Marston wrote: 'I think the majority of the members present agreed that there was a big future for the rod of moderate weight – 5oz to 8oz, according to length.'

One of the most striking alterations in the argument can be dated from the arrival at the office of *The Fishing Gazette* of two light rods, of 8ft 6in and 5¾oz and 9ft 6in and 6¼oz, sent by Hardy Bros for comparison with American examples. Marston must have been very startled when they suggested showing them to Val Conson (whose real identity was of course well known to Hardy Bros). The letters of J.J. Hardy had shown a perceptible change month by month, from being deeply offended, angry, ill-tempered, derisive, then alarmed by the weight of evidence, and at length moving wearily towards admitting that the progressive party might have a case. Once Hardy began to make at least a partial retreat the ranks of the heavy rod supporters were bound to falter. Some never wavered, such as William Baden-Powell, who thought there was no evidence for the reputed excellence of the Leonard. Charles Payton, well known as British Consul in Calais for many years, and familiar with the chalk streams of Picardy and Normandy, maintained that he was happy to continue using a single-handed trout rod weighing 1lb. There seems to have been an impression with older anglers that there was something effeminate about these slender rods from America: true Englishmen should have backbone and so should their rods. In his interesting book on the rise and progress of the bamboo rod, *Casting a Spell*, George Black has identified a similar prejudice twenty years earlier in America. At first some critics could not get used to the appearance of these slender wands in the earlier tournaments in New York, and scorned them as unmanly and un-American. But the logic of the new rods was bound to prevail, just as in Britain a good deal later.

Skues reported his impressions of the Hardy offering in *The Fishing Gazette*. It was a good example of his rational and even-handed summaries. He admitted that he did not yet own a Leonard rod, a piece of news that may have surprised some readers. He arranged a meeting with Coggeshall at his house in Kensington, taking the rods with him for a trial. He also took his Houghton rod, made some time before by Hardy to his order, 10ft in length in three pieces, with a weight of 12oz. This substantial rod could cast a good distance but was 'most trying to the hand'. Coggeshall also provided two Leonard rods from his own armoury for Skues to compare. The first Leonard put into his hands was a rod of 10ft 6in, about fifteen years old and weighing 6¼oz. Skues immediately encountered something mysterious in the feel of this rod. It appeared on first inspection to be disappointingly lacking in backbone. Coggeshall explained that the action of getting out line and progressively passing the load further down the length of the rod produced a sensation of mounting power. This was probably a result of the minute attention paid by the maker to the taper of the cane. A proper trial in a Kensington drawing room was not possible, so Coggeshall then challenged Skues to put himself in the place of a hooked fish and defied him to break the rod by pulling as hard as possible. Something of the terror of Skues can be detected in what he described as

> a series of tests of strength and reliability so extravagant that I dare not subject the Hardy rods to anything like the same tests. With the strain put on the rod any gut short of sea-trout must have smashed, and I every moment expected the rod to go into splinters or to break off short like a carrot ... From these strains the rod sprang back as straight and true as ever. He claimed that his rods were unbreakable unless they were run against a wall or run over by a cab. I could come to no conclusion but that this 6¼oz Leonard was in point of power equal in every respect to the heavy-built 12oz Houghton, while there was a soft ease and sweetness about its action which made that of the Houghton appear dull, clumsy and uneven.

The second rod was 10ft and 5¾oz, and was similar to the rod with which Mansfield had made the prodigious cast mentioned earlier. In Coggeshall's hands it had been heavily used for two years and had killed fish up to 7lb. Skues described it as an exquisite piece of work, dwelling upon the neat suction ferrules which did not allow the sections to twist, in contrast to the lockfast collared ferrules of his three heavy Hardy rods, which had all shared this fault. And for the second time he used the damaging word 'clumsy'. If Hardy had been hoping that his intervening and providing test rods was going to result in a striking victory he was disappointed. Skues finished his long letter (1,800 words) with a pessimistic summing-up:

> I went to the trial hoping that it would prove that Messrs Hardy had done something which would – for the credit of our English manufacturers – make a good showing by the side of the American work, but though I think that in making these light rods they are moving in the right direction, it is no good pretending that they have not a lot of leeway to make up before they reach the standard of the best transatlantic work. If I know them they will at once set about it, and make a good bid to accomplish it.... I have never handled split-cane rods of such sweetness of action and temper as these Leonards, and I intend to treat myself to one at the first opportunity.

Marston added a bewildered note at the end: 'Val Conson's statement of his belief that the 6¼oz Leonard is "in point of power equal in every respect to the heavy-built Houghton" is so startling that I should immensely like to see the matter tested.'

Many other readers of *The Fishing Gazette* would have echoed this feeling. The swing of opinion had begun, but there was some way still to go. A real test in practice was more than a year in the future.

Meanwhile Skues was able to achieve his desire to own a Leonard rod before the new season of 1903 began. On a windy day in February, some time after the Kensington indoor trial, he and Coggeshall went to the River Wandle at Mitcham. Handicapped as he was by his permanently damaged wrists, Skues was not made for distance casting but, in his own words: 'I put out 24 yards of heavy Halford line with that rod against a stiffish breeze.' Another (unnamed) friend with them achieved 26 yards. This was decisive enough for Skues: these were the sort of rods he wanted. Pointing up the obvious lesson from the Wandle experience Skues wrote in *The Fishing Gazette*: 'All these gibes about "toys" and "ladies' rods", cotton reels and threadlines are really off the point ... I have yet to see the lady's rod that will ram such a line 24 yards into a brisk breeze and pick it off the water with the utmost ease as this Leonard did.'

Louis Bouglé continued to be an invaluable supporter of Skues during this period. Apart from his much greater knowledge of the technical side of rod-building he also had a much wider connection in Europe and America. He derived a good many of his ideas about American rods from the well-known writer and activist in angling matters C.G. Levison of Brooklyn, whose correspondence with Bouglé in the previous two years had run to 800 pages. Levison's opinion was that the rods of Payne could be as good as those of Leonard at half the price. Another of Bouglé's American friends also recommended the work of Payne, adding cryptically that their work was more 'conscientious'.

Bouglé had almost decided to get himself a Payne rod when he took fright at hearing rumours of sudden unexpected breakages. Some examples were also said to be top-heavy. If Skues had been pondering a similar purchase he was quick to abandon the idea upon hearing of these problems. It must have been a further cause for alarm when Bouglé warned him that by no means all of the Leonard range were free of faults. One of the heavier models made for a friend, the Comte de la Chapelle, was found to be '*très défectueuse ... excessivement* top-heavy, *très fatigante pour le poignet*'. There were shortcomings in other respects as well. Bouglé criticized the fittings, particularly the ferrules, which tended to come apart in use. He also complained that the rings of nickel alloy or 'German silver' of one of his rods had been deeply grooved by the line within a few weeks of use. After this experience he asked Mills to put English rings on any Leonard rods made for him. So choosing a Leonard rod meant entering a minefield, and good advice would be essential. Nevertheless Bouglé was emphatic that, at their best, these rods were the wonder of the age, distinguished by their power, lightness and durability. The comparison of the rods with those of Hardy was, he wrote, 'the difference between a thoroughbred and a donkey', adding prophetically that the rest of the world would gradually come round to that opinion.

Skues was fortunate to have this effervescent and knowledgeable Frenchman as an adviser. He had been considering the idea of a rod of 10ft 6in weighing 7¾oz, an interesting indication that he was only slowly moving towards the shorter rod. Bouglé deflected him from this – another top-heavy weapon. He was aware that Skues had been pondering over Leonard's rods in the catalogue of William Mills, and in April he proposed sending to him three rods from his own armoury for comparison. He had also now learned about the fabulous light rod of 10ft weighing 5¾oz which Skues had tested on the Wandle. Bouglé regarded this as '*très curieux*', for he had always been convinced that a rod of this length would have to weigh at least 6oz. However, this model possessed '*un nerf et une puissance merveilleux*', and it was the rod of choice for Reuben Leonard, who had used it to achieve a switch cast of 90ft at a tournament. Although he was, himself, an habitué of the tournament scene, Bouglé was well aware that fishing a river was a different game, and warned Skues against what he called 'tournament monstrosities'.

Skues had been somewhat discouraged by the high prices of the Leonard rods in Britain. Even though he was by now a junior partner in Powell's firm, he still needed to be careful with money. But in 1903 he came into a small legacy, and felt able to ask Coggeshall to arrange something for him with William Mills. Coggeshall had a waiting list of friends, including Irwin Cox, who were eager for the American product and placed an order for four rods. As a result Skues acquired the first of the six Leonard rods that he possessed in his lifetime. He had decided on the heavier 10ft rod: his favourite and most famous weapon, the 9ft, 5oz Leonard was not acquired until 1905 (see below).

The war of words over weight continued until the end of March 1903, by which time thirty-six more letters and four articles had appeared in

The Fishing Gazette. As in the previous year, some of these were of considerable length. Skues had intervened five times, with letters designed to keep up the momentum of his party. In April a dazed silence fell upon the battlefield and the flow of letters ceased for several months, although Skues could not resist coming back in September with a small piece of triumphalism. Making use of one of his 'Jottings' series of articles he described how his new 10ft Leonard had performed on his trip to Bavaria, catching 200 trout in a fortnight in weedy water. The tackle firms began to relax a little, though without any loss of resentment on their part. Truly, as Bouglé had written to Skues in January of that year, 'You will make mortal enemies of all the English tackle makers.' J.J. Hardy continued to insist against all the evidence that light rods were for women and children; in fact he never forgave Skues. However, the light rod supporters knew that they had made a lot of ground.

The Tenth International Fly and Bait Casting Tournament was held at the Crystal Palace on 22 and 23 July 1904. Both sides looked forward to this as a real chance to settle the light rod argument. Skues was appointed one of the organizers and threw himself into the planning with enthusiasm. As a preliminary flier he wrote to *The Fishing Gazette* in April to make sure that everyone knew of the interesting results of the recent Anglers' Tournament of New York. His letter began: 'The attitude of one who says "I told you so" is not deemed gracious.' Nevertheless he was going to tell all. The winning cast in the class for rods under 4oz achieved 88ft 9in, and in the 5oz class, 94ft. In another class the Englishman Edgar Shrubsole had thrown a line of 90ft with a 10ft rod, but it had been built especially for tournaments and weighed twice as much as the American rods.

The Committee of Management for the Crystal Palace event included several of the leading British anglers of the day. Apart from Skues it included C.H. Cook, the angling author Philip Geen, A.C. Kent (editor of the *Journal of the Flyfishers' Club*), the Revd G.E. Mackie and R.B. Marston. Kent and Marston both elected to compete. Skues allowed himself to be persuaded into entering the light rod distance event, in which of course he had no chance at all. More promisingly, he put his name down for the dry-fly accuracy event, where his damaged wrist would be less of a handicap. Cook, Geen and Mackie decided (perhaps wisely) to stay out of it. Skues must have been uneasy as the time of the competition approached, for it appeared as if no one from America would be competing. Coggeshall worked hard to bring over some of his countrymen, and rather late in the day Marston was able to report that Edward Ringwood Hewitt had entered, and that Eddie Mills, grandson of William Mills, would also be there, accompanied by his father Thomas Bate Mills. Even so, as was pointed out afterwards, the Americans were not sufficiently represented, although several English anglers used Leonard rods.

Marston played the chief part in organizing the tournament, using *The Fishing Gazette* to carry notices of the preparations. Prizes were donated from many quarters. By modern standards they seem unexciting: tea sets, fly-boxes, fly-lines and a pair of Cordings' celebrated boots. T.B. Mills brought an unofficial prize in the form of a 9ft, 3¼oz Catskill rod, the gift of his firm.

The Fly and Bait Casting Tournament, upon which so much was reckoned to depend, began at 12 noon on Friday 22 June 1904. A week later *The Fishing Gazette* devoted three and a half pages to a detailed record of the results in each event. Apart from trout-fly casting there were competitions for salmon fly, light and heavy bait, float and sea rod casting. Of the seventeen events only four were likely to provide data for the controversy over light trout rods.

At 2.15 that afternoon Skues watched, no doubt with anxiety, Competition C, the trout-fly casting for professionals. No rod was allowed to be more than 11ft 6in long, or weigh more than 1¼oz per foot. J.J. Hardy, veteran of many competitions, won comfortably with three casts of an aggregate of 101yds, the best two casts being each of 34yds. Hardy's nephew L. Hardy came second with an aggregate of 88yds and 1ft, best cast 30yds, and Eddie Mills, upon whom the hopes of Skues and his friends rested, came third, with 85½yds, best cast 29yds. The rod used by J.J. Hardy was unfortunately not specified. L. Hardy used a Hardy rod of 11ft 6in with a steel centre, weighing 12oz, as did two of the other contestants. It is quite likely that his uncle did the same. The rod used by Mills was one of the more heavy-duty Leonard rods built specially for tournament work, at 10ft 6in and weighing 8oz. Apart from this rod no other rod in Competition C was less than 11ft in length.

The next relevant trial for the light rod was at 12.30 on the following day: Competition M – trout-fly casting for amateurs, with the same rules for rods as with Competition C. There were eighteen contestants. Most of the rods were made by Hardy, and were of the type described by Skues as 'wrist-breakers', of weights varying between 11½oz and 13oz, but there were two of Fosters' curious steel-ribbed weapons. Marston came tenth (aggregate 73yds and 2ft) with a 13oz Braddell greenheart. Skues came fourteenth with his Leonard of 10ft and 6½oz, but he cannot have expected to do well in such an event. His aggregate was 67yds and 2ft and his longest individual cast was 23yds and 2ft. His brother Charles came twelfth, and the well-known Dorset angler Hardy Corfe came fifteenth. These and several other also-rans were surpassed by the phenomenon of the two-day event, Miss R. A. Newham, using the lightest rod of the event, ironically one of the new Hardy light rods, of 9ft 3in and weighing 5¾oz. She came ninth with an aggregate of 74yds and 2ft, her two longest casts each being 25yds. The winner was Fred Shaw, later a well-known professional casting coach. Using a Hardy rod of 10ft 9in and weighing 11oz, he achieved an aggregate of 90yds and 1ft. Second came Hewitt of New York (84yds and 1ft).

Competition N for ambidextrous casting followed. This was for all-comers, professional and amateur, but Skues preferred to be a spectator. Marston entered but only succeeded in smashing his greenheart rod.

Competition O, Light Rod Fly Casting, was governed by the same rules as C and N, save that it was restricted to rods of 5¾oz or less, and was open to all-comers. Skues did not take part but he must have watched with tremulous interest, for this event held out the best hopes. The first two events had given the victory to rods of brute strength over finesse. Here was a chance for a fair contest in which every contestant was armed with a light rod. But once again the unbeatable J.J. Hardy came first with an aggregate of 86yds, using a rod of 9ft 6in and 5¾oz. His two best casts were each 29yds. Fred Shaw ran him close with an aggregate of 85yds and 6in. Eddie Mills achieved an aggregate of 84½yds with a 10ft Leonard weighing 5¾oz. Hardy, who had donated one of his firm's best rods, value four guineas, for first prize, now received it back. Fred Shaw carried off the prize of the Leonard Catskill rod, an extra award for the best amateur participating.

Once again Miss Newham, described rather patronizingly in *The Fishing Gazette* as 'little more than a child', astonished the spectators by coming eighth out of seventeen contestants, incidentally beating her own father, a professional. Some fairly mawkish poetry, likening her to the Roman goddess of hunting, appeared soon afterwards in *The Fishing Gazette*, the work of a nameless admirer.

In Competition P – Dry Fly Casting for accuracy – for amateurs, Skues must have felt that at last he had a chance for a good performance. Such a contest also had much more relevance to fishing on a river. Rods were allowed to be up to 11½ft, not more than 1¼oz to the foot, and had to be used single-handed. Casts were to be of single gut, not less than 2yds or more than 3yds long, with a white-winged dry fly 'of moderate size, to be approved by the judges'. The target buoys were placed at 30, 40, 50 and 60ft. Once again seventeen contestants lined up for their allotted five minutes of casting. There must have been some astonishment when Skues was observed to be casting underhand with his Leonard. At one point he appeared to be winning, but a gust of wind blew his final effort sideways, and he was placed second, no doubt to his disgust. His reaction to his prize of Nottingham lace curtains has not been recorded. Marston came third. Once again Miss Newham was more than halfway up the list, beating ten men, including Charles Skues.

So ended this historic tournament: two days of interest and delight for the spectators, although the judges, toiling for hours under a burning sun, may have felt otherwise. But it left a feeling of puzzlement and inconclusiveness. J.J. Hardy and his admirers at first rejoiced in what seemed an obvious triumph. English rods had won the distance events with both trout and salmon rods. The problem for Skues was how to explain and dissect the results and to draw out some lessons to counter the jubilation of the other side. Now he intervened with a long, closely reasoned article in *The Fishing Gazette* of 6 August, emphasizing the great difference in weight between the English and American rods and the surprisingly small difference in achievement. He picked out the performance of Fred Shaw who, in one event, managed a cast of 30yds and 2ft with a Hardy rod of 10ft 9in, weighing 11oz, and in another a cast of 29yds with a rod by the same maker of 9ft 7in, weighing only 5¾oz. The difference in weight between the two rods was striking, but in performance was small. Skues had identified the important point that tournament casting and fishing on a river are very different things. One could fish all day with a Leonard rod without the least fatigue. The English manufacturer, he wrote, had not yet achieved the success of building a first-rate light rod which was at once a fishing rod and the equal of the Americans' light rods in casting power, foot for foot and ounce for ounce.

Having argued his way through two columns of careful analysis of cases taken from the tournament Skues summed up: 'I hope I have made it clear that on an examination of the facts the victory of the English made article is more apparent than real, and that the English manufacturer will not for a moment relax his efforts to regain the supremacy that once was his.'

If J.J. Hardy was infuriated by this letter, the wave of support for the opposition that followed must have left him speechless. One contributor pointed out that the performance of the light rods in the hands of Eddie Mills, Miss Newham and even J.J. Hardy himself amply demonstrated that 'a light rod can do all the work necessary'. Fred Shaw wrote in praise of the miniature Catskill rod which had been his unexpected prize, with which he had already killed twenty-three trout. Eddie Mills wrote to refer to the record cast of Walter Mansfield in 1900, which had been surpassed by an even more phenomenal throw of 140ft by F.C. Golcher in a private club event, using a Leonard of 10ft 6in and 8¾oz. Marston's editorial of support on 13 August showed the world that he acknowledged Skues as the leader of the light rod movement:

> I believe 'Val Conson's' sole object is to spur English rod makers to make rods like those made by Mr Leonard. He says, and I quite agree with him, that there is something about the make of a Leonard rod that our makers do not give us. I hope Mr Hardy will note that I do not say 'cannot' give us, because, having only recently been over his splendidly-equipped establishment at Alnwick, I believe there is nothing his firm cannot do.

Hardy's state of mind by now can only be imagined. His simplistic attitude might be expressed thus: 'We have won, therefore there can be no further argument and splitting of hairs.' His angry riposte of 13 August in *The Fishing Gazette* was his most violent of all in the controversy. It filled three columns, each divided in half, creating a small problem for the journal's compositors. In the left-hand half-columns were those parts of Skues' article of the previous week to which Hardy particularly objected, and on the right were Hardy's irritable rejoinders. He wrote that he had read the remarks of 'Val Conson' 'with interest and not a little amazement … and while everyone must endorse the kind feeling which prompts him to find an excuse for the defeat of our American friends, I think it is only fair to ask him to draw correct instead of incorrect conclusions from the records'.

To Skues' suggestion that 'the victory of the English made article is more apparent than real', he responded with a demand for an explanation – where was the evidence? 'It is an unwarrantable attack on English manufacturers generally, and is quite untrue, and I feel sure that British anglers will resent this attack on their manufacturers in no small degree.'

No reaction in detail to this thunderous piece came from Skues. Perhaps he thought that he had said enough for the time being, and that the lessons of the tournament and the many thousands of printed words of the past three years should be pondered. However, a week later he could not resist adding a subtle footnote by recording a visit he had arranged for Eddie Mills at Abbots Barton. Skues spent the greater part of the day looking after his guest and providing him with flies. Mills brought two Leonard rods with him. One was a very light rod weighing 2⅛oz described by Skues as 'a piece of magic', which for a trial was put into the hands of the keeper, the popular and capable Humphrey Priddis. With this slender rod, of the type ridiculed by Hardy as a plaything for girls and children, Priddis cast 23yds and, in weedy water, captured a trout weighing (by a happy coincidence) 2lb 2oz, i.e. 2⅛lb. An even more significant event of that day was Skues' introduction to the second of the rods brought by Mills, a 9ft, 5oz rod 'of fascinating action'. For Skues this was love at first sight, and he resolved to get an example of this wonder rod at the first opportunity.

It was not until 1905 that an item in his professional work put him in a financial position to achieve his heart's desire. Skues had done a complex piece of work for a client called Bertram Falle, later created Lord Portsea of Portsmouth. The Falles were a Jersey family with a long pedigree. In his memoir Skues did not, of course, say what this work was: perhaps he had to sort out the tangled problems of a family settlement. Whatever it was, it was clearly a service of considerable value, for when Skues presented his firm's account the grateful client wished to add an additional sum of £200 as a personal present. Skues felt that this offer would not fit with his notion of the ethical standards of his profession. The client, himself a barrister of the Middle Temple, was sympathetic to his embarrassment but eager to show his gratitude somehow and proposed giving something of money's worth instead. Skues saw the opportunity to acquire his dream rod, and the client insisted on adding a reel and line to the gift. Even allowing for the high price of the Leonard rods imported into England the value of this complimentary present was only a fraction of the money originally offered.

This rod served Skues for the next forty years for most of his occasions. When the wind was troublesome, a fairly frequent event on the exposed banks of Abbots Barton, he resorted to his stronger 10ft Leonard. He damaged one of the two tops in the early 1920s and arranged a repair. Not long afterwards it was smashed, this time beyond remedy. After he gave up fishing in 1945 he passed on the rod, with its remaining top section, to his brother Charles. (In 1952 Paul Barbotin, who had befriended Skues in the last two years of his life, wrote after his death to William Mills & Son to enquire about their pre-1914 rods. Their cordial reply can be found at Appendix 5.)

Skues has recorded that eventually he possessed six Leonard rods, thus creating a curiosity and some research among angling writers. He claimed that he acquired all of them by the same indirect means from grateful clients, although one was in fact a gift from Coggeshall's widow. The task of settling a definitive list still remains to be done.

The battle died down in the last months of 1905, and the tackle trade, licking their wounds, gave more attention to making lighter rods. In September Skues appeared before the readers of *The Fishing Gazette* to report on the recent tournament at Chicago. He was probably still feeling sore at the failure of the Leonard rods at the Crystal Palace to romp home easily in advance of the Hardy rods, and wished to remind readers that the result had not been truly representative of their capabilities. In the distance event at Chicago Eddie Mills had made a cast of 120ft (40yds), using a Leonard tournament rod of 10ft 7in. Of the nine contestants (who all used Leonard rods), seven equalled the best performances at the Crystal Palace the previous year and five exceeded them. Hardy responded, as he felt he must, but his reply contained little that was new, except the ludicrous suggestion that perhaps these phenomenally long casts could be explained by some different quality in the atmosphere of America! Skues was kind enough to ignore this obvious target, merely intervening the following week to tell Hardy that if he wished to equal the recent achievements at Chicago and other American tournaments his firm would have to produce a fly rod of 10½ft and 8½oz capable of casting 120ft, and a 4oz rod capable of casting 96ft, adding soothingly: 'No-one would be better pleased than I if this can be done.'

The indoor rod trials at Olympia in February 1906 can be seen as the last major milestone in the affair. J.J. Hardy came armed with a number of light rods of a type he would not have troubled to make ten years earlier. One was a rod of 9ft weighing a fraction under 3½oz. Marston thought that these trials proved that Hardy's had caught up with the Americans, a judgement with which Skues was not able to agree. For him there was always an intangible quality about the Leonard that could not be equalled. The final convert was Harry Cholmondeley-Pennell, a formidable angling authority of an earlier era. He announced his change of heart after purchasing a 9ft Leonard of 4oz: 'I was surprised by its power in hooking and playing.' Pennell had been writing on angling since the 1860s, and could remember prehistoric two-handed trout rods of enormous weight, but he was open-minded enough to acknowledge that the light rod was a great step forward.

Many other British anglers were also converted. At the Houghton Club, Arthur Gilbey encouraged members to introduce themselves to the Leonard experience. Some years later John Waller Hills was one of those who joined in, although it took him a little time to get used to the unfamiliar feel of the rod. At Abbots Barton, Skues observed the rods on the rack in the fishing hut: 'I saw five or six Leonards to one Hardy.' For years after the great dispute the possession of one of these rods was a mark of an advanced angler and connoisseur.

The argument declined in the next three years and eventually subsided. Hardy began to be more conciliatory, admitting that perhaps the old 11ft Test rod had been too heavy. He even conceded that the controversy had done some good, though without ever forgiving its very effective leader.

The light rod controversy showed Skues at his best. He made a few mistakes but his contribution was important. He moved the debate on every time it showed signs of flagging, convinced waverers by his accurate use of language and goaded the other side. Whenever a summing-up of 'progress so far' was needed he intervened with a carefully worded statement. The once shy and retiring young man had, in his middle years, become a mature and practised controversialist, at least in print. A verbal confrontation was never going to be his scene of choice.

7

Sunk Flies – the Era of Rebellion

I T IS TEMPTING to see the angling life of Skues in the first years of the twentieth century as an inevitable and purposive path towards the nymph. The letter to *The Field* of 1899 (see Appendix 3) turned out in the event to be prophetic, but it did not at once produce a radical change in his methods. For some time he contented himself with the dry fly and its endless possibilities, and only turned to the sunk fly when conditions demanded it. Furthermore, for some years these sunk flies were not the nymphs with which his name is now associated, or even anything much like them, but wet versions of dry patterns made from absorbent materials and sharing the design of the flies of the Tweed.

His progress with this new idea was both slow and rather puzzlingly oblique. Fishing for nymphing trout with sunk winged flies seems odd to us now. Fortunately the fish did not seem to mind – although, as I record below, Skues did at times wonder why they took these flies. The discouraging dictum, repeated more than once in Halford's writings, that the wet fly on the chalk stream *might* work, but only as a sort of occasional fluke, probably still haunted him. Did he wonder if his new wet-fly successes were perhaps all flukes?

Signs of accelerating development and growing independence of mind appear in Skues' fishing in 1904, and by 1907 his articles in *The Field* and *The Fishing Gazette* begin to look more like a joined-up campaign to restore the sunk fly to the chalk stream, rather than a series of occasional successes. But these successes were not being achieved with nymph patterns as later defined, but with the Greenwell, the Rough Olive and the Iron Blue, all tied with upright wings. Only the Tup, which became a sort of hinge fly leading to more obviously nymphal forms, was tied without wings.

It was about this time that he yielded to the encouragements of Louis Bouglé, and of H.T. Sheringham, the angling editor of *The Field*, who had observed in Skues' work signs of increasing focus, out of which could be derived a new and fruitful programme. The influence of these two friends had a good deal to do with the writing of *Minor Tactics of the Chalk Stream*. True nymphs began to creep into the story soon afterwards.

Skues' work on the dry fly between 1890 and 1910 has largely been forgotten, probably because of the much greater attention paid in modern times to his wet-fly experiments. In fact he was, in this period, becoming one of the great dry-fly men of all time, and his thinking about the manufacture of dry flies was becoming more and more profound. Other leading anglers were glad to have the chance of sharing ideas with him. Skues' habit was to keep a watchful eye on the pages of *The Field* and *The Fishing Gazette* for signs of original thinking and for the chance to get in touch with other workers in the field. Three of his correspondents stand out in the period before the Great War – Robert Austin of Tiverton, Theodore Gordon and Louis Bouglé, whose part in moving Skues on to the Leonard rod has already been examined.

Skues opened correspondence with Austin after reading several of his articles in *The Fishing Gazette*. At an early stage in their association, which was to last for over twenty years, Skues realized that Austin was a clever deviser of new fly patterns, and there was nothing more calculated to arouse his interest. Robert Stanway Austin had been a gunner in the Royal Artillery and had served in the Crimean War before Skues was born. He had reached the rank of sergeant and had retired with a small pension. Subsequently he had lived in several places, including Donegal, but eventually had retired to Devonshire, where he set up a tobacconist's shop at 10 Gold Street in Tiverton on the River Exe. The making and marketing of flies would have provided a welcome addition to his trade, and he was able to impart his skill to one of his three daughters.

The Skues–Austin correspondence began in 1888 or 1889 – Skues later admitted that he could not remember which – but the earliest letter in the papers now deposited in the library of the University of Princeton is dated April 1891. There is a small mystery here, one of many in the Skues story. In 1913 Skues wrote that moth had got into the collection, and that he only possessed letters from 1907 onwards. As there now exist at Princeton some pre-1907 letters from Austin it may be that a small cache of lost letters had come to light elsewhere in his house after 1913.

The friendship between the two men was almost entirely by letter. Skues only met Austin twice while on a trip to the West Country in 1897. Austin's letters, although with formal beginnings and endings after the fashion of the age, have the air of a friendly respect between equals. It is one of the attractive aspects of Skues' character that his admiration for talent would override the rigid class boundaries of that era. It was much the same with J.W. Hills and William Lunn, or Sir Grimwood Mears and Frank Sawyer. Austin's achievement was the more remarkable in that it developed against a background of considerable difficulty. Not much income, it may be guessed, could be generated from a small shop, even adding the money from fly-tying. Austin decided after a while that he could not even afford to buy the weekly numbers of *The Field* – required reading for a keen fly-fisherman – when he noticed that he could find them at the Tiverton Conservative Club. His small personal library of fishing books, which included such authors as Best and Aldam, must have been built up slowly and with considerable effort. But his lively, well-written letters show that some education had come his way. Perhaps this was partly through his own efforts: in that harsh age many of the Victorian working class were imbued with the principles of Samuel Smiles, whose book *Self Help* was to be found in many homes.

Unusually for an angler in Devonshire, his interest was chiefly in the dry fly. Some of his views were curious and subtle. In an early letter he admitted that his flies had a 'nondescript' look. He liked a fly that had been used a little so that the colour had begun to fade, and recommended to Skues red hackles that had become brassier when exposed to fierce sunlight. In another letter he enclosed hackles with a suspicion of rust in the colour. In 1907 he suggested to Skues the use of bear's hair which, when mixed with red mohair, made an excellent Red Spinner. Tied on a no. 2 hook, he reported that this fly worked well on the Exe, adding: 'I took the pattern from Best's book.' This may have been helpful to Skues, who in 1908 began to use bear's hair for one of his early nymph imitations. Austin's ideas coincided with those of Skues in several ways: in August 1908 he recommended for nymphing fish a small Blue Upright or a small Half Stone. A month later he wrote: 'Your pattern of the nymph is more sparsely dressed than mine [Skues' marginal note says 'shorter hackle'] and I have copied it for future reference.' He also mentioned the use of split shot on the line above a wet fly or – an improvement – lead foil on the hook of a sunk grayling fly.

Austin's letters frequently contain samples of plumage, dubbing and finished patterns, and many original ideas and dodges, including a good method of winding on two cock's hackles to look as if they were one. Some of his ideas were local to Devonshire, and may have descended from Hewett Wheatley, whose interesting book *The Rod and Line* appeared in 1849.

Austin's flies were in demand by anglers in Devon and were effective for many fishing situations in waters much further afield. Sadly, most of them are forgotten nowadays. Skues was particularly admiring of his little pale 'Gnat', 'an admirable representation of the Coenis [sic], the only good representation I have seen'.

The one pattern out of a large number invented by Austin which has survived into our time is the well-known Tup's Indispensable. This was for Skues the most useful fruit of their association, and he had an important role in advertising it to the world. In 1900 Austin had become a nine-day wonder locally by capturing a group of large trout which inhabited a piece of river at the confluence of the tributary Loman with the Exe on the outskirts of Tiverton. These difficult fish were well known to the anglers in the town and could be seen feeding every evening, eager for natural flies and contemptuous of all artificial offerings. In the course of several evenings Austin succeeded in confounding the local talent by capturing them on the new wonder fly. In his account of this achievement, written many years later in the *Journal of the Flyfishers' Club* (summer 1934), Skues wrote that one fish exceeded 5lb, and three others weighed 3lb ½oz, 2lb 8oz and 2lb. There is a discrepancy here however. In a letter written about the time they were caught, Austin wrote that the total weight of the four fish caught on the second evening was 5lb (see Appendix 4). 'The first evening I used this fly, I got six fish, weighing 4 ¾lb in the pool … biggest fish 1lb 7oz. The next night I had four weighing 5 lb, biggest fish 3lb ½oz.' Well, even if there was no five-pounder, this was an unusual piece of work, and a 3lb trout is big in Devonshire.

It was a mark of friendship and trust for Austin to reveal the recipe for the Tup to Skues, and to send him a sample of the magic dubbing material (see Appendix 4). The original tying was:

Hook   sneck bend
Silk   yellow, showing two or three unwaxed turns at the tip
Hackle pale spangled blue cock
Whisks as hackle
Body   a mixed dubbing, i.e. the 'tup' mixture.

The secret of the dubbing was also revealed to C.A. Hassam, at that time regarded as the most accomplished fly-tier of the Flyfishers' Club. One ingredient, the wool from the scrotum of the ram, or 'tup' in country speech, became known fairly soon, and the fly was named by Skues accordingly. As a result of the publicity he gave to the fly this name caught on and was accepted by Austin. Some fly-tiers have supposed that the natural oil of the wool was important as a floatant, but in fact Austin emphasized that it needed to be thoroughly washed to remove all this, otherwise it was too difficult to deal with in the tying. However it was almost impossible to wash out all the grease, which is very tenacious. To this was added cream-coloured seal's fur and, to help the process of spinning two rather awkward materials on to the silk, some fur from the poll of the hare. Also included was a small amount of red mohair to produce a pinkish shade, and some yellow fur combed from the ears of a lemon-coloured spaniel. Fur or hair from dogs had been used by other fly-dressers in the past; in the seventeenth century Charles Cotton had mentioned the idea of combing the neck of a black greyhound: 'The down which sticks in the teeth will be the finest blue you ever saw.' Also, for that matter, using scrotal wool from a ram is mentioned by Alexander Mackintosh in *The Driffield Angler* (1806). The pink mohair, sometimes altered to seal's fur in later versions, was thought by Skues to give an impression to the trout of a nymph bleeding from the thorax. This was a rather odd notion: haemoglobin is present in some insects, but not in ephemeropteran flies.

Skues' first trial of the wonder fly was on the Wandle near his home in Croydon in the late summer of 1900. Without shifting his position he cast over and hooked no fewer than eighteen trout, although an overhanging tree prevented him from striking effectively, and only a few were landed. One April day the following year, fishing the unforgiving waters of the Itchen at Abbots Barton, he caught fourteen trout. Humphrey Priddis, the efficient and popular keeper, stood by transfixed by this performance, and told the tale in his next report to *The Field*. In the first issue of July Skues added his own version of his achievement, and the Tup's Indispensable was launched on its stellar career, eventually catching trout all over Britain, and in America, South Africa and New Zealand. The notion of secret ingredients, with its flavour of alchemy or witchcraft, seems to have tickled the fancy of the angling public. No doubt admirers of Beau Brummell's boot polish or Escoffier's famous sauces yearned to know their secret ingredients (in Brummel's case reputedly the finest champagne). A wave of orders descended on Austin from Britain and abroad, and he later confessed to Skues to being wearied at being called upon to tie hundreds of dozens of these flies.

Winchester College: Chamber Court (late fourteenth century). The dwelling place of the young Skues for five years

Winchester College: Chamber Court (late fourteenth century)

Skues at fourteen, in his Winchester College scholar's gown

Skues the newly qualified solicitor. This photograph shows that his notion that he was ugly was not justified

Entry in Skues' commonplace book: handwriting of the 1880s

Alexandra Kitchin as a child in the early 1870s, some years before she became the object of Skues' 'hopeless love'

The Strand: Law Courts to the left, entrance of Essex Street just off picture at the right hand side *c.* 1910

A leaf from Marryat's fly book (the Portmanteau), in which Skues thought there was 'an enormous predominance of patterns better calculated to fish wet than dry'

The prescription in Skues' handwriting for the Tup's Indispensable

Flies (*c.* 1900) tied on double hooks, which assisted the sinking of Skues' prototype sunk flies

Louis Bouglé bait casting (c. 1906). Bouglé won or was placed in a number of fly or bait casting competitions in France before 1914

Half-title of Skues' first book: a presentation copy to F.M. Halford. This was the final straw that brought about the quarrel in the Flyfishers' Club

Letter of Louis Bouglé. Fly at top possibly Coch-y-Bonddu; writing obscured by fly below says 'Olive Dun'

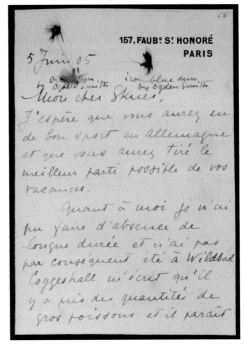

MR. G. E. M. SKUES CASTING IN COMPETITION P. DRY-FLY CASTING FOR ACCURACY.

Skues competing at the Crystal Palace, July 1904. He narrowly missed winning the accuracy competition

WALTER D. COGGESHALL ESQ.
President 1918.

Walter Durfee Coggeshall (Coggie), probably the man behind the pseudonym of 'Viator' in the light rod controversy

H.L. Leonard, prodigy among rod makers. Thanks to the intervention of Skues and Coggeshall, Leonard rods made a considerable impact in Britain

Theodore Gordon and companion. The girl he described as 'the best chum I ever had in fishing' may have been the one in this picture

Skues in fishing clothes, with Leonard rod, white cotton bag and net with six-foot handle (1927)

Picture taken on the same day by Dr Barton. This is the most frequently published picture of Skues

Skues transfigured: image created and touched up by Howard Coster, 1927. An attempt to provide what Skues considered would be a more acceptable version of his appearance

Skues' house in Croydon from 1894 until 1940, when he withdrew to Wilton at the time of the threat of German invasion

In the event, the wonder fly may have been a slight disappointment to some purchasers, especially the sort of angler – present in every generation – who imagines that he will one day discover the ultimate fish-catching device for all occasions, irrespective of the fly on the water. The Tup, dry or awash, will turn out to be ineffective in many situations, but comes into its own during a hatch of pale watery duns. Austin thought that its main usefulness was from April to June. It is odd that he at first called it a type of Red Spinner. Skues added to it a number of variations and discovered a few seasons later that it could be adapted into a killing nymph. This was the most important advantage of the Tup. Some of his most effective sunk patterns were derived from this fertile source.

Austin died in September 1911, and Skues contributed to *The Field* an affectionate tribute to a man for whom he had a deep respect:

It is with sincere sorrow that I have had the news of the death of Mr R.S. Austin, of Tiverton. I am but one of many anglers all over the country to whom he was a friend, and his place will not be filled again in this generation. For upwards of twenty years I kept up a correspondence with him on matters connected with fly-dressing and fly-tying, and he always dealt with the subjects under discussion in the open spirit of an amateur and a sportsman, putting his wide and varied knowledge at the service of a brother angler.

A little later Skues announced to readers of *The Fishing Gazette* that he would soon be able to reveal the true ingredients of the fly. But this was not to be, and the angling public had to wait for another two decades. Skues learned that Austin's daughter intended carrying on her late father's business and had asked that the professional secret be kept. In 1913, when seeking permission from Austin's son and executor to publish a series of four articles in *The Fishing Gazette* on Austin's work, Skues received a further reminder from Austin's son and executor: 'I appreciate your remark that the secret of the Tup's Indispensable will not be disclosed, as that has become an important business asset to my sister.' Years later, in 1934 the daughter wrote to Skues to say that she was retiring from the business of fly-tying, and gave leave to make public the mystery of the dubbing. In the meantime a number of attempts had been made to imitate the fly. Most of these were fairly wild: Eugene Connett in *Random Casts* wrote that 'great crimes have been committed in the name of Tup's Indispensable'. And in more modern times commercial versions of the fly often seem to have only a sketchy connection with the original. Too much silk is shown at the tail, the dubbing is often of a violent pink shade and the hackle is seldom correct, often of a clear electric blue. As mentioned above, Austin was fond of hackles with a freckle in them that others might have rejected.

As with Austin, the letters between Skues and Theodore Gordon are mainly about flies. Having taken up the dry fly with enthusiasm, Gordon seems at first to have been slightly puzzled by Skues' enthusiasm for the wet fly, and may have thought it a retrograde step. However, Gordon and most other Americans were much more likely than British anglers to be open-minded about the wet fly; indeed they were, in the early years of the twentieth century, only just coming to terms with the dry fly. Thaddeus Norris and no doubt others whose names are lost had fished upstream and tried to keep their flies dry. Gordon fished the wet fly early in the season and at other times whenever conditions called for it, but was eager to learn more about the construction of the new dry fly, and had some years earlier turned to a man who might help him. In November 1891 he received from Halford a kind and courteous response and a packet of samples, laid out on two sheets, of forty-eight different dry flies. Gordon was so delighted with this collection that he kept it unblemished as a keepsake as well as a guide. Soon he was developing his own patterns and ideas in this area, and in due course became the first true interpreter of the art to his countrymen. However, a general correspondence, involving an equal exchange of ideas and experience, does not seem to have ensued between them. Halford did not have much desire or curiosity to learn about North American angling practice, feeling no doubt that it had no real relevance for him. By contrast Skues was fascinated by the details of Gordon's fishing, even though it was in a faraway land that he would never see, and he was eager to know all that Gordon could tell him.

Skues had been aware of Gordon as a correspondent of *The Fishing Gazette* for several years before writing to him in December 1905. They soon discovered that they had many characteristics in common. Both were fascinated by the minute details of fly-tying. Gordon once wrote: 'Surely the subject of fly making can never be exhausted.' Both men perhaps, at times, took it beyond the bounds of practical angling needs. By this date it was for Skues an art form. It was no accident that, when he began to appear in the pages of *Who's Who* some years later, his pursuits were listed as fly-fishing and fly-tying, as if each was capable at times of an independent existence. There was, of course, a shared area, or his fishing would have become meaningless, but the making of more and more subtle simulacra of life at times became almost an activity pursued for its own sake. Gordon had equally demanding standards. He once wrote that one needed a dozen different shades of olive hackles.

Both men had also begun to think about what it is that trout really perceive. It probably made an impression on Skues when, in September 1903 (that is to say, some time before he was in touch with Gordon), he read in one of Gordon's stimulating articles under the title 'American Notes': 'The more I study the imitation of the natural fly and the various books on the subject ... the surer I am that trout have a wonderful eye for colour but a very indifferent notion of form.' Skues had been puzzling over this problem since the 1890s, and returned to it in *The Way of a Trout with a Fly* in 1921. Gordon's view on the subject altered with time. After his untimely death George La Branche, another great name in the history of American angling, wrote:

> His imitations of the natural insect were about as perfect as human hands could make them, and he was a strong believer in the efficacy of colour.
>
> I think, however, in the last few years he was more inclined to a representation of the fly as it appeared on the water, paying more attention to the size and form of the fly than to exact shades or tints, but he could never quite abandon his ideas of some colour imitation.

Another matter over which their views coincided was the artificial stocking of rivers. Skues, it is true, would let himself go when on holiday abroad, and was quite happy pulling out large numbers of farmed trout in Germany – 250 fish in a fortnight on one trip in Bavaria. But this seems to have been a relaxing sort of fun rather than genuine sport. Equally, when later he fished on occasion on stocked fisheries on the Test, such as Dr Barton's piece at Leckford, he almost never made an article out of such expeditions. They simply did not provide interesting material. It was the beginning of a stocking programme at Abbots Barton in the 1930s, something against which he held forth with bitter but ineffectual eloquence, which became one of the factors that decided him to leave the syndicate and go elsewhere (see Chapter 12).

By the time Gordon died in 1915 Skues had amassed a deskful of his letters. At first they ranged over angling experiences, fly-tying ideas and all the detail beloved of the dedicated fly-tier. After a while more personal details creep in, and Skues must have built up in his mind a picture of this romantic recluse, lonely and unwell, living a quiet life in the countryside by the Neversink River, and generously sending flies, materials and advice to friends and strangers alike. Fresh air was about the only prescription contemporary doctors could think of for tuberculosis sufferers, and it was surprising that Gordon survived for as long as he did, since winters were severe in Sullivan County. In 1906 he wrote to Skues that 'the wood burning stove is my only companion', and lamented that fly-tying became impossible in really cold weather: the wax would not melt, it was too cold to sit in a good light by the window and if he retreated to the stove in the middle of the room it was too dark to see properly. Several times he refers to the awesome feeling of isolation of a North American winter. But much of the time, even in spring and summer, he was fighting off the same feelings. In May 1908 he wrote to Skues: 'I am very lonely tonight, and am writing to you for the feeling of companionship.' In 1909 he wrote apologetically: 'Loneliness may explain the length of this letter.' But although he lived in isolation passing anglers knew that a great angler was to be found thereabouts and would seek him out. Many notables of the next generation, such as Roy Steenrod, and Reuben Cross, owed much to his influence. And occasionally there was female companionship. In 1906 he wrote, somewhat wistfully, in *Forest and Stream*: 'The best chum I ever had in fishing was a girl, and she tramped just as hard and fished just as patiently as any man I ever knew' – and he recorded that she was not frightened of wading without waterproofs.

Gordon's contributions to *The Fishing Gazette* were valued by a wide circle of the readership. He, in turn, had a high regard for the paper: in 1902 he wrote that it was 'a great educator', and thought that American anglers owed much of their knowledge of new fly-dressing methods to it. John MacDonald, who in 1947 edited the letters and papers of Gordon, wrote that his articles in *The Fishing Gazette* were surprisingly sophisticated writings, more so than his pieces for *Forest and Stream*, 'perhaps because Gordon was counting on the most exacting audience of fishing critics ever gathered around one paper'.

At the beginning of their correspondence Gordon did not realize that 'Val Conson' and Skues were the same person. In April 1906 he wrote that he hoped to see more articles by 'Val Conson' – 'I have taken a great fancy to that gentleman'. Skues seems to have relished the comic side of this situation, and allowed it to go on until May. The astonished Gordon wrote to Skues: 'You and Mr Halford have been my piscatorial gods for many years', and signs himself 'Faithfully your pupil'.

Although Gordon was able to provide certain plumages for Skues, he soon came to realize that far better hackles were to be had from Britain, and he envied Skues for his fruitful expeditions to Leadenhall Market. In 1912 he wrote: 'Your account of the abundance of good reds and gingers makes me a little envious.' His own memories went back years to the market in Savannah, where the hunt for materials was as much a pleasure as the acquisition.

Although their exchanges were for some time mainly about dry-fly matters, Gordon became aware that Skues was moving towards something equally exciting – the re-establishment of the sunk fly on so-called 'dry-fly streams'. A voracious reader, Gordon had long ago picked up what he could from the British school, including fishing upstream in the manner of Stewart. And his thinking was not far behind that of Skues. On two spring afternoons in 1906 he caught thirteen trout up to 2½lb by fishing with 'a thing intended to resemble a large larva or nymph'. As his enthusiasm increased for the new practice there was a noticeable waning of his earlier uncritical admiration of Halford. He was puzzled by his hostility towards the wet fly, and began to dislike the preaching of the master. To what extent Skues contributed to this feeling of disenchantment we cannot know, for most of his letters were lost in a fire at a local storage at Liberty, and the rest were destroyed as a public health precaution after Gordon's death. Gordon acknowledged the pioneering work of Halford in former years, but even here a note of criticism began to show itself. In a letter of 1915 to Roy Steenrod he referred to the earlier days when he was 'saturated' with Halford detail and had arranged for a rod to be made according to English ideas 'that nearly killed me', and had filled his fly-box with imported patterns that were of little service in American waters.

His experience closely paralleled that of Skues: once he had emerged from the hypnotic state induced by Halford's first two books he regained confidence in his own ideas about dry flies for American waters. The 'New Patterns', as Halford called them, first appeared in *The Field* in 1903, and eventually in book form in *Modern Development of the Dry Fly* (1910). They did not impress Gordon. A lover of natural colours in hackles, he wrote in April 1912 that he did not care for Halford's 'wholesale adoption of the dye-pot', or for his excessive use of quill and horsehair instead of dubbing. When Halford died in March 1914 Gordon recorded his regret in a letter to Skues, but added: 'The tone of his last book was unfortunate.' However, he was magnanimous enough never to forget the good and useful side of Halford's work to codify the tactics of the dry fly.

It is sad that the two men never met. Skues never crossed the Atlantic again after his childhood voyage in 1861, and Gordon, who hungered to see the chalk country and Winchester in particular, was never confident enough about his health to attempt the journey. In a letter to Skues of 30 April 1915 he wrote cheerfully about a plan to make him some Mayflies; a postscript adds: 'Am writing in bed.' He died the next day and, in John MacDonald's sad and kindly phrase, 'was swept from sight like a spent spinner', leaving behind a priceless legacy for fly-fishers in America and much further afield. An important part of that legacy resides in his contributions to *The Fishing Gazette*, and in his correspondence with the most original angling thinker in Britain at that time.

Skues learned of his death from R.B. Marston and commented:

I have corresponded with many angling enthusiasts, but never with any so persistent and enthusiastic as he. I have in my desk shoals of his letters ... seldom did I have a letter from him that had not some little gift in it – a batch of summer duck feathers, samples of American woodcock hackles, or offers of American squirrel, or fox or hare.

Marston added: 'I never knew an angler who was more ready to give information.' George La Branche wrote to Marston from New York:

Isn't life the most uncertain of all things? To-day was the day fixed for a trip to the Neversink to fish a few days with my dear old friend Theodore Gordon, and instead I am writing of his untimely death ... I think that Mr Gordon was, perhaps, the greatest student of fly-fishing in this country, and without exception the best flytier I have ever known ... I had hoped that he would give his ideas to the fly-fishing public in permanent form, but it seems that was not to be during his life-time.

Nor was it to be after his death. There had, it seems, existed a manuscript which Gordon intended to send to La Branche to read. If the relatives would pass it to him, he wrote, he would arrange publication. But it must have been part of the prudential destruction of his effects referred to above, thus adding to an already sad loss to the world.

The third member of this trio of correspondents was Louis Bouglé. His lively letter style has already been noted in Chapter 6. A typical paragraph might contain a bold sketch of some new idea, ending with the words: 'What do you think of that, monsieur?' And the letters always have a serious purpose – to get hold of the best information on the latest discoveries and ideas.

The well-filled box of his letters at Princeton – 300 in number – begins with a query about flies. Addressed from 157 Faubourg St Honoré, Paris, Bouglé's letter of May 1902 plunges straightaway into his recent experiences in Germany with the little pale blue, as the small pale watery *Centroptilum luteolum* was sometimes called at that date. The Wutach at Bad Boll was a stocked river, but the trout could be difficult; this fly hatched in huge numbers every day, and he had tried nine different patterns in sizes 0 and 00 without much success. He had been alerted by reading Skues' long article in *The Fishing Gazette* of the previous December titled 'The Little Pale Blue of Commerce'. In this Skues had described several frustrating days some years earlier on the River Coquet (which he calls the Hussy, another of Skues' numerous jokes: elsewhere he called it the Flirt). As had been Bouglé's experience in Germany, there were profuse hatches of pale wateries, but no response to his offerings. No amount of tinkering at the fly vice in the evening availed. And there were other similar failures in later times. These eventually decided Skues to research the question as lawyers might, by going to the authorities, and eventually another of his impressive portmanteau articles was born.

By 1901 Skues was probably the most learned living historian of the artificial fly, and his long and detailed article (7 December) went back to the *Treatise*, Barker, Cotton and many others, finding nothing helpful even in his beloved Chetham of Smedley. The first pattern – and not a very good try – was in the second edition of Thomas Best's *Concise Treatise on the Art of Angling* (1789). Others followed: Bowlker, Bainbridge, Ronalds, Shipley and Fitzgibbon, 'Arundo', Theakston, Jackson, Foster, and Pritt were all looked at and dismissed. Halford was given short shrift ('Curiously he gives no imitation except the Little Marryat, which clearly he did not think was good enough'). It was not until his German holiday of 1901 that Skues felt that at last he was getting this fly nailed down. He did not have with him a copy of Walbran, but reproduced (from memory!) his tying:

Wing Small pale gull (no sea-swallow in stock)
Body Pale yellow silk dubbed loosely with hare's poll and ribbed closely with coarse primrose silk unwaxed
Legs pale blue hackle

In respect of the body, 'loosely' was the important term: the fur would push up between the ribs and, when wet, spread in a soft film over the yellow silk.

No other contributor to the angling press at this time could have produced an article of the standard of 'The Little Pale Blue of Commerce'. Bouglé had been impressed by it but, doubting his own fly-tying abilities, asked Skues to suggest the names of English fly-dressers who could provide him with a good imitation of the pale blue and also of the willow fly. Skues advised him to send to Robert Austin for the Tup and to George Holland for the Pale Watery of Walbran. Skues may have supplied his own version of the artificial Willow Fly, one of his first and best inventions, going back to 1888.

Armed with flies from England, Bouglé returned to Germany in the summer of 1902, but of the little pale blue there was no sign on the water. This did not prevent him from catching 350 trout and thirty grayling, mainly by fishing the wet fly. In Bavaria his fish averaged ¾lb, and in Würtemberg rather less. He also fished on the Baubeuren near Ulm, a place recommended to him by the well-known French angler Albert-Petit, but here the fish were even smaller.

The run of letters in English did not last long. The fourth letter was written entirely in French. Bouglé explained that it was now the Christmas season, the entire family was with him and he was of course very busy. Perhaps M. Skues would not mind if he wrote in French. Bouglé owed his faultless English to having spent a year as a youth at St Augustine's College at Ramsgate: even so the effort of composition must have been considerable – he wrote that it took him four times as long to write a letter in English, 'and I remember that you told me in one of your letters last spring that you have no difficulty in reading French' (my translation). Even so, the arrival of a long letter in French may have occasioned from Skues a slight exclamation of surprise (it certainly did with this writer). Having employed this excuse Bouglé never wrote in English again. The remainder of the correspondence (296 letters) are all in French, ending with elegant valedictions such as '*Mes sentiments les plus dévoués*' or '*Bien cordialement à vous*'. Needless to say other avalanche-paragraphs occur, with the ending '*Que pensez-vous de tout cela, monsieur?*'

For some years Bouglé provided the latest information and a digest of expert opinions from others about equipment, as described in the previous chapter, while Skues countered with detailed and learned information about fly-making. Bouglé never became fully confident about his own efforts, and would send to George Holland, Ogden Smith or '*la demoiselle de Wimbledon*', his name for Holland's former assistant Miss Farley. He was interested (and enraged) to find that flies from England were much cheaper than in France. In Paris the same patterns would cost two or three times as much, and furthermore would be of wretched quality ('*Les mouches les plus détestables*').

The two men were in agreement on many points. Both preferred blind hooks on gut for their wet flies, neither liked dyed hackles, and both were in agreement with Gordon that they did not care for Halford's 'New Patterns'. Holland had sent Bouglé some samples of these and he wrote to Skues: 'These patterns do not satisfy me at all.' He usually praised Skues' flies, which he thought had 'a "chic" and a remarkable allure which indicates the hand of a great artist'. However, when he wished to criticize he was no respecter of persons. In the spring of 1905 he received one of Skues' many attempts at imitating the dun of the blue-winged olive, something at which Skues never really succeeded. The wings, thought Bouglé, were too heavy in appearance, too opaque and dark, and lacking the necessary blue-violet sheen. Skues may not have liked this much, particularly as Bouglé's letter enclosed one of Halford's 'New Patterns'. This, Bouglé had considered to be a better imitation, so he was not prepared to dismiss everything designed by Halford.

On the other hand, Bouglé was full of excitement and praise for Skues' experiments with the sunk fly on the Itchen. From 1904, as recorded earlier, Skues' work in this direction was increasing, and his fishing outside Britain also provided interesting lessons. It was in Germany, as he wrote some years later,

that I first began to have some glimmerings of the idea of working up a wet-fly theory for chalk streams on dry-fly lines, and my friend M. Louis Bouglé, of Paris, great angler and great gentleman, with whom alike on the Itchen and on his Norman waters I have had delightful days, encouraged me to persevere.

Bouglé never lost his admiration for the wide and deep knowledge of his English friend, and recorded his pleasure in December 1903 upon seeing that Skues had been given a place among the best living fly-fishers in *Baily's Magazine of Sports and Pastimes*. The list, which included cricketers and other categories of sportsmen, was called 'The Twelve Best', and had been settled by a plebiscite of the readers. Halford came first, William Senior second and Edward Grey third. Skues came sixth equal with C.H. Cook, Harry Cholmondeley-Pennell and two others. A decade later the order of merit might have been different.

Skues' foreign expeditions have an interest in themselves, although it was mainly the German experience that was relevant to his developing thought. He first began to think of fishing further afield in 1897. At first he carried out a lengthy and minute examination of guides and maps. He then placed a letter in *The Fishing Gazette* over the signature of 'Stroke' (an early use of this pseudonym – after the Great War he promoted himself to Capt. Stroke), asking for information about fishing for trout and grayling in Bosnia, also about suitable fly patterns and even the fineness of the gut. Later that year he and a companion, Harry Tomlinson of the Paymaster General's Office, travelled on Thomas Cook tickets by way of Ostend, Cologne and Banja Luca. After some hunting around they lighted upon the River Pliva near Jezero, about sixty miles north-west of Sarajevo, later to acquire an unfortunate notoriety, but at that time a place unknown to most people outside Bosnia. A little later they moved on to the River Sana at Kljuc. The blue rivers and lakes of an amazing clarity must have delighted the Englishmen. Skues used his trusty 'wristbreaker', a 10ft Hardy 'Perfection', while Tomlinson favoured a 12ft Malleson from the Civil Service Stores. Most of the fish they caught were grayling. Trout were to be found in the Lake of Jezero, but the larger ones seem to have eluded them.

The chief interest of the piece Skues wrote for *The Field* the following January is the light it casts on social life in this part of the Balkans, almost unknown to most Europeans in those quiet times. Personal comfort and convenience were not to be thought of on such a holiday. The accommodation was primitive, the diet of dumplings and jugged hare uninspiring, and the sanitary arrangements were best forgotten. Life for the local people was hard, and poverty and disease were everywhere. The girls were beautiful but worn out with toil by thirty years of age. But he praises the natural courtesy and friendliness of the local anglers, who fished with tackle that was coarse and a skill that was refined.

In 1899 Skues and his youngest brother Charles journeyed to Norway and caught between six and seven hundred trout and grayling on the headwaters of the Mandal river. These were brought back to the grateful proprietor of the hotel. The encounters with the fish were straightforward and the methods conventional; mainly wet fly based on the enormous appearances of the stonefly. The fishing was exciting, and the memory was enough to tempt Skues back to Norway in July of the following year. On this trip he planned to explore an area further north and east on the Swedish border, where a combination of lake and river on the headwaters of the Rena seemed promising. Charles could not get away on this occasion, and Skues made up a party with a friend, his wife and another lady. As was customary with Skues, his account is informative about the fishing but silent about his companions. In 1947, in the *Journal of the Flyfishers' Club*, he recalled that the fishing was impressive, particularly on Lake Storsjoen at the mouth of the Rena, where the grayling were numerous and large. For Skues, the grayling at Winchester were no more than grayling, but their Scandinavian cousins were another order of fish. One weighed 4lb, and thirteen others were over 3lb. Hardly any were under 2lb. Sedge flies of two types were abundant: one was dark and mottled, the other was paler and resembled the grannom. Skues made up some patterns and fished three to a cast, which worked well. Trout of 2lb were daily events, and there were several 3lb fish.

The return visit in 1902 was a sad anticlimax. Low water conditions were to blame, and the fish were scanty and small. He records the catching of one good trout of 3lb 12oz on a stonefly and a few smaller fish. Of the big grayling there was no sign at all – the largest was only 1lb 9oz.

The Norwegian experience, delightful though it had been, was simple and straightforward holiday fishing. It did not, any more than the Bosnia trip, give Skues food for thought about chalk-stream technique.

With Germany, things were rather different. The first visit was in 1899, and was so successful that he went there, generally accompanied by Charles, almost every year until 1909. More research with guide books and geological maps enabled him to identify a limestone area north-east of Nuremberg, on the borders of the former Kingdom of Bavaria with the Duchy of Franconia. The Skues brothers conducted a reconnaissance and found a number of waters which they rejected as only holding coarse fish. Eventually they found the sort of water they were seeking.

In his article on Bosnia Skues was prepared to reveal the place, but he chose to wrap up the identity of his German hideaway in a series of whimsical names. The river (which was, in fact, Pegnitz) he called the Erlaubnitz, from the word *Erlaubnis*, meaning leave or permission, which was readily granted by riparian owners on the understanding that all sizeable fish were kept and handed over to them alive. This involved employing an attendant or *Fischer* with a *Fass* or barrel, who would trot away at intervals to fill up the fish box with fresh water from the river. The fish would then be sent away by rail to the big towns, or passed to the hotels in the valley, to stock up the glass tanks in the dining rooms. Connoisseur diners would identify the fish they thought most promising, which would be scooped out and borne away to the kitchen to be cooked. For the angler this solved the problem of what to do with the heavy bags of trout, for this stream teemed with fish. Most of them had, of course, been put there: there had long been a tradition of fish-rearing in Germany and other central European countries.

The two Britishers who appeared in the valley in 1899 were quickly recognized as being far ahead of the local anglers in effectiveness on the river. Soon, the owners were imploring them to come back and catch more fish. Another attraction of the place was the low cost of living. At one hostel they found that it was possible to live for 3s 10d a day. The drawback was that, although picturesque from a distance, the villages smelt bad and were full of tuberculosis.

In the next few years Skues and his brother returned to the valley, made many friends and entertained the locals with the fishing skills of Hampshire. On one reach they met a German angler who had caught one 8in trout by spinning. He insisted that it was too late in the year for fly-fishing. The Skues brothers set to work and captured seventy-eight trout. In 1904 Skues caught and handed over 249 live trout in fourteen days, including eight days of atrocious weather, and in the following year 265 in thirteen days. His brother's contribution in that year raised the total to 458. In most other parts of the world the brothers would have become deeply unpopular, but by involving themselves in the local restaurant-economy they were hailed as heroes. Truly, as T.B. Thomas wrote in 1986, they were unpaid fishmongers' labourers.

T.B. Thomas also went to some trouble to decode the elaborate language – some may have found it amusing, others irritating – in which

Skues concealed the whereabouts of his German paradise. The words were mainly in common currency then and now, in public notices in the street or on shops. The 'Erlaubnitz' was described as being in 'Wurstphalia' (*Wurst* is German for sausage). Skues advised the would-be angler seeking the place to travel by the '*nicht-hinauslehnen* State Railway' (Do Not Lean Out Of The Window) to the town of 'Wartesaal' (waiting room): the best fishing is between 'Wartesaal' and 'verbotener Eingang' (No Entry). There were several other (more or less humorous) names which defeated the decrypting skills of Thomas.

There is a small puzzle here related to Skues' German exploits. Why did he, who was fastidious about artificially stocked fish in England, and only interested in difficult challenges on the river, alter his approach and become frankly slaughterous abroad? In a letter years later he admitted that the Bavarian trout were 'absurdly easy'. From time to time he experienced similar days – although not on the same extraordinary scale – on stocked fisheries in England. When invited to the Kennet or to Dr Barton's fishing at Leckford on the Test he would cheerfully haul out a heavy weight of trout, but he seldom wrote about such exploits. Perhaps such days were a glorious escape from the slowed-down tactics of a difficult and tense day on the Itchen; a sort of explosive release or catharsis. There is a distinction between good sport and good fun. Even a hard-line purist can enjoy an away day by the seaside with the mackerel. But Skues wrote that he always returned from these expeditions to the austere regime of Abbots Barton, convinced that 'this was the real thing'.

The last visit of the brothers to their stock-fish paradise was in May 1909. On arrival they were shocked to see the evidence of the devastation caused by the *Hochwasser* of the previous February. It was called the flood of the century, and is now part of the history of the region. There were other disquieting signs of change: urban development was creeping along the valley from Nuremberg, smart villas were appearing, and 'Erlaubnis' was no longer freely available on some reaches. They resolved on no further expeditions. The visit did, however, produce for Skues a trout of 4lb 6oz, the largest of his career. Between them the brothers also secured three more over the 3lb mark, and a grayling of 3lb. These were all caught in early June at the end of the holiday but, in spite of these successes, the average size overall was considerably down on previous visits.

Skues never seems to have gone abroad or, indeed, anywhere in Britain as a sightseer or cultural tourist. The idea of visiting French cathedrals or the galleries of Florence or Venice would have held no charm for him. Nor would he have been drawn to the lazy round of the Edwardian moneyed class at Como, Cannes or Biarritz. He was a single-minded enthusiast, and holidays had one serious purpose – the pursuit of the trout.

I have described the German experience as fun rather than serious sport, but one aspect of it struck Skues forcibly – the readiness of trout in limestone streams to respond to the wet fly. He noticed this particularly on the 1904 trip, for which he had prepared by buying a stock of wet Alder flies from Peeks of Gray's Inn Road, tied according to the pattern of Charles Kingsley, with a wing of brown mallard or dark hen pheasant tail, a body of peacock herl and a black hackle tied in front of the wing to give the impression of the humped back of the natural. Kingsley mentions a good variation of this fly, using the mottled wing feather of the game hen. The effectiveness of the Alder probably depends on which river is being fished. Skues could not make it work for him on the Itchen, and it has never been well regarded on the Test, but large trout on the Kennet have been caught on it, and it works well on the streams of the Welsh border and on some streams of mixed chalk and other beds, such as the Nadder of Wiltshire, where Skues once had four wild days during a Whitsun holiday before the Great War, catching 104 trout.

The experience of the Pegnitz in 1901 provided one other useful tactic, called by Skues the wet-fly oil tip. This involved anointing the gut cast with paraffin down to the last link, to act as a floating indicator of the underwater take of the trout, and was in fact devised by his brother Charles. He thought that it was only suitable for fishing directly or almost directly upstream. Fishing across a strong stream was apt to produce an ugly drag.

The slow development of Skues' move towards the wet fly and the nymph has already been mentioned, and it remains one of the puzzles of his life. As I have recorded in Chapter 5, finding the horde of 'creepers' in the mouth of a trout had given him an idea:

> I took him in a sharp current, and have ever since been vowing to try there with an imitation of the larva of small Duns, and I have even gone so far as to dress a few; wingless, almost legless, and with short whisks. I daresay some day I shall carry out my resolution, and then we shall see.

The 'creepers' had been seen in 1888, and the idea had only come to him a few years later. A question therefore suggests itself: if Skues had been able at this early stage to make nymphs in a style that was almost the same as his later patterns, why did he revert to wet flies with upright wings, bearing far less resemblance to the real thing, and moreover persist with them for a period of years? It seems an illogical side road, even retrograde.

The slowness to get started at all on sub-surface techniques, whether with flies winged or wingless, is equally strange. The hypnotic influence of Halford's writings had a lot to answer for. No general theory to guide one's fishing could be founded on the odd fluke occurring on what Halford liked to call 'a happening day'. As I have suggested, the encounter with Halford at Abbots Barton in September 1891 had the effect of planting in Skues' mind a small germ of doubt about the competence of the leader on the river. By 1897 the uncertainties in Skues' mind had increased, but those doubts centred mainly on small points of disagreement about fishing technique and fly-tying. After 1904 his views about Halfordian infallibility become much clearer in his mind. After all, what he was now doing on the river was not an affair of small points – it was a radically new technique. The German experience had accelerated his previously slow development. His experiments with the sunk fly at Abbots Barton became more confident and numerous, as did his articles recording the success of the new practice.

This process was accompanied by a step-by-step deterioration in his relationship with Halford, once so cordial. Eventually it became an outright rupture (a detailed examination of which is the subject of Chapter 8). It was inevitable that this should be so, for increasingly Skues seemed to be unable to resist including more and more criticisms of Halford in his writings. This aspect of their growing antagonism has perhaps not been sufficiently noticed. Broadly speaking, the somewhat blunt-edged view in modern times has been that Skues was entirely justified in the controversy, and that Halford was wrong and deserved all he got. The unfortunate result has been to obscure much of the useful work done by Halford and Marryat in getting dry-fly fishing rationalized and explained to the world. Halford would have been less than human if he had not become irritated. He never knew, as he opened his latest copy of *The Field* or *The Fishing Gazette*, whether yet another article by Skues might be waiting for him, casting doubt on one of his cherished principles. Yet, for some years, he kept a dignified silence: criticism about his methods at the fly-tying bench were not worth his notice. But articles advocating the use of the wet fly on the chalk streams, occasional at first but becoming more frequent, must have stoked a long pent-up heat.

During the first decade of the twentieth century Skues' articles dealt with new dry-fly patterns, tackle improvements and the shortcomings of British fly rods already considered in Chapter 6. But the writings that aroused most interest – and with some readers the most irritation – were accounts of his successes at Abbots Barton and the lessons to be drawn from them. These articles generally followed a common form, driving home the lesson that it was unprofitable to cover nymphing fish with dry flies. In the 1890s his method had been to attack them with the hare's ear or the Pope's nondescript. Now he had found something better.

After the drama of the 1899 letter Skues let the subject lie for a while. But in 1901 he opened the season at Abbots Barton at a time of wild weather. On Easter Monday the wind had raised waves a foot high. 'There was nothing for it but the wet fly, and for nearly an hour I pegged away, first with a Red Palmer and later a wingless Hare's Ear, intended to resemble a hatching nymph.' This passage, with its interesting implications, shows that Skues was prepared, at least at this date, to 'fish the water', and indeed in other places he writes of putting the sunk fly into 'likely places' where no rise had occurred and no fish were visible. This is, of course, the essence of wet-fly fishing in rough freestone rivers, but it requires, at least in its most skilful form, some rivercraft to know where such places might be. But in the chalk country it was frowned upon in those days – as indeed it is on many reaches nowadays.

In the 1930s, when a wave of opposition confronted him, he might have regretted frank admissions of this sort, and there was a danger that purists with long memories might come back at him. It was because of this that, in later years, he adopted a less reckless line in his writings (if not in his practices) and laid down a more restricted code of practice on the river. In *Nymph Fishing for Chalk Stream Trout* (1939, p. 34), his final statement of best practice, he wrote: 'In nymph fishing the artificial nymph has to be presented with the maximum of precision to selected individual feeding fish in position.' This definition certainly did not quite cover some of his tactics in earlier times. And in the same book (p. 66) he was careful to agree with Halford by further distancing himself from the practice of fishing the water, ignoring the fact that he had done this on the occasion mentioned above and, indeed, on many others.

Halford would have read the 1901 piece with irritation and alarm. His advice had always been to refrain from fishing altogether under such conditions: better to retire to the fishing hut or hotel and read the paper. In fact he once told Skues that he thought that a day of wind and rain could often make things too easy – 'a duffer's day' was his term for it, but gave no explanation. The idea of withdrawing from the river if conditions were not right for delicate dry-fly work did not commend itself to Skues, and similar opinions had been voiced by others since the rise of purism in the 1880s. Such days do not always occur. Many of Halford's most devoted followers were men of leisure who could afford to lose a day when the weather was less than perfect, but many less fortunate men with limited time for days by the river would have to make the best of things, and would tend to experiment with methods not approved of in the Halford directives.

At least on that day Skues was able to report that no fish were caught by these methods. After a fruitless morning he found some rising fish in a quiet corner away from the wind, substituted a well-oiled Rough Olive for the wet Hare's Ear and, after losing two fish because of a rotten sample of gut, at last landed a trout of 1½lb. He stayed out doggedly in the storm until 4.30 but caught nothing else. Meanwhile, 'my friend industriously flogged away with two wet flies in the roughest water in vain'. Rules at that date were more lax at Abbots Barton than on other fisheries nearby, and the keeper, Humphrey Priddis, would actually advise rods at a loss on a rainy day to put on two flies and fish downstream. This was, in fact, the method normally used by the two nephews of Irwin Cox when faced with a day of such weather (though they did not, in fact, catch anything very big), and it is another example of the fact that, contrary to the general impression today, purist ideas were not universally followed in Hampshire at that time.

In the next few years the pace of Skues' practice with sunk flies increased, and the assembling of the material which was later to be marshalled into the text of his first book can be seen. In April 1903 he began to introduce his team of likely flies for wet-fly use. These derived from the Tweed and Clyde styles of dressing, as described in David Webster's book *The Angler and the Loop Rod* (1885). These flies, with their upright wings of solid feather (blackbird, starling and snipe), compare rather oddly with the true nymphal imitations that Skues began to design a few years later. The hallmark of the latter was a minute attention to detail, whereas the former do not appear to modern eyes to be accurate representations of nymphs rising in the water to hatch. It could be argued that, at the moment of eclosion, a nymphal case with a fly shooting up its new wings might be imitated in such a way. But that would only apply if the artificial were actually sitting in the surface film. Some modern writers have suggested that this is, in fact, where Skues wished his sub-surface imitations to be, but the evidence we have is unclear. As early as 1902 he wrote: 'There are occasionally days on a dry-fly river when the trout will touch nothing but a more or less well-sunk wet fly', which indicates that his new Scottish-inspired flies were, some of the time anyway, more than just an inch or two beneath the surface. And as his sub-surface practice developed, it is quite likely that his flies were fished at several different levels, even at this early stage in his experiments.

Many of his new experiences appeared in his long-running series entitled 'More Jottings' in *The Fishing Gazette* and followed on from his earlier series 'Some Jottings of an Amateur Fly-Dresser'. These articles are all of the greatest importance in understanding Skues' development, particularly when he was on the road to the nymph. In 1904 the wet Tup figures more often in his published accounts. An article in June praises the nymph-like translucency of the pattern, and describes a morning on the Itchen when the trout came readily at it 'sunk or semi-sunk'. But the article shows that he was still unclear as to what exactly he and the fish were doing: 'Why they came I cannot say, for the fly bore not the least resemblance to the nymphs on which they were gorging. I have, however, noticed that a spinner seems to be welcome to trout during the hatch of the subimago.'

There is a puzzled and dissatisfied flavour to the above account. Skues liked to think that trout had at least some discrimination, and that he was giving them the best imitation of the natural. After spending years paying minute attention to the build of dry flies, he may have felt that, with his new wet flies, he had gone back to lures – mere instruments to catch fish. Throughout his life he was always irritated if fish behaviour ceased to make sense. He once wrote that if he did not think that a trout had taken his fly as the best imitation of the real thing on which it was feeding, then the real pleasure of fishing would be greatly diminished. The first time his friend W.D. Coggeshall came to the Itchen, Skues was amused to find that he proposed to attack the cautious fish of Abbots Barton with large American patterns several times the size of the fly on the water. When these flies began to catch fish his amusement turned to bafflement.

There are two more intriguing points in the article of June 1904. They may have gone unnoticed at the time, but both acquired significance later.

He wrote: 'I sometimes wonder whether on such occasions a hook tied on with waxed yellow silk and a couple of turns of hare's ear dubbing at the shoulder, picked out and trimmed short, and without wings or hackle, might not take fish.' This was an idea that, if carried forward, would have produced something very close to the no-hackle nymph of Frank Sawyer. Nothing quite like it was followed up for several years. It makes one wonder once again why Skues did not simply get on with it. He was, in fact, describing in 1904 the more complete nymphal form that he was not to devise until 1908, but for some time he continued with his practice of offering Scottish wet flies to Hampshire trout. Moreover, when he did begin to develop a range of nymphs he provided them all with hackles.

The second point is equally startling. Skues states in more than one place that he did not discover the marrow spoon and the baby plate until the early 1920s, probably in June 1921 and therefore too late for inclusion in *The Way of a Trout with a Fly*. These became important items for him on the riverbank, because they gave information about the current feeding of the fish, and also a chance to avoid the horror of a bankside autopsy, about which he had an almost pathological disgust. He once wrote that if he wished to be remembered for anything it would be for the great discovery of the marrow scoop, and he lamented the lost opportunities of the years before that discovery. It is therefore the more mystifying to find at the end of the article mentioned above the following:

> Mr Tod states in his book that he is led to infer that trout sometimes take the insect ascending to the surface to hatch, but that it is impossible to prove it. Let him try a marrow spoon down the throat of his trout, and let him turn out the contents into a glass of water.

Making an important discovery in 1904, forgetting about it, and rediscovering it in 1921 seems rather bizarre. So within the same article we have more material to add to the long list of insoluble puzzles about Skues.

In August 1904 Skues produced another wet-fly bulletin, describing the taking of four brace of fish on a semi-submerged Tup, which showed that he was thinking increasingly about the level of the fly in the water: 'The fish would not stand to be cast to with a floating fly in general, but the half-sunk fly did not seem to scare them.' The discovery that a small wet fly presented delicately caused less disturbance than a dry fly was also an important point, particularly in the quiet and clear conditions of summer. This would have been a further cause of uneasiness for Halford. It had always been an important article in his purist belief-system that the delicate arrival on the water of a carefully-presented small dry fly was an important factor in rendering permanently obsolete the wet fly of the former age. For him the old technique was a clumsy affair, sometimes of two or three flies on thick gut, cast often at random up, across or down, and likely, if pursued in the new reformed age on the chalk streams, to spread a contagious alarm throughout the fishery. To find in the journals a series of articles praising a new variation that advocated the use of small flies of the same size as his own cherished patterns, but used discreetly underwater, must have given him an alarmed sense of having been outflanked.

1904 was an important year for Skues, and there were signs that he was becoming bolder and more direct in his approach about the place of the wet fly on the chalk stream. What had formerly been an occasional series of suggestive papers began to turn into a purposive and joined-up campaign. The encouragement of Louis Bouglé mentioned earlier was important in the path towards publishing his work in book form. In April Bouglé wrote to Skues: 'It seems to me that you are on course to revolutionize the chalk-stream technique.'

In the same month there appeared an article called 'A Wet-Fly Day on a Dry-Fly River', a good example of the sort of coat-trailing titles which Skues was to use in the next few years to make his point, along with a highly effective new use of language. It is true that some of it may have been lost on many anglers, but more perceptive readers would have got the point of this and many other apparently innocent sallies. To such people the unspoken questions must have quickly suggested themselves. What exactly is a dry-fly stream anyway? Who calls it so? And what is his warranty for saying so? Halford's supporters would have said that the question had been settled for years. A dry-fly stream was a stream thus defined by the master himself, and carried his authority. Was Mr Skues intending to set himself up against the Halford system? Many anglers could see that this process had already begun. He had, as shown above, at first been attacking the outworks of the citadel by criticizing Halford's ideas about fly-tying in many interesting but non-essential respects. Now the main assault over a matter of principle was beginning.

The article just mentioned appeared in *The Field*, in itself a small provocation, for Halford had been publishing in it since the 1880s and regarded it as a safe house. Skues described arriving at Abbots Barton on a day of heavy rain in April. The large dark olives were on the water and the fish were moving, but not to the winged fly. Having made this diagnosis Skues applied the treatment – the wet Rough Olive, one of his new discoveries. Three good fish were landed, weighing 5lb 5oz in total. Then his last two copies of the killing fly were lost through hasty striking. The hatched fly was still not being taken, but Skues was forced back to using dry flies, needless to say without result. Skues pegged away for the rest of the day without success. This article, with its obvious moral, would have annoyed the purists, but must have made an impression on many more open minds, for it emphasized the futility of hammering fish which were obviously feeding beneath the surface.

A piece in *The Fishing Gazette* the following November widened and deepened the attack. This was not in his usual form – another factual description of an outing on the Itchen with suggestive ideas drawn from events – but a discussion of principles. Again, it is a piece worth analysing as a text for the use of effective language. He pointed out that from time immemorial

> before it [the dry fly] became the rage anglers fished those sacrosanct streams with the wet-fly and made baskets upon them which the dry-fly angler of the present day would deem himself fortunate to rival. It is absurd to suppose that the trout changed their habits and their times and place of feeding with the new fashion of the dry-fly ... the angler should be catholic in his methods and hold himself free to fish wet or dry, big fly or small fly, according to the conditions of the day, and not bind himself rigidly by the limitations of a cast-iron system.

And he added a final challenge to the opposition: 'The dry-fly was a great discovery, but it has its limitations.' A reader of the above, particularly if a purist, would not have failed to notice the lack of becoming reverence in the use of the terms 'rage', 'sacrosanct', 'fashion' and 'cast-iron system'.

As time passed, these radical articles became more direct. Some of them contained matter that might, in the light of later events, be thought a little rash. In a piece in 1905 called 'In Default of a Rise' he depicted himself arriving in Winchester at 5 p.m. on a Friday evening, and finding (as one would expect at such an hour) that there was almost no activity in the fish world. This would have been one of the first occasions when he was using the newly acquired Leonard – of all the six rods that he eventually owned the most used and most beloved ('delicious to cast with even if one is catching no fish'). After experimenting without result with a pale watery he mounted a small Tup to gut. Dressing this creation of Robert Austin on double round bend hooks as recommended by E.M. Tod, was a recent idea of Skues: unfortunately each one took twenty minutes to tie. With this new device he began to search the water. The title of the piece only indicated half the story. There was not only no rise; there were no fish visible either. This was, therefore, blind fishing. The evening became more prosperous, and Skues began to get his fish. Although four sizeable fish were landed so, also, he recorded rather unwisely, were five undersized fish. Of course, fishing into places where a fish might be was one of the tactics which caused disapproval among the purists, because it was thought to result in catching fish below the size limit. This factor was to reappear in the 1938 debate; in fact on that occasion fishing blind with a dry fly was also held up as objectionable. The purists had long memories, and Skues may have regretted some of the matters that he had so carelessly mentioned.

At the close of this article Skues summed up in a style that was by now becoming increasingly confident, rejecting the idea that the dry fly was the only permissible method:

> That raking the water with a team of flies to be fished down-stream is to be deprecated, and may properly be barred on such a water, is, I think, indisputable, but it is difficult to believe that such wet-fly work as here described, where the fly is always directed upstream to a particular fish, or at least to a place where he may be expected to be, should come under the ban of the most rigid of purists.

It was in an attempt to stem the flow of sunk-fly articles that Halford published, in April 1906, his most direct and angry article so far (see Chapter 8). But if he thought that he had brushed aside this stinging gadfly he had not long to wait to learn otherwise. Three weeks later another breezy article advocating the use of Tweed-dressed winged patterns appeared in *The Fishing Gazette*, over the signature of the unabashed 'Val Conson'. The provocative title was not calculated to reduce the temperature of the debate, viz.: 'Wet-fly Patterns for Dry-fly Rivers'. Some of the sentiments expressed in it were provocative too: 'In course of years there has grown up a theory among anglers of the Hampshire school that to fish their streams other than with the dry fly is a profanation. For them the dry fly has become a fetish.' And he emphasized again the inutility of presenting dry flies to fish feeding on nymphs.

This article provoked criticism from a correspondent from Romsey calling himself 'Ballygunge'. Skues was never able to identify him but it is possible that he may formerly have been a judge in India. He had been a member of the Houghton Fly-Fishing Club, the breakaway group that secured the Houghton water from 1875 to 1892. This meant that 'Ballygunge' was, for some years, a fellow member with Halford. He insisted that dry-fly men do not in fact hammer away with floating flies over fish obviously not taking surface fly. Anglers had been sinking their flies for years. However, the letter makes clear that the writer was thinking of spinners rather than nymphs, and was recommending the use of spent patterns. As for bulging fish, he did not think it likely that any fly had ever been or would be discovered to catch them. It was, in fact, in some respects the sort of letter that Halford might have written. Skues replied, expressing surprise that anglers were so adaptable as to fish wet flies upstream – this had not been his experience of his fellow anglers. Besides, he added, Mr Halford had recently written in *The Field*, 'strongly deprecating the practice of wet-fly fishing on dry-fly streams, [and] shows no consciousness of the fact that wet-fly fishing could be pursued on them otherwise than by long-lining down stream or across and down'.

Halford's frontal attack in 1906 had no effect on Skues, who was now pressing forward in his campaign to liberalize chalk-stream practice. In his enthusiasm he made several other risky suggestions which later he might have regretted, and which would certainly have caused fresh bouts of wincing with the purists. In a 1907 article he considered the question of the weighted fly. This arose out of earlier letters in *The Fishing Gazette* about the ease with which such flies could be used as poaching devices, especially in the case of large salmon flies. R.B. Marston intervened twice in this correspondence to give his opinion that wrapping lead wire around a trout fly or adding split shot to the gut was not 'fair and square fly fishing'. This might have warned Skues that the area was dangerous, but it did not. In a 'Jottings' article in the issue of 11 May he plunged into a discussion of the most efficient way of sinking a fly. On occasions he would use a heavier hook or a double hook. How did that differ in principle from adding a lead shot? After all, it was done by Francis Francis (also, though he did not know it, by H.S. Hall). And he quoted the case of a certain Midland angler who was accustomed to fish for trout with a float, a shotted line and a wet Coch-y-bondhu: 'It may be objected that this is not fly fishing as commonly understood.' But the fly was the same; only the method of transmission was different. One would feel instinctively that it was wrong, 'but it is difficult to formulate the reason why'.

He went on to raise another interesting point: How deep is it permissible to sink a fly in a chalk stream? Why is it unfair to use it near the bottom in deep water and not in shallow water? Questions of this sort exercised the minds of anglers for many years in the first part of the twentieth century. As late as 1947 T.A. Powell, in *Here and There a Lusty Trout* (1947), recorded knowing of waters where the sunk nymph was regarded as 'only being one degree less obnoxious than a night-line'.

Bearing in mind the particular belief-system that was shared by many chalk-stream anglers at that date, Skues might have been better advised to confine this sort of thing to private musing, or at least to conversation with a trusted friend, instead of exposing his ideas in print. He was, of course, pursuing a simple philosophical monologue along the lines of 'If A can be allowed, why not B, which is almost the same, and then C, and so on', but such a journey will soon take one an alarming distance away from the starting point. He sought to cover himself by pointing out that he was not advocating the practice of fishing the deep nymph, merely searching for a principle 'with a desire to find some logical basis for a rule'. This was to ignore the danger that many readers would not stop to consider that this was merely a meditation on meanings, but an alarming suggestion for a new practice.

More practically he suggested that the danger of poaching was not the same as with a large salmon fly: a weighted trout fly could not be used for snatching. Marston added a reproving footnote: 'Why not? I am sure "V.C." is in error on this point. I am sorry that he considers "fly-fishing" covers sinking a trout fly with shot.'

Skues found a fellow sympathizer three weeks later in a correspondent named R.W. Vernon. Vernon was also inclined to question the disapproval of the weighted fly. He could see no problem in logic: if one wished to imitate the hatched fly by using paraffin and even sometimes cork to float the artificial, where was the difference if one used lead to sink the artificial if one wished to imitate the nymph? Besides, an angler 'would be a mighty fine craftsman to snatch a trout on a 00 hook'. Marston again added a worried footnote, reiterating his view: if it was a free-for-all fishery where worms, minnows, etc. were allowed, weighting an artificial fly presumably would be acceptable, 'only let us not call it fly-fishing'.

This must have been something of a setback for Skues, and a warning to be wary where he put his feet. So far, he had been carrying this prominent editor with him; a valuable asset. It was some time before he won back the lost ground and recovered Marston's support.

Bruised as he may have been by these reproofs, Skues did not entirely refrain from living dangerously, and there were several other such risky discussions in *Minor Tactics* in 1910. It was not until some years later that he set to work to purge the tactics of his nymph practice, screening out elements that would provide any justification for the purists to condemn and reject. The programme set out in his final statement in 1939 – *Nymph Fishing for Chalk-Stream Trout* – contained a final and much narrower statement of acceptable tactics, and provided an interesting contrast with his pre-1914 writings.

Other papers followed in the two main journals, too many to be considered here in detail. They usually shared similar features – the pointlessness of flogging nymphing fish with dry flies, the importance of identifying exactly what was happening in the fish world from hour to hour of the fishing day, and the subtle delight of responding to the almost imperceptible take under water.

The use of the wet flies with the Scottish profile continued, and it was not until 1908 that Skues moved on to true nymphal forms. In August 1908 he was at Abbots Barton for seven days of interesting fishing (Saturday to Saturday – Sunday fishing was not allowed until 1917). He had timed his visit to get in ahead of the late summer weed cut. By this date his knowledge of this difficult fishery was so comprehensive and his skills as an angler so advanced that he had come to prefer the fishing of August almost more than that of any other month, at a time when most anglers would have been baffled by the conditions. Towards the latter part of his life he would stop fishing at Abbots Barton at the end of August, feeling that the fish soon became too easy as the time of spawning drew nearer, and they began to feed more intensely to build up for the approaching spawning season.

The exploits of this week were recorded in an interesting article called 'In Advance of the Chain Scythe'. Readers must have marvelled at the variety of tactics used to catch the fish. There was a good deal of dry-fly work: fish were caught on the Hare's Ear Sedge with landrail wings, Little Red Sedge, floating Tup's Indispensable, Orange Quill, Pope's Green

Nondescript and Dotterel Dun. But whenever the fish turned to nymphing they would soon find themselves examining wet versions of the Tup and the Greenwell. Skues explained: 'The *modus operandi* was to let the fly trail in the water, well below me, till thoroughly soaked, and then to dispatch it, with a flick sufficient to float the gut, not the fly, to the neighbourhood of the rising fish.'

Tuesday was an eventful day in an eventful week. On that day he discovered in the mouth of a trout a nymph, and dressed an imitation with dark greenish-brown olive seal's fur, very fine and close, mixed with a little dark bear's hair from the roots of the fur, and ribbed with fine gold wire: whisks from a soft, darkish dun hen's hackle, and hackle a very small dark blue cock's hackle, about half the usual length of fibre for hackling on a 0 hook. He did not (or could not) identify the natural at the time, but later in *Minor Tactics* called it 'a dark olive nymph'. By the time he was assembling the elements of *The Way of a Trout with a Fly* he had become more familiar with the little dark fly that becomes plentiful on some summer afternoons, and which he named the July dun. It is now called the small dark olive or *Baëtis scambus*.

By 11 a.m. on the following day this new pattern had caught six fish. In the course of the week he accounted for forty-nine fish, a result which many of the rods on that difficult fishery would have regarded as satisfactory for the work of a whole season. Again, the intended lesson of this long and delightful article was that, whatever the detractors might say, the wet fly used carefully at the right time was as effective and also sporting – an important word in that era – as the dry fly.

By 1909 Skues' postbag must have been considerable, as people wrote with questions and encouragement. It is sad that most of these early letters have not survived. Occasionally he would publish one of them. In the summer of that year he reproduced in *The Fishing Gazette* a letter he had received from an angler in New Zealand, who had been inspired to pursue his local trout with Skues' new method by the 1906 article mentioned above, 'Wet-fly Patterns for Dry-Fly Rivers'. This correspondent had also been an avid follower of the 'Jottings' series: when was Mr Skues going to resume them?

In fact Skues wrote fewer articles in 1909, no doubt because he was working hard to prepare his first book for publication. Also, it may have been that he was by now in a hurry, because he was becoming aware of a serious competitor in a field that he had come to regard as his own. The activities of a number of other users of wet flies on the chalk streams have already been mentioned, but their efforts had not been systematic, and none of them had gone as far as Skues. By 1909 Skues had revealed himself in a number of articles, and it was clearly prudent to publish as quickly as possible.

The dark horse coming up behind Skues was Dr Mottram, who had become known in the pages of *The Field* over the pseudonym of 'Jim Jam', and who was to be a preoccupation for Skues at intervals for the rest of their joint lives. James Cecil Mottram was born in Holt, Norfolk in 1880. During his medical career he moved towards cancer research and became one of the noted pioneers in radiography treatments. After his death in 1945 he was described in the British Journal of Radiography as 'the outstanding pathologist in this country'. It was natural that his approach to the problems of angling, as well as to the problems of river management, would be thorough and scientific. He is best remembered nowadays for *Fly Fishing: Some New Arts and Mysteries* (1915), which was a collection of articles previously published in *The Field* and the *Journal of the Flyfishers' Club*. He had dealt with several topics that had already interested Skues, such as the importance of form, colour and transparency as they might appear to fish. He may have been the first to explain by diagram how the upright wings of the hatched fly appear first to the waiting trout below, to be followed by the image of the body of the dun as it is carried downstream on the surface. His theories of how trout see led him to design different types of dry fly for use at different times of the day to take account of light angles and directions. He also gave some thought to imitating underwater creatures, and his ideas have continued to intrigue experimenters down to the present day. Paul Schullery's 2008 edition of some of Mottram's writings quotes Ernest Schwiebert, who wrote in *Nymph Fishing* (1973) of the debt owed to Mottram by Marinaro, Swisher and Richards. But he is not widely known today, and one regrets that he had not written more on the nymph.

Some of his ideas were worked out and published before the publication of Skues' first book. An article in *The Field* included one of Mottram's early attempts at a nymph, which for that date was fairly advanced. One of them included a picture of two advanced flies – one of which was a Pale Watery Nymph, tied on a heavy wire hook (to aid efficient sinking) in size 0 or 00, with straw-coloured silk built up to form a thorax, then narrowed and tapered towards the tail end of the fly. Three fibres of badger supplied the whisks. There was also a drawing of his idea of a gnat larva, in form little different from modern standard patterns. This paper appeared in

January 1910. Skues, aware that his own work was being prepared for publication, must have had a further moment of unease.

Mottram modified this nymph plan when preparing his own book several years later, and divided the single pattern into two designs. For fish taking the nymph at or near the surface, which he called 'dimpling fish', he devised a pattern called 'the resting nymph'. The form of it was based on the idea that nymphs on the edge of hatching have no perceptible activity or movement. It was therefore provided with legs, four in number, from fibre from the wing of a hen pheasant, leaving the fragment of quill at the base of each to imitate the foot of the natural. Four legs he considered to be enough, as he had not yet, he observed drily, 'found a trout that would only take a hexapod'. Three guinea fowl barbs were to represent the cerci or tails. This, with an abdomen of herl and a thorax moulded to the correct silhouette from a number of turns of Pearsall's silk completed this device.

His second type was intended for a different form of fish behaviour. The actively moving nymphs being intercepted by bulgers would have their legs clinging to the body and thus scarcely visible. No hackle would therefore be needed. This version, which he called 'the swimming nymph', had points in common with the minimalist pattern, the Pheasant Tail, developed by Frank Sawyer many years later. For this nymph the same guinea fowl barbs as before stood for the tails. Floss of the appropriate colour, the choice being left to the fly-dresser, was continued forwards in a taper and built up in the area of the thorax. The tips of two dark grey cock's hackles were tied in to point over the top rear of the thorax to represent wing cases.

Mottram had worked out different techniques of fishing the two patterns. The 'resting nymph' was to be cast upstream to nymphing or 'dimpling' fish and drifted down to them, with the last part of the cast submerged. For bulging fish he decided that the nymph needed to be energized instead of inert. It should therefore be fished dead square across or from above at an angle of about 45 degrees, so as to swing across in front of the fish. Thus the first mode was the same as that used by Skues. The second is definitely not, and he expressed his disapproval of it.

The accusation of dragging has some force, for Mottram called for the 'swimming nymph' to be placed 'two or three yards above the fish and beyond it, so that as it swings down and round with the current it will cross in front of the fish. How far beyond the fish depends on the strength of the current and the amount of the drag you expect.'

Two decades later, in a 1935 number of the *Journal of the Flyfishers' Club*, Mottram extended the scope of this tactic into something resembling the Leisenring Lift, a technique, as with many others in angling, which may have been re-invented several times. He wrote:

The leaded nymph is often far more attractive than the unleaded, because with it you can imitate the rising of a nymph from the bottom. To do this, oil the gut and line to within two feet of the fly, cast well above and a little beyond the trout, allowing the whole to drift down to the fish without drag. As it passes the fish, gently draw on the line, causing the nymph to ascend through the water in imitation of a natural, and if all goes well the trout will follow it up and take it.

This newcomer had several other advanced ideas. He had produced several other sunk fly patterns, commonplace enough today but novel a century ago. These included imitations of the pupae of various diptera. For Mottram, whatever a fish was feeding upon was fair game for an imitation. Skues had thought about shrimps, as had Halford at an earlier and less developed stage of his thinking, but neither of them would have designed an 'Alevin Fly', with beads for eyes, a design that Mottram had picked up in Japan.

Mottram's pioneering work was therefore surprisingly radical for his time. It involved a rejection of purist behaviour on the river, and is the more surprising in view of his change of heart in the late 1930s. In one respect he moved more rapidly than Skues, for he described the use of true nymphal forms at the beginning of his work, instead of passing through the intermediate stage of winged wet flies. This may, however, have been because he had profited by reading of Skues' earlier experiments.

Perhaps it was a pity that Skues could not bring himself to make an approach to Mottram as a fellow member of the Flyfishers' Club and work to pool their knowledge, but that was not his way. Throughout his life he worked alone: there was no equivalent of the Halford-Marryat partnership. In the past he had been generous to some workers in the field, such as McClelland, but he seems to have regarded Mottram as a competitor and a threat, and from time to time in the next few years criticized him in the journals, eventually drawing his remarks into the text of *The Way of a Trout with a Fly* in 1921. In the section 'Ex Mortua Manu' he wrote:

I am aware that a book called *Fly Fishing: Some New Arts and Mysteries* (J.C. Mottram) has set out an interesting method of nymph fishing. I do not wish to be understood as disparaging his flies or his methods in any way, as I have never tried them. In theory they seem to me to have the defects of rigidity, density, and dullness of colouring and a tendency to fall heavily when cast, by reason of absence of hackle. Moreover, they are used dragging.

This passage is an example of Skues in one of his less than generous moods. To assure the reader that he is not disparaging Mottram's nymph designs was an unconvincing ploy when he then proceeded to do exactly that. In the same book he returns to the subject in the same disparaging manner:

I hope I may be forgiven for saying that I do not think his method presents the right line of approach to the best theory of imitation or representation of nymphs, for his patterns were intended to be fished downstream and dragging, and they therefore make an appeal to the same propensity in the trout which attracts him to a spinning minnow or a dragging, winged wet fly.

Having thus thoroughly disapproved of Mottram's nymphs – somewhat unfairly, for it was only the 'swimming nymph' that was designed to move in the water – Skues wrote some years later to add the name of Mottram to a list of authors whom he considered to be interesting but whose writing style was devoid of wit or humour. After all this it is something of a relief to find Skues describing him as 'that very interesting writer and skilful angler, Dr J.C. Mottram'. Whether the hostility was returned, and may even have contributed to the position taken by Mottram at the debate of 1938, it is impossible now to know. The debate has usually been seen as a closing of the ranks of the purists, but Mottram did not really fit that description, even after he had changed sides. An angler who fished leaded nymphs downstream could hardly have been called a Halfordian purist.

Just as Halford, preparing his first book in the 1880s, might have fretted about the possible competition of H.S. Hall, and discovered that there was nothing to worry about, so Skues launched his remarkable book at the world without competition. Mottram's book did not appear until 1915, and in any case dealt with a miscellany of subjects, of which the discussion of sunk flies occupied only a small part.

When, after this long and complicated period of gestation, *Minor Tactics of the Chalk Stream* saw the light, the great change in the chalk-stream world began to accelerate.

8

Minor Tactics and Major Discord

S KUES' FIRST BOOK, *Minor Tactics of the Chalk Stream*, appeared in
the shops in March 1910, well presented in cloth of a suggestive
dark olive colour. Marston thought it was 'a handsome volume'
and was surprised that it only cost 3s 6d.

Skues must have spent some time pondering the style and approach of
the book. Hitherto, his articles on wet-fly methods had been descriptions
of fishing days, in which had been placed useful hints on how the reader
might do better on the river. He would have known that bringing them
together between hard covers would result in a major difference. It would
be seen by the fly-fishing public as a manifesto for change, and possibly
controversy might arise. The manner of drafting such a document would
have to be approached with caution. If the chalk-stream world was to be
converted, this missionary knew that he would have to proceed with tact,
gathering in a few souls at a time. As he looked over his papers published
in *The Field* and *The Fishing Gazette* it might have occurred to him that
he had been somewhat unwise in certain of them. Their combined effect
might resemble an aggressive frontal assault which would alienate the
friends as well as purists. It would be necessary to be gentler and more
conciliatory and, like Agag, to 'walk delicately'.

In this he was extremely successful. One of the striking things about
Minor Tactics of the Chalk Stream was the persuasive and reasonable tone
of the book. The dedication was 'To my friend the dry-fly purist, and to my
enemies, if I have any.' Even those who might have been disposed to come
out and fight were left bemused and silent. The most surprising example
was Halford himself, who would have much enjoyed annihilating his
enemy. In the event, as I show below, even he seems to have felt that he had
nothing he could effectively say. He was, no doubt, startled to find in the
Foreword to the book a graceful tribute to himself and to his published
work. Skues had been careful to write that he, like most of his fellow

anglers, thought that *Dry-Fly Fishing in Theory and Practice* had been the last word on the art of chalk-stream fishing, 'so clear, so comprehensive, is it; so just and so in accord with one's own experience ... the greatest work, in my opinion, which has ever seen the light on the subject of angling for trout and grayling'. And the tone of *Minor Tactics* as a whole continued to be mild and for the most part not challenging, in spite of the subject matter. Skues' experience as a family solicitor must have come to his aid here. He was accustomed to avoiding unprofitable confrontations and to soothing his way towards compromises and out-of-court settlements and similar arrangements. Even the title of the book was odd, implying that the sunk fly was to be secondary and subordinate to the major tactics of the dry fly. A curious concession, perhaps, by a man who knew quite well that trout did most of their feeding below the surface. This concession worked well at the time, and most people seemed to have been taken in by it. In fact the effect lasted for decades. As late as 1958, Wilson Stephens, then editor of *The Field*, provided an introduction to Frank Sawyer's *Nymphs and the Trout*, in which he wrote that nymph tactics were not 'minor', but of the same validity as dry-fly fishing. He wrote:

> To Sawyer nymph fishing is a distinct technique; an alternative to the dry fly, its equal in sporting appeal and in the fair balancing of the odds between man and fish, but different. In his eyes the nymph is the dry fly's partner, not its poor relation. That this is a divergence from the view of Skues is implicit in the title of the latter's classic work.

This notion arises from a misunderstanding of Skues' real though not advertised view at the time, which he was careful not to insist upon. He did not think of the new tactics as minor at all or regard the nymph as the poor relation of the dry fly. But he knew well that, in the climate of opinion prevailing in 1910, it would be wiser to allow readers to think that way. Largely as a result of Halford's enormous prestige the dry fly had, at least for the time being, taken the lead. Halford, 'Detached Badger' from his pulpit at *The Field*, must have appeared to have constructed an impregnable position through his books and his prolific journalism – over two hundred articles by 1910. The wet fly could only take a deferential and limited place. The purist citadel was too strong to be taken by a *coup de main*. But a long and subtle piece of siege work might achieve something one day. Who knew what the future might bring?

The Foreword continued, carefully worded but now slightly critical. The effect of the 'triumph of the dry fly' had been to obliterate in the course of two or three decades the wet-fly knowledge which had been good enough to serve on the chalk stream for many generations. Skues admitted to have been dazzled by this triumph himself: he found it 'stunning, hypnotic, submerging'. He thought that, except for 'a few eccentrics', almost no one imagined that a wet fly would be of any service on the chalk stream, so great was Halford's influence. This was not quite true. As I have shown elsewhere, the evidence is clear that a number of rebels were using wet-fly methods, often with considerable success, during the era when the dry fly was on top. Skues was by no means the first to rebel against Halford – in fact it was quite some time before Skues joined in. The purpose of *Minor Tactics*, therefore, would be to tell how he had awoken from his enchanted sleep and made good his escape. In the process he had found a way of bringing the wet fly back to the chalk stream in a modern and acceptable form.

Having set out his stall in this clever and disarming way, Skues moved on to introduce his new system of accurate fishing upstream or across without drag, to fish that were evidently feeding on insects beneath the surface. It would not be any threat to current practice, he hastened to assure his readers, and would be available to supplement but not to supplant 'the beautiful art of which Mr F.M. Halford is the prophet'. Halford was paid other compliments elsewhere in the book but, as later events were to show, he was not mollified. Skues' attempts to mend bridges between them had come too late.

The first chapter of the book concerns Skues' own early experiences which had led to a dawning line of thought – that is to say the incident of the sinking Large Dark Olive in 1891 (mistakenly identified by him as 1892), and the similar event a little later with the Blue Dun with mole's fur dubbing and snipe's wing. But even in this seemingly innocent passage Halford's irritation must have been aroused, for one of Skues' basic principles appeared immediately in the text, namely that the angler should observe and experiment for himself, rather than rely blindly on tradition and authority. Dead knowledge, which was reliant on books, should be distinguished from live knowledge, which was experience and self-reliance. To a man such as Halford, who had been energetically purveying knowledge (frequently dogmatically) for a quarter of a century, this must have seemed an obviously personal reference. And the use of the word 'authority', which seemed with Skues to suggest a portentous quality, appeared several times in the book. It carried with it more opprobrium than any other term to which he could lay his pen, and in after years he scolded correspondents who incautiously applied it to him. 'Please do not call me an authority' occurred frequently in his correspondence. He was, however, quite happy to write about his former state of blindness and to admit that he had followed authority for some years before his eventual happy enlightenment. A fairly typical passage occurred at the beginning of Chapter V: 'Years ago, before the spirit of revolt was in me, when I followed as closely as I knew how the maxims of the apostles of the dry fly, and knew no other method for chalk streams, I suffered many blank days ...' Again, it would not have escaped Halford that Skues was adopting an oblique way of saying, in effect, that he was angry at the many opportunities he had missed over a long period through allowing himself to be blinded by the influence of the man everyone regarded as The Authority.

From his earliest articles and through *Minor Tactics* onwards to the end of his writing career, Skues adopted the practice of providing suggestions and advice rather than inviolable precept. He was not writing manuals of practice. In fairness to Halford, it should be said that if he had been challenged about his own books he would have pointed out that many anglers did not have the time or abilities – or perhaps even the inclination – to carry out extended experiments. So, Halford might have concluded, a manual containing rules of practice was exactly what they wanted.

A reader in 1910 might have found *Minor Tactics*, charming and stimulating though it was, to be a little confusing. It is sometimes alleged today to be a pioneer book about nymph fishing. However, artificial nymphs make only a very limited appearance in *Minor Tactics*. Skues' main weapons of attack in the years before 1910 had been the winged flies tied to sink and constructed on Scottish principles. The coloured frontispiece, praised by some critics (though not in fact liked by Skues) showed eight of these winged patterns and one nymph (an Olive). There followed four hackled flies occupying a sort of transitional position between the winged flies and the nymph. If he had written the book a few years later the main emphasis of it would have been upon nymphs alone. Even one year later Skues' mind was beginning to change radically. He wrote long afterwards that it was the hot, dry summer of 1911, when underwater fishing alone produced any result during the day, which moved him more decisively on to true nymphal forms. His useful article in *The Field* later that year, with illustrations by St Barbe Goldsmith, was the first to explain methods of constructing the new nymphs. These pictures appeared again in 1921 in *The Way of a Trout with a Fly*. It may be that he was aware of having produced a book which, however successful, was advancing a theory that was not quite complete, for in the fourth chapter he wrote defensively: 'It might be supposed .... that a hackled pattern would better suggest the nymph stage than a winged pattern. This may be true, but the theory has yet to be worked out in much detail before one can dogmatize about it.' This passage raises the interesting question, never entirely solved, of Skues' choice of the Scottish-style wet fly for his main armament in *Minor Tactics*, rather than the more advanced nymphal forms which he had briefly considered in 1888, 1891 and 1904 and then laid aside.

The matter of drag would have been examined inquisitively by the watchful purists. In a section in the fifth chapter called 'Of the Trout of Glassy Glides' he mentioned the question. Elsewhere he had already said that he did not deliberately move the nymph, but he was well aware that it did not, of itself, always follow a dead drift, and that it might be moved by pressure on the line by the current into a contrary path. This movement, if not too considerable, could be an advantage: what would be unacceptable in a dry fly might be attractive in a sunk fly. He described the case of the steep glide, smooth but rapid, often found just above a broken run, tenanted by good trout which were impregnable to the dry fly because of the drag problem but, he discovered, negotiable with the wet. It was in fact close kin to the induced take (albeit involuntary) of a later age.

Minor Tactics was not entirely about the sunk fly. The book's subtitle *and Kindred Studies* would have told the new reader to expect to find discussion of a number of other matters. There were sections on tactical studies, and on fish behaviour in many forms. Skues also referred to the light rod question, which by 1910 he treated as entirely settled: 'The light rod has won its place, and has come to stay.' For a seminal work which has always carried the reputation of opening the door to subaqueous fishing, there was also a surprising amount of material on dry-fly fishing. Artificial nymphs only made a fairly limited appearance, in fact on only five pages out of a total of 133. Ken Robson wrote: 'These are, undoubtedly, the most sensational pages in the book, and must have sent shock waves out to the ranks of Halford's disciples' (Robson (1998), p. 81). In this section Skues began with the Tup's Indispensable and his discovery (also accidental, it seems) that it answered well as a wet version. Eventually he began to convert it into several nymph patterns by adapting Austin's original design. In one variation the dubbing consisted of medium olive seal's fur and bear's hair on primrose silk, the legs a single turn of the blue hackle from the merlin, and the short, soft whisk from the spade hackle of a blue dun cock. He then plunged on rather incautiously to deal with ideas that most anglers of that time would find alarmingly radical, such as the Alder Larva. At least he had avoided describing it in detail: having regard to the trailing tracheal gills on either side of the abdomen, his pattern would probably have been tied as a palmer. It had worked effectively one day in Germany, and his three samples were quickly worn out. But what could be permissible in fun-fishing in Germany would not do at Abbots Barton: 'It was not quite the game to imitate the insect at this stage,' he conceded.

Years later Brigadier H.E. Carey wrote of the alder on the upper Hampshire Avon in his book *One River*: 'I have not felt it lawful under our rules to fish it sunk.' Carey, a good friend to nymph patterns derived from up-winged flies, was the Secretary of the Officers' Fishing Association, on whose water Frank Sawyer was keeper for many years. A hostility to the sunk alder persisted into modern times and has not yet faded away everywhere. Perhaps Skues was wise in 1910 to conclude by writing 'I am therefore not giving my recipe. Nor do I give that for making a caddis or gentle which I once tried, with mad success for a few minutes, but gave up, conscience-stricken.' This rapturous experiment took place on the Teme in 1895. It would have been, to contemporaries, the most startling part of the book. It was also slightly confusing. Gentle is the name for the larva of the house fly, a terrestrial creature, in other words a maggot. It is not synonymous with the larva of the caddis, although it may resemble it superficially.

This dynamite-section closes with mention of the artificial shrimp, but Skues was careful to claim not to have actually used any of his experimental shrimp patterns. He certainly did some years later, but without making much reference to the fact. He was well aware of the often-heard objection, that a shrimp was not a fly, which many believed at the time to be a serious objection.

Minor Tactics contained many examples of practice, but eventually returned to questions of definition and principle in a section called 'Ethics of the Wet Fly'. Skues recorded that, in conversations with other (no doubt purist) anglers, they would remark in a shocked tone: 'But that is wet-fly', as if it were 'a high crime and misdemeanour to use a wet fly on a chalk stream'. How, he asked, had the wet fly come to be so discredited?

First, it was widely believed to be unsuccessful on chalk streams, a belief he considered from his experience that he was entitled to deny. It was also accused of being 'a duffer's game', not, one imagines, in terms of results, or the two judgements would exclude each other, but because of the clumsiness of the technique. This would mean casting across and down, often with more than one fly, resulting in pricking and scaring trout, catching many undersized fish, disturbing too much water and, as a result, spoiling the sport of other anglers. All this, Skues conceded, was true of clumsy downstream wet-fly fishing in the old style, and had no relevance to the technique he was describing. The wet fly was much like its dry counterpart, except that it was more sparsely dressed and caused to sink, and was cast upstream or across to individual fish. He slightly spoilt the effect of this last definition by adding a candid but, in the mental climate of the day, unwise admission. It was, he thought, permissible to cast 'to places where it is reasonable to expect that a fish of suitable proportions may be found'. This was something that was bound to excite disapproval among the purists looking for weak points in his argument. As late as 1938, at the debate in the Flyfishers' Club, one speaker thoroughly objected to speculative casting even with a dry fly into 'likely places', as well as with a nymph.

The important argument of the book was that the new art could restore the wet fly to the chalk stream in a fresh and more delicate and discreet form that would not be subject to any of the objections raised by the purists, and which, especially in high summer, was less likely to disturb the water than a dry fly.

A further advantage was that by fishing over trout moving to underwater creatures, or even just casting to likely places, the amount of fishing time in an otherwise slow day would be extended. Skues was well aware that not every angler was a private gentleman living on his own means who could come to the river at any time. There were many others in his position, tied to professional work during the week, who had to take their days when they could. It was unreasonable to condemn them to a day of bankside loitering because there was no hatch of fly. Even if a hatch developed, bulgers swirling over the weed beds, or perhaps, at a later stage, fish moving quietly at nymphs near the surface could be fished for, sometimes for an hour or so, before the first hatched flies were being taken.

This interesting section closes with another polite contention with the master:

> Mr F.M. Halford, with every desire to be absolutely fair, has, I think, in Chapter II of "Dry-Fly Fishing in Theory and Practice", done more than any other man to discredit the wet fly on chalk streams, by the implications, first, that the principle of the dry-fly method – viz., the casting of the fly to a feeding fish in position – is not applicable to the wet-fly method, and secondly, that on the stillest days, with the hottest sun and the clearest water, the wet fly is utterly hopeless. On both these points I respectfully join issue with him.

The final chapter, called 'Apologia', finds Skues bowing out and about to withdraw behind the curtain, but unable to resist the odd Parthian shot in the usual direction. Again he warns his readers against relying on any authority, 'whether it be that of Mr F.M. Halford or another'. At the end of this chapter and indeed the book he leaves a testamentary statement about his own liberal and to us very modern view about his work and influence:

> In giving records of my own experience by the water-side rather than in laying down a system, I am not asking others to do as I do because I say it, or to accept anything from me. I would have no weight allowed by any man to tradition or authority until it is proved by himself; no man's words accepted as final because they are his; everything questioned, tested, and brought to the dock of practical experience. If I have ventured, indirectly, to preach at all, the sum of my preaching is not a system, a method, but an attitude of mind – the importance of being earnest, the power of faith, the observant eye, the unfettered judgment, independence of tradition, and above all, the inquiring mind.

In the area of general ideas rather than specific points, this is one of the finest things that Skues ever wrote. It expresses his position or credo in fly-fishing. It could equally stand for a reasonable enough guide for life in general. Taken together, these two texts provide an essential clue in understanding two men and two very different and unfortunately antagonistic approaches.

Skues had for some years been trying to correct Halford in some points of detail, and to warn him off from trying to belittle his own achievement in restoring the sunk fly. But, in attacking Halford's somewhat oppressive handling of doctrine and mode of writing and preaching, he was getting much nearer to making a personal attack. Halford may have thought that the younger man was trying to supplant him in the leadership of the chalk-stream movement. It is doubtful if Skues was really trying to do this, but he was clearly irritated by Halford's rather over-developed self-belief. As with the slave crouching behind the victorious general processing in his chariot in triumph through the streets of ancient Rome, he felt it was his role from time to time to whisper to Halford: 'Remember thou art mortal.'

In the few days following publication of his book, Skues distributed several presentation copies. One of the first went to his old school. The copy in the library of Winchester College bears the date of 12 March, and sits alongside *The Way of a Trout with a Fly* and *Sidelines, Sidelights and Reflections*. Close at hand rest the books of Halford: *Dry-Fly Fishing in Theory and Practice*, *Dry-fly Entomology* and *Modern Development of the Dry Fly*. Once metaphorically locked in combat, these old volumes now sleep upon the shelves in silent reconciliation and goodwill, a past chapter in angling history while, nearby on the Itchen, anglers, probably without reflecting on the once-great controversy, apply the systems of both antagonists, now long dead.

Sheringham, who had long ago adopted a liberal and pragmatic attitude to chalk-stream fishing, wrote warmly and generously of this striking new publication in *The Field*. Skues had published extensively in it, and some of his pieces had provided material for *Minor Tactics*, so Sheringham began his long notice of the book by explaining that he felt debarred from providing a full critical review. He nevertheless managed to indicate a good measure of approval:

> Readers who have already learnt to look above the signature of "Seaforth and Soforth" for articles in which suggestive trains of thought are followed with logical clearness, in which useful hints as to flies, tackle, or methods are given freely, and in which the saving grace of humour has a prominent place, may turn to Mr Skues' book with full confidence of finding all these excellencies as prominent as ever.

His fishing did not include the clumsy raking of two big flies in windy conditions, Sheringham continued. The new method was subtle and delicate and a good way of achieving success on an otherwise hopeless day. He identified a drawback however: 'One conclusion is that all this is a mighty difficult business' – a sixth sense on the part of the angler is needed to know when to connect with a fish. But overall he believed that:

> Altogether there is more variety between these covers than is often found in volumes of thrice the bulk. That the book is one of the most important yet written on the subject of chalk-stream fishing our account of it will have suggested. Its author says something new and opens fresh fields of exploration to the angler who cares to enter them.

Altogether a notice of unmixed praise from a discerning writer who had begun by saying that, for reasons of propriety, he was not really going to write a review.

R.B. Marston, another angler who was at ease about the sunk fly in the chalk country, even though he was not quite convinced that it worked there, gave a kind reception to *Minor Tactics*. Although, as with Sheringham, he began by indicating that he was not about to write a review as such, the main effort being left to E.M. Tod in a later issue, he was sufficiently carried away by his enthusiasm and fascination with the new book to provide an account – whether review or no – running to three and a half columns of his own opinions. In dealing with the sunk fly, he noted, rather damagingly for Halford's point of view:

> Mr Halford states most positively that the thing cannot be done, that the difficulties are insuperable, the fish will not look at this imitation in this way. Surely it follows, then, that if somebody comes along and, after years of experiment, proves conclusively that it *can* be done, so far as *art* goes, it must be a finer art, than deceiving a trout with a fly fished dry.

He mentions three matters where issue might be taken. He had an anxiety about the slaughterous possibilities of the new art, at least in capable hands. If fish were to be open to attack from wet as well as dry flies, the period of danger for them during an angling day would be greatly extended and they would never have any peace. This was to be another point urged against the practice in the debate of 1938. Marston also mentioned the difficulty of responding to the subtle take of a fish to wet fly. And he warned that many anglers simply believed the dry fly to be the summit of the art and did not wish to know any other. Nevertheless this was a supportive article.

Perhaps the most generous article of all came a month later from the pen of E.M. Tod in *The Fishing Gazette*. Ewan Tod, the former bank manager from Leeds and expert in the wet-fly lore of Yorkshire and the North, was already a confirmed follower of Skues. He had previously shown his colours in a slashing review of the second (1899) edition of Halford's *Dry-Fly Fishing in Theory and Practice*, with damaging phrases such as 'self-satisfied complacency'. *Minor Tactics* fascinated him from the first page, and he gave it the unusual amount of five columns, or well over 4,000 words. Tod welcomed the sunk fly as 'a powerful auxiliary to the dry fly', noticed the abundant evidence of Skues' accurate observation of trout behaviour, and the reasoning that he derived from it, and admired the examples of his 'generalship' in dealing with complex angling situations. Tod's review must stand as one of the most admiring and laudatory notices ever written of an angling book. It is therefore all the more surprising to find at the end of it: 'I trust that nothing I have said may wound the author in any way.' He entered one small caveat, that the book would not have much value for the streams outside the chalk country, but conceded that Skues had not intended it to be applicable anywhere else.

There were one or two querulous letters in the press. Two appeared in *The Fishing Gazette* at the beginning of April. A correspondent, sheltering behind the pseudonym of 'Hyandry', referred to Marston's point of over-fishing: 'the time has arrived when we must husband what is left of our chalk streams in every possible way'. He was also sorry to see Skues recommending the practice of 'fishing the water'. Another correspondent, A. Severn, was worried about the new art leading to other methods, including the use of strange lures such as 'an artificial water shrimp (or something worse)' and referred to 'the most terrible poaching things sold for this kind of fishing, which must result in fish hooked foul'.

'Hyandry' had not finished with Skues. On 16 April he returned with another objection, one which was to recur in angling journals and no doubt in discussions in clubs and fishing huts for the next half-century. It was a matter of interpreting a definition: how could a device used beneath the surface be defined as a fly? By definition a fly lived in the air, not in the water. Many anglers were impressed by this piece of logic-chopping, and it was to come back at Skues more than two decades later.

Skues can be seen, therefore, to have got off fairly lightly with the critics. Later mentions of the events of 1910 have sometimes alleged that there was a storm of controversy over the book, with much bitterness, vicious attacks in the press and broken friendships. It has become accepted fact in angling folklore. This is, however, incorrect, and has probably arisen from a careless copying of some brief allusion to the later conflict in the 1930s. Controversy did eventually arise, but not for many years – not, in fact, until the mid-thirties, when it had a good run leading up to the 1938 debate. When a second edition of *Minor Tactics* was published in 1914 Skues was able to add a note at the beginning recording his surprise that:

> In the fifty or so Press notices, short and long, I find, without exception, an absence of the harsh word, and a pervading urbane and kindly spirit which is of the true Waltonian still. Such fault as has been found has in the main been that I have shown undue timidity in dealing with the pretensions of the dry-fly purist ... I take leave to hope that the interval since the first publication of "Minor Tactics" has brought a good few of them round to the view that, without ousting the dry fly from pride of place as major tactics of the chalk stream, the wet fly has its subsidiary, but still important, place of honour in chalk-stream fishing.

The one review that would have aroused his interest and apprehension did not appear. The idea of presenting Halford with a copy of *Minor Tactics* may have given Skues pause for thought, having mentioned his sometime friend several times in the text. Might it not look too obviously personal or challenging? Or perhaps he thought the High Priest might at last be converted, or at least set possible personal feelings on one side and treat the subject objectively. We cannot know, but he hesitated for nearly three weeks before sending him a copy, even though he must have known that a friendly response was unlikely.

Halford, however, already had a copy, which he had purchased fairly soon after publication. He may have been a little surprised, having regard to the coolness existing between them, also to receive one from the author, with a compliment in the customary classical form on the fly leaf: 'F.M. Halford ex dono G.E.M. Skues 31 March 1910'. He passed on his first copy to Martin Mosely and settled down to read the second.

Halford's state of mind as he worked through the book was not recorded, at least as far as is known, but a good deal can be inferred from other factors which we can know. He must have felt a sense of alarm as he began to read what was clearly an attack upon an important element of his system. He would have begun to take stock of it and to marshal his arguments in his mind. By 1910, indeed for years before, he had decided that he did not like Skues. For some time, perhaps up to 1896 as I have previously suggested, Skues' comments about his mistakes were received by Halford without rancour. After all, many of them were small points. As Skues himself once wrote, Mr Halford was a good-natured man. As late as 1904, in a speech at the annual dinner of the Flyfishers' Club, Halford had praised the work of Skues and Fred Ohlson on the sub-committee which looked after the Club's collection of fly-dressing materials. This was a magnanimous gesture. Only a month earlier Skues had picked out a small point for criticism in Halford's recently published autobiography. It would not have improved things that a little earlier, when Halford was known to be pondering a title for his book, Skues had suggested what he imagined would be a humorous form of words: 'Attachments and Detachments of a Badger'. Halford responded to this suggestion with some asperity. It was a predictable encounter between a man whose wit did not always commend itself to everyone and someone who had no sense of humour at all.

There was one criticism in particular to which, once he had raised it, Skues returned endlessly. It concerned the correct identification of the Welshman's Button. Halford had applied this name to the small day-time sedge fly *Sericostoma personatum*, which can be a useful alternative on the river when chalk-stream trout are gorged with mayfly. Skues objected several times to what he considered a misuse of the name. In 1908 he wrote a letter on the subject for *The Field*, as well as an article in *The Fishing Gazette*, criticizing Halford for misleading the angling public and pointing out that the name had, from the eighteenth century, been applied to a beetle. Halford countered that all chalk-stream fishermen had accepted the name for the sedge fly, and such was the power of his name that it remained. We have here another interesting example of the essential difference between the two men. Skues, with his deep knowledge of angling history, had discovered a great deal of evidence about the Welsh beetle. By contrast, Halford never had much use for the historical background to angling – his preoccupation was always with the present. Skues returned several times, both during Halford's lifetime and after his death, to a question to which most anglers had probably become indifferent. Skues was still pertinaciously raising it in the 1920s, and it surfaced again in 1939, when Martin Mosely was on hand to defend his old mentor.

These small pinpricks continued through the first decade of the century. They were not all in one direction. Halford began to disparage the Tup's Indispensable. It did not fit into his rigid system, and he was tired of hearing glowing accounts of its success from the pen of his rival. It was, he maintained, a fancy fly and of very limited use. But he was sufficiently shaken by the well-known reputation of the fly to break his iron rule of only using his 'New Patterns' at Mottisfont and to give the Tup some secret trials. And when, in 1905, he intervened in the argument about American rods, no one could have been surprised to find him in opposition to Skues, with a piece in *The Field* bearing the scoffing title 'The Light Rod Craze'. He had been upset by the large number of British anglers who were praising the American makers, and even more so that Skues had appointed himself their chorus leader. Some firm intervention was called for. He had been handing out advice on rods as upon every other aspect of fly-fishing, and his preference had always been for weapons of extreme power, even if they involved a good deal of weight. His two Eaton and Deller rods, made for him in 1882, were still in use, although he had made some concession to changing ideas by having them cut down three times. These fearsome weapons were originally 10ft 6in long and were, by 1905, down to 9ft 6in, with a weight of 12½oz. He was obviously proud of the power of these dinosaur-rods, and was irritated that they were of the type ridiculed by Skues and other correspondents in the journals. It was only after he had been exposed to three years of light-rod discussion in the press that he resolved to try one of them.

As was usual with Halford, he went into the test with reluctance, and in a half-hearted manner which was likely to prejudice any chance of an open-minded result. It was a cardinal point with him to reach a conclusion after a good deal of research, and then stay with it. So, as might have been predicted, he was not about to send for one of the new very light Leonard rods. Instead he purchased a more substantial example of 9ft 9in weighing 8½oz. He took the opinion of J.J. Hardy, and together they proceeded to disparage it. They decided (incorrectly) that its lighter weight was achieved entirely by a great reduction in the weight of the fittings and the handle. A trial on the river reassured him that British was best: he believed that a Hardy copy of one of his old Eaton and Deller rods performed better than the Leonard which, he thought, required more force to drive a heavy line across the river.

This in-fighting, much of it on small points, seems to the modern eye to be a little foolish. But these men were more than just enthusiastic anglers: they had made angling their main purpose in life. To them these things were important. And, for Halford, the position of leader of the chalk-stream movement was very dear to him, and to be constantly lectured by a man he had once looked upon as a recruit and disciple had become too much.

If anyone had ever buttonholed Skues and suggested that he should leave Halford alone, he would no doubt have explained that this was how the business of sorting out difficult and interesting problems was carried on. There was nothing personal about the expression of contrary views. Sentiment and personal feelings ought to be immaterial: only ice-cold logic would serve. Skues was probably more able to adopt this line in life than most people. He was familiar with the spectacle, always a matter of curiosity to outsiders, of barristers spending a morning tussling in court and lunching as friends afterwards. The need to shut out personalities in a dispute was, and is, a fairly familiar argument. One has to look pleasant, even though that adjective does not always quite describe one's inner feelings. But in this case the criticisms must have seemed rather frequent, and Halford would have been less than human if he had not wondered if there was not, in fact, something personal going on.

However, although towards the end of the 1890s a coolness had grown up between them, Halford still kept his temper, outwardly at least. By that time he had a considerable prestige in the angling world, and so had the dry fly. For many in the south it was 'normal' procedure. His fellow authors deferred to him, and would insert into their texts remarks such as 'you cannot do better than follow Mr Halford's advice about flies'. He had devoted his life to setting up a system which would provide workable methods for everyone. Skues, however, had for some time been undermining that system by dismantling some of the details, no doubt in a disinterested search for truth. But in the last years of the nineteenth century there was something different, when Skues began his occasional wet-fly attempts. This was not peripheral but central to Halford's doctrine, particularly as he knew quite well that it was being practised by other anglers on chalk streams. In the eyes of the purists, Skues was giving encouragement to this process: he had over-reached himself. At last the master had a clear objective, and a salvo was delivered in 1906 at the man and the practice. It had, however, been preceded by a chain of disapproval at first, that developed into hostility. This was not his first pronouncement: he had written a fairly mild article on the subject in the same journal in 1886. In an article in 1899 he adopted a more severe line. In 1906 he fairly lost his temper altogether. The sunk fly was not simply of little or no use on the chalk stream; it was improper, even morally wrong.

It is worth examining the stages in Halford's thinking, because his various pronouncements were to dog the footsteps of Skues for the rest of his life, and to have a profound effect on the course of angling history.

When Halford joined the Houghton Fly-Fishing Club in 1877, his chalk-stream education was still at an early stage. There were dry-fly fishermen in the Club, but others still practised the old method of fishing wet downstream with long, double-handed rods, although some may have fished upstream in the manner of Stewart. Fishing on the Test was in a period of flux, and Halford would have seen various styles in use. At first he may have been pragmatic in his approach, and probably took a little time to settle to his well-known style. The first page of his diary, which began in 1879, records him using a wet Alexandra, a technique which later in his career he would have regarded as contemptible. It is amusing to find him, in 1889, reflecting with prim horror in *Dry Fly Fishing in Theory and Practice*: 'What a profanation to bestow on this monstrosity the name of one of the most charming and amiable princesses of this century.' He and Marryat certainly used other sunk forms, but Halford does not appear to have had much success. To fish the wet fly upstream is a difficult skill and not given to everyone. Even with the dry fly, results for Halford came rather slowly, in spite of a great deal of concentrated effort. He was never going to be an intuitive performer, and to the end of his life he was always better at theory than practice. There was none of the quick perception and imaginative reach of a Marryat or a Skues. It is, for example, difficult to imagine him writing anything like the well-known piece of subtle guidance written by Skues in the *Flyfishers' Journal* about responding to the almost impalpable signs of a fish that has taken a fly under water ('The Draw', 'The Flash or Gleam', etc.).

So Halford seems, quite early in his angling life, to have found it simpler to reject the wet fly. It was better to concentrate on the dry fly, the details of which he had begun to describe in the pages of *The Field* from the mid-1880s, and to treat all wet-fly fishing as clumsy behaviour.

Much later, his way of rationalizing his practice during this earlier period of his life was to admit that he and Marryat had killed a few fish on sunk fly, but desisted after a while, thinking it improper to use such tactics 'on waters *reserved for dry fly*' (my italics: no discussion followed as to how chalk streams had come to be reserved exclusively for the dry fly).

An honest, frank memoir from Marryat might have given posterity a very different version. Marryat probably achieved a great deal with the wet fly on chalk streams, no doubt when Halford was not standing by watching him. He was, however, on one notable occasion taken by surprise when Halford unexpectedly came round a corner. I have recorded this event in *F.M. Halford and the Dry-Fly Revolution*. On that day Halford, Marryat and a third (unnamed) angler were fishing at Newton Stacey on the Test on a day when the mayfly were thick on the water. Halford, who was fishing on another part of the river, had achieved little, and went in search of his friends for a consultation. What followed had a comic element that must have been entirely lost on Halford, who was not famous for his sense of humour. The two rods had between them captured eleven trout for 27lb. Marryat explained – could he have had tongue in cheek? – that they had both been using a small fly, 'half dry', so that it began to sink as it came downstream to the fish. Marryat's playful style was well known – it frequently went with a deadpan countenance. Halford solemnly recorded this in an article in *The Field*: 'The reason for this idiosyncrasy neither of us could fathom, as anything more opposed to the action of the fly could not be imagined.' This baffled comment is enough to show that Halford had not grasped the significance of fish taking emerging flies.

Halford and the wet fly were never going to come to a successful partnership. Lacking the skill needed, he could not accept that the method was of much service. He came to this opinion quite early and held to it for the remainder of his life. If he could not do a thing, he honestly believed that no one else could. His strong measure of self-belief was one of his most striking characteristics.

The articles of 1886, 1887, 1899 and 1906 give valuable clues as to the changing and eventual congealing of Halford's mind on this topic over time. In 1886 Halford's approach had been one of practical efficiency. In a piece in *The Field* in February he insists as his main point that the sunk fly does not work – he simply does not want the angler to waste his time on the river. He did not deny that the sunk fly might catch a fish or two on certain days, but it was a matter of chance and not a result upon which one could rely.

This passage was more or less repeated in *Dry-Fly Fishing in Theory and Practice* (1889), in a chapter called 'Floating Flies and Sunk Flies'. Parts of this chapter have been admired by later writers and quoted, mistakenly as it seems to me, as examples of Halford's tolerant attitude. It is true that the chapter includes one of his usual disclaimers designed to disarm opposition: 'In treating of the advantages of dry-fly over wet-fly fishing, I am most desirous of avoiding any expression which should tend to depreciate in any way the skill exhibited by the experienced and intelligent followers of the wet-fly.' And he goes on to quote the well-known dictum of Francis Francis: 'The judicious and perfect application of dry, wet, and mid-water fly-fishing stamps the finished fly-fisher with the hall-mark of efficiency.' If one reads further, one finds that this is a piece of Halfordian sophistry, and has no reference to chalk streams. He continues: 'Whatever advantages can be claimed for the sunk fly elsewhere, however, there are streams and conditions of weather in which it cannot be considered as having the smallest chance against the floating fly.' So that is his position: he has nothing against the sunk fly in its proper place, that is to say, well away from the chalk country. It has been a mistake in modern times to find tolerance in this area of his writing.

Another passage in an article in *The Field* in September 1887 cast a long shadow into the future, and raised its head at the nymph debate at The Flyfishers' Club in 1938, long after Halford's death. He described a common enough scene on the river – trout feeding ravenously underwater, swimming vigorously around making waves and bulges in the water in pursuit of free-swimming nymphs:

> Some readers may inquire why the dun in the nymphal state should not be imitated ... it is my opinion that the difficulty does not lie in dressing an artificial grub fairly resembling the dun nympha, but in imparting to that imitation the motion and direction taken by the natural insect at that stage of its existence. Some authorities recommend the use of a large sunk fly when trying bulging fish, but personally I have never found this advice of any assistance ... On rare occasions one hears of a brace or two of bulging trout, or grayling, having been killed by a comparative novice with a wet fly dragging, or even fished downstream: and once or twice I have positively seen such a thing occur [He may have been thinking of

Major Carlisle or Thomas Andrews, both keen wet-fly men on the Test].

Once again, the sunk fly is condemned as a waste of time. Halford is not, at this date anyway, regarding it as unethical – although there is a hint that it is inappropriate in the reference to 'a comparative novice' (who would know no better) and in his show of astonishment at the occasional success of such a crude procedure. He drives home his lesson by stating his view that attempts to deal with bulgers will not be made by 'the more experienced and probably the more earnest votary of the art'.

The use of language in this passage was therefore likely to attract support, as was the encouragement not to toy with bulgers – would not every angler reading this immediately make a resolve to be numbered in the ranks of the 'experienced and earnest votaries of the art'? Halford's writings are less readable than those of Skues, but his words could, at times, be deployed effectively.

Most significant of all was the reference to the mobility of the ascending nymph. In later writings he would express it more colloquially, quoting Marryat's view that 'one could imitate the nymph but not the wriggle'. Some modern writers have taken this seriously as a maxim, although it may only have been one of Marryat's witticisms or merely a casual remark at the time. But it was taken literally and with enthusiasm by many in and outside the purist ranks, and was to carry serious implications for Skues' work for decades.

In March 1899 Halford returned once more to the question of the sunk fly. His opinion had hardened over the years, and his approach now was one of reproof rather than friendly advice. Even the title of the piece, 'The Ethics of the Dry Fly', sufficiently indicated his new angle of approach. The wet fly was not merely ineffective; it was a breach of the code of good sportsmanship: 'No doubt anything like fishing the stream either with sunk or floating fly is an unmitigated nuisance on the chalk stream. It rarely fills the angler's basket, and will, if persevered in, render the trout so shy as to be almost unapproachable.' Those who were content to wait patiently until the rise comes on were termed 'the most advanced school among dry-fly fishermen', an appealing idea to readers, who would no doubt at once wish to be described as such.

An important element in Halford's world view was that a chalk-stream fishery was a jittery place where highly strung fish could easily be stampeded or simply rendered mistrustful and impossible to catch. This is why he and 'the advanced school' had outlawed the older brand of wet-fly fishing. For him it was just bungling, and he never changed his view about that. In any case, he insisted, was not dry-fly fishing the most delicate and satisfying method? What was the angler's true purpose in his pursuit? Did he not, in fact, wish to do something reasonably challenging? The object of fishing was not just to catch fish. And Halford, the successful businessman, identified the economic factor, which would have met with approval in many quarters. It was because the practice of the dry fly was so attractive that people were prepared to pay good money for it, an important argument for owners worried about serious loss of income from land as a result of the agricultural depression. They would therefore be unlikely to welcome wet-fly fishermen on their waters. Even Theodore Gordon wrote to Skues that he could see the force of Halford's argument (which may not have pleased him).

In 1906 there appeared in *The Field* over Halford's signature a much more aggressive article than anything written by him in 1887 or 1899, as well as being more personal. It was his most extreme attempt so far to make safe and hold on to the protocol of correct behaviour which he hoped was already in place. For some time he must have been observing, with mounting alarm, evidence of widespread mutiny against the guidelines he had so carefully laid down. The writings of Skues were not the only threat to his peace of mind. There was a long file of rebels who preferred to think for themselves and to sink the fly when it seemed appropriate. It has sometimes been said that the purist dominated in the chalk country in the years before the Great War. J.W. Hills wrote that in 1902 'he reigned a despot: nothing was admitted but the dry fly'. However, this is far too sweeping a statement: clearly Hills did not know what was happening in some quarters. Most alarming of all must have been the fact that, prior to Sheringham, the last three angling editors of *The Field* in succession had not, by any means, been as sound on the matter as he would have hoped. Francis Francis fished wet or dry according to the conditions. So did William Senior and C.H. Cook ('John Bickerdyke'). R.B. Marston, who had at first been an admirer of Halford's work, kept an open mind about some aspects of it, and gave increasing support to Skues as each season passed. Halford may have regarded Sheringham as the worst threat. To have the current angling editor of the paper in which all his journalism had appeared for years giving open support to Skues must have been the worst blow. It had become necessary to rise up and smite the opposition.

In this piece 'Sunk Fly on Dry Fly Streams', Halford proceeded to ignore the delicacy of the practice (which Skues had been careful to describe in detail in his articles), and to misrepresent it even more forcibly. He drew an imaginary picture of an owner fixing a date with a guest to come and fish: no doubt he had in mind his own fishery at Mottisfont. If the day turned out to be propitious, with flies hatching, fish rising and taking hold, 'then everything is *couleur de rose*'. Unfortunately, he admits, such occasions are not common. This was an unwise admission, and good ammunition for the other side, for one of the important arguments for the use of the sunk fly was that it gave the angler a better chance on an otherwise hopeless day. Halford then, not for the first time, describes with approval the correct reaction of the true purist: 'The past master will in such case possess his soul in patience and wait for the appearance of the duns, and if they should be conspicuous by their absence, will shrug his shoulders and hope for better luck next time.' He reserves his scorn for the man 'who is not so able to bear up under adversity'. Such a one cannot wait to start fishing and proceeds to the top of the fishery and flogs it steadily downstream with a wet fly. Such tactics, he insists, were in the very worst of taste. No 'old hand' would do such a thing, 'because he knows that the unwritten law of the dry fly purist on a Hampshire chalk stream is to eschew any but the legitimate method'. The visitor may fluke the odd fish, 'and go away and talk of having wiped the eye of the dry fly man, or even fly into print, and announce, *orbi et urbi* [sic – Halford's mistake: the quotation is *urbi et orbi*], that he has made the discovery that sunk fly will at times kill on the south country chalk stream.' This is of course, he concluded, a delusion.

Again the use of language is artful. The terms 'past master' and 'old hand' are inserted. The man who cannot cope with the disappointment of a hopeless day is not only guilty of impatience and bad manners, he is lacking in moral fibre in not being able to endure adversity. Further, he is a vainglorious exhibitionist, who cannot wait to go public and boast of having solved a problem through a chance success. And, worst of all, the imaginary angler here described with such scorn is a guest! The behaviour of this abandoned character is thus dramatically contrasted with the self-abnegation of the 'past master' or the 'old hand'. By the use of such language were the faithful kept in awe and new converts corralled with them.

As with many of Halford's pronouncements, there was some truth in what he was saying, but he spoilt his case by a combination of

over-emphasis and misleading statements. In particular, in order to show
up the wet-fly user as unsafe on the river, he had to depict him as a clumsy
down-streamer. He considered that it had been an important part of his
life's work to have outlawed such practitioners from the chalk stream.
But in so doing he had set up a straw target, for Skues had made it clear
that blind fishing downstream was not what he was doing. Even so, there
were some points in Halford's article that might have made a reader
thoughtful. There is some substance in the criticism of the over-active
angler, restlessly pacing the bank and irritating others fishing the river.
Such a one was effectively lampooned by William Caine in *An Angler at
Large* (1911) in the fictional (but relevant) character of Blennerhassett. It
still resonates today.

Skues was not named in Halford's article, but there could have been
no doubt in any reader's mind as to who was in his gunsight. Halford
knew what he was doing: after this the two men could never be friends
again.

The last two attacks must have indicated to Skues what he was up
against. The forces of prejudice were being marshalled against him, and
they had a leader who was not above making unfair points. He replied in
The Field a week later, correcting Halford's factual errors, and claiming
that the delight of responding to the underwater take of the trout was
equal to that of the surface rise to the floating fly. Halford did not reply.

Skues must have been aware that Halford had played a new and
dangerous card, that of morality. In 1886 and 1887 the wet-fly user had
been told that he was wasting his time and spoiling his own chances.
Now he was being told that he was spoiling the chances of his fellow rods
as well, by breaching what Halford called the 'unwritten law' of the chalk
stream. His attack therefore came from two different angles. Readers
who might resist a piece of moral teaching could be approached by way
of the etiquette argument. This accorded well with many of the concep-
tions, or perhaps the obsessions, of the age. Throughout the nineteenth
century golf, tennis, and a host of other leisure pursuits acquired their
rule books, so that there was more and more to learn. The correct code of
social behaviour within a country sport became as important as mere
skill. Not to know these rules would mark one out as ignorant and
socially suspect. In an age which was probably the most class-conscious
in history this was a very powerful influence. Social life was hedged about
with a multitude of little rules. It is true that there was a more genuine
and worthy side of social etiquette, having been developed to smooth

social relations and to avoid giving pain to one's fellow beings. But, for many people, it was a way of appraising the badges or signs that would enable one to identify the social class of an individual. To be considered not to belong to the right group was unthinkable. Children of well-to-do families were reared in this atmosphere, with constant reminders from parents as to 'how it's done'. The refinements of conduct must have seemed endless: it was important to know how to enter a room, how to be introduced, to master all the modes of address to people of different rank, or to manage an introduction. Even such matters as the exact size of a visiting card, the length of time of an afternoon call or the mode of holding a teacup could be worrying. It is doubtful if anyone in the nineteenth century lost money from publishing an etiquette book.

It was therefore a clever stroke on Halford's part to bring etiquette into his system, by suggesting that the use of the wet fly on the chalk stream was dubious in terms not only of one's efficiency as an angler and of moral behaviour, but also of one's social status. It would strike a chord of unease and worry in the mind. A fundamental part of his argument was that fish were pricked or lightly hooked, and therefore made shy by the practice of wet-fly fishing. The highest praise at that date was to call someone an unselfish angler. By employing the wet fly, the fishing was spoilt for other anglers, therefore wet-fly fishing was selfish and, most importantly, not the act of a gentleman.

The reaction of Halford as he began to look into Skues' book needs to be seen against this long and developing background. Skues cannot have been unaware of this, but he resolved nevertheless to send a complimentary copy to Halford. Did he hope that he could rely on the soothing effect of his non-confrontational style, which he had been at such pains to employ? If so, there was no foundation for his optimism. Halford had made up his mind about Skues. He was defending himself as well as his life's work.

There were other factors about Skues' first book that were likely to increase alarm in Halford's mind. In several ways 1910–11 was not a good time for Halford. He had, for some time, been preparing what he intended to be the last book of his career, *Modern Development of the Dry Fly*. Here would be set out his final testament, the result of decades of work. He had settled upon his idea of the contents of the fly-box – the essential team of thirty-three chalk-stream patterns. He had laboured for some years over this, and the materials had been selected with enormous care. He considered that the excellence of his 'New Patterns', as he called them, had been conclusively proved by tests going back to 1903 on the lower Itchen and from 1905 at his laboratory-fishery on the Test at Mottisfont.

Unfortunately, Halford's new book did not have a good start. The publication had been confidently planned for 1910, but matters did not turn out that way. Skues' book was first off the press, which was annoying, but that was nothing to what followed. Halford's book was beset with problems of production, serious delays took place, and it did not appear in 1910 at all. This rather odd story has been told in more detail in my introduction to an edition of *Modern Development of the Dry Fly* produced in 2005 by the Flyfisher's Classic Library. In summary the problem lay in the constant intervention of Halford in the production process, mainly over the quality of the colour plates. Eventually the complete book came out at the end of February 1911, even though the title page, already printed, still bore the date 1910. It had cost Halford (and Messrs Routledge) many months of irritation.

But his cup was still not full. Halford must have hoped that his last offering to the public would be received with respectful tenderness. His heart must have sunk when he opened his copy of *The Fishing Gazette* on 18 March and saw the familiar name of 'Val Conson', whose review he most feared. Here was a review of more than three thousand words, not many of which were complimentary. The beginning was kindly enough, describing the book as 'brilliant, stimulating and interesting from cover to cover'. This welcome did not last long – six lines, in fact. Then Skues got down to serious matters:

> Yet some malign influence has always dogged Mr Halford and persuaded him not to do what would have added enormously to the interest and value of his successive works dealing with flies and fly dressing, namely, to illustrate, life-size, in colour, side by side with the coloured artificial he portrays, the insects of which they purport to be imitations.

This ideal arrangement was used with great success by Ronalds, but had not been adopted in any of Halford's three previous books with plates of artificials. This would have greatly enhanced their appearance, and would also have given the beginner some idea of what he should aim at in fly-dressing. Halford would have been further affronted at being reminded in the second paragraph that he was, after all, the Chairman of the Natural Fly Committee at the Flyfishers' Club, as if to imply that he ought to know better.

Then followed a minute and exhaustive analysis of the thirty-three 'New Patterns', now no longer exactly new, having first made their appearance in *The Field* some years earlier. What followed must have read (and reads today) like a lengthy reprimand. The questions rained down: Why was the grannom not included? Why use condor quill 'to the entire sacrifice of translucency'? Why was dubbing rejected, with the excuse that it absorbs water, floatant now being easily available? What about seals' fur and mohair, both more water-repellent? Why wind the silk the reverse way from that employed by the professionals? Why perform the winging operation in such an inefficient way? Why recommend the Thompson vice, which was so difficult to obtain in Britain? And if Halford was aiming at exact imitation, as seemed likely from the 'extreme meticulosity' of his designs, then why put on hackle so thickly – two hackles for small flies, three for mayflies – to imitate a creature which has only six legs? Why use gallina, which is much too thick, for whisks? And why use four whisks when no dun has more than three? And of course Skues could not resist mentioning the Welshman's Button again, adding the withering adjective 'so-called'. And there were other disapproving remarks about colour and shape of flies. To Halford the catalogue of grouches must have seemed never-ending. The text was 'insufficiently explicit', and in some cases at variance with the illustrations. Particularly damning was the innocent enquiry: how could the 'New Patterns' be said to be the last word in effectiveness if only they and no others had been subjected to years of river testing on a fishery? In the absence of a fair comparison no such claim could be made. It must have seemed as if bordering on the insulting to the author of *Modern Development* to suggest that perhaps, in all the circumstances, it had been better not to place the New Patterns next to their natural counterparts in the plates. Otherwise their shortcomings would have become too obvious.

Halford had never been the subject of a slaughterous review like this. Odd particulars of praise turned up here and there in the review, but they were not numerous. The standard colour chart was valuable, Skues conceded. And he admitted that imitating the exquisite products of nature is an impossible task – only a sort of post-impressionist version could be achieved. It was lucky for the angler that trout were 'not so mighty particular'. At the close Skues, conscious perhaps that he had written a negative and somewhat sour piece, wrote an olive-branch offering:

I owe much to his writings in the past, and if in the above columns I have dealt somewhat critically with some of his theories advanced in this book, I hope he will believe that it is in no hostile spirit, but in the search for truth, and that, with all his other readers, I hope that his foreboding that it is scarcely probable that he will write another book may prove mistaken, and that he may long live to enjoy his favourite sport upon the waters he loves so well, and to give to his brother anglers the benefit of the observations and experience of his acute and original mind.

This rather forlorn appeal, reminiscent of the famous final quarrel in the House of Commons in 1791 between Edmund Burke and Charles James Fox ('I hope there is no loss of friends') had no effect. About this time there took place the famous row between the two men in the Flyfishers' Club. In 1946 Skues told Otto von Kienbusch that it was in 1911. It is a pity that almost no detailed information has ever come to light about the actual ingredients. If Halford ever left any record it has not come to light. Skues made no effort to provide a good description of the scene. This is a pity, for it must be classed as one of the important events in fly-fishing history. But then Skues had a shrinking from what he would have called 'personalities', a tendency shared with many of his generation and, in his case, reinforced by the usual caution of the lawyer. It is noticeable in his writings, where initials appear in place of names of people, often in entirely innocent contexts with no suspicion of defamation about them. In addition Skues, who could contrive a good account of a fishing day, was a poor hand at describing the behaviour of his fellow men. It is odd that he had once had ambitions to be a playwright. For him it remained a painful event – something for a brief reference rather than an extended blow-by-blow account. The fragments of such evidence as survive are set out below.

In September 1945, in a letter to Sir Tom Eastham, Skues referred to his earlier relationship with Halford as having been cordial, and 'it was only on the use of the sunk fly that he became nasty'.

A little more detail appeared in a letter to R.B. Marston, referring to the forthcoming second edition of *Minor Tactics* (for the full text see Appendix 11). It was written on 10 March 1914, a week after Halford's unexpected death. It made reference to the quarrel, indicating that it derived from the publication of Skues' book, but is otherwise short on detail:

Though I hoped and believed I had done all that man could to avoid giving offence, yet to one friend of many years standing the book was a cause of a, to me, incomprehensible bitterness. I had hoped that time and the sense of the drift of opinion around him would have brought reconciliation. But now he has passed beyond the opportunity of that. I never ceased to have a cordial kindness for him and it is a sincere sorrow to me that for the last four years of his life our relations should have been clouded. I owe him gratitude not only for his work for angling, but for many kindnesses, not least being the putting of me up for the F.F.C.

This sad letter was written a week after Halford's death. It indicates that Skues, in his search over the years for pure truth in the most minute detail, had never realized that he might have seemed, to Halford, to have been a threat to his work and his peace of mind. The clash between an honest seeker and an inflexible authority figure was always likely to end thus. But there is no doubting the regret in this letter as well as the puzzlement.

Another clue, though not in my view entirely reliable, also comes from the latter end of Skues' life in 1949, and long after the event itself. It was contained in a letter from him to the now extinct journal *Angling*, the editor of which had asked him to write something about the great angling names of the past. Pleading old age, Skues declined to do this, but proffered instead a letter of which the following is part:

For some years prior to that [i.e. the publication of *Minor Tactics*] I had been fairly intimate with Halford, but as my views widened with experience he became hostile and after publication of the book he took me aside and said, 'You know, Skues: what you say in that book can't be done. Mind, I'm not arguing, I'm telling you.' I replied 'Halford! What good do you think you are doing by telling me a thing can't be done which I have done scores of times.' He got up and left me and never spoke to me again.

This bleak encounter took place in the Flyfishers' Club, in those days at 36 Piccadilly, perhaps one late afternoon when no one else was about. As a piece of reporting of the actual words it has a slightly too neat and unconvincing flavour, more an air of 'what I would like to have said'. A riposte of that sort has a decisive and masterful ring which one does not associate with Skues, who was excellent on paper, but much less effective in a man-to-man confrontation. And the terse epigrammatic 'Mind, I'm not arguing, I'm telling you', has a distinct look of an invention, a sort of shorthand version of Halford's style in the interview rather than an actual record of the words used. Skues may have unconsciously been imitating the well-known words of the painter and art critic Whistler who, when locked in serious argument (which was quite frequent), was accustomed to use this smart form of put-down. It was often quoted or used from the late nineteenth century onwards, as if it were something new. J.W. Hills used it (with proper attribution) as late as 1936 in *My Sporting Life*. The words may, however, have summed up the sense of what was said: the impression one receives from Skues' account has a brevity about it which is not quite credible. If we take as literally accurate the forty-five words of description used by Skues the interview would have been over in a minute or less. This seems difficult to believe: it would surely have been too short a time for the development on Halford's part of 'incomprehensible bitterness'. It is more likely to have lasted for at least a quarter of an hour, beginning as a discussion and gathering in intensity as the minutes passed. In the end it must have got out of hand, for underlying Halford's point about the impossibility of frequently catching Itchen trout with sunk flies was a clear implication of lying. R.B. Marston had already picked this up in his notice of *Minor Tactics*, pointing out that this was something rather serious of which the public should take note. Perhaps Halford, the one-time monarch of the chalk-stream scene and conscious that his sceptre was passing from him, realized that he had gone too far, for he left abruptly, perhaps an admission that he was losing the argument.

There is, however, no doubt that this rupture was a profoundly distressing event for Skues. After his death, his brother Charles said that he often referred to it and never quite got over it. One wonders if Halford stayed away from the Flyfishers' Club after this. He was not present at the annual dinner on 25 February 1911 in the Whitehall Rooms of the Hotel Metropole. Later he would have been able to read in the *Journal* the account of the evening, the usual ten-course marathon (consommé duchesse, saumon, cailles à lucullus and other good things), a parallel marathon of eight speeches and the company of nearly one hundred and fifty people, many of them his close friends such as Mosely, Sheringham and William Senior. Both Skues brothers were present.

Halford was absent the following year as well, otherwise he would have been compelled to listen, in a speech by Marston, to words of praise for Skues for presenting the Club with 'a set of his new special under-water patterns of nymphs and mermaids to captivate trout by minor tactics on chalk streams'. And he would have felt increasingly alienated at witnessing his heretical adversary not only tolerated but positively praised, and thus realizing that he had a following of many friends. The serving of oysters and of the entertainingly named Bombe Doria would not have been enough compensation. He was not seen at the dinner in 1913 either. Was he also avoiding such once-pleasant occasions as the convivial soirées on Thursday nights, at which Skues was a constant attender? The once-dominant figure of the chalk-stream world was becoming a rather sad old man, even a figure of fun with some, such as the humorist William Caine.

But Halford was not finished yet. He was aware that he still had a large body of followers in the angling world, even though they had not so far found much to say in his support. Perhaps they could be mobilized and led back into the breach. He had previously proclaimed that *Modern Development* was to be his last work: now he began to change his mind. Throughout 1912 he was busily assembling the materials for yet another book, which was to be positively his last throw on the board. If it was intended to suppress Skues it certainly failed of its objective.

The Dry-Fly Man's Handbook went to the shops on 10 March 1913. Critics praised parts of the book, but there was a wide agreement that it was seriously marred by unfair criticism of the new wet-fly/nymph developments on chalk streams. At least Halford was careful not to mention Skues by name. Chapter 3, 'The Ethics of the Dry-Fly', was the final prospectus of his belief system, but it contained nothing that was new. In the main it followed the form and actual wording of the broadside of 1906. Once again there was the bland and friendly statement that he had nothing against fishing the wet fly, without making it quite clear (as would have been more honest) that he believed that it should be confined to 'wet-fly rivers'. A little further into the chapter it once again becomes clear that, on the chalk stream, the sunk fly was anything but respectable. Dry fly was the only acceptable way, and the aim of the angler should be to aspire to the conduct of the ultra-purists and purists. Halford defined ultra-purists as those who would only cast over a rising fish. Purists were those who would occasionally cast over a fish in position, though not actually rising. A measure of tolerance might be accorded the latter species of angler, but Halford was less enthusiastic about them: their conduct might be enough to scare a trout on a much-fished stream.

Casting a dry fly into likely places, which he regarded as 'at random', would not do at all. Casting a wet fly in the same way was even worse. And he resurrected the imaginary disgrace-scenario of the guest who is so ill-mannered and ignorant of the established protocol that he will fish the water downstream with a wet fly throughout the day. Even though he knew that Skues was not interested in such a pointless tactic, he proceeded to devote three pages to demolishing this straw target.

Halford was well aware that there were other less offensive ways of fishing the wet fly. He turned to the practice of upstream fishing, as advocated by Stewart in his book of 1857. This method had spread throughout the north and west of Britain: the angler would use his rivercraft and move upstream, searching the likely places. Halford rejected this – it would not do in the slower transparent water of the chalk stream. A much greater length of river is needed for a day of fishing, and fish are likely to be frightened. Finally, and no doubt unwillingly, he compelled himself to consider the new Skues method:

> I am told, however, that there is a school of fly fishermen who only fish the sunk fly over a feeding fish or one in position if it will not take a floating fly. This, they urge, is a third method of wet-fly fishing, the other two being the more ordinary of *fishing the water* with sunk fly either upstream or downstream. Candidly I have never seen this method in practice, and I have grave doubts as to its efficacy.

This passage, with its deliberate misunderstanding of the method, and its condescending tone, did Halford more damage than anything else, and critics were harsh in their judgements. *The Field*, which he regarded as a safe house and which had been publishing his work for many years, thought that the 'I am told' passage should be removed from any future edition, and added: 'the school of flyfishermen, of which Mr Halford is "told", has had its doctrine admirably expressed by Mr G.E.M. Skues in *Minor Tactics of the Chalk Stream*, a book so familiar to all serious students of the sport that Mr Halford does ill to ignore it so loftily'.

The Fishing Gazette singled out the same passage. R.B. Marston, Halford's colleague on the Committee of the Flyfishers' Club, was a friend of many years, but nevertheless showed that he was no respecter of persons. 'What is a "Dry-Fly Purist"? – that unfortunate denomination which seems to invite derision', he asked. Halford had suggested that it was 'unwritten law' that fishing on chalk streams meant dry-fly fishing, and that it was unnecessary and indeed 'insulting' to mention it on a fishing ticket, as if to imply that a visitor was ignorant of a generally accepted fact. This was nonsense, wrote Marston, and was an overestimate of Halford's influence in attempting to establish a norm. If a fishery owner wished to maintain such a rule he should state the fact on a ticket. He continued: 'In this and in some few other matters I think Mr Halford is rather too inclined to make a business out of what should after all be a recreation.' And, as did several other critics, he quoted the 'I am told' passage, criticizing Halford for condemning as if on hearsay, and with no personal knowledge, a new method pursued by 'a whole "school" of first-class fly-fishers and first-class sportsmen'. He continued:

> He cannot pretend that he does not know that this no longer very new school have claimed in the sporting press and in books that they use the method he refers to with success; and there seems to be only one inference to be drawn from his remarks – namely, that he does not believe it. It is to be hoped that in the next edition of his admirable work he will modify his chapter on ethics on this point. Good sportsman as he is, had he read the book he is condemning he could not possibly have made his 'candid' statement.

This very directly aimed passage must have made Halford extremely uncomfortable for, as we have seen, he had in fact read *Minor Tactics*, and he could be accused of alleging that the descriptions within of the success of Skues with the sunk fly were simply invented, or in plain English, lies.

But there was another interesting fact, unknown to the angling public at the time. Halford did, in fact, know rather more about the use of the artificial nymph than he had revealed. For a period of two seasons on the Test he had become a nymph fisherman, albeit surreptitiously. The papers by Skues in *The Field* and *The Fishing Gazette* celebrating the advantages of his new technique had caused Halford to become baffled and alarmed. Eventually, and no doubt in a very unwilling and disgruntled state of mind, he resolved to give it a trial. For this he called in the help of the faithful Martin Mosely, who would have been sworn to secrecy. There can be no doubt of that: having regard to Halford's reputation, and to the fact that he had expressed public distaste for the sunk fly, he simply could not afford to be exposed to public view in the matter. It would have been seen as hypocrisy, and a cry of derision would have been heard in the angling community. The experiments needed to be carried out in the most complete privacy. So began one of the most extraordinary passages in Halford's career as a fly-fisherman.

It is curious to reflect that, in one way, he could have given himself an excellent chance of success, for it may well be that he was armed with some useful flies. Halford did, after all, know a good deal of entomology, and between them he and Mosely probably fashioned some good imitations. Unfortunately no examples of the patterns used have survived, but the evidence of his diary shows that he paid no attention to sunk versions of winged Scottish patterns, which occupied the main part of Skues' sunk fly team at that time. Instead he went straight to nymphal designs and used examples tied by Mosely. This was not, however, going to be of much service to him.

There were two possible reasons why the trials did not work. One was that Halford's skills lay in a narrow groove. Flexibility was a quality unknown to him. He probably imagined that a man who had mastered the high art of the dry fly would have no difficulty with what he saw as the lesser and more clumsy work involved with the nymph. He had indicated in one of his earlier articles that he and Marryat had made some nymph prototypes back in the 1880s, but had abandoned their use as being inappropriate on the Test. But fishing the nymph requires some apprenticeship, and neither he nor Mosely had the experience to acquire this subtle technique. They were also debarred by Halford's terror of public exposure from getting the help of Skues, the one man who could have shown him the way.

Secondly, Halford's attitude would probably not have been conducive to success. A man of his type, whose attitudes, once arrived at, congealed like concrete, would not have gone into such an experiment with the open mind which might have led to success. Privately he wished it to fail, and to prove his long-held theory. It would have been a half-hearted test, similar to his test of the Leonard rod.

The nymph trials were therefore hardly comprehensive. They took place at Mottisfont on three days in 1908 and two days in 1909. The diary does not make it clear for how long they were persisted with on each day. A few fish were caught, so it was not entirely a waste of time. On 22 April 1908 Halford began with a grannom pupa, perhaps his 1886 tying, catching a fish of 1lb 4oz. The diary records 'Tried this fly as fish were flooping. Autopsy showed nothing but olive nymphs.' On 9 May he caught a respectable trout of 1lb 8oz on 'Martin's nymph' and returned an undersized one. Three days later he recorded that the fish were bulging, but he stuck to dry fly and no doubt missed a good opportunity. On 12 June he wrote: 'Killed a breakfast fish in Norman Court with Martin's nymph.'

In 1909 Mosely began with a fish of 1lb 7oz and a grayling, and returned a small trout. On 27 April Halford had a fish of 1lb 9oz – 'fish fighting and bulging in both streams'. On 19 June a guest had a fish on a Tup's Indispensable, the fly about which his host had been so dismissive, but whether it was on or below the surface was not recorded.

Some anglers might have considered this modest result as something upon which to build and improve, but Halford seems to have decided that he now had no grounds for uneasiness, and that his original diagnosis had been correct. Had he not always allowed that the thing was feasible on odd occasions ('happening days')? The performance had not been substantial enough to provide a foundation for a worthwhile angling technique. It perhaps also provided fresh material for his theory that the movement or 'wriggle' of the nymph was impossible to imitate. So the man who, throughout his career of teaching other anglers, had been following the line of Dickens' Mr Gradgrind in *Hard Times*, and dealt only in 'Facts, Facts, Facts', was reduced to purveying a fiction.

It was a pity that Halford's 1913 book was marred by the ill-natured attempt to hold on to the purist programme by the use of arguments that were not straight, and which for many left a sour taste. We do not know if he was swayed by the arguments of the critics to amend the objectionable parts of the chapter on ethics. It seems unlikely. In any case he had no chance. A year later he was dead.

9

Consolidation 1911–1922

THE YEARS AFTER the publication of *Minor Tactics* and before the outbreak of war in 1914 were in many ways the best part of Skues' life. His stature had been steadily increasing for two decades. As a result of his prolific journalism he had become widely known as a creative fly-dresser, and the relevance of his patterns was appreciated far beyond Hampshire. In the new century he had played a major part in a significant controversy over the merits of the light rod. Most importantly he had almost single-handed conducted his own campaign to restore the sunk fly to the chalk stream, and his articles and his first book had marked him out as an original thinker. Now his position in the angling world was fixed and his stature and confidence as a person had increased. He never entirely lost his shy and wary manner, but at least the once reticent and awkward young man was more relaxed and assured. He had also become a practised controversialist – at least in print, for he was never at ease in verbal confrontations. The acclaim that came with the production of a major book was helpful in cementing his position and continuing the work of converting people to the sunk-fly practice.

Minor Tactics did well. The first edition was sold out by 1914, and the publishers were sufficiently encouraged to bring out a second. Oddly enough Skues did not take the opportunity to follow the advice tendered in 1910 by R.B. Marston to produce a good index for the next edition. Nor did he modify the text to take account of the important changes that he had made in his methods since 1910. Soon after the publication of his book the process of moving away from winged wet flies and towards true nymphal forms began to move much faster. The process was accelerated by the hot summer and low water of 1911, which produced abnormal conditions everywhere. The countryside everywhere was burnt up and green leaves were hard to find, and singing birds fell silent. In July – the warmest since 1868 – the temperature in places reached 34 °C, and in August 37 °C, by which time the newspapers were reporting a considerable mortality from the effects of heat, particularly among children. The chalk country was seriously affected. By the autumn the Kennet was drying up below Marlborough and as far down as Ramsbury, an event unknown in living memory. The Test and Itchen ran low, and the main river at Abbots Barton had hardly any current in it. By August only the sunk fly would serve, at least during the day. In the evening the trusty Orange Quill was as effective as ever.

Skues has not told us about his 1911 experiments in any detail. The main clue we have for the work is his description which appeared in *The Field* of the two alternative methods of dressing the typical nymph, with excellent illustrations by the artist St Barbe Goldsmith. This article was reprinted in 1921 as an important part of *The Way of a Trout with a Fly*. Otherwise, with his usual caution, he was not going to give patterns to the world until they had been thoroughly tested and, apart from the Carrot Fly (another of Skues' jokes) in 1912, and the Iron Blue nymph in 1918, no further nymph patterns were published until 1923, although a number of prototypes had been tried out.

In the years immediately before the Great War, Skues was still living in 'Hyrst View', the leasehold house in Croydon acquired in the 1890s to accommodate his family. In the early years after the premature death of his parents it does not seem to have given him much joy. He wrote cryptically, as he sometimes did when treating of subjects upon which he did not wish to dwell, that 'the Croydon ménage did not entirely answer'. To have suddenly become head of a household of six siblings aged between seventeen and thirty-three must have been trying. We have no information as to how they lived: the house was probably a bear garden. But by 1910 there were fewer people jostling for the space at 'Hyrst View', and the pressure would have lifted a good deal. Frederick was working in Africa. Minnie had gone to Newnham College Cambridge, and went into school-teaching, eventually becoming headmistress of Newark High School. Charles (C.A.M.), Elsie and Gertrude had all married. Gertrude had three children before dying in 1905, the second of Skues' sisters to be carried off by the dreaded tuberculosis. Mary alone remained as housekeeper at the Croydon residence until 1940.

Apart from the regretful reference recorded above, Skues scarcely ever made mention of his Croydon life. The house seems to have been hardly a home in the usual sense – more of a convenient suburban box in which to dwell, eat, sleep and tie flies in the evening while inconveniently compelled to work for a living in London.

Skues was fifty-two in 1910, and in good health. He regarded the serious crisis of the early 'nineties as having 'cleansed a lot of rubbish out of my system'. Whether or not this is a medically safe judgement, he was nevertheless able in the 1920s to tell Dr Barton that, since 1895, he had not paid out more than 5s in doctor's bills.

There do not appear to have been any women in his life at this date, nor indeed at any subsequent time, apart from sisters who kept house for him and were breezily referred to as 'my womenkind' or 'my womenfolk'. He was certainly not unaware of women, or they of him, but by this date he had left all that behind. He was settled in his life, and could make his own unencumbered decisions. His angling, and the continuous hunt for new ideas, was the main drive in his life. It was all he wanted, and he was sufficiently content until the loneliness of old age closed in upon him after the Second World War.

Skues fished in a number of different places in his life. For some time he took a fishery, sharing it with some friends, on a stream at Shalford in Surrey called the Tillingbourne. He occasionally refers to it in his writings, calling it the 'Thrillingbourne'. It enabled him to have somewhere to fish near home when time was limited. In his earlier years it was even easier, for he could walk from his house in Croydon to the Wandle. Eventually, as the Croydon pollution increased, it became obvious that the days of this once peerless stream were numbered. He also knew some fisheries that are scarcely mentioned by him in his writings. When he got to know Dr Barton he fished with him on his stretch of the Test at Leckford, which Barton shared with Sir Frederick Still, the distinguished child physician. Here, he several times had bags of two-pounders which had been reared in the nearby stew ponds. But we seldom hear from Skues about these visits. By this date his skills had reached such a level that only the most challenging fishing satisfied him. As with many men who have been tested on a tough fishery, when let loose on a stocked paradise he could be dangerous. Many anglers will have been familiar with this sort of experience. In his book *The Guileless Trout* (1950) Dr H.B. McCaskie remembered a nightmare day on a private fishery adjacent to his club water. In a short time he caught 'as many trout as I could decently keep', broke off the business part of his hook, and continued to cast, presumably out of curiosity. When he had risen over seventy fish he crept away, 'completely bored, and longing for the morrow when I could resume my hopeless pursuit of the permitted three brace'. Elsewhere in the same book McCaskie pointed out to the no doubt puzzled layman that 'we do not offer up prayers that the trout, on each and every day, should behave like a shoal of mackerel'.

After nearly thirty years Skues knew every reach and corner of Abbots Barton, and it might be supposed that he would have exhausted all its possibilities and moved on to another fishery. Some of his friends found their excitement in fishing all over the British Isles and in the wider world beyond. His was an inverted approach – he preferred to know one place in depth. He wrote that he was aware that this was a paradox, but decided that, although there was an apparent sameness about Abbots Barton, he was constantly surprised at the subtle variation through the year in the riverbank and the reaction of the underwater world to the changes of weather and season. No two days were alike. In a piece called 'Variety' he wrote:

> I have fished a good many waters – British and Continental – some of them many times, but never have I found the same locality so infinitely various as in the south country, and in particular in the Hampshire water meadows. It is never when revisited quite as I recalled it. Always after the interval between two week-ends there is some subtle change which seems to make a different stream of it and sets much of the experience of many years at naught.

At Winchester one's powers of observation need never slumber, and this interesting place remained his laboratory for decades. More than that, it was his main retreat, the place on earth where he was most happy. Here a lonely man, now no longer young, could find peace for his spirit.

The fishery was still in the hands of the amiable Irwin Cox, who allowed Skues, Sheringham and several other fortunate men to use it at will, imposing no restraint on the number of trout caught, only a 12in size limit. In August 1911 Skues published in *The Fishing Gazette* an account (more familiar to us now in *Itchen Memories*) of a week of fishing there, while the heat-wave mentioned above increases each day. On this notoriously difficult fishery, in what, for many anglers, would have been unpromising conditions, he catches forty-two trout in six days.

For the reader nowadays this piece could stand as a good picture of that period before the catastrophe of the Great War. It is a self-portrait of an angler who knows exactly what he is doing on a river and uses a wide variety of flies and tactics, but there is also a lyrical element not often seen in Skues' writing, and an appreciation of the charm of the river and the meadows by the old town. It is evident on almost every day of the diary of this week. He notes the tall spikes of mullein and the huge patches of ragwort, the green veined white butterflies ('Never saw so many'), the smell of the hunting weasel and the consequent danger to the fledgling birds, the young toads in the grass, the spider's web that must be searched for duns and spinners and the glow-worm found after dark as he returns to the hotel. The horses are beaten by the heat and retire under the trees and the cows get into the river where they can ('glad I had foresight to order in large supply of syphons [sic]'). Yet in spite of the temperature he retires to his hotel for dinner in the early evening and comes back – a considerable walk – for the late rise. And afterwards he is not too tired by a long day to miss the last sights of nature, writing, in a passage which reminds us of the 'Incognita' piece and the unattainable love that inspired it years before: 'At night, when one knocks off, the life in the air is a wonder. Big ghost swifts, male and female (the white and yellow bustards of the north), and an innumerable array of moths and sedges are buzzing around all intent on the business of life.'

In his later writings we find less and less appreciation of natural beauty. No doubt he would have been aware of it, but his interest declines and increasingly gives place to the serious pursuit of fish. So perhaps this piece of 1911 may have been one of the last glimpses of Skues as a romantic. There is something boyish about the suppressed excitement in the words of the opening day: 'Could not sleep; up at five and out in the meadows.' And at the end of the holiday on the second non-fishing day, when most anglers would have been stepping onto the train for London, he cannot bear to leave this well-loved place, but makes his way to the meadows again, and for hours watches a group of trout nymphing.

No information has survived about Skues' feelings during the July Crisis of 1914. Perhaps, as with many observers at the time, he thought a diplomatic solution might be discovered. If so, events quickly disabused him, and the war began to touch him very closely when a letter came to him, bearing that most ominous of all dates – 4 August 1914:

My Dear Skues
In fifteen days I shall be 50 years of age, and consequently I will not be called up, but my feeling is that in these present circum-stances it is the strict duty of all men capable of marching and

firing a rifle to come forward and to offer their services. I have
enlisted therefore as an ordinary soldier for the duration of the
war, in a marching regiment, if they are willing to do me the honour
of accepting me.

I hope for better times

Your sincere friend

Louis Bouglé

Having done his compulsory service as a young man, for Bouglé the
induction back into military life did not take long. By the latter end of
October he was sent off to the trenches and within a short time was in
action helping to drive off German attacks. One letter described the
regiment firing all night at the German trench two hundred metres away,
without really being able to see them, no doubt to discourage them from
making a surprise attack by dark. A small flash of humour indicates his
chalk-stream principles: firing at random without seeing the quarry, he
wrote, was hardly the custom. He was only in the trenches for twenty
days. At the end of that time he was invalided away to hospital at Chateau
Thierry. He had lost 4kg of weight and was seriously ill with dysentery.
For some time his life was in danger, and his convalescence was to last for
more than two years.

At first many people tried to treat the war as an unnecessary intrusion.
It would not do to be too flurried or put out. Anyway it would soon be
over – by Christmas, some said. The watchword everywhere was 'Business
as usual'. No doubt Skues' ability to withdraw into his own world was a
comfort to him. He went away to Abbots Barton for a week at the end of
August 1914. This happened to be the week when the first actions were
being fought on what was to become known as the Western Front. Seven
German armies were already carrying out the long-planned manoeuvre
known as the Schlieffen Plan, and the British Expeditionary Force had
taken up their pre-arranged station on the left of the French, and facing
the German First Army of 320,000. On 23 August the advanced group of
English soldiers collided with part of an enemy formation, three times
their number, at the Battle of Mons. On that historic Sunday morning, a
non-fishing day, Skues was in the Winchester meadows conducting a
reconnaissance for his own campaign for the week. He began his week of
fishing on the following day, while the weary survivors of the B.E.F. were
retreating from Mons. Skues later wrote several interesting pages on his
holiday (see *The Way of a Trout with a Fly*, pp. 172–6), chiefly to examine

the question of the effect of moonlight on evening fishing. On Wednesday 26 August he recorded that the sun set at 7 p.m. and the waxing moon rose at 8.28, and after catching a single trout in the evening the moonlight defeated all his subsequent attempts to get near a fish. On that day the German hordes caught up with one of the two retreating British corps, who turned to confront them, and the hard-fought battle of Le Cateau followed. The contrast between these savage events and the peaceful scene in Hampshire is curious and sad, but no mention was made by Skues in this account or anywhere else of this bizarre contrast – no ironical reflections or heavy moralizing. The effect of a rising moon on the trout of the Itchen was more important to him. Why should he not withdraw his attention from the world and this distressing spectacle of modern barbarism?

But the war was to obtrude more and more: there was no ignoring the paradox of the nearness of these stupendous happenings. When mobile warfare came to a halt the trench system developed and the left wing of the Front rested on the Belgian coast only seventy miles from Kent. The sound of battle was often heard across the Channel. On 30 June 1916, members of the Houghton Club who were fishing the evening rise could clearly hear the sound of gunfire. What they were hearing was the week-long bombardment that was reaching its appalling height in preparation for the Somme offensive on the following morning. A year later, at 3.10 a.m. on 17 June 1917, the explosion of nineteen mines containing 500 tons of ammonal produced the greatest man-made bang in history up to that date, only to be surpassed in the atomic age. The concussion was heard over a large area of the south of England, causing many people to wake up in alarm: in his house in Croydon Skues would probably have been one of them.

This was surely a new sort of war. It became unusual not to know someone who had lost a relative. As the news of death and disablement came ever faster the angling community was not immune. R.B. Marston stayed away from the AGM of the Flyfishers' Club in July 1916, agitated at not having had news of his son, who had been wounded on the Somme. Confirmation of his death came a few days later. Marston's younger son survived until the final weeks of the war, dying shortly before the Armistice. John Waller Hills, a major with the 20th Battalion of the Durham Light Infantry, was wounded on the Somme in September 1916 and brought back to England. Leonard West's son was killed when his aeroplane was attacked from behind, according to the account, by 'two swift German aeroplanes', and was shot down in October 1916. In the summer number of that year the *Journal of the Flyfishers' Club* published a list of 145 members serving in the forces, in which appeared the name of C.A.M. Skues, serving in the Royal Artillery. Skues took over the Club's secretarial duties from his brother, with help from another member. It was a way of 'doing his bit', and of helping to maintain a semblance of normal life. His style was well adapted to administrative desk work of that sort. However, he never became President. He knew he was not president material and resisted three attempts at different times to propel him into that role.

Louis Bouglé was also on that sad list in the *Journal*, so many members of which did not survive the war. A.-P. Decantelle, his friend and adversary in many pre-war casting tournaments, was wounded but recovered and went back to the front. By February 1915 Decantelle's unit, originally of 350 men, had been kept at that figure, but only by bringing in reinforcements totalling 750 more men, so considerable had been the slaughter.

Bouglé recovered his spirits a little in 1916 and began to discuss fishing matters again with Skues. He was now convalescing at a chateau. He complained that there were no fish thereabouts except some carp in an ornamental pond. The place had once belonged to Talleyrand, and the excellent library had some interesting books, including Fabre's book on insects. He wrote to Skues that he now wished to acquire copies of the first edition (1681) of Chetham and an example of Scotcher, perhaps not realizing that the latter was a choice and rare item. By 1917 he was in Paris and sufficiently well to be employed in a desk job at the *Centre d'Action Propagande contre l'Ennemi*, an office that did not close down its operation until September 1919. When Bouglé proposed resigning from the Flyfishers' Club Skues persuaded Marston and Coggeshall to arrange his election as an honorary life member. His correspondence with Skues, which was more important to him than ever, continued for several more years. In 1919 Skues enquired for the correct term in French for a rise. '*Montée*' replied Bouglé, although '*gobage*' (verb '*gober*') would be more likely to be used locally. He wrote that '*fausse montée*' could be applied in the case of bulging fish, and this phrase was taken up and used by Skues in *The Way of a Trout with a Fly*.

There were other ways of keeping despair at bay. Men began to realize as never before the benefit of escaping to the peace of the waterside. The editor of *The Fishing Gazette* revealed that Marshal Joffre, the French Commander-in-Chief on the Western Front, relaxed with rod and line whenever he could get away, and that anyone who could help men on leave to take up fishing opportunities would be doing a kindly act, as also would be the gift of waders to soldiers in the waterlogged trenches of the Front Line. The Houghton Club began to allow visits by servicemen on leave, and in May 1915 Sunday fishing began on their fisheries. Some members may have considered this latter move a benevolent change, while others might have seen it as yet another attack on an ancient custom that should have been inviolable. Skues discovered a wartime trespasser at Abbots Barton, fishing with float tackle and bait, but the young man was in uniform and no doubt soon to be at the Front. In his own words: 'I could not bring myself to do my duty to the other members of the syndicate by interfering', and he even colluded in the trespass by withdrawing and attempting (without success) to catch a grayling to give him. The atmosphere of war and national calamity had enabled a man who was a lifelong Tory to submerge his conventional social ideas in a feeling of community.

Fishing journals struggled on, attempting to make their contribution to normality, decreasing in quality of paper and increasing in price. Sheringham noticed that angling books also continued to flourish. Some of Skues' wartime articles were later used again to assemble the text of *The Way of a Trout with a Fly*, and he joined zestfully in any available controversy. They were, however, small-scale matters compared with the battles over the light rod and the sunk fly. In June and July 1915 he got into an argument with Marston about the exact shade of the iron blue dun, and several polite letters ensued. In early 1916 he once again entered the lists on the subject of Halford and the misnaming of Welshman's Button (seven letters on this), a subject that he could never leave alone for long.

As for the fishing at Abbots Barton, the conditions of wartime eventually began to bring about a serious alteration. For two years Skues did well. In 1916 he had a run of five successive Saturday evenings which provided fishing that he remembered all his life. He described it or referred to it on a number of occasions, the last time being in 1947. This was the fruit of the discovery of the Orange Quill in 1894. He admitted that the credit was partly due to Halford, for it was in that year that, while searching through the flies on the counter in George Currell's shop for Red Quills, a favourite pattern of Halford's, he came upon an example with an orange rather than a red body, an obvious mistake. Even when he found how effective it was in the evening he was slow to connect it with the appearance of the blue-winged olive, and to realize that he had found good medicine for a difficult fly. There has been discussion for more than a century over this apparent match, for there seems no very obvious resemblance between the Orange Quill and the newly hatched dun: the female has the body colour of a ripe greengage, although the brown colour of the male is perhaps nearer. It has been suggested that the artificial has more resemblance to the spinner, which deepens to a golden orange colour. It is often on the water at the same time, but Skues claimed (confusingly) that the artificial was effective in the absence of the spinner. Anyway, however the Orange Quill worked, Skues caught three and a half brace of good trout each evening, resulting in a total of thirty-five fish.

These successes did not last, and things began to change at Abbots Barton in 1917. The season started well for Skues, with good fishing during hatches of iron blue and pale watery. He was, at that time, experimenting with a sunk variation of the pale watery derived from the Tup's Indispensable, but he did not publish the prescription for this or indeed any other nymph for several years, except for the imitation of the iron blue nymph previously mentioned. It is tantalizing not to have more information about the early nymphs of Skues. We do not know any detail about the exhibition at the Flyfishers' Club mentioned in May 1912, which, amongst others, featured Skues' Mayflies, Spent Willow Flies and 'his unique nymphs'. He was perhaps not sufficiently confident in these early experiments to allow them to appear in print. But with the Iron Blue Nymph he was happy that he had arrived at the best artificial, and he published it in the *Journal* of Autumn 1918. This was the well-known pattern, dressed on a size 16 hook to gut, a body of mole's fur dubbed onto crimson silk, with a tiny wisp of a jackdaw throat hackle and soft fibres from the saddle of a white cock.

The fine beginning of the 1917 season was not maintained, and by late summer a serious shortage of stock became noticeable. Larger fish of 2lb and even 3lb were to be had, and this in a fishery where a two-pounder had in former times been a prize. The *average* size which, in earlier times, had been an ounce or two above the pound also increased but, whereas there had always been plenty of trout to fish for, now the overall numbers were seriously diminished, and there was a worrying absence of smaller fish.

Skues was able to test his impression towards the end of June, when heavy hatches of the blue-winged olive would normally have brought on a general rise and enabled him to make a fairly reliable census. His impression had been correct: fish numbers were declining badly. Since the 1890s, by which time Skues had acquired his full measure of formidable skill, he had been able virtually to eliminate blank days. In 1918 they became familiar events: the season began with five blank weekends. Skues was not used to this sort of thing. It was clear to him that it was caused by inadequate river work. The pike had got out of control because of the wartime shortage of labour. Netting had been conducted in a slipshod manner, and the spawning pike had not been harried with spear and snare as in the days before the war. Not until November 1917 had a stop net been used, when the keeper who had stoutly rejected the idea of a pike problem was nonplussed to witness a haul of 98 pike in one day of netting. In the winter a further 120 were caught, and 85 more were removed in March 1918. Skues came down to Winchester to help, and was troubled by the complete absence of trout in the nets.

It is not, of course, impossible – although Skues did not consider it, at least, not in writing – that enterprising persons from the neighbourhood had done some surreptitious netting in the dark hours of the night. Abbots Barton was vulnerable because of being adjacent to a large centre of population, and it was known that there was a certain level of poaching before the war. There was now an additional motive, for there was a very real danger of starvation in Britain. The German U-boats ruled supreme in the Atlantic and, with each month, the dismal tale of merchant ship tonnage sunk rose higher. In April 1917 875,000 tons of shipping were lost, and only six weeks' supply of corn was left in the country. It was officially (though secretly) estimated that the limit of British endurance would be reached before the end of 1917. About this time the angling press was promoting the idea of freshwater fish for food because of the advancing famine. Even Skues began to eat more fish. In the past he had given most of his trout away. The Itchen trout of 1918 were better than usual on the table, comparable to sea trout. No doubt this was because of their smaller numbers, allowing more space and less cause for competition. In the same year he reported eating a pike which, he claimed, 'ate as good as a turbot'.

The fishing of 1918 may have been slow – thirty trout in sixteen visits up to mid-July – but their quality was extraordinary by comparison with pre-war years. By the end of the season Skues' tally of fish over 2lb had risen to twelve. The Pheasant Tail, Tup's and the July Dun were all effective, but something was also amiss in the natural fly world. Sedges were scarce, also the blue-winged olive. When conditions were right the nymph was of more service. He mentioned a 'dark nymph' in a *Journal* article without giving particulars, but it was probably an early version of the nymph no. XVIII mentioned in 1939 in *Nymph Fishing for Chalk Stream Trout*, with a blue hen hackle and a body of cow hair the colour of dried blood.

One Saturday morning in September 1918, when many wondered despondently if the war was going to last until 1919, Skues was sitting in the Essex Street office, no doubt discontented at being at work on a case when he would rather have been on the river. A curious reminder of that other place, a female pale watery spinner, appeared on his window overlooking Fountain Court in the Middle Temple. It must have been carried by the wind for many miles from its natural home outside the London sprawl. He recorded this pleasing event in *The Fishing Gazette*. If he regarded it as a sign of hope and a good omen for possible better times ahead in the world, he did not say so.

The angling world had been touched by many tragedies in the war. Hugh Tempest Sheringham, author of some of the most charming of all fishing books and lampooned by Skues in humorous pieces in the *Journal of the Flyfishers' Club* as 'Scaringham', was never the same afterwards. His wartime post as Editorial Director of the Ministry of Information, a job involving much hard work and stress, had taken a severe toll of him, and he had a major breakdown. The remainder of his life until his premature death in 1930 at the age of fifty-four was clouded by periods of depression.

The health of Louis Bouglé also never recovered, and his letters to Skues told of intermittent fever and weakness. But he also wrote of the memories of their long association and of their fishing in Hampshire, Normandy and Picardy. The good times before the war seemed now long ago. Thinking of them, Bouglé quoted Talleyrand, an enduring object of his admiration, who had once said that unless one had lived under the *Ancien Régime* before the French Revolution one could not have known the '*douceur de vivre*'. He wrote in November 1923, recording his pleasure in reading Skues' article in the *Journal* on Marryat and the evolution of the floating fly. This was the last time that Skues heard from him: there were to be no more of the zestful letters from this agreeable man, with endings such as '*Je vous prie de me croire toujours très cordialement votre Louis Bouglé*'. He died in 1924, a victim of the Great War as much as if he had been killed ten years earlier in a trench on the Western Front.

A bitter anger was everywhere in Britain in 1918. Towards the end of January the normally good-natured Flyfishers' Club held a Special General Meeting, at which it was resolved that no person of German parentage or nationality should henceforth remain or in future be elected a member of the Club. It is not known which member or members were behind this. Skues continued to carry on as Secretary for some time after the ordeal of war had ended and the country could begin to deal with the problems of a shattered society. He eventually gave up in the summer of 1919, when a live-in Secretary, Colonel Wickham, was appointed. This was a new departure, to be paid for by an extra guinea on all subscriptions. The *Journal* wrote generously of Skues' caretaker regime: 'At the same time we must not forget to thank our energetic late Acting Secretary, Mr G.E.M. Skues, who has done so much to keep the Club going during the difficult and strenuous times caused by the war; indeed, it has been a puzzle to everyone how he has managed so well.'

Small scraps of praise like this may have been helpful, for Skues, like many others, emerged from the Great War in a state of weariness of spirit, perhaps even mild depression. He wrote to Louis Bouglé that he had arranged a holiday but could hardly trouble himself to go. The war had left behind an exhaustion and a malaise of spirit everywhere. If Skues and men like him imagined that they could get back to life as it was before 1914 they fairly soon found that many things had changed for ever. Even in the realm of fishing this was true; in fact it might be said that Abbots Barton was permanently affected by the Great War. Horace Cox Ltd resolved to sell *The Field*, and in 1919 it was acquired by the Runciman family. More importantly for Skues, Sheringham and their friends, Irwin Cox gave up Abbots Barton, and the old easy days of giving leave to friends came to an end. The fishery was taken by a new landlord, and a small syndicate was formed, which survived until halfway through the next war. Irwin Cox also gave up the presidency of the Wilton Club, formerly the Hungerford Club, of which he had been a member since 1879, dying in August 1922 at the age of 84. His memory should always be cherished by chalk-stream fishermen for having made Skues free of the ideal fish laboratory of Abbots Barton for three and a half decades, and thus opened the door to a new style of fishing.

The new syndicate at first had six members, but after some years it fell to four. Skues now had to pay for fishing which, for many years, had been a free gift. The combined cost of rental, rates on sporting rights, the wages of two keepers and expenses of netting, weed-cutting, mudding and other smaller outgoings was considerable. When asked towards the end of his life what his share of the annual cost had been Skues could only remember the figure for the last years of his membership after the rent had been raised when the head landlord, Colonel Barrow Simonds, had bought the east bank of the main river. At this time his quarter share varied between £120 and £140 a year.

At Abbots Barton the new syndicate varied in number between four and six for many years. The lease at first was held by James Rolt, then, after some years, by Gavin Simonds. The membership is not entirely clear, for no lists seem to have survived, and we have to rely on scattered references in Skues' writings. Some of them were friends of Skues, but not all, as will be seen. James Rolt, KC, of Frog Hall, Wokingham, was a senior barrister with a large Chancery practice. His fishing career went back to the 1890s, when he fished with Halford and got to know Basil Field, one of his partners in the Ramsbury fishery. Field, a well-known solicitor in London, acted for the executors of G.S. Marryat, and secured from his effects his enormous fly-book, known to friends in his lifetime as 'the Portmanteau'. Field kept it for several years before passing it on to Rolt. After a disquietingly adventurous career, this priceless piece of angling history now rests in the Flyfishers' Club.

Rolt was a patient and effective fisherman. It was his habit at Abbots Barton to lie in wait for a rising fish by a particular riverside stile upstream from the fishing hut known to members as 'Piscatoribus Sacrum', but generally to go no further upstream. This may have been because he had lodgings at Kingsbury near the top end of the fishery, and could easily get back to base at the end of a tiring day. The stile came to be known as Rolt's Stile for many years before the Second World War.

Judge Cecil Lilley is mentioned occasionally by Skues with the humorous (though incorrectly spelt) pseudonym of 'Fleur-de-Lys'. He had been given leave to fish it some years earlier by Irwin Cox and knew the fishery before the syndicate was formed. He already knew Skues, having been a member of the Flyfishers' Club since 1912, and Skues volunteered, or was asked by Cox, to show him the way on his first visit to Abbots Barton. Some years later Lilley wrote a humorous piece in the *Journal* about this event called 'Of a Master, his Book, and his Disciple', by F. De L. In this sketch the expert, who is called Mentor, has pressed upon the writer the loan of a certain book called *Minor Tactics of the Chalk Stream*, 'which, he said, had been written of this very fishery by a master. This, said he, I must read, mark, learn, and inwardly digest. Then would all things be made clear, and I should be heir to the wisdom of the ages and the lord and master of great fish.' On the great day he, of course, knows the book by heart, including Skues' characteristic maxims, so that he can recognize a rise as 'dace-like', although he has no idea what a dace might be, and knows also that a 'kidney-shaped' rise must mean the engulfing of a blue-winged olive, although he is dismayed when the keeper assures him that they would not appear for another month. When he gets into tangles and loses flies he is unable to agree that 'to repair damages was the work of a few moments', another ironical quotation from the book. After an unsuccessful morning he makes his way to the fishing hut, encountering his Mentor who has, of course, caught a brace of substantial fish.

This article was no doubt written as a riposte to one written by Skues in the previous issue of the *Journal*, called 'The Evil Influence of Fleur de Lys', by Integer Vitae, but good-natured contentions of this sort were not serious. Skues once went to the trouble of finding a copy of the first edition (1836) of Ronalds for Lilley. He and Skues seem always to have been on good terms. Other members, as will be apparent in Chapter 12, were less well disposed.

Another member, H.B. Harris, who joined in 1924, has been briefly described by Skues in *Itchen Memories*. He came as a refugee from the Kennet, and only fished for one season at Abbots Barton before resigning his membership. The explanation offered by Skues was that although Harris did well enough on the Itchen, he wanted to get back to 'the four-brace days which he was accustomed to get on the Kennet at Ramsbury'. It is perhaps a little unfair to produce the evidence of the Ramsbury fishery log, but the true record for H.B. Harris indicates that the 'four-brace days' were not customary at all. The entries show that he began as a paying rod of Colonel Grove-Hills (brother of John Waller Hills) in 1914 and fished there for the next ten years, a total of 149 rod days. Only four of these were days of eight trout and one of nine. An accurate fishing record can be a stern corrective of rose-tinted memories.

The curious change in the quality of fishing at Abbots Barton persisted for years; in fact it never really seemed to get back to the pre-war level of numerous but smaller trout. This was to be the beginning of difficulty for Skues on the Itchen, which was to have consequences in the wider world of angling. Few of the members of the new syndicate had the skill to make headway against a much smaller population of large and experienced fish. They became discouraged and disgruntled, and, as the years passed, resentment against Skues began to develop. The withdrawal of Irwin Cox had deprived Skues of a patron, and after 1918 he began to be aware that he was without protection. Differences of opinion over matters of management and rules for members arose in the syndicate, and he generally found himself isolated and out-voted. He was prepared to admit that the stock in the river had fallen so low that a bag limit was necessary. This move had never before been contemplated. In *Itchen Memories* he described a day at Winchester before 1914 when he and Lamorna Birch caught fourteen trout between them and added, with sad memories of better times: 'Those were the days before any limits on baskets were imposed.' In a scheme of management which the members had asked him to prepare for the season of 1919 he admitted that the size limit should rise from 12 to 13in, and that the bag limit of fish between 13 and 17in or two pounds should be a meagre two brace. Above 17in no limit needed to be fixed. He made it clear that this policy ought only to be followed during what he hopefully called 'the period of recovery'. The size and bag limit was agreed, but his objection to adding artificially to the fish population came up against the solid resistance of the other members, and was not adopted. He wrote:

> I do not advocate re-stocking. The upper shallow is a fine spawning ground, and there are more up Mr F.'s Scotch burn and below the W. Mill. The Itchen has stocked itself despite enormous losses to the town below for all the years that I remember it, and I think wild fish, bred wild, make far better sporting fish than any stew-fed trout.

No record seems to have survived about this clash, the first of many defeats, but the other members had probably pointed out that, whatever the spawning beds might once have contributed, the evidence now was that they were not producing much.

In 1921 *The Way of a Trout with a Fly* appeared. It has been the opinion of posterity that this was Skues' best contribution to the literature of angling. However, just as some critics have always preferred the first of Halford's books to the second, so there still can be found some Skues enthusiasts who have an affection for the freshness of *Minor Tactics of the Chalk Stream*. By the 1920s his ideas had moved on and he began to regard it as a piece of juvenilia that was better forgotten. After the appearance of the third edition in 1927 he asked the publishers not to think of another. The 1921 book, with its far greater range, was always considered his best work.

It had been some time in the making. A&C Black had hoped to publish it in 1918 but were defeated by the severe paper shortage at the end of the war. A good deal of it had already seen the light of day in the form of papers printed in the angling journals. For most of us it would qualify as a 'book', but Skues, with his usual combination of logic and personal modesty, insisted that it was therefore not a book at all – it was merely an anthology of his previously published material. His next book, *Sidelines, Sidelights and Reflections* (1932) was similarly constructed from his former writings, and Skues continued to maintain that he had never written (or, as he put it, 'been guilty of') a book. For him, his first three publications had merely been edited compilations. He wrote that he doubted if he was capable of writing a book. Not until 1937 did he sit down to plan and construct something that he could allow to be a 'book'.

These technicalities aside, *The Way of a Trout with a Fly* was and remains one of the most significant contributions to fly-fishing literature in the past five centuries.

The Foreword, with its magnificently sonorous opening – 'Authorities darken counsel' – sets forth the author's policy. For him, dogma is a thing to be avoided. Free enquiry into all problems is to be preferred, and the enquirer ought to keep in mind the essential fluidity of the process of knowledge-gathering, rather than aiming for certainty and finality. He was not quite the first angling writer to see the value of this idea; there had been a few earlier writers holding liberal views. Alfred Ronalds had, in 1836, suggested to his readers that to cling blindly to someone else's list of flies has little value: better to use such a list 'as a *help*, not as an *oracle*, and it will assist and facilitate your studies'. Skues was prepared to admit that, when he was a beginner, in what he liked to call the stage of his 'aboriginal dufferdom', he had relied heavily on such lists and had regarded established writers (particularly Halford) as oracular. By the middle of the 1890s he had begun to abandon this belief. In the years that followed he had become actively resentful of his own earlier simplicity and credulity, and of the amount of time he had spent in the Reading Room of the British Museum working through all the angling books published since 1496, and uncritically absorbing the statements of so-called authorities. In the course of time he came to see that most of them consisted merely of repetitions of former information, much of it fallacious and inaccurate:

It was not until I realized this that my reading became any use to me ... From that point on an author became merely a suggester of experiment – a means of testing and checking my own observations by the waterside, and no longer a small god to be believed in and trusted as infallible. [This admirable foreword, a model of its kind, continued in a firm, reasonable but hard-hitting style:] An authority who lays down a law and dogmatizes is a narcotic, a soporific, a stupefier, an opiate. The true function of an authority is to stimulate, not to paralyze, original thinking. But then, I suppose, he wouldn't be an authority.

There can be little doubt as to the identity of the 'small god' Skues had in mind.

Skues then returned to a matter that he had aired before in the journals: his early ambition to write a major book on fly-dressing. After some years, he admitted, two problems had brought him to a halt. The first, already referred to, was his growing suspicion of the value of the so-called wisdom of former ages. He still nursed this project for some years, but around 1900 he became aware of another serious difficulty. In order to construct some worthwhile theoretical framework to act as a guide for the art of fly-dressing, an author would need to have some idea, based on good science, as to how trout vision operates. It was typical of Skues to worry about this problem. Many fly-dressers past and present have not bothered their heads with principles, being content to work on a simple trial and error basis: if this or that pattern seems to work they are happy. This was not enough for Skues: he wished to enquire more deeply. However, he was aware that, although he was a reasonably equipped observer and field naturalist, he was not a trained scientist. Nor was he a trained philosopher, or he might have waded deeply into Plato's ideas on ideal objects and imperfect copies. He could only deal as far as he was able with the more practical matters of the biology of trout vision and the physics of light, and defer to any specialist who he might help him out.

At times he lamented his lack of scientific education, for he had been thinking about these problems for many years before 1921. In one of his first letters to *The Fishing Gazette* in 1887 he pointed out that the dry fly 'being in a different medium (the air), must present a different appearance to the fish under the surface to what it would if it were sunk'. In 1904 he had corresponded with Louis Bouglé on the same subject, and a year later in *The Fishing Gazette* he had written: 'The longer I fish the more satisfied I am that the sight of trout, though amazingly quick, is also imperfect, in so far as it does not enable him to distinguish form.' Although, by that date, an accomplished fly-dresser, he had come to wonder whether the attempt to achieve a perfect finish in a pattern, particularly with wings, was quite worth the trouble. Colour and size were the important factors. One day in 1912 he made a journey to Ipswich with Sheringham to visit Dr Francis Ward at his laboratory, in order to view his experimental water tank. Both men came away feeling that they had improved their understanding of the underwater world. Some of Ward's ideas, set forth in a ground-breaking article in *The Field* in 1912, were taken further in his book *Animal Life under Water* (1919). But, to the end of his life, Skues never felt satisfied with his own progress in understanding these questions. Because of his doubts and hesitations the second half of the Foreword of *The Way of a Trout with a Fly* is presented rather apologetically to the reader. Skues' approach was that he could only present the best working theory of fly-dressing in the present state of scientific knowledge, in the hope that other investigators might do better. Ten years later he regarded his friend Col. E.W. Harding as a thinker in this category, and Harding's book *The Flyfisher and the Trout's Point of View* (1931) as one of the most important of its kind of the century. In 1935 in the third edition of *The Way of a Trout with a Fly* he made mention of Harding's theories and regretted his premature death. He several times referred to Harding as 'a great angling mind' and was therefore dismayed some years later when George Monkhouse, a director of the Kodak company and well informed about optical problems, cast doubt on some of Harding's ideas (see Chapter 13).

Two books by other authors appeared in the years after the publication of *The Way of a Trout with a Fly*, both of which Skues thought to be worth noticing in later editions of his book. The views of Colonel Harding in *The Flyfisher and the Trout's Point of View* are mentioned in the third edition of 1935. In the second edition in 1928 he mentioned *Sunshine and the Dry Fly* (1927), by the aeronautical engineer and philosopher J.W. Dunne, also known for *An Experiment with Time*, a speculative book on the significance of dreams. Skues was interested in anything about the relationship between trout vision and fly construction but, like many another angler, he found Dunne's use of fragile and easily degradable artificial silk impractical on the river. Also, he was not keen on Dunne's way of clipping hackles, remarking to Dr Barton: 'A man who would cut hackles would cut a throat.' He was, however, impressed by the effort to deal with the problem of translucency, and therefore refused to criticize the book. It was, as usual, Skues' habit to perceive the drawback in Dunne's procedure and then attempt to improve it by trying out the use of the more durable artificial raffia. In 1929 he made his own brief contribution to the discussion in an article in *The Field*, pointing out that the translucency or opacity of a floating fly depends on its position in relation to the fish and the source of light.

Another significant contribution came in 1939 with the appearance of *Random Casts* by the American Eugene Connett III, which Skues considered had taken up Harding's ideas and moved them on a good deal. At the front of his copy was a handsome tribute: 'To G.E.M. Skues, in appreciation for the many valuable lessons I have learned from his delightful writings. Sincerely Eugene Connett.' Skues wanted the publishers to add yet another note praising this book in his *Nymph Fishing for Chalk Stream Trout* but, by some oversight, this was not done. Eventually it found a place in the fourth edition of *The Way of a Trout with a Fly* in 1949, shortly before Skues' death.

The first section (called a Division in the original) of *The Way of a Trout with a Fly*, numbering thirty chapters, discusses the above-mentioned and other problems. There is a concerted attempt to get beneath surface appearances and search for significance and real meaning, involving the reader in a chase through thickets of logic and semantics in the search for essence. These chapters contain more in the way of question than of solution. Having cleared the ground, Skues moved on to an area in which he was more at home. It might be a fair guess that most readers turned with some relief from the content of the first Division to the less difficult and more entertaining material in the second. Here are gathered a number of short pieces, many of them based on days by the riverside, where interesting and effective tactics are discussed to provide good examples which might lead the reader towards success in the angling day. Some of Skues' best writing can be found in these pages.

If the book had been published a year later, it would have included an account of another of Skues' discoveries, namely the occasional importance of the large spurwing or blue-winged pale watery – *Centroptilum* (nowadays called *Pseudocentroptilum*) *pennulatum*. It came to his notice soon after the appearance of his book. It is odd that he had never been aware of this fly before, and he only decided to add an account of it in the fourth edition. It seems only to occur occasionally, but when it does it can bring on a general rise of fish, perhaps more so than the blue-winged olive. He recorded its appearance only three more times between 1921and 1938. When he migrated to the River Nadder in 1939 he began to see the fly more frequently. It was perhaps this that encouraged him to persuade his publishers to add an extra chapter to the fourth edition of the book in 1949. In this, he described his first encounter with the large spurwing in June 1921. Two consecutive evenings with trout rising wildly at every fly except the angler's left him baffled. The trusty Orange Quill was of no service at all. The following weekend he and his guest Dr Norman McCaskie were defeated by a similar episode. Skues and Cecil Lilley caught nothing: McCaskie, urged on by Skues to break the rules, retained an undersized trout for autopsy, and that evening in a Winchester hotel the mystery fly was revealed in a saucer of water: 'several largish duns of a species I had never before seen, with wings of the same dark blue as the B.W.O., but with bodies white, long and tapered, flat on the underside, with faint brownish markings on the rounded upper side of the last two or three segments'.

The following morning Skues tied several imitations of the new fly with dark blue hackles and a white wool body and, armed with this new weapon, the three men went out onto the river. As evening came on the fish began to behave in the same way as before. It says a lot for Skues' fixation with the blue-winged olive that for some time he made no attempt to use the new fly, but battled on with no success with what he described as 'the proved B.W.O. alternatives', which must mean in the main the Orange Quill. Lilley, however, caught with the new fly a difficult fish of 2lb 9oz that had defeated Skues and McCaskie in the morning. There was just time for Skues to profit quickly from this information, return to a fish over which he had been casting in vain and, shortly afterwards, to discover that it weighed 2lb 6oz. McCaskie had also done well, with a fish of 3lb 2oz.

There is a small problem here. Skues may not have remembered with complete accuracy what happened. His account quite clearly states that the biggest fish of the evening also succumbed to the imitation of the spurwing. However, McCaskie says not: his angling diary has survived, and his account of the evening's fishing includes a note: 'Caught my 3/2 on pheasant tail spinner.'

The killing imitation of C.P., as Skues called it, was recorded in the *Journal* (summer 1941):

Hook   No.13 Bartleet 7362
Silk   White, waxed with clear wax
Hackle Dark blue hen (like wing of natural B.W.O)
Whisks Pale blue dun
Body   White lamb's wool

[He added a note: 'Discovered 21st June, 1921. Very deadly on the rare occasions when the natural insect is hatching.']

A year later the fly was observed by J.W. Dunne hatching on another river (Skues thought it might have been the Kennet) and shortly afterwards Martin Mosely provided a positive identification of the mystery fly.

The notices in the angling press of *The Way of a Trout with a Fly* were somewhat disappointing and inadequate, as if the writers had not been able to perceive the importance of the book. To a certain extent this was true for reviews of all Skues' books, including (it is painful to record) the perfunctory efforts at reviewing in the *Journal*. One is left with the impression that Skues was so far in advance of his generation as a theorist and a practitioner that it was difficult for editors to find reviewers who were up to his weight. The review in *The Scotsman* was clearly written by someone who had no idea at all what the book was about. *Nature* praised the book, emphasizing one of the main suggestions: 'If your trout be only feeding on larvae or nymphs, then let them have it underwater.' The most discerning review came from R.B. Marston in *The Fishing Gazette*. A cautious convert to the sunk fly in the early years of the century, he was now a generous supporter, pointing out that the practice had since 1910 'achieved deserved popularity'. He liked the discussion of the trout's sense of form, and thought that the chapter on rise forms was the best in the book. He allowed himself a little gentle mockery of Skues' attempt to analyse the reasons why fish take flies, which does seem to traverse some fairly obvious ground. But he emphasized that 'in every chapter Mr Skues sets the reader thinking'.

The publication of his 1921 book sealed Skues' reputation for all time. As often happens to authors after the publication of a major book, he acquired an increasing number of new acquaintances, some of whom became friends. Invitations to new fisheries arrived. He had already some experience of the Test. Now John Waller Hills, who had first made trial of the sunk fly on the Kennet in July 1914, saw an opportunity to observe the method in the hands of the master, and brought him to the waters of the Houghton Club. In June 1922 Skues was a guest at the annual dinner of the Houghton Club at Claridges, being placed next to Dr Pryce-Tannatt, whose strong round-bend hooks had always excited his admiration. And in 1927 he caught the largest grayling of the year from the Houghton waters. Skues always maintained that grayling were vermin, but a big grayling would always make his pulse quicken, particularly the giant specimens he encountered in Norway.

For Skues this was a prosperous and stable period. The dark memories of the Great War were beginning to fade, and he enjoyed achievements with both rod and pen. The problems within the syndicate at Abbots Barton and with purism in the angling world at large remained, but they had not yet run out of control. It was the Indian summer of Skues, a pause before the deluge.

10

Equipoise 1923–1936

T

HE PERIOD BETWEEN the wars was, in the main, a happy time for Skues, at least until 1936, when a real threat to his peace of mind announced itself. The man who once thought that he was going to die in 1891, and later imagined that he might with reasonable luck reach his sixtieth year, was as tireless as ever on the riverbank throughout the 1920s. But he was approaching old age now, and in the next decade he began once again to be pessimistic about his expectations of a long life, writing in August 1932 to his friend Major Evans:

> My feet seem to be giving out and it looks as if I should not be able to go on fishing much longer and I certainly do not want to dribble into the grave. I had a Grandmother who died at the age of 88 and a Grandfather who died at the age of 77, but I have no particular desire to emulate them.

In spite of these gloomy forecasts he had thirteen more seasons of fishing to come. However, his health did begin to alter. He wrote to a correspondent: 'Whether I shall be able to stand the fatigues of the water meadows next year it is difficult to say.' But his overall constitution was still sound. In the winter of 1933 he went to the funeral of an old client of his firm and, in the freezing cold of the church, he caught a chill, which soon turned into pleuro-pneumonia. The same thing happened to his neighbour in the congregation: that man died but Skues survived. Later, a bout of influenza involved a secretary in a trip from Essex Street to Croydon for several days to take dictation, and he caught the odd cold from time to time, something from which he had been free for years. In 1936, when he was seventy-eight, he was irritated to notice feelings of tiredness after a long day on the river, and there were also occasional falls in the meadows, one of which, in 1931, called for the attention of a masseur. He wrote to

Evans: 'I wish I could say that I thought he had been successful.' In fact the discomfort from this injury was still with him in 1946.

He treated these events as unimportant. More disturbing than these temporary setbacks was the deterioration in his eyesight, which had never been entirely reliable. By 1932 he found he could not see spinners on the water in twilight, and in rough water could not see a floating fly at all. In 1935 he wrote to Tommy Hanna: 'my eyesight is deteriorating as I get older, and I miss so many rises to my nymphs'. By the end of the 1930s evening fishing was no longer possible. His hearing, also, was failing. All the speeches at the annual dinner of the Flyfishers' Club in February 1932 were lost on him, including, to his great regret, the address by the guest of honour, John Buchan. So, also, was the speech of Lord Grey at the Fishmongers' Hall in June of the same year.

In the Essex Street office there was one major change. James Powell retired in 1925, Skues became the senior partner and a young solicitor was recruited into the practice. The firm continued for many years under the new style of Skues and Graham Smith. The stock of handsome, cream-laid headed notepaper, after the parsimonious practice of that age, was not scrapped for pulping, but was used for long afterwards, with the name of Powell neatly crossed out each time a letter was sent. One drawback of becoming head of the practice was that Skues' workload increased and leisure time was drastically curtailed. Abbots Barton visits were, of course, sacrosanct, and he was determined to get there every weekend, but anything more ambitious was not possible. The last long holiday of his working life was in 1924, when he went to Norway for a month. From that time onwards, only weekend absences from London were possible.

His success in his profession and, after the publication of his second book, his assured position in the world, had given Skues an added confidence. He continued to publish stimulating articles in the angling press. From them, readers could learn new and subtle ideas about tactics, and could marvel at the ever-lengthening list of nymph patterns. In this way he hoped to bring about, quietly and without aggression, a revolution in thinking about the place of the nymph on the chalk stream. Perhaps he thought that his prestige could be useful in moving on the process of conversion. More and more was he being regarded as one of the most influential men of ideas in the world of fly-fishing. In 1928 he was made an honorary member of the Anglers' Club of New York (several years in advance of a similar move by the sister club in London).

For Skues the disadvantages of a rather unsatisfactory start in life were less important now, although he never lost a reserve and a reticence with people. For him, acquiring a new acquaintance would need some sort of vehicle or agenda, rather as many people pick up friends in the workplace. Skues was not going to add non-fishing people to his circle unless they could join in his rather specialized type of conversation. For his social life he knew he owed a debt of gratitude to the Flyfishers' Club, where he was often to be seen at a fly-dressing session in the corner – which, however, he would abandon to join in the conversation of a group of newcomers. Ill-timed familiarity would always annoy him, and he never entirely took into his confidence new acquaintances who too obviously claimed an intimacy that he felt was not justified. Into this category later came George Monkhouse, who wrote a long sycophantic letter of introduction in 1939, and thereafter pursued him so energetically that Skues was never able to shake him off.

There were, however, a host of friends and acquaintances who encouraged his work and brightened the life of a confirmed bachelor who had little use for the house-parties and conviviality of social life. They were a second generation of contacts in Skues' life, to take the place of Bouglé, Coggeswell and Sheringham. Some were companions on the river, while others were correspondents whom he never met. Some of them influenced his thinking, but there is little doubt that the intellectual traffic moved mainly in the other direction and that his friends and correspondents were the fortunate learners. Of those who were interesting theorists as well as being competent on the river, mention might be made of Major J.D.D. Evans of Usk who, among his many talents, had a deep knowledge of forestry; C.A.N. Wauton, a former President of the Flyfishers' Club and author of *Fly-Fishers' Ephemeridae* (1921), extended into a larger version as *Trout Fishers' Entomology* (1930); J.W. Dunne, author of *Sunshine and the Dry Fly* (1924); and George Benson Stewart, artist, Harley Street dentist, inventor of a useful hand vice, and characterized in a series of Skues' humoresques in *The Journal* as 'the Novice'.

There were others who were effective practitioners, but are not known to have recorded anything theoretical, such as Samuel John ('Lamorna') Birch and A.D. Chaytor. Next in rank come the good but not brilliant performers such as Dr E.A. Barton, J.W. Hills, Dr Norman McCaskie, Captain C.F. Struben RNVR, Colonel Jesse and Dr Arthur Holmes. In a class by himself was Colonel E.W. Harding, author of *The Flyfisher and the Trout's Point of View* (1931), a book much admired by

Skues. There were also many overseas correspondents, mainly from America, some of whom came to fish with Skues on the Itchen, such as Henry van Dyke, G.M.L. La Branche, Baird Foster, Edward Boies (who was President of the Anglers' Club of New York in 1925 and 1926), Franklin B. Lord (who had an impressive library which included a copy of that notable rarity, Scotcher's *Fly-Fisher's Legacy*), Dr Warren Coleman and Richard Carley Hunt.

It is worth looking at these men. Skues was cautious in his acquaint-anceships, and warmth and affection did not come naturally to him: if we are looking for the friends in his life, this is the nearest we will get. Acquiring a sense of these relationships is not easy for us today, sixty years and more after his disappearance from the scene. Like Halford, with whom he has more points of resemblance than is sometimes realized, Skues did not intend to be known in too much depth. When C.F. Walker published his useful collection of Skues' letters in 1956, the Foreword by John Evans applauded Walker for sticking rigidly to angling matters and for eliminating all material of a private nature. Evans had loaned more letters to Walker than anyone else. He wrote: 'Skues was a sensitive man and I think he would have been greatly displeased if many of the personal remarks in his private letters had been made public in this book.' Such delicacy was appropriate in 1956 when Walker's book appeared, and when many friends of Skues were still alive. Of course, what Evans referred to as 'personal remarks' are exactly what a biographer does need if wishing to get nearer to the real man. Skues is now not a recently deceased hero but part of history, and the reasons for such reticence have lost their relevance with time.

But the search for evidence about the man behind the angler is still difficult. One reason is the factor mentioned above, the reticence of Skues himself: even his letters, when one gets a sight of the same material carefully deodorized by Commander Walker, lack the personal detail one would wish to find. The second reason is a similar unwillingness of his friends in their letters to examine the deeper wells of his conduct in life. The result is that there is little in the way of record of even his ordinary conversation and habits. He had no Boswell constantly by his side to recreate for us his table talk at the Flyfishers' Club or the fishing hut, just as he had no Marryat working with him on new ideas. There are, however, some fragments in the surviving papers of friends, most notably Dr E.A. Barton, which tell us more about the human being as well as the angler than anything else. With the eye and approach of a doctor, Barton could see deeper into this odd man than many more superficial observers. Some of this can be gleaned from Barton's published work and from his letters, but more so from his eighteen annual diaries covering the years 1922 to 1939. These provide probably the richest source of all.

Barton first met Skues at the Bear Hotel in Hungerford in 1917, recalling years later: 'I was at once attracted to him by the something in his conversation and manner which drew men towards him ... I realized that in my new acquaintance I was meeting a master angler.' Barton became Skues' most frequent angling companion and, at length, his closest and kindest friend. For the next thirty years he was able to observe Skues and his method of carrying to his fishing the same spirit of deep enquiry that appeared in his professional life as a lawyer. Barton wrote in an obituary piece: 'No slack thinking, no guess work was allowed, but facts and facts only were permitted as the basis of his deductions.' Skues had early realized that Abbots Barton, more than most other fisheries, demanded the best in fly-dressing and the quality of the flies tied by him astonished Barton: 'No fly but with the closest approach to an exact similarity to the real insect was of the slightest use.' When he stayed with Skues in Winchester, Barton would often find that his host had got out of bed much earlier in the morning, and was already in a corner of the breakfast room, bent over his fly-dressing materials, watch-glass in his one good eye, making the flies appropriate for the day. In the 1890s he had designed an elaborate fly-dressing table, which had then been made up by his brother Charles. In later years he increasingly used a more convenient campaigning apparatus. This consisted of elephant files, eventually three in number, any one of which would normally be left at his hotel. A smaller travelling packet was set up for riverside fly-tying and for journeys: his dressing of flies with a hand vice in a railway compart-ment under the gaze of bemused fellow-passengers is, of course, now part of the Skues legend.

For posterity, the most valuable contribution lies in Barton's descrip-tions of his fishing days with Skues. His impression, which is supported by similar memories of the colonial judge Sir Grimwood Mears and others, is that when on the river Skues was a driven man, allowing no time to be wasted. This did not mean that he was one of those over-active anglers who imagine that the fly must be constantly in the water. He would begin by wandering slowly about, even when fish were rising, in order to get the feel of the day. But he was dogged and thorough once he had started. They mounted a combined assault one day on a particular trout, 'an old friend of Skues' observed Barton in his diary, taking turns to cover the fish with four casts each. In this way they showed sixteen flies to the trout. In spite of all this attention the fish remained in the river.

Skues' rather eccentric riverside equipment excited a good deal of comment from Barton and other friends. In the period between the wars he had settled to a system that suited him and he wanted no other. He did not use the usual compartmented fly-boxes, preferring to use small matchboxes. In the days when non-safety matches had a habit of choosing their own moments to ignite, match boxes were of tin, measuring 2x4in, and Skues had armed himself with several of these. They contained a number of slips of paper, into which the flies were pinned. Barton wrote: 'but I never knew him at a loss when changing his fly'. A mackintosh and the rest of his tackle, including a tobacco pouch which did duty as a cast damper, were stowed away in a large white cotton bag (sometimes two) secured at damaged places by safety pins and string, together with his catch of fish, wrapped in dusters or napkins. There was also a straw market basket and a canvas fishing bag, and a shooting stick for pausing to watch the river or for sitting out a long siege over a difficult trout. Finally there was a long and, one would imagine, cumbersome net, made up from a broom handle he had purchased in the 1880s for sixpence. We are not surprised to learn from Barton that, on the riverbank and indeed in the streets of Winchester, Skues looked from behind like the White Knight in *Through the Looking Glass*.

For a fishing day Skues took a small packet of sandwiches and little else in the way of food with him. According to Barton, although it borders on the unbelievable, he took almost nothing to drink. He would begin the day with an enormous breakfast, including a chop and other sustaining items, and this plan would enable him to keep famine at bay from ten o'clock in the morning until dinner in the evening. The Corner House was not a particularly good example of Winchester accommodation, but at least it seems to have been flexible about meal times. In April and May Skues (and perforce his guests) would dine at the end of the fishing day at seven to eight o'clock, but as the days lengthened he would come back for a quick supper as early as five o'clock in order to get back onto the river before the evening rise.

Anyone fishing at the Abbots Barton water, which lacked shelter from trees and which, on many days, became a natural wind tunnel, had to devise some way of getting a line into a headwind. On the morning of a fishing day Skues would pay more attention to the weathervane than to the barometer. To counter the effects of fishing in such conditions Skues had devised his own unorthodox style. Barton described it as being something between a switch and a roll, with the rod neither vertical nor horizontal but in between, inclining more to the lower level. This technique was known to be so characteristic of him that it enabled him to be recognized on the river at a considerable distance. No doubt many anglers of the time, schooled in Halford's teachings, would have adopted Marryat's downward cut. Skues, perhaps without planning it, had developed an alternative but effective trick of withdrawing line at the moment of full extension of the cast. Skues wrote: 'I do it by turning the wrist at the end of the cast so that the back of the hand is downwards, then drawing back the whole hand sharply to the side. This seems to curl out the fly quite straight into the wind in quite a remarkable way.'

If he was addressing a trout feeding underwater his method was to get out the line in a series of flicking movements, allowing the nymph to enter the water each time so as to retain its moisture. Barton and other observers wondered at this apparently casual and informal performance, and even more at the accuracy of the final delivery. He wrote in 1923: 'I noticed that though Skues cannot throw as long a line as I can – (he says 'it is my wrist') – yet he casts far more delicately and accurately.' Barton was a much more energetic caster, and Skues approved of Barton's powerful wrist action and also of his 9ft 4in Leonard. Barton added: 'But I liked his casting much better than my own. His line was much straighter and more wire-like than mine and he made it run along the water uncurling as it went, the fly falling last at the end of quite a straight gut. It was very pretty.'

Skues had also devised a method of recovering the line from the water by aerializing it for a moment before beginning the back cast, a manoeuvre he called 'picking it off'. As the day advanced his line presented more resistance because, although he greased it in the morning, he seldom troubled to treat it again. Barton commented on his host's sunken waterlogged line emerging from the river accompanied by a fountain of moisture. 'Picking it off' and getting the line free of the cling of the surface before using full power was therefore a good method of avoiding placing unfair strain on the tip of his precious Leonard. Skues was concerned about the load Barton placed on his own rod and tried hard to teach him the technique, but without much success. Barton wrote in his diary: 'Skues says I shall break the heart of my Leonard by too-violent casting.'

Throughout these years Skues continued to rely mainly on the same rod – the 9ft, 5oz Leonard procured for him from America in 1905 by Coggeshall, which he called 'the joy of my life'. He was fascinated by the workmanship of the makers, and acquired other Leonards, although it may be that some of them spent more time in the cupboard than on the river. As for gut leaders, he relied on the trade rather than making up his own, merely modifying what he could buy. Most of his casts were tapered to 3x or 4x. In many parts of the slow-moving main stream at Abbots Barton the trout cruised rather than holding their position, so it was unwise to use a short cast and he generally used one of 11 or 12ft. He wrote to Captain Evans in 1932 that he avoided casts with too thick a butt: 'I hate a stout end to my cast. I seldom use anything stouter than Refina.' In the scale for nylon in modern tackle Refina would be 1x or .010 of an inch, rather finer perhaps for the butt-end of a cast than present-day anglers would care to rely on for achieving a good turnover in casting. However, gut that had become soaked in water is likely to have been heavier than nylon of the same diameter, and may have achieved a similar result.

Barton learned a good deal about fly patterns from Skues. He was a moderately effective fly-dresser and would send some of his attempts to Skues for his judgements. In 1923 Skues wrote: 'Your effort at McCaskie's Green Cat is on the small side, but not unlike McCaskie's performance, bar that it has not the disconsolate and dishevelled air which probably constituted its supreme attraction for the grayling.' For Skues this was a fairly mild response. Anyone incautious enough to ask for Skues' opinion of their fly-dressing had to be prepared for anything: his strictures were apt to be devastatingly frank.

Barton was an accomplished photographer and would take his camera with him on fishing expeditions. He provided most of the illustrations for the *Journal* for many years, the best of which were gathered together after the Second World War and published in *An Album of the Chalk Streams*. He was naturally anxious to secure as much of a record of Skues as possible, but here he came up against the almost invincible camera-phobia mentioned earlier. Apart from being a very private sort of man Skues was sensitive about his baldness, which came about fairly early in life, and he could never rid himself of the conviction that his appearance in general was odd. If Barton was about to take a shot of a stretch of the river Skues would edge out of the line of view, and accost him a little later, enquiring anxiously: 'I don't come into it, do I?' The small number of the Abbots Barton shots of Skues that have survived are mostly the fruit of some surreptitious work on the part of Barton, lurking unobserved in the background. In fact there are very few images of Skues in existence at all, either at Abbots Barton or anywhere else, so the same pictures are frequently repeated in books and journals. The late Ken Robson succeeded in securing some new examples of Skues as a child and a young man, and his book *The Essential G.E.M. Skues* is the best place to see a small collection not available elsewhere.

Being well aware of this problem, Barton was startled one day to be consulted by his friend about a proposed photographic session. Skues explained that the Anglers' Club of New York, several of whose members knew him and had fished with him, had asked for a photograph. He was now in a fix and needed help. For anyone else it would have been a simple matter of arrangement, but this had a personal as well as a practical element: only someone in whom he had an absolute trust would do.

The session got away to a slow start. Barton arrived at Skues' house in Croydon, found him in his everyday office outfit and dispatched him upstairs to find his usual fishing clothes in a tweed the colour of willow bark. The result was the small selection of pictures nowadays familiar to us. Predictably, Skues did not like them. When Barton showed them to him a few days later he was shocked and mortified, saying: 'I don't really look like that, do I?' Barton assured him that they were true likenesses: 'It is you exactly.' Skues at once resolved not to use them, and extracted a promise that they should never be seen in his lifetime. A little later he attempted to solve the matter by visiting a professional photographer, who took several shots and did some 'improvement', brushing out the craggy contours of the face and providing what Barton called a 'school-girl complexion'. The Anglers' Club of New York must have acquired an impression of Skues that was out of date by decades. Barton, however, was pleased with his own results, one of which he published in an article in the *Journal* after Skues' death. In this he bids us, with the practised eye of a medical man, to observe the high domed forehead, the drooped lid over the left eye which had almost no sight after the botched operation of 1867, the projecting bone of the radius joint at the wrist where a proper re-setting had never taken place and the prominent fingers capable, in spite of their size, of making the smallest fly.

Although the strength of their friendship was never in doubt, Barton always felt ambivalent about his visits to Winchester. Of one he wrote glumly: 'I had not looked forward much to this expedition, which is always a very exhausting one.' Once, after a hot day working in University College Hospital, he had got to Winchester at 6.45 p.m. and had spent a fruitless session trying to make something of the evening rise. The following day he was too tired to fish and spent most of the time sleeping under the trees at Ducks' Nest Spinney.

Abbots Barton was a challenging place in which to catch fish, and its layout was daunting, with its main and side streams strung out over a wide expanse of open country, and in most places devoid of trees for shade in hot sun or to deflect the wind. On one occasion – there were several similar – rain began to fall heavily and Barton crept into the boathouse for shelter. It was impossible to stand up inside and he crouched miserably for a long period while the rain rattled deafeningly on the tin roof. Meanwhile Skues could be dimly discerned in the distance, unconcernedly fishing throughout the storm.

Barton confessed that he did not even care much for the look of Abbots Barton: for him it was an open, dreary moorland site, lacking charm. He only rarely took his camera there. By contrast he preferred the pretty fishery at Leckford, where everything was more restful and there would be a respectful keeper to carry at least some of the baggage for the day, including his heavy wooden camera. He wrote: 'Skues' invitations I value much, as I learn much, but it is a very tiring place.' The fact that Skues (who was five years older than Barton) was impervious to fatigue made it worse. Even when he was well into old age he would range tirelessly up and down the two miles of water. Barton commented: 'I am dead beat after two hours, but at 5 p.m. he suggests "one more look round above the hut" which means the top of the water again – not me! I said to the keeper I would give all I possessed for a bath chair home.'

Skues' notion of appropriate places at which to lodge was another deterrent. He had, over the years, tried a number of hotels in Winchester, eventually settling in the 1930s on the Corner House Hotel, apparently for no better reason than for its nearness to the railway station. As he was there almost every weekend from March until the end of the season, he could arrange to store a good deal of his possessions, including fly-dressing materials. At times he even took the trouble to hire a private sitting room, if a guest had been invited. None of this weighed with Barton: more important was that the standard of accommodation was in several ways rough at the edges and there was not much talent to be found in the kitchen. Skues cared little for these matters, but Barton appreciated good food and the comforts of civilized life. Of all the doubtful choices of Skues in Winchester, the Corner House was the least favourite for Barton.

Situated at the junction of five roads, the racket of modern times was hard to bear. On a hot evening conversation at dinner was impossible with the window open. Thunderous lorry traffic continued throughout the night, shaking the whole building. There was a garage next door where cars were repaired noisily far into the night and again from 6 a.m. the following day. Skues was unaware of these drawbacks, ate heartily and slept deeply throughout the tumult of the world outside. Barton observed: 'I am sure that he will sleep soundly through the last trump and rise too late for any subsequent events.'

It cannot therefore be surprising that Barton received invitations from 'old Skues' with mixed feelings. It might have been better if he had been able to be more effective on the river, but the fishing in the 1920s was becoming slow and testing, and only the most advanced practitioners were getting fish. Apart from the problems inherited from wartime, the great drought of 1921 brought fishing to a virtual halt in the summer. 1922 was not much better because of the accumulation of mud from 1921. Occasionally, Barton got fish when Skues did not, but these were rare triumphs. As for the hotel problem, Barton became more restive as time passed and began to take a quiet survey of the local alternatives. It was not until 1935 that he felt confident enough to announce that he preferred to stay at the Hyde Abbey Hotel, which was marginally more acceptable, going over to meet his host at breakfast-time. Skues accepted this strange arrangement.

If one were to read only the complaints with which these interesting diaries are filled, the conclusion might be that the relationship between the two men was almost one of hostility. In fact, Barton's regard for Skues never failed. In one passage in his diary, after he had relieved his feelings of irritation in a diatribe of half a page, he ended by reminding himself that he would rather fish with Skues than with anyone else. The best clue to their long association is in their letters, which contain many tokens of affection. In 1924 Skues wrote: 'I enjoyed having you down immensely', and a year later: 'Shall I see you at the Club on Thursday? If not I daresay I shall not go', and in 1926: 'I should regard the year as a failure if you did not come down for one weekend at least to me.' In 1925 Barton presented Skues with a tiny monocular Zeiss glass, which improved his observation of nymphing trout, particularly when they were lying deeper. In his letter Skues thanked him for 'your charming little gift of a waistcoat pocket telescope. It is a thing which would never have occurred to me to acquire. You always seem to be planting little things on me, and I have not the knowledge or imagination to be able to hit you back in the appropriate place.'

It is clear from these passages (and others of the same sort) that, apart from his brother Charles, Edwin Barton was Skues' closest friend. In one of his letters Skues speculated how much longer his own life might last, and added: 'whether it be long or short, I hope it will always be marked by frequent enjoyment of your company by the riverside, at the fly-dressing table, at the dinner table and at the Club'. He entrusted Barton with the task of publishing after his death the list of his original ideas and inventions. Significantly, it was to Barton and – as far as can be known, to no one else – that Skues revealed the sad secret of his impossible love for the mysterious Alexandra Kitchin – the deepest personal wound of his life.

Samuel John Birch was another valued friend and fishing colleague. He was a member of that talented community of Cornish artists in the first half of the twentieth century. His style was in the Constable tradition, with a good understanding of light, shadow and the effect of wind on water. He called himself Lamorna Birch after Lamorna Cove where he lived (Skues always called him 'The Cove'). He was familiar with waters in many parts of the British Isles and elsewhere, even as far afield as New Zealand. By chance he met Minnie ('my schoolmarm sister', in Skues' own words) who, in 1911, was on holiday near the artist's house. Birch was adept at getting alongside new acquaintants, especially if they were women. He had already read *Minor Tactics,* and quickly used the opportunity to get to know Skues through his sister, taking as a gift one of his landscapes to their first meeting. Skues described their expedition to Abbots Barton in April 1913: the artist at once made an impression on him. Armed with a Leonard rod – a good beginning for getting into his host's good graces – he collected eight trout in a short time, and was able to set up his easel and record the scene. Skues always liked having a guest who was a skilled practitioner. To the last part of his fishing life, he was always prepared to learn something from others. He was particularly impressed with the powerful and accurate casting of the artist, and his friend's experience on the overgrown streams of Cornwall meant that he seldom got caught up. But the Cornish trout are not noted for their size, and Birch welcomed opportunities to get access to other areas such as the Itchen. Years later, in the 1930s, he got to know the artist colony around Salisbury, including Henry Lamb, Algernon Talmage and Wilfrid and Jane de Glehn. Here he became a frequent guest; some quick reconnaissance in the area followed and before long he had got leave to fish on the nearby River Nadder at Compton Chamberlayne.

Birch came to London each summer to exhibit at the Royal Academy, before or after which Skues would carry him off for another visit to Abbots Barton. After a while he found the George Hotel in Winchester to be too expensive for him – later Skues came to the same conclusion – and transferred to the Cart and Horses at Kingsbury. Later still, he discovered that one of the Abbots Barton rods living nearby had a gardener who would put him up, and he arranged a further saving by moving to Northleigh Cottage. Several pictures exist of the fishery, generally painted in the latter part of the day after a successful morning of fishing, for Birch seems to have been a rapid performer in both activities. He was also prolific: during his working career of seventy years he is believed to have executed 20,000 pictures in various media. Critics have suggested that some of his work was commercial rather than inspired, but a good deal of it was sufficiently impressive for him to be admired by leading contemporaries such as Alfred Munnings, Dame Laura Knight (who used to call him the Infant Samuel, because of his youthful energy), Augustus John and Dorelia McNeill. He became RA in 1934 at the same time as Walter Sickert who, along with Courbet and Pissarro, had always been an important influence on his work.

On one of his annual visits to London, Birch encountered an aspect of his friend and host of which he had previously been unaware. Mention has been made elsewhere in this book of Skues' intense involvement in one area of interest and his lack of engagement in virtually all other subjects. This was not likely to matter when they were lunching at the Flyfishers' Club or in the fishing hut at Abbots Barton. But when Birch came to London for the Royal Academy exhibition in 1934, Skues persuaded him to dine with him at home in Croydon and stay overnight. The evening was not a success, at least not for the artist. Keen fisherman as he was, he found the continuous dwelling upon fishing matters wearing after a while. That he was a heavy smoker in a house which, unusually for those days, was a non-smoking zone, increased his unhappiness. At last, in desperation, he sought leave to withdraw and view the back garden in order to have a cigarette. To his relief this was allowed, but he afterwards described the evening's entertainment as 'the very dullest experience'. It is unlikely that Skues noticed anything untoward.

Skues wrote later of Lamorna Birch that 'he more and more impressed me with the quality of his fishing, ranking with two other friends of mine as unsurpassed by any other rods I ever saw at work either on that or any other water'. Skues does not say who the other two performers were, but he may have been referring to A.D. Chaytor and John Evans. The former is mentioned in admiring terms. In a letter to Evans he admits to a recent day of failure, while 'young Chaytor' got five trout. Skues wrote that they were both using the same pattern – a hackled spinner with orange floss silk over a bare hook, but that Chaytor's fly had a soft hackle and sank, whereas Skues used a fly with a sharp cock's hackle. He added: 'It shows how absolutely essential it is on that tricky water to have exactly the right thing.' But days with Chaytor are not described in any detail in Skues' writings, except when they fished together on the Nadder at Burcombe. About Major J.D.D. Evans we can know much more.

Apart from Dr Barton, John Evans of Usk was probably the most ideal companion for Skues. A finished performer on the river, he was also deeply interested in all details, even the most minute, of the pursuit. As with Skues, he was interested in pushing the frontiers, and had been thinking about nymphs since the 1890s. He was also a thoughtful and progressive maker of trout flies. According to Norman McCaskie, Evans had promised himself that he would never use a fly that he had not dressed himself. In 1919 he had sworn a mock oath to stick to this plan and had signed it over a halfpenny stamp before a fellow member of the Flyfishers' Club, Sir Colchester Wemyss. Skues also preferred to fish with his own tyings, but he was not going to take such a hard line with himself on all occasions. He told Evans in 1932 that he did not object to buying from the shops some straightforward dry flies, particularly the Pope's Nondescript, the Red Quill and his standby for the evening appearance of the blue-winged olive, the Orange Quill.

Evans' fascination with artificial flies made him an interesting correspondent for Skues, and their letters were full of many points of detail that would have been far beyond most anglers. Skues had early formed the view that the colour of the spinner should be taken as the model for tying the dun and even the nymph of the same insect, and was delighted to find that Evans had independently come to the same conclusion. There was even a short exchange of letters about the virtues of hedgehog fur. Evans was an experienced breeder of gamecocks, and this provided another strong element in their correspondence. He was a man of means, with land in the valley of the Usk, and had opportunities that Skues must have envied. Skues looked back on his own abortive breeding experiments in the past without much satisfaction. He described to Evans the success of the system of a particular breeder before the Great War:

> His principle was to keep the birds he mated in separate pens and weed out those whose colours did not prove satisfactory, and turn them into a general barn-yard, where, by reason of the fighting strain in them, they monopolised the hens, and he used to obtain, he said, wonderful crosses of all sorts of colours.

Skues had begun operations at home, and had produced 'some birds with lovely necks', but a small garden in Croydon was not a convenient place and he then made the arrangement mentioned in an earlier chapter to keep cockerels at Chilworth, which ended so disastrously. He told Evans that if he was ever able to retire with some money he would like to get back to breeding for good colours, and this was probably in his mind when, in 1940, he withdrew from London to a small hotel in Wiltshire, which was intended only as a temporary lodging while he searched for the small house of his dreams. This he was never able to find, and the breeding plan was stillborn.

In the inter-war years Skues and most other amateur fly-dressers found increasing difficulty in getting plumage of the quality they wanted. The once-joyful plundering expeditions at Leadenhall Market produced less and less of value. Every generation since the abolition of cock-fighting in 1849 had complained about the decline in the supply of good hackles: perhaps every generation in its time was correct about this. As he got older, Skues became increasingly fastidious about the quality of fly-tying materials. But fortunately there were several leading amateur breeders active at this time. The trio of Evans, Thomas Hughes and John Henderson led the field and between them published several pioneer articles in the inter-war years. The contributions of these men are an important part of angling history and could perhaps merit republishing as a pamphlet. Evans was aware of his friend's difficulties in finding good hackles, offered help and received a prompt shopping list. Skues reported that he was well supplied with very small hackles, having secured a good deal of loot from the effects of C.A. Hassam, for whose estate he had acted professionally. Skues was not short of large hackles either. His real need was for hackles in the medium range, and a rescue package from Evans arrived soon afterwards. Predictably the contents called forth a measure of gratitude, but it was followed by a small barrage of detailed criticism about hackle quality from Skues.

In January 1932 he began to think more widely about the problem of plumage supply and asked Evans for the names of any breeders known to him. A week later he reported that his suggestion that the Secretary of the Flyfishers' Club should write to *The Fishing Gazette* and *The Field* inviting all the breeders to come into the scheme had been taken up. This excellent idea produced little result and the feather famine continued.

When Colonel E.W. Harding appeared on the scene as a new angling writer Skues immediately gave support. In *The Flyfisher and the Trout's Point of View* (1931) Harding had tackled the problems of trout vision and optics which Skues, for want of a scientific training, had only been able to touch upon in *The Way*. He wrote: 'I do feel grateful to the gods that Harding has come forward in my lifetime to tackle the numerous puzzlements which baffled me in *The Way of a Trout*.' It is therefore curious, as Frank Elder pointed out in *The Book of the Hackle* (1979), that he made no effort to revise the 1935 edition of his book to take account of Harding's work. But he was pleased to find that Evans shared his high estimation of Harding. He wrote:

I am sure he is a man who will be grateful for any instructive criticism on his work, as he is far more anxious to get the right deductions for the angling public than to effect a personal triumph … Most of the reviewers, I fancy, are incompetent to review his work and either write stupid stuff or do not write at all.

It may have been because of encouragement from Skues that Harding consented to deliver a lecture to the Flyfishers' Club in February 1932. Skues worked hard to give him support and fresh information, and encouraged Evans, as the most knowledgeable person he could think of, to write to him with useful points well before the lecture. Evans duly sent Harding a list of his thoughts, whereupon Skues set to work with his usual method and added a gloss to Evans' version of twenty-one different comments of his own. Harding wrote to Skues: 'I appreciate Evans' comments enormously. They are very fair and broadminded. He doesn't niggle at every little possibility of disagreement and he has so entirely grasped what I meant to be the spirit of the book, that it should be suggestive rather than dogmatic.' In the event the lecture was something of a disappointment to Skues. He wrote to Evans: 'Harding had a good crowd last night, but it only really touched the fringe of the subject.'

Harding's book was received politely in Britain but it did not sell well. In America, however, there was a more enthusiastic response from Eugene Connett III. He called it 'the most interesting, most valuable, and most thought-provoking volume on trout fishing that we have ever read ... a milestone in the history of fishing literature'. Connett took the subject of Harding's research further in his book *Random Casts* (1939), and several writers after the war, mainly American, have added to the body of knowledge. But Skues never altered his view that Harding was a great man, that his book was one of the most important works of the century and that the author had not been sufficiently appreciated amongst his fellow countrymen. Privately, he shared with one or two close friends the view that Harding's performance on the river was extremely maladroit.

Harding's ideas on the subject continued to develop after his book was published, and he began to prepare new material and to sort out certain corrections, in order to produce another and more mature version. But death overtook him soon afterwards. Skues wrote his obituary, calling him 'the most competent and brilliant student who has ever turned his attention to our sport'. He looked over Harding's notes to see if the task could be completed, but they were not in a form that enabled them to be adapted into a revised version.

In December 1939, however, he co-operated with the publisher Seeley Service to make another attempt. For this he needed a copy of the 1931 book to annotate and enquired whether Douglas Service could provide one, perhaps an unbound copy? By this date Service was aboard a ship of war in the Atlantic and had other things to occupy him, so he asked Skues to deal with his brother Ian at the Shaftesbury Avenue office. No copies at all, either unbound or bound, were left and Service, no doubt reluctantly, authorized the dispatch of his own handsome copy with attractive bookplate. Skues set to work with his customary minuteness, and within a few days had corrected all the typographical errors in red ink in the book, and also, in violet ink, identified the more important changes in Harding's notes which could be decoded, some in the text and some in a separate notebook. But these notes were probably only a small part of the story, and furthermore Skues found that his lack of a scientific background prevented him from interpreting them properly. He wrote on 18 December: 'Unless you get a competent editor to lick these into shape, I fear they can be of little use. I certainly do not feel equal to the task.' No revised version which might have advanced Harding's ideas ever appeared. Skues commented sadly: 'The death of Colonel Harding, leaving his work unfinished, was a great loss both to the fly fishing world at large (which even now does not appreciate fully the great work he did) and to me as a personal friend.'

Evans began to extend his angling library in the 1930s and, realizing that Skues was in touch with a wide range of second-hand booksellers, began to rely on him for advice. He badly wanted a copy of Edmonds and Lee, *Brook and River Trouting* (1916) and the much rarer work of W.H. Aldam, written in the Derbyshire dialect, *A Quaint Treatise on "Flees, and the Art a Artyfichall Flee Making"* (1876), two items for which Skues could give no help. In July 1933 he did better, advising Evans to consult the latest catalogue of James Tregaskis & Son. This offered a run of useful books, mainly from the library of John Waller Hills. Second-hand and antiquarian booksellers of the inter-war years offered books at prices which would astonish a modern collector, but even by the standards of the day Skues was justified in describing those of Tregaskis as 'ridiculously low'. For Pulman's *Book of the Axe* the price was just 7s 6d and his *Vade Mecum of Fly Fishing for Trout* was on offer for 3s 6d, the Walbran edition of Theakston's *British Angling Flies* (1883) for 2s 6d, while Martin Mosely's *The Dry-Fly Fisherman's Entomology* (1921) soared to 5s. Skues added: 'I should think they would be snapped up by somebody', and Evans began buying. Two days later he asked Skues to reserve copies of Blacker, Pulman, Chetham and Theakston, and he soon became an active collector. He added a pencil note to Skues' letter: 'I bought quite a bunch of these books, which remain in my library here.' He then became fascinated with one of the great books of the nineteenth century: Ronalds' *The Fly Fisher's Entomology*, which had by the 1930s run to twelve editions. Over the next few years he managed to get his hands on the first edition of 1836 for a guinea, and eight other editions. Skues was rather puzzled by this. He was no collector of books as antiquarian objects, only a buyer of material that would advance his knowledge. But Evans was both a collector and a reader, and soon appreciated Ronalds' wide grasp of the subject, noticing for example that he had realized as early as 1836 that there were two species of March brown. He shared this piece of information with Martin Mosely, who was a little nettled not to have noticed it himself in his copy of Ronalds.

Evans' literary output was limited to a few articles in the *Journal* and

The Salmon and Trout Magazine. That he never wrote a book was a matter of regret to Skues, and perhaps to some later anglers.

In his earlier days, Skues had been a useful committee man in the Flyfishers' Club and had served the members well as Secretary on a temporary basis in the place of his brother during the Great War. After the Armistice he found a new interest in helping to develop the bond with the Anglers' Club of New York, presenting himself as a sort of one-man reception for American members coming to London. In this way he was able to add to his team of friends and correspondents a number of well-known American anglers who wanted to know more about British fly-fishing. Some of them received the coveted invitation to Abbots Barton and wrestled with the problem of deceiving the most difficult trout of the chalk country. In his book *A Trout and Salmon Fisherman for Seventy-Five Years*, Edward Ringwood Hewitt gave an honest account of his two days at Abbots Barton in August 1925. Hewitt was one of the leading names in the eastern school of American fly-fishing; a subtle angler and not one to be easily beaten. In spite of all his skill with small flies and a long, light leader (14ft, tapered to 6x or .005 of an inch) he had a discouraging first day. August is notoriously a challenging time, which is why Skues found it so rewarding. For a newcomer it could be heart-breaking. Hewitt found that the disdainful trout of the Itchen were easily put down, or were missed or pricked at the strike. He wrote, after being defeated by several trout, that 'it began to dawn on me that it was a man's job to catch these fish at all'. The difficulty of selecting the right fly seems to have astonished him: every trout was different and 'each had its own preference'. At the end of the day, having seen large numbers of fish in the water, he had caught one trout of takeable size, several below the limit and a moderate grayling. He came back to his hotel very tired but, in his own words, convinced that 'here indeed was the great school for fly fishermen'. On the second day he fared no better. He must have been relieved to move on to Stockbridge the following morning, where Hills had given him two days on the water of the Houghton Club. Here, the stock fish were more easily caught, and his self-respect was restored.

Skues' connection with Hewitt was brief. A correspondence did not ensue, and he decided that he did not care for Hewitt, though he did not say why. His relation with another well-known American was cordial and long-lasting. Edward Baldwin Boies had been active in building up the Anglers' Club of New York in its early days, and became President in 1925. In 1932 he was elected President of the Fish and Game League of

South Western Connecticut. At the time of his death in 1947 he was affectionately remembered at the Anglers' Club for his charm and courtesy, the ingredients of an ideal clubman. The arrangements for their first fishing together were briskly set up by Skues at Whitsun in May 1930: 'The hotel where I stay in Winchester is the Hyde Abbey Hotel, Hyde Street, Winchester, and I should like you to arrive by ten on Monday morning if you can manage it.' Boies recorded his day in a piece in the *Bulletin* 'A Catskill Rod in England'. He wrote little of his own performance and much about his fascination with Abbots Barton and the compelling ambience of the place, once the haunt of Marryat and Halford: 'As I strolled beside the stream, with the shades of these departed anglers, I could not escape the inspiration of the hour.' He was impressed by the accurate casting of Skues and his pains to identify the right artificial for the moment. Skues would only use the fly for six casts, and during a hatch of fly which lasted for four hours Skues was casting and changing the fly 'at least three-quarters, if not practically all, of the time'.

For the next seventeen years they exchanged letters, fifty-three of which have survived. Skues was always glad to acquire correspondents in America. On receiving a brochure from Boies on American flies and how to tie them he wrote: 'I am looking forward to reading the book with the greatest interest. I am always interested in foreign views on such matters and foreign methods, in the hope that I may have something to learn from them.' But the exchange of letters between them was more than that, for a warm friendship soon developed, which lasted until the death of Boies in 1947.

Unfortunately for Skues, his new friend was not in England very often, and his letters contain anxious enquiries about the next visit. Having been disappointed in 1931 and having been dismayed to find that George La Branche did not intend a visit in 1932 Skues wrote plaintively to Boies: 'Will there be any chance of seeing you?' In fact he had to wait until 1934 to see his friend again. Boies was well received by the Flyfishers' Club and Skues secured his election as an honorary member with the help of Dr Barton. In a letter in the *Bulletin* in February 1935 Boies wrote of the kindness and courtesy of Skues and Barton and the 'dignified simplicity' of the customary Thursday evening dinner. After tea one afternoon at the Flyfishers' Club he witnessed an impromptu test of two Leonard rods, made by attaching weights to the tips, and decided that the atmosphere there was very similar to that of the Anglers' Club of New York. He returned later that year and was once again invited to be at the usual Thursday dining night. However, Skues had to confess with some embarrassment that a day on the Itchen was now not possible. He explained that the syndicate had 'passed a self-denying ordinance not to have any guest days, and latterly I have given a promise not to bring down any more friends'. This was part of the ominous slow-burning campaign against Skues in his own syndicate, a process which is discussed in detail in Chapter 12.

Part of the correspondence between the two men strayed outside fishing matters, an unusual experience for Skues, and is interesting as providing a glimpse of his political ideas. As a staunch supporter of the Republican Party, Boies was interested in what was happening in British public life. The Great Crash of 1929 and the depression which followed on both sides of the Atlantic must have occupied his mind a good deal, and he applied to Skues for an informed view of conditions in Britain. The response from Skues, a lifelong Tory, was fairly predictable: his ideas look a little naïve in the twenty-first century, but for many of the middle class in the 1930s Socialism and Communism were only different terms for the same thing. In September 1931 he responded to Boies' enquiries: 'I should not be a bit astonished if the legislation and taxation to be imposed by this government did not antagonize so many interests, that the Socialists, led by Henderson, may come back with a working majority: and then goodbye to prosperity and any hope of recovery in this country.'

In fact he need not have worried. In the general election of September most Labour candidates were defeated in a wholesale massacre, the Conservatives came back with 473 members, and a new National Government of the parties was formed to deal with the crisis. In Ramsay Macdonald's new cabinet the name of Arthur Henderson, until recently Home Secretary, was nowhere to be seen. Skues' next report to Boies was ecstatic:

> Thank you very much for your letter of the 29th instant congratulating our people on the way in which the challenge of the Socialists has been met. Had the Election gone the other way the country would have gone up in smoke, and in three months we should have been starving. I agree with you, however, that the verdict was too magnificent....After all, the Socialists, if they are entitled to votes at all, may reasonably have a grievance that their total voting power represents one third of the aggregate poll and is only represented by one ninth of the members returned.

Skues' regard for Edward Boies never faltered. When, in 1936, Boies and his wife left London and journeyed to France, Skues responded to their friendly letter of thanks: 'I am sure I have done nothing that you would not have done equally for me if I had been a visitor to your part of the world.' In 1937 he was going through one of his periodic glooms about possible early death. As Boies and his wife embarked on the *Aquitania* for America he wrote what he imagined might be a farewell letter:

As it is not improbable that by the time you pay the Old Country another visit I may not be here to bid you welcome I use this occasion to assure you that the visits of yourself and of several other members of the N.Y.A. to this country and the F.F.C. have added enormously to the pleasures which I have derived from the society of brother fly-fishers.

The response of Boies was a letter of such warmth as to astonish Skues, who replied: 'I am proud indeed to have such an assurance of your regard....You may be sure that if I am a going concern when next year you are over here you will be as welcome as ever.'

In 1932 Skues' third book appeared before the public: *Sidelines, Sidelights and Reflections*. It followed the custom of his earlier works, that is to say it was once again derived from his previously published articles in the journals and therefore, according to Skues' rather tough method of classification, was not entitled to be called a book at all. Skues never really cared for *Sidelines*, and it owed its publication to the persuasions of his friends, and to Seeley Service and Co., the publisher. By 1932 Skues had created a massive amount of published work; any bibliographer attempting to list all his articles would have to set aside a substantial period of time. The thinking behind his choice of articles for *Sidelines* is intriguing. Having selected 114 articles he divided them into nine sections. Most modern readers would, I imagine, react well to the memories of incidents on the river and to the short biographies of the long-dead personalities of the chalk-stream story. The fly-dressing and technical sections and the tactical studies are also deeply interesting. The longest section of all in *Sidelines* – thirty-three articles in a hundred pages – was devoted entirely to Skues' humorous pieces. Some puzzled readers may have wondered whether these pages might have been dispensed with. But humour is a matter of opinion: the fact that he went to the trouble of rescuing these from the pages of the *Journal* and to place them before the public again indicates that he thought well of them.

The final section, entitled 'Oddments and Dreams', which contains the 'Incognita' piece referred to earlier, contains seven imaginative essays, in four of which Skues, who does not seem ever to have possessed much in the way of religious enthusiasm, was reaching out for the mystical and the sublime, and aiming at some deeper meaning in life. He actually asked friends to read the pieces in this section, but only those, such as Dr Barton, for whom he felt a real trust. He also wrote to Edward Boies and his wife asking for their opinion of the piece called 'As Pants the Hart', 'even if it be a bit out of the usual line of matter for an angling book'.

Having consented to the publication of *Sidelines* he regretted it, writing to Evans in 1933: 'My opinion that the work would be a flop appears to be thoroughly justified.... Another time (if there was to be another time) I should rely on my own judgement, and not allow myself to be over persuaded', adding gloomily: 'but there won't be another time'. Although he grumbled about *Sidelines* for some time afterwards its performance was reasonable, and 590 copies were sold in its first year, 250 of which went to America. It has survived in the favour of the public, and it was republished in 1976 with the title *The Chalk-Stream Angler*, with a useful introduction by Conrad Voss Bark.

Some of Skues' acquaintances carried on a correspondence with him for years for advice or support in their understanding of fishing and fly-tying problems. As I have recorded earlier, they soon found that there was a price to pay. He was straightforward and at times quite alarmingly direct in his comments. For him, such issues were far too important to be fudged by considerations about people's feelings. Skues' relationship with Tommy Hanna produced a number of examples of this trait in him. It was entirely carried on by letter, for Hanna lived in Moneymore in Northern Ireland, a place that Skues never visited. From these letters, fifty-three in number, which ran from July 1932 to July 1939, it is clear that Hanna valued the advice and opinion of the master, even though at times he must have reflected that there was a great deal of criticism and not much praise.

Skues' letters provide an interesting light on an area of social history as well as fly-fishing. In an age governed by formal codes, the manner of beginning a letter was well understood. An example of the familiar way with one's friends, especially if they were members of the Flyfishers' Club, would be 'Dear Evans', or if it was a warm friendship, 'My Dear Barton', etc. Skues' habit with people he did not much care for was subtly different and intended to create a certain distance, e.g. 'Dear Mr Monkhouse'. Those of a different social class, in this case a man such as Hanna, who was running a fishing tackle shop in the back of a drapery store, would be addressed as 'Dear Sir'. Such an attitude would arouse no disapproval at that time. It did not imply disrespect towards Hanna, only what would have been generally thought of then as 'maintaining proper distance'. In fact Skues soon acquired an admiration for Hanna and his progress in fly-dressing and when, in one of his early letters, he dispatched a selection of his own nymphs, he apologized for their lack of neatness. Courtney Williams thought that Hanna's work was 'full of originality'. However, when Hanna proffered samples of his work Skues lost no opportunity of pointing out the defects. A Sherry Spinner was rejected ('I would not call that a rich red ant colour'), as were some dry flies with clipped wings ('I could never bring myself to use them'), and all the Irish patterns were dismissed as being too large for southern England.

Skues never seemed to be aware that people had feelings: surely, he would reason, they were as interested as he was in getting things right. Hanna must have learned fairly early in their acquaintance that judgements had to be accepted quietly and without affront. But he could not help being hurt at the response when his book *Fly Fishing in Ireland* was published in 1933. Skues wrote: 'I have read it with exceptional interest, and I hope you will forgive a few comments.' The comments, about twenty in number, were mostly critical and ran to six pages. The letter ended: 'Please forgive this bombardment' (see Appendix 6). Hanna's reply has not survived, but he must have shown that he was offended, because there was a sudden alteration in Skues' next letter. It looks as if Hanna may have written something to the effect that, if Skues' comments were correct, he would have to regard his book as of little worth. Skues became apologetic:

> I do not agree at all in the opinion you have expressed of your book. You have evidently brought much mind and thought to bear and the books on angling of which that can be said are rare. If your book had been a dud [probably echoing a term used by Hanna] I certainly would not have been at the pains to write to you about it.

About the same time Skues wrote to John Evans, who had also been reading Hanna's book:

There are no doubt a good many respects in which it could be criticised, but I do think that the man has some ideas and is trying to work out something of value to the fly dresser and angler ... Hanna is quite a young man still [in fact he was 25] and I do not despair of his doing something of value as I am sure he is a trier, and some of his fly dressing is extremely neat.

This mollified Hanna and, fortunately for posterity, the correspondence continued for another six years, with many items of interest about Skues' habits and views. Skues believed that translucency was of less significance in the nymph than in the floating fly, as it and the fish would generally be on the same level, or nearly so. On the other hand, colour would therefore be more important. He also revealed in one surprising passage that he seldom fished a nymph downstream, to which the purists might have responded: 'Seldom indeed? Why at all?' He wrote that he preferred to fish 'either directly upstream or slightly up and nearly directly across'. In 1935 he wrote: 'I don't work my nymphs.' For many years he adhered to the idea that nymphs coming up to hatch were inert and comatose, and imparting any form of movement was therefore not needed. There is even a little more to be gleaned about the fishing depth of Skues' nymphs: 'My rivers are not fast, but still I could not get a nymph (unless heavily leaded) over a foot under the surface', an indication that he did use the leaded nymph at times in order to fish it deeper.

There are also indications in letters to Hanna and to other correspondents of nymph patterns that have never been published. The fact that Skues did not persist with some of these ideas may indicate that he was not satisfied with them. Two mystery nymphs appear in a letter of July 1935. One is a variation of Overfield no. 17. The other does not appear in any of the published lists. His letter to Hanna described a natural nymph

with a definite red head and shoulders. I have been imitating it successfully this season thus:

Hook	no.15 Pennell Down eyed Sneck.
Tying silk	white under lower part of body, waxed with colourless wax or drenched with celluloid varnish.
Whisks	pale ginger hen.
Tying silk	for shoulder and head – orange exposed at head.
Thorax	rabbit's poll dyed in Red Ant colour (Halford).
Hackle	honey dun hen with red points, quite short, 2 turns.

Dr Edwin Barton (left) and Charles A.N. Wauton aka 'Tup' (right) were leading fly fishermen of their day, and friends of Skues

Sir Tom Eastham. A successful lawyer, but a self-confessed novice in fishing, he learned a good deal from his long correspondence with Skues

Major John Evans. Skues regarded him as one of the most accomplished fishermen of his acquaintance

Abbots Barton: Skues fishing the main river

Abbots Barton: Skues fishing below Duck's Nest Spinney

Abbots Barton, 2008: syndicate member James Gilman (aged ninety) taking his ease by the Upper Barton Carrier

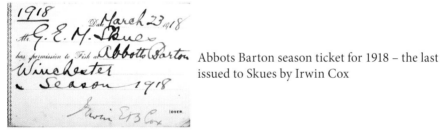

Abbots Barton season ticket for 1918 – the last issued to Skues by Irwin Cox

Abbots Barton, Duck's Nest Spinney, 2008. Skues used to fish from the far bank, switch casting to avoid trees. This is not feasible today because of reeds growing in the water

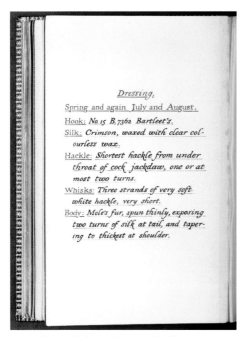

Dressing:

Spring and again July and August.

Hook: No. 15 B. 7362 Bartleet's.

Silk: Crimson, waxed with clear col-
ourless wax.

Hackle: Shortest hackle from under
throat of cock jackdaw, one or at
most two turns.

Whisks: Three strands of very soft
white hackle, very short.

Body: Mole's fur, spun thinly, exposing
two turns of silk at tail, and taper-
ing to thickest at shoulder.

Iron Blue Dun.

Pages from Col. Pack-Beresford's manuscript book of Skues' nymphs, the black tulip of the collection in the Flyfishers' Club

Sir Joseph Ball, Skues' formidable adversary in the nymph debate of 1938

The Mouth Vice. The tortoiseshell base, if held in the teeth, should present the fly being dressed at the level of the eyes. There is no evidence that this was ever used by Skues: probably one of W.D. Coggeshall's jokes

Frank Sawyer on the banks of the Upper Avon. Skues recognized his talent and encouraged him to publish his ideas

The River Nadder at Burcombe, 1938. Skues waiting for Mayfly Hatch

The same pool on the River Nadder today

The Nadder Vale Hotel, Ugford, Wilton: rear view today. (Now a private residence.) Skues' room was at the rear

Paul Barbotin, noted French angler and last major correspondent of Skues

The Lattice Bridge, Ugford, on the River Nadder today. This bridge was directly below the Nadder Vale Hotel. Skues would halt at the bridge before beginning to fish in order to examine the spiders' webs for clues as to the flies of the day

Skues' handwriting in old age, minute and shaky, a trial of patience for his correspondents to decrypt, but considered by them to be worth the trouble

Beckenham, 1948 or 1949: Last known picture of Skues, taken by George Monkhouse (probably surreptitiously)

I did this from the natural insect from a trout's maw, and found it very killing during the latter part of May and June when the natural insect was on.

Hanna's work may have been neater and more professional than Skues' in appearance, but he probably acquired a more subtle insight about form and variations of colour and shade from their correspondence. They soon began exchanging gifts of materials. In 1934 Skues offered Hanna some albino moleskins, part of the effects of Colonel Harding, for whose estate he was acting.

When Hanna began to publish articles on fly-dressing in *The Fishing Gazette* he cannot have been surprised to hear from Skues, who wrote having seen the first three of the series. The letter began by congratulating Hanna on his papers: 'You have said well a number of things which required to be said', but after this amiable beginning continued more ominously: 'But I have some comments to make on no.3.' Hanna may have braced himself for another detailed mauling, but the objections this time were fairly mild, mainly about technique in winding hackles. Two years later Hanna began to prepare another series, this time on the winging of trout flies. Remembering that Skues had offered to look over any of his material before publication he submitted them for comment. Skues wrote in November 1936: 'I am writing on the assumption that you genuinely desire my opinion, not only on the general scope of the articles (which I heartily approve) but also in matters of detail.' The letter which followed is a good example of the sort of thing in which Skues revelled – an examination of the fly-dressing process in a detail that would be far beyond the comprehension of most fly-fishermen. It is a paradox that its minuteness, and in places its severity, was a sign of Skues' respect for Hanna. Towards the end of the 1930s he urged him to get his papers together and to publish another book, but this never happened.

For much of the inter-war period, Skues' life seemed to be on a plateau. As he approached old age he must have looked back on his work with some satisfaction. More and more anglers were giving him support. Surely the final triumph of the nymph was at hand. At the annual dinner of the Flyfishers' Club in February 1935 Dr Walshe, a firm supporter of Skues, proposed the health of the guests, and in his speech looked back to the days when the dry fly–wet fly argument raged:

To fish with a dry-fly was like eating marmalade for breakfast, the sure sign of a gentleman; to fish with a wet was like eating peas with a knife, the hallmark of an outsider. [Loud laughter.] How this feud was composed is an epic in itself. The occasion produced the man, and a genius appeared – still happily amongst us [applause] – who ... found the solution. He took the horrid wet-fly – the lure, as its traducers called it – gave it a haircut, and called it a nymph. [Great laughter.] The disguise was perfect, the name irresistible and now your dry-fly fisherman may fish wet with a clear conscience, when he can't fish dry.

A later speech by the guest of honour, Lord Justice Roche, included an affectionate reference to 'fishing such as I enjoyed on the Itchen, on the water where my friend and your fellow member, Mr Skues, practises his minor and other tactics – [applause]'. At least on that occasion there was no sound of dissentient voices. Skues must have known that not quite everyone was on his side, but the die-hards would surely soon convert and fall into line. In 1936 he told Dr Barton that he thought that a general acceptance of the nymph practice was not far off. But if he thought that he had successfully given purism notice to quit, he was soon to learn that things were not going to be so simple.

11

Nymphs – the Final Achievement

IN THE EARLY 1920s Skues was at the summit of his skill and knowledge, and everything was in place for assembling a team of effective nymph patterns intended to cover all situations he was likely to encounter at or beneath the surface of his beloved Itchen. In 1921 he wrote in *The Way* (p. 123) that he wished 'that some wet-fly enthusiast would set to work and make exact reproductions of nymphs and larvae in the same way as Mr F.M. Halford treated the floating fly'. Soon afterwards it must have occurred to him that no one could supply that need better than he could. At this stage of his life his deep knowledge of fly-dressing technique, his minute attention to detail and his fastidious views on materials were all a byword at the Flyfishers' Club. Commercial suppliers of plumage were well aware that he was their most exacting customer. By the 1930s they were in despair at their inability to please him. The well-known firm of Messeena became alarmed and offended at his straight-talking letters and refused to send him any more hackles. He wrote in 1933 to Tommy Hanna that Veniard was also avoiding him 'although he knows what I want'. The subtlety of some of his ideas must have been incomprehensible to many of his fellow members at the Club as he sat in the fly-dressing corner devising something diminutive and deadly while delivering pungent views on the shortage of good materials. In 1932 he wrote to Tommy Hanna:

> The only way to get hackles small enough for nymphs is to pick them yourself from the bird, the firms specialising in fly dressing materials know nothing about them. For some purposes henny feathers from cockerels are better than hens' hackles. Especially where you get a good dark webby centre, so that the centre suggests the thorax and the points the legs.

As explained in Chapter 5, Skues' early work on the sunk fly had been surprisingly slow. Some might say that it lingered for some time in a blind alley. In later years he looked back ruefully to the days when he cast macaw tags, which were really fancy lures, along the edges of the rafts of cut weed, or up-winged wet flies over trout taking nymphs. He had, after all, become aware of the existence of the immature underwater stage of ephemeropteran flies quite early in his fishing career, and had even sketched on paper a likeness of a passable imitation. Why this led nowhere at that time is beyond anyone's guessing and, more than once in his mature years, Skues was inclined to blame himself for such slow progress on his part, but unfortunately his later recollections were hazy and we know little about this early stage of his thinking. Two factors combined to make his recollection rather hazy. In 1936, in the introduction to the Pack-Beresford nymph collection, referred to later in this chapter, he wrote: 'The processes of thought and experience that led to the evolution of the practice of nymph fishing for trout and grayling have been gradual and long drawn out, and, unfortunately, I have kept no precise record of its development.'

The first recorded example of a true artificial nymph rather than an up-winged Scottish-style wet fly dates from 1908. This was twenty years after gazing at the 'tiny pea-green creatures' in the mouth of a newly caught trout on that spring morning in 1888 at Abbots Barton. It was to be another ten years before he published his next pattern. In 1936 he wrote that he had, by 1910, developed 'some definite nymph patterns'. However, his references to the tying of them on pp. 31–2 of *Minor Tactics* were incomplete. There is an important clue in his observation in the same book: 'It is evident that on this subject I am only at the beginning of inquiry.' So it would seem that, in his attempts to move on to the next stage and develop nymphal forms, he had not yet acquired enough confidence to lay everything before the public. For some time he continued with his use of wet flies, although he was disturbed by the fact that they were hardly faithful copies of the natural larvae. It seems as if he was still in the main a dry-fly fisherman who regarded the wet fly/nymph as an extra weapon on a difficult day, rather than as something of much wider application. He admitted years later that, in the earlier days, he had still not realized quite how extensively trout fed on nymphs. Full confidence about artificial imitations of nymphs therefore came only slowly. After the vaguely described 'definite nymph patterns' of 1910 mentioned above no notification of a new Skues nymph pattern appeared in print until 1918.

In the 1920s a radical change appeared in Skues' nymph programme, and during the next two decades he assembled a team of effective patterns. From the summer of 1921 onwards he made frequent use of the marrow scoop and baby plate, and urged his readers to tie nymph patterns with a natural nymph beside them in a saucer of water. Shape, proportion and colour should be noted carefully, and the hook placed alongside the natural to check for length. As time passed he increasingly sought the most minute accuracy in making his patterns. In 1932 he wrote to Tommy Hanna: 'I have been devoting myself for the past two or three years to an effort to represent nymphs as they look to the trout, and I think I can claim a good deal of success.' In *Nymph Fishing for Chalk Stream Trout* (1939) he was able to refine his discoveries down to twenty, of which three were B.W.O variations.

Most of these nymphs were included in a useful list (though marred by some mistakes of copying) in Donald Overfield's excellent book, *G.E.M. Skues: The Way of a Man with a Trout* (1977), required reading for Skues enthusiasts. However, he seems to have derived most of the patterns only from the pages of the *Journal*, thereby missing those mentioned in the unpublished letters. Skues' restless mind was constantly devising new ideas at the fly-dressing bench, and many nymph experiments may only have been mentioned in items of correspondence now lost. Also, patterns that did not work well would soon have been discarded. This means that the task of settling a final list would be virtually impossible. However, the main lines of his work on nymphs were set forth in the *Journal*, which after the Great War carried most of his writings. *The Fishing Gazette* heard from him less and less, particularly after the death of R.B. Marston in 1927, and by 1932 he had ceased to correspond with them. Relations with *The Field* deteriorated after a major row with the editor towards the end of the 1930s. Skues wrote to Evans in January 1939:

I won't write for *The Field*. When they played that dirty trick on me of publishing in "The Field Flies" a set of alleged nymphs, including "Bloody Butcher", "Professor", etc, in the same No. as a bespoke article on nymph fishing by me and would not publish a disclaimer, I wrote that I would have no more to do with them, and I won't.

Evans' reply, which has not survived, looks (from Skues' next letter) to have been an attempt to defend H.D. Turing, who had been, since

1930, the angling editor of *The Field*, having succeeded his brother-in-law Sheringham. Somewhat mollified, Skues replied:

> Apropos of the behaviour of "The Field", I don't hold it against Turing. It was a weakness on his part. He allowed his better knowledge to be overruled by Eric Parker. I considered it a shocking case of pandering to the Advertiser. Such a thing could never have occurred in the days when "The Field" was a client of mine. Neither Senior nor Cook nor Sheringham would have stood it.

When he began detailed nymph experiments, Skues found that some species presented more difficulties than others. The large dark olive, the July dun and the iron blue were solved straight away. The pale wateries, however, were a problem family, and the medium olive gave him endless trouble. Imitations of the blue-winged olive, whether wet or dry, have seldom been satisfactory for most anglers, including Skues.

The Iron Blue of 1918 was the first published nymph in the *Journal*, with the exception of the Carrot Fly in 1912. The latter was in one of Skues' humorous articles and so not intended to be taken as a serious pattern (although it has been known to catch fish). The Iron Blue, however, was an excellent nymph and remained one of his most effective patterns. He altered it in 1931, but only slightly, calling for the Bartleet B7362 hook instead of a hook to gut. By this date he had virtually abandoned the use of blind hooks, which formerly he preferred for any sunk fly, claiming that they enabled the fly to swim better. Skues' regard for the Bartleet hook and its holding property fell only just short of idolatrous. When production ceased in 1932, because of the amalgamation of Bartleets with Milwards, he seems almost to have taken it as a personal affront. He did, however, admit that they were never so good after the Great War: before 1914 'they were admirable and practically unbreakable'. His pattern recipes after this date increasingly recommend the down-eyed Pennell sneck.

As for size, Skues' nymphs were generally tied to hooks of 15 or 16 Redditch, or 0 and 00 Pennell (confusingly, he sometimes expressed the sizes in one scale and sometimes the other). Size 14 or 1 and 17 or 000 were less often seen in his nymph box. Size 17 would, at that date, have been considered as getting down to the limit for chalk-stream fishing, and would have made most anglers nervous. Nowadays the use of a size 20 hook would not be seen as a serious problem, and large fish have been caught on smaller hooks than that. Towards the latter end of his time at Abbots Barton, Skues succeeded in landing fish in the neighbourhood of 3lb on size 17 and even 18 (or 0000) hooks, which made him wonder whether he should have taken more account of the minute *Caenis* tribe.

No new nymphs seem to have been devised until 1923, when Skues published three useful types, two of them attempts to deal with the problem of the blue-winged olive, in articles in the autumn and winter numbers of the *Journal*. The first 1923 nymph was a sunk version of the Green Cat. The dry-fly version was the invention of Dr Norman McCaskie, who had been using it for some years. The vital ingredient was fur from a cat called Tim, a member of the McCaskie household. The rather violent shade of green was achieved by dyeing the fur in a picric solution. Skues exercised his wit in the article, imagining his friend's pet condemned to a coat the colour of a billiard table, and adding menacing remarks about the RSPCA. The first article was mainly about the dry-fly version, and only mentions the nymph at the end (which caused Donald Overfield to overlook it in 1977). The tying of the nymph followed that of the floating pattern except that a soft henny hackle was called for. In the winter 1923 issue of the *Journal*, a much more subtle B.W.O. nymph appeared (mistakenly ascribed by Overfield to winter 1928). Here, the brilliant electric effect of the green cat fur was tempered by mixing it with brown olive seal's fur. Skues described it as 'the most nymph-like pattern I have ever turned out'. At its first trial it caught thirteen grayling. In 1939, in the final list included in *Nymph Fishing for Chalk Stream Trout*, the cat contribution appeared again in two more B.W.O. nymphs: one in a green version, the other with the cat fur mixed with six other ingredients.

Skues' attempt at dealing with the pale watery tribe was also published in the same issue of the *Journal*. It was the first of many: eventually he made fifteen or sixteen versions, and no doubt enjoyed the process of tying and testing. He thought that the newly hatched pale watery usually got off the water more quickly than other species, which had a discouraging effect on the trout. The nymph was therefore likely to be more effective. In the 1939 list he included four dressings to take account of the variations in the different species of pale watery, which is a good indication of his conviction about getting dressings absolutely right, but also of his sheer delight in experimenting. There were (and still are) many anglers who can never quite accept that such minute attention to detail is necessary: for them, presentation and all other tactical precautions when addressing a feeding fish are far more important. But Skues was always insistent on accuracy, at least as he saw it. Paradoxically, flies tied by Skues would probably not win prizes in fly-dressing competitions nowadays. His friends noticed that there was a lack of 'finish' about them, a point mentioned by Overfield in his 1977 book. However, if they were somewhat rough at the edges, perhaps because of the speed with which they were made, no one could doubt the impression of life which made them so effective in use. Flies tied by practised professionals are distinguished by their neatness, but often the indefinable element is missing, which derives from intuition rather than mechanical skill. The thirty-three flies in the deluxe edition of Halford's *Modern Development of the Dry Fly* are good examples of this – well constructed but somehow lacking in liveliness.

In fact, Skues participated in several fly-dressing competitions. These were 'friendlies' or 'fly-dressing scraps' as they were called, held at the Flyfishers' Club on Thursday evenings. He was usually defeated by several other members, particularly C.A. Hassam, who produced flies of an artistry that has seldom been surpassed. I doubt if Skues minded: a pattern, whether dry or wet, needed to look good to the fish. For him, Frank Sawyer's nymphs would probably have looked a little too simplified and basic, especially the grayling bug with a body of wool, deadly in use though it undoubtedly was.

At first the nymph campaign was intermittent. It was three years before the next group of nymphs were revealed to the world (*Journal*, autumn 1926). Two of these (omitted from Overfield's list) were attempts to imitate the pale watery of autumn, a small, feeble fly needing a 17 hook. In the same issue (pp. 72–3) two other nymphs appeared. They were not named, but were evidently intended to represent the nymph of the medium olive. One of them was slightly unusual in having a body composed of amber floss silk wound over the bare hook. Most of his nymph patterns were made with various dubbings, mainly rabbit, hare, opossum, mole and seal's fur, either natural or in various colours. He also liked the blue fur found at the root of the coat of the English or red squirrel. Skues mixed these colours a good deal, rather as an artist would consult his palette to get the exact shade. His final attempt in 1939 to crack the B.W.O. problem contained five different shades of seal's fur, with the addition of fur from a hare's poll and the now indispensable green cat fur. Other materials, such as herl and quill, were used far less frequently. The process of tying these later nymphs was simplified, and attempts to imitate the thorax with material of a different colour surmounted by a slip of feather to represent the wing cases were henceforth abandoned.

Skues had a brief flirtation with another material popular at the time. He wrote to John Evans in 1933 that he had been experimenting with a Pale Watery nymph with a body of white rubber ribbed with fine silver wire and, during a difficult weekend, had caught three fish, 'all of them pretty decent'. He had never cared much for rubber until he saw good use made of white and yellow samples by the ingenious Tommy Hanna. Skues was particularly pleased with the effect of translucency. But the deliquescent habit of rubber soon showed itself, and he decided not to add the white rubber Pale Watery to his running list of published discoveries. He wrote later to Evans: 'Like you, however, I have always come back to silk, fur and feather.'

In 1928 three more new nymphs appeared before the public. Skues was becoming more purposive and methodical in his pursuit of the perfect list of new weapons, and henceforward his articles begin to look as if they were part of a definite campaign. He recorded in his review of the 1928 season: 'On the whole I made little use of the floating fly during the season, not because the trout were seldom taking on the surface, but because I wished to do all I could to ascertain what dressings of nymphs were really attractive to the trout from time to time.' He adds, with his usual candour: 'But I cannot say that I got very definite results, though I caught a good many of my trout on nymphs' (*Journal*, winter 1928).

In an article entitled '1927 on Itchen' (*Journal*, summer 1928), Skues wrote: 'much of my execution was done with a new pattern of nymph of the medium olive dun which I evolved as the result of an autopsy of a trout at the end of May' (Overfield no. 21, but called by him the Tup's Indispensable Nymph). This was a considerable advance on the Tup protonymph of 1910 pictured in *Minor Tactics*. Skues apologized to readers that he could not give the pattern in full, as this would involve disclosure of the secret of the Tup mixture, but admitted that he had, in any case, varied it by using brown-olive seal's fur instead of the red of the original. He added that 'the pattern proved often irresistible'.

In an article called 'Occasionally It' in the same number of the *Journal*, Skues recorded yet another attempt at solving the problem of the blue-winged olive. One evening in the previous year he was having a bad time on a Test fishery (probably Leckford), until he lighted upon a pattern with a fat dark body and a dusky blue hackle. This was part of a collection of old wet flies given him years earlier by a friend who had fished mainly on Devonshire streams. This produced three good fish in quick time before darkness fell. Characteristically, he raged over the wasting of time: 'I might easily have brought in another leash of trout and possibly two brace.' This odd pattern scored again on the River Nadder. He then began to devise his own pattern, using the dark brown hair with a shade of purple sometimes found on barbed wire where cows had been scratching themselves. This is the first mention of the cow hair 'the colour of dried blood', to the value of which he referred several times in later years. To this he added a blue hackle: the words 'to match the B.W.O wing' make it unclear whether this fly was meant to be fished on or below the surface. The article shows that the Devon collection came into his hands at the beginning of the century, and could have been modified into one of Skues' more primitive team of sunk flies with wings. Later versions constructed in true nymphal form were to prove of great value on blue-winged olive evenings when big trout were feeding eagerly. In its final version it appeared in 1939 as the first of three versions of the B.W.O. pattern no. XVIII in *Nymph Fishing for Chalk Stream Trout*.

The pale watery problem was again attacked in 1928, and a pattern with a dubbing of squirrel fur was the result. Skues described it as 'serviceable', but although it survived in the Pack-Beresford collection of 1936 it was rejected in the final list of 1939. He must have pondered the problem during the close season of 1927/8, for another shot appeared in the spring 1928 number of the *Journal*. Tied on a size 17 hook and with a body of undyed baby seal's fur, it was another attempt to imitate the small pale watery of autumn.

In 1930 Skues felt sufficiently confident in his method of simplifying the tying of nymphs, already carried into effect in 1928, to announce that he was to some extent going to abandon the finer detail of some points, which were perhaps unnecessarily precise. He referred to one of the 1928 team, a Medium Olive nymph, in which three turns of deep blue hackle were used to get the effect of legs and wing cases in one operation. The woolly centre of the hackle would then suggest the wing cases, and the smoother tips the legs. He suggested to Hanna in 1933 that the wing cases of the natural nymph are not fixed down but are, in fact, slightly mobile, and therefore can be suggested by short hackles. The Medium Olive of 1930 used the same method, and picric-dyed heron herl was substituted for the Tup mixture. He added: 'I have never had a more attractive type of nymph.' His mind must have been teeming with ideas, for the ink was scarcely dry on this piece of praise for his own invention when, later in the same article, he introduces another pattern with a body of stripped peacock quill (not from the eye), commenting 'I expect to be finding it soon replacing the heron herl nymph described above.' Two more Pale Wateries completed the 1930 offering to the public.

In the following year, readers of the *Journal* for autumn 1931 would have been startled by a fresh wave of new nymph patterns, eleven in number. This avalanche raised the score of nymph inventions since 1918 to twenty-nine. No new species of natural were addressed: the same ground was covered, but with more subtlety. This extraordinary list was the result of an extensive attempt by Skues towards refining his personal collection of essential patterns. Four were for the medium olive and three were for the pale watery group. The reason for such a large number of alternatives was, at least in part, to deal with alterations in the appearance of the natural at different stages in the season. The three remaining patterns on the list were intended to imitate: the iron blue (identical to the 1918 version save for being on an eyed instead of a blind hook); the large dark olive (the first attempt since the primitive version in *Minor Tactics*); and another imitation of the July dun, Skues' name for the small dark olive (*Baëtis scambus*).

It is a pity that we do not have much evidence about the reaction of the fly-fishing public to Skues' work at this stage of his life. Most of them must have wondered about the relevance to them of this increasingly intricate series of new flies. The average angler would have been looking for fairly simple solutions on the river. There certainly was a small coterie of admirers who took up Skues' ideas and applied them, but they were men of the advanced school. For the majority, Skues must have occupied another and more rarefied world. They admired him but could not keep up with him. In his defence, Skues would have pointed out that Abbots Barton was a special place, where often only the most accurately devised imitations and the best of tactics would do. On many other chalk-stream fisheries, especially if stocked with hatchery trout, something less complicated and intellectually demanding would serve well enough.

Two more patterns appeared in 1935, and one more in 1937 (all unfortunately unnamed). These complete the tale of those Skues nymphs that can be identified, approximately forty in number, before the refined-down list of twenty was extracted and published in *Nymph Fishing* in 1939. Mention should, however, be made of the Shrimp pattern, which he published in *The Field* in 1931, and again in a reprinted article in *Sidelines* (1932). Shrimps would have been numerous everywhere at Abbots

Barton, but Skues had discovered two particular playgrounds for them, where gaps in the riverbank had been filled. In these gaps, repair work of cement bags, unattractive no doubt to the human eye, had become popular to a large shrimp population and, as a result, a common place of resort for trout. Fish caught thereabouts were found to be full of shrimps. Skues' pattern was to be tied with a body of pale olive and orange seal's fur, with the dressing carried some way around the bend of the hook to echo the curved shape of the natural shrimp, an idea which was to be frequently followed by fly-tiers in later versions.

Shrimps had, of course, awakened interest years earlier. Charles Walker, in *Old Flies in New Dresses* (1898), had praised the shrimp and thereby annoyed Halford, but on chalk streams there had always been a feeling of reserve about the use of such patterns. So advertising a shrimp pattern in the 1930s may have been a somewhat risky idea. If, as seems likely, a good many ill-disposed persons were scrutinizing Skues' articles at this time, they may have felt that they had discovered yet more objectionable material to store up against him. If they were taking their cue from Halford, as many still did twenty years after his demise, they would have turned the pages of *Dry Fly Fishing in Theory and Practice* and reminded themselves of the pronouncement: 'Honestly, I doubt if the artificial shrimp would under any circumstances prove killing.' That was Halford's view in the 1880s. By the end of the nineteenth century his view had altered and become more severe. He now considered that the use of the shrimp was bad for the fishery.

Skues said little about his deep nymph practices, and his tying of the shrimp in *The Field* does not mention fuse wire (as used by Dr Barton), lead foil or any other weighting material, but no one could pretend that an artificial shrimp could be intended for fishing near the surface, or indeed anywhere else but deep down. The anonymous author of a rather foolish article in the *Journal* in 1922 wrote: 'A man who would lead a fly is, I think, beneath contempt.' In any case, argued some, a shrimp was not a fly anyway. This argument, pedantic as it may seem in the twenty-first century, was to become a dangerous weapon in the controversy of the late 'thirties. And twenty years later Dr H.B. McCaskie apologized for mentioning 'anything so abhorrent as an artificial shrimp'. He may have had tongue in cheek, though one wonders why writers in the past had to be quite so jokey and fearful about the matter. But these and many other public expressions of opinion caused Skues to adopt a cautious line, and to take care not to give any hostages to fortune.

There are, however, a number of references in Skues' articles to fishing the nymph at a surprisingly deep level. A passage in *Itchen Memories* (pp. 33–5) mentioned the habit of the Winchester trout of lying out 'deep under the banks in anticipation of the ascent of nymphs to the surface', and of his success in catching four trout one morning, which had been lying at some depth in a run '6 or 8 feet deep'. It is a pity that he did not tell us how deep the trout were, but from his account, in which the word 'deep' occurs five times, they must have been a long way from the top of the water.

There are other examples that suggest deep nymph practice scattered through the writings of Skues. In May 1933 he advocated fishing McCaskie's Green Cat well sunk, but this may have been before the hatch had begun. Elsewhere he agreed with Evans that, when the hatch was well under way, the B.W.O. nymph should normally be fished near the surface as 'at the time of the take you see trout sucking away for all they are worth quite close to the surface, and if the fly goes below them they are apt to miss it'. This may be food for thought, for it has been frequently claimed by authors in more modern times that Skues' nymphs were intended to be fished in or very near to the surface of the water, in order to imitate the natural nymph in that vulnerable moment just before or at the moment of emergence. Donald Overfield wrote in the *Journal* in 1984 that Skues' nymphs were 'near-emergent'. Similarly, it is often stated that it was left to Frank Sawyer to fill the gap and complete the nymph revolution with the development of the Pheasant Tail Nymph ballasted with copper wire.

Perhaps part of the confusion may have arisen because the tying of the typical Skues nymph included a hackle to suggest the legs, albeit a hackle which was short, frequently soft and mobile and also short in the flue. It suggests to us the idea of a creature which is quiescent rather than active, and consequently within a second or so of hatching. The other reason may be that, although one can detect by a close reading of Skues' writings the indications I mention above of deep fishing, he did not unequivocally recommend it. It could therefore easily have been forgotten after his death. Skues knew in the 1930s that he had to be careful what he put on paper. Some of the ideas discussed in Chapter 7 were certainly rather wild for their time: an example would be the article in which he asked himself what would be wrong or reprehensible about fishing a nymph at the level of the bed of the river, but this was in 1907, and mercifully seems to have been overlooked by his adversaries in the 1938 debate. Other examples of debatable items, such as the corixa or water boatman, were quietly abandoned by Skues and forgotten in the 1930s as the purist tide flowed more strongly. The corixa had been suggested to him in discussions half a century earlier with his brother and with Dr C.E. Walker, the author of *Old Flies in New Dresses* (1898), which had explored some daring ideas about flies.

Skues' natural caution showed itself in other ways in the 1930s. In 1928, as mentioned earlier, he had admitted in an article that he was getting into the way of fishing the nymph more and more, sometimes almost exclusively. Later he was wise enough not to advertise the fact too much. He probably regretted having given himself away in former times, although he would still discuss his tactics with trusty friends. His fellow rods at Abbots Barton knew well enough how he was getting his impressive bags of fish, and a certain restiveness was growing in the syndicate and in the angling world beyond. To him, however, the technique made sense. It had been no secret for decades that trout took most of their food beneath the surface. Skues was well aware that interesting fishing was to be had on cool moist days in the spring, when the hatched duns rode down for many yards before escaping into the air. At such times the dry fly scored well. In early summer he noticed that, although a good hatch would have begun, the fish were still taking nymphs at or near the surface. He formed the view that the fish would only begin genuine rising to the hatched flies when they outnumbered the nymphs beneath. This might take some time, during which the purist could do little but wait, or perhaps follow Halford's advice and offer the Gold Ribbed Hare's Ear to the fish. The third stage in the angler's year, the dog days of summer, bright, hot and with a drying wind, was above all else the time of the nymph. Even if there was a show of fly, on hatching they would get away to safety at once. This was particularly true of the pale wateries. His knowledge of these different sorts of conditions was enough to convince him that he was doing the right thing. A growing following of anglers thought the same – but not all of them.

In 1936, Lieutenant-Colonel H.D. Pack-Beresford, a senior member of the Flyfishers' Club – he had joined in 1908 – approached Skues with an interesting suggestion. Not much is known about Pack-Beresford, but he was obviously an admirer of Skues and his liberal and open-minded approach, and he deserves to be remembered as having rendered an important service to angling posterity. His proposal was that the Skues patterns of nymphs should be preserved for all time in a made-up book, following the method of W.H. Aldam's famous collection of 1876. It would be kept permanently at the Flyfishers' Club, with the condition that it should never leave the premises.

Skues happily fell in with this idea, and undertook to dress the patterns. He also added an autobiographical note which, though brief, adds a few more details to our knowledge of the nymph story. The thirteen patterns were dressed on down-eyed Pennell snecks, with the exception of the Iron Blue and one of the Pale Wateries. They were placed in sunk mounts on thick cardboard pages faced with parchment, one to each page, with the dressing described on the opposite page in elegant manuscript by an accomplished calligrapher. They were then bound up into a book in handsomely tooled calf by the firm of William H. Robinson of 11 Pall Mall. It now lies safely in the Flyfishers' Club, one of the choicest items of the collection, having survived the wrecking of the Swallow Street premises by a land mine in April 1941.

Skues' feelings about the setting up and promoting of a sort of standard nymph team must have been mixed. On the one hand, it had always been an important part of his approach to trout problems that laying down the law was inappropriate, and that there was certainly no such thing as finality. The true investigator ought to proceed by means of a series of fresh experiments in pursuit of an ever-moving frontier of knowledge. On the other hand, the suggestion of Pack-Beresford had been too tempting to ignore. It was a chance to leave behind a tangible record of his contribution, to lie beside his published work. He was now in the latter part of his life and also under the impression, not for the first time, that he had not much longer to live. It was probably about this time that he began work on his memoir, another element in his personal testament.

Other nymph designs followed, a sufficient indication that the period of invention was not over. Another unnamed nymph, called 'the dark nymph', appeared in 1937, with a thorax of mole's fur and an abdomen of mixed mole and yellow seal's fur. In 1941 he devised an imitation of the grannom pupa, and in the same issue of the *Journal* he published a pattern for the spurwing or, as he called it, the blue-winged pale watery. His first experience of this strange fly had been in 1921, but subsequently its appearance had been only occasional.

Overfield included in his list two nymphs mentioned in *Itchen Memories*. The first is not called a nymph in Skues' account, and from the dressing

(*Itchen Memories*, p. 45; Overfield, no. 81) appears to have been a more conventional form of wet fly. The second (*Itchen Memories*, p. 53; Overfield, no. 82), probably invented after the Second World War, has some resemblance to a Pale Watery of 1931 (Overfield, no. 34), having a body of greenish floss silk, a thorax of hare's ear and a hackle of honey dun. The hook size prescribed is, however, larger: 14 instead of 17. At its first trial this new pattern produced a trout of 2lb 13oz. Soon afterwards Skues hooked a much bigger fish, apparently more than 4lb. After a hard fight it broke away. Skues was so downcast at the loss of this fish, which would have been his own personal record at Abbots Barton, that he felt unable to go on fishing and went sorrowfully back to his Winchester lodging.

Skues' final list, shortened and refined after extensive river tests, is to be found at the end of *Nymph Fishing for Chalk Stream Trout* (1939). For the first time in his life he was putting together a manual of practice, something that he had always avoided, rather than a series of interesting suggestions and examples. As with the Pack-Beresford collection, Skues must have felt once again that he was in some measure doing violence to his principles. This was the sort of thing that Halford used to do. But there was no help for it. He felt that there was still so much ignorance about good nymph practice on the river, and so many grotesque patterns masquerading as nymphs to be found in the shops, that a decisive intervention on his part was called for. At least the appearance of the 1939 book has given posterity a chance to see where his nymph project had arrived as he entered his eighties.

The list of 1939 closely resembled the selection in the Pack-Beresford pattern book. It contained patterns to cover the six leading types of chalk-stream ephemeropteran flies – the large dark olive, the iron blue, the July dun or small dark olive, the medium olive, the blue-winged olive and the pale watery group of four. The first three had always been regarded by Skues as straightforward, and were given only one pattern each. The next three had given him problems and no doubt a great deal of pleasure. What he called the medium olive seemed to change its appearance at different times in the season, but this may have been because he was looking at more than one species of olive. Skues, as we have seen, was a good field observer, but he lacked the guiding book-knowledge of entomology.

To cover all situations with this fly (or group) he devised no fewer than seven versions. The pale watery group also needed, or seemed to him to need, a complicated treatment, and seven patterns were judged by him to be necessary. There were three attempts to get on terms with the nymph of the blue-winged olive. One of them – uniquely in this list – was for grayling; it was of no use for trout. Skues was fond of calling grayling 'vermin', but he spent a good deal of time in the autumn fishing for them, thinking that it was good for the river. This completed the tale of Skues' final offering of sunk-fly weapons to his public. There were no nymphs of the mayfly, or of the broadwing group (*Caenis*), or of the pale evening dun (*Prochloeon bifidum*). The mayfly had died out at Abbots Barton many years earlier. He had never made much use of the broadwings, and if he had experienced an evening appearance of the pale evening dun he would, no doubt, have identified it as a pale watery. There was to be nothing speculative in his list. He had confined himself to what he knew from half a century of experience, but only of one fishery.

The preference for fur dubbing for the bodies emerges clearly in the list. Fifteen of the twenty patterns call for the fur of seal, mole, fox, squirrel, lamb, hare or rabbit, as well as cow hair. Quill and silk appear twice each, and herl only once. Half of the patterns are given a thorax, but there is no sign of the slip of feather to represent wing cases. This unnecessary extra, after a brief flirtation in the early 'twenties, had long ago been dropped. The basic design, refined over several decades, was now settled.

Skues had been dismissive of *Sidelines*. Now he decided that he did not much like *Nymph Fishing* either. In 1941 he wrote to a correspondent: 'I am quite resolved to write no more books. I am really not a natural book maker ... my last, the only deliberate attempt at a book, was as dull as ditchwater.'

There is a marked contrast between this detailed list of finely crafted flies and the simplicity of many more modern patterns. Frank Sawyer thought that a large number of complicated nymphs was not necessary, and promoted the Pheasant Tail nymph as the chief player in the game on chalk streams. The Grey Goose stood for the pale wateries, and some years later he designed a third type with condor herl for the body. Many members of the angling community must have sighed with relief: perhaps something as complex as Skues' selection was not needed after all. To be fair to Skues, he would, in his defence, have said that Abbots Barton was rather different from many other places. He was fond of quoting William Senior's opinion that it was the most difficult water he had ever known. There was a swarming population of invertebrate life, and the fish would often become locked onto one species. He thought, therefore, that it was important to aim for a precise likeness of the natural nymph of the moment, and that getting form, size and colour as correct as possible was crucial. Several of his friends, particularly Barton and Evans, were sure that his success, on days when other anglers caught nothing, was a consequence of his beautiful patterns, both wet and dry. But we may suspect that, as time went by, there was another more personal factor: he was in love with the complexity of the pursuit of excellence in fly-dressing, and simply devised more and more alternatives for the sheer joy of it. In 1939 he wrote to John Evans, quoting from St Paul's opinion of the intellectually restless Greeks: 'I agree that it is a mistake to get into a groove in fly dressing. I am like an Athenian, always seeking and trying some new thing.'

12

Confrontation 1936–1939

S UNDAY 31 MAY 1936 was a fateful day for Skues. It witnessed the beginning of a conflict which was to cast a shadow over his last years, as he fought for the acceptance of his life's work. He had imagined that, apart from a few myopic diehards, the struggle for the nymph was virtually over. He was wrong, and it was on that day that he was forced finally to realize the fact.

The fishing had gone well enough, with no warning of what was to come. He had enjoyed a prosperous afternoon on the reach below the railway bridge at the top of the Abbots Barton fishery. Nothing had happened until shortly after midday, when six trout began to take the hatched fly. Five of these took Lock's pattern of the Whirling Blue Dun and were landed, and the sixth rose and kicked off. An hour later he had a cock fish of 2½lb on a Medium Olive Nymph.

Later in the day, as he was walking downstream to Winchester for an early evening dinner, he encountered Gavin Simonds. It is likely that this was not a chance meeting, and that in order to bring it about Simonds had been loitering on the riverbank for some time. Skues described the event in a letter to Barton two days later:

> On the way back I had an unpleasant interview with Simonds, who said in his opinion it was a breach of our agreement to use the artificial fly only to fish with nymph. Of course, as the agreement is in his name I must accept his interpretation: but it cuts out the main interest of the fishing for me. I don't think there is much to be learnt about dryfly fishing and I am still working out nymph patterns, so I shall not renew for next year. I imagine Simonds' view is aggravated by the fact that this year and last there have been comparatively few fish seen moving. This is true enough and I have had few fish under 1½lb and have killed 9 two-pounders up

to the present. But I fancy that the scarcity is due to the two preceding short water years resulting in the spawning seasons being failures. The results are singularly like those when the pike got such a hold during the war.... But I don't doubt the recovery of the water. Anyhow, it is a sad ending of my long experience of the water.

Not an angry or complaining letter, but there was an unmistakeable element of quiet misery in it. The idea of banishment from a fishery to which he had had such a long attachment must have been very bitter.

It is a pity not to have more information about this momentous meeting. How long did it last? What sort of defence did Skues make? The only clues we have are that Skues said afterwards that he had pointed out to Simonds that, for generations, the chalk streams had been fished with wet flies, which in many cases must have been taken by the fish as nymphs. Simonds, however, stuck to the narrow legalistic point that fishing the nymph was not fly-fishing at all, just as a nymph was not a fly any more than a caterpillar was a moth or a butterfly.

This bizarre idea would not have come as a surprise to Skues. He had heard it before, and had referred to it in *The Way of a Trout with a Fly,* in a section called 'The Excommunication of the Dry Fly'. In this seminal passage he dealt with many of the objections raised against the nymph, and had reflected ironically on the change of stance of his opponents, from the earlier notion, derived from Halford, that the sunk fly did not pay on the chalk stream. Now they had moved to the view that in fact it worked very well. Therefore, he wrote, the purists were forced back to the foolish semantic argument that it was not fly-fishing. As he tersely put it: 'This is a mere verbal distinction culled *ad hoc*, and as an argument it leaves me cold.' Skues was capable of being robust, even annihilating, on paper, but in a face-to-face encounter he would not have been nearly so effective. We can only guess at the way in which the conversation with Simonds went. No detailed record exists in the surviving Skues papers, nor would it have been likely that he would have penned a description of such a distressing event. The important fact was that he had been cornered by a formidable adversary.

In 1936 Gavin Turnbull Simonds was a rising star in the legal world. Born in 1881, he had had a much more propitious start in life than Skues. He was the second son of Louis de Luze Simonds, the brewer magnate, of Audleys Wood near Basingstoke, and one of the founder members of the

Flyfishers' Club. He had been educated at Winchester College and New College Oxford. In 1906 he had been called to the Bar and became King's Counsel in 1924. His career accelerated in the latter part of the 1930s: he became a judge (with the customary knighthood) in 1937 and a law lord in 1944. In 1951 (rather to his astonishment) he became Lord Chancellor and was created Viscount Simonds of Sparsholt.

It is true that, on that day in 1936, some of this was in the future, but he was clearly already a heavyweight, and it was beyond the capacity of Skues to defend himself effectively. It was to be the same at the nymph debate in 1938 when Skues faced the attack of Sir Joseph Ball, a close colleague of the Prime Minister. For most people today the names of these once-prominent men are fading, whereas for anglers it is different. The name of Skues is honoured in memory by fly-fishermen all over the world. Surely, we feel, he could have pulverized them in argument? But in the world of that era status was important, and in the scheme of things his status was far below that of these successful men. Add to this his diffidence of manner, particularly in confrontations, and it becomes clear that Skues could not prevail against carnivores of that type.

Simonds' view of his role as a judge has been the subject of discussion by legal historians, which can give us some notion of what his attitude might have been towards the propriety of novel fishing methods. He had a first-class mind, and is still regarded nowadays as one of the great judges of the twentieth century, but he was very obviously in favour of the established order of things, and was orthodox in his judicial decisions. This meant that he disapproved of – and at times went out of his way to reject – the idea that judge-law could be used in a creative way to keep pace in a society which was changing rapidly. A judge should be sound rather than radical, and any important alteration in existing law was a matter for Parliament. It was inevitable that, after 1945, he would have been alarmed by the decisions of Alfred Denning. Denning quickly became the darling of the journalists as a forward-looking judge on the side of the common man, but he was also seen as the bane of many of his brother judges. They, in turn, regarded him as being too cavalier towards the accepted rules of procedure in arriving at his judgments. Simonds in fact became their unofficial leader, and some of his asides from the bench were deliberate rebukes directed at Denning. In a case in 1954 he said: 'It is for the legislature … to determine whether there should be a change in the law and what that change should be.' One author has described Simonds as 'the foremost twentieth-century exponent of judicial conservatism'. If this attitude extended into other areas of his life and his thinking then it would not be surprising that the dominant figure in the Abbots Barton syndicate should have been a thoroughgoing Halfordian with no time for perilous innovations such as nymphs.

The other prime mover in the attempt to restrain Skues was also a member of the syndicate, N.F. Bostock. Dr Barton was of opinion that he may have been more of a fire-breather even than Simonds, but that the two men had conferred and had decided that the bankside interview would be better conducted by Simonds, who was presumed to carry more weight and gravitas for the occasion.

Neville Bostock also had a successful life outside angling, as part owner of Lotus Shoes, and managing director of its great factory in Victoria Street in Northampton. He had fished a good deal in foreign parts, including Norway and New Zealand. He was well known at the Flyfishers' Club, having been a member since 1906. In 1923 the Committee of the Club included Bostock, John Rennie (a close friend of George Joseph Ball, later Sir Joseph Ball), Dr J.C. Mottram and Martin Mosely. All these men were devotees of the dry fly and, with the exception of Rennie, were closely involved in the nymph controversy from 1937 to 1940.

For some years Skues regarded Bostock as a friend, and in some respects their principles were the same. Like Skues, he found fishing for stock fish unsatisfying, and described the average trout of the Test as lacking in vigour when hooked and likely 'to come in like a piece of string'. In a piece in the *Journal* in 1928 entitled 'A Dry-Fly Fisherman's Lament' he wrote of his distaste for the heavy stocking policies now found on many parts of the Test, which were causing a decline in the wild trout population:

> It is the rarest thing to get a proper Test trout ... A fish caught in the Itchen in a certain well known stretch where there has hardly been any stocking for years is worth two brace of any Test fish I have caught for some years. He fights like a seatrout and is a picture to see when landed.

The fighting qualities of the Itchen fish were often praised. Skues' friend Arthur Holmes, who had a wide experience, considered them the best fighters of river trout, only to be equalled by those of the Deveron.

Bostock could be very effective with the dry fly at Abbots Barton, at least when rising fish were to be found. In one weekend he caught five of the much-admired two-pound fish. But even he became depressed by the shortage of trout prepared to feed on the hatched fly, and began also to agree that Skues and his guests were on the water too often, and that their methods were not quite fair.

The semantic argument that a 'nymph' can, by definition, not be a 'fly' had been heard before and had generally been dismissed by many as a piece of sophistry. Sheringham, H.D. Turing, for some years editor of *The Salmon and Trout Magazine*, and several other writers had rejected this idea. For them it was merely a term of art. John Evans probably spoke for most anglers when he wrote that anything assembled upon a hook from the usual fly-tying materials was a 'fly'. In the 1920s Arthur Ransome wrote an article in the *Manchester Guardian*, later reproduced in *Rod and Line* (1929), describing a frank exchange of views which he had witnessed on a riverbank. Four men were fishing, one of whom was noticeably more effective than the others. By lunch time the successful rod had caught eleven trout, while the other three had only four between them. An indignant meeting composed of the three less fortunate anglers was unanimous that the fourth man had been fishing with a nymph (in fact, a Hardy Pale Watery Nymph) or, as they chose to term it, a 'grub'. Later that afternoon, by which time he had caught three more fish, the happy angler was ambushed by one of his disgruntled colleagues. In the dialogue which ensued there is no doubt as to where Ransome's sympathies lay. The successful party explained that the fish were feeding beneath the surface, which was where he presented to them something more attractive than a dry fly. To the accusation that he had no right to call a thing without wings a fly, any more than a creature with two legs could be called a quadruped, his response was brisk and effective: 'Come, come. We have neither of us been fishing with either flies or grubs but with hooks decorated with scraps of feathers.'

Skues must have made his way back to the Corner House hotel in a state of bewilderment. If he had recollected some of the arguments at the annual meetings of the syndicate since the Great War he might have been struck by instances of an increase of tension. At first it had been slight and he probably had not perceived it, or else had brushed it aside as something irrelevant. But the problem did not go away, and the atmosphere became more brittle in the 1930s. We can only know the tale in outline. Skues merely alluded to a series of events in three separate entries in *Itchen Memories*: he was not going to enter into the detail. The trouble, in his opinion, began upon the admission to the syndicate of 'a certain wealthy member'. Restrictions on the number of days when rods might bring guests were steadily increased. In the third entry in *Itchen Memories* Skues indicated that he regarded all these restrictions as unnecessary, and to be laid at the door of the new member, 'whose activities from the first had not been conducive to the maintenance of the happy spirit which had hitherto prevailed among the members'. The influence of this unwelcome colleague seemed always to have prevailed in the syndicate meetings and Skues would be outvoted. Even after the withdrawal of the member from the syndicate the 'uncomfortable spirit' remained. The member in question has never, I believe, been identified. It may have been a man called Innes, who had made it clear that he disliked Skues' nymph methods, and in particular objected to the small double-hooked Greenwells that he found so effective. It must have been particularly galling for Skues to feel harried by anglers who, he felt, were far behind him in knowledge and experience. The sense of personal injury never left him. In 1944 he wrote: 'On Abbots Barton I suffered much from restrictions imposed (quite needlessly, to my mind) at the instance of other members not the most competent or knowledgeable.'

At the annual meeting in February 1933 it was agreed the season would henceforth begin in the middle of April. This must have been a hardship to Skues, who liked to begin on the first weekend of the month, in order to make good use of the heavy hatches of the large dark olive. In fact, such was his longing towards the end of each winter that he would begin to spend weekends at Winchester from the beginning of March, wandering about without a rod, in order to 'walk the course', but also simply for the sake of being in what was, for him, that most loved of all places on earth.

In spite of tougher rules, no member in 1933 was able to record catching a two-pound trout, even though the river had plenty of flow after a wet winter. 1934 was a drought year after a dry winter, and again no member or, indeed, guest had a two-pounder. Guests were now only allowed for two consecutive days, with the concession that on a weekend visit the evening rise on Fridays could be added. Later, a further restriction only allowed a guest for each member on alternate weekends.

Eventually guests were banned altogether, unless they were prepared to accept the idea of rod-sharing. Skues found this less of a burden than did his friends. In an article written as far back as 1902 he had pointed out the advantages of consultation over difficult fish and choice of flies, a second pair of eyes and agreeable companionship. 'There are far worse ways of fishing than sharing a rod.' Some of his acquaintance may have thought differently, particularly Dr Barton. In April 1936 he wrote in his diary: 'This is an invitation I am not keen on, as I never do much down there.... To make things worse I had to share his rod ... I would rather share a rod with Skues than most men but I loathe sharing a rod at any time.'

On that weekend he did not bother about sharing the rod, 'and let old Skues have it'. Instead he spent some time in photography, having secured help with his heavy camera from Avery the keeper. For the next two days Barton only had the rod for half an hour, and spent some of the time sleeping off the effects of a busy professional week. This seems to have been a fairly frequent pattern of his weekends at Abbots Barton. At 2.30 p.m. on Sunday he made an excuse to escape to London: 'Glad to get into the train', he wrote.

The thunderclap of 31 May 1936 was the climax of the discontent within the syndicate, and of a gradually extending series of policy changes to try to deal with the problem of a fishery that was not producing a good enough result. In the late 1920s the other members concentrated on trying to improve things by river work. By 1930 they were beginning to regard Skues as part of the problem, but for some time they proceeded in a polite and very English fashion. If there was murmuring in corners there was nothing direct involving bitter arguments and confrontations. Indeed, so slowly did the danger signs increase that Skues seems to have suspected nothing. His failure to notice the growing element of hostility in the syndicate is perhaps another example of his myopia about human relations to which I have already referred. The fact that he was fairly consistently successful on days when other members caught little or nothing may have caused irritation. Some of his guests were also very skilled at getting fish, in particular Lamorna Birch, John Evans and A.D. Chaytor. An additional factor was that Skues published frequent articles describing his and their successes on the river. This was, in part, intended to underline his teaching that, in spite of what Halford had written, the nymph was effective. It did not seem to occur to him that some anglers, both inside the syndicate and in the angling world beyond, were beginning to think that the nymph was perhaps a little too effective.

The withdrawal of Cecil Lilley ('Fleur de Lys') in 1934 may have been important in the conflict. There was now no one in the syndicate who could be called a close friend, and the secret discussions must have become more ominous in their intent. Eventually it became personal.

They believed that the activities of one of their number ought to be contained. The problem, as they saw it, was twofold. One was over-fishing; the other was the use of the nymph. In a letter to Wauton in June 1937 Skues admitted that the stock of trout at Abbots Barton was 'deplorably low'. He added: 'Simonds professes to consider it is due to hard fishing', a point of view that Skues did not wish to accept, as it was of course aimed at him. The real reason, he claimed, was that no effective netting for pike had been possible in 1935 and 1936. He was happy enough about the state of the fishery, even though fish were less plentiful than in pre-war days. In 1936 he killed forty-two trout, of which twenty were two-pounders, a low score in numbers but a high average weight.

As for the second objection, Skues reluctantly gave a promise not to use nymphs for the remainder of the season. It is not quite clear when this promise was extracted from him. The interview with Simonds occurred at the end of May whereas, in a letter to his friend Captain Struben RNVR, he mentioned that he had given up using nymph patterns 'about the middle of July'. At that time of the year this would have been a great handicap, and it is clear that he bent his own rule a little, from the intriguing words which follow in his letter: 'but as the trout continued taking under water I found I had to use sunk flies to get any fish at all'. This may mean that he had resorted to using dry flies adapted to sink rather than true nymphal forms. His last fish in August took a midge on a 0000 hook. He continued to arrange his life so as to be at Abbots Barton every weekend during the season. He then finished his season, as had been his custom for many years, at the end of August, having long ago decided that trout in September became far too easy to catch.

Although, in his sorrowful letter to Barton, Skues had spoken of resigning, the other members relented a little and encouraged him to stay on for the seasons of 1937 and 1938, mainly because they feared that it would be difficult to get a new member onto a fishery with such a meagre population of trout. Skues, meanwhile, had been investigating the chances of getting a rod elsewhere. He had not been successful in this, so he was no doubt relieved to be allowed to reappear on the Itchen in the spring of 1937. In 1938 he at last secured access onto the Nadder, and was able to spend several weekends there, thus removing pressure from Abbots Barton. Eventually, when the gates finally closed for him at Winchester, he settled at Wilton.

Relations at Abbots Barton in 1937 must have been a little strained, but having decided that they needed Skues' membership for a little longer his colleagues let him alone; in fact at the usual February meeting of the syndicate the matter was not mentioned and no attempt was made to extract a fresh promise from him to fish the dry fly only in 1937. He may have been expecting the worst at the meeting, for he had written gloomily to John Evans a few days earlier:

> I expect my colleagues will be as averse to nymph fishing as they showed themselves last year. It is a pity. I wish they would read what Hills says about it in his new book, *My Sporting Life*, but it speaks so absurdly highly of me that for very shame I could not ask them to read it. It is all the more annoying in that at my age I have so little time still before me to pursue my studies of nymphs and their imitations. I *should* like to carry them a bit further.

So Skues quietly resumed his former courses and stuck stubbornly to them for his last two seasons at Abbots Barton.

The pattern of the previous few years was repeated. The fish were larger and in excellent order, but they were few in number. In 1937 Skues killed twenty-one, of which twelve were over the two-pound mark. They included two trout of 3lb 5oz and 3lb 14oz. This last fish, caught on a nymph on a 00 hook, was the biggest Skues ever caught at Abbots Barton in his entire career, although he had several times been in temporary contact with larger fish. For years he had dreamt of a four-pounder. Other fish of that size were taken there in his time: one was caught by a schoolboy from Winchester College who had been given a guest ticket for the day. Another, a fish of 4lb 7oz, was caught with bait by an angler fishing from the back of the cottages near the downstream end of the fishery. But such examples were very rare.

If Skues was at all discontented with his total bag in 1937, it is likely that his colleagues fared worse. No doubt there were fresh murmurings about over-fishing. It is curious that the syndicate never followed the common practice on other chalk-stream fisheries of assigning each member a particular day of the week, or even of allowing a maximum number of days for each rod in a season, as did the Bemerton Club. This would have outraged Skues, who wished to have the freedom to be on the water at any time. Simonds had become so exasperated at the low stock of fish in the river that he had installed a stew by putting screens into a side stream near the top of the fishery. By the beginning of that season fish purchased from hatcheries were being fed on a diet of horse meat to prepare them for release into the river. Skues had always been against the idea of stocking, preferring challenging to easy fishing. He wrote to Wauton in June 1937 of a day at Abbots Barton when no one could catch fish at all:

> Still, I would rather have them difficult like that than be catching a lot of stew-fed fish which is the expedient to which the minds of some of my colleagues seem to be turning ... I daresay I shall not persuade my colleagues, in which case I feel inclined to put up my sub. in full for 1938 and resign, for I dislike the idea of fishing for stew bred and stew fed trout.

In *Itchen Memories* he wrote scornfully against putting such fish into a river: 'I always hated the idea of feeding up young stock to be killed, as much as I dislike the idea of feeding young pheasants till the end of September and shooting them on 1ˢᵗ October.' He noticed with disgust that the stock trout thrust their heads far out of the water to take the fly, a vulgar habit that they had acquired in the stew pond.

Skues had been slow to realize the danger in his own syndicate, but he was in no doubt of the rising tide of disapproval of nymphs in the angling world at large. His fellow members at Abbots Barton were not expressing their views in print, but many other fly-fishermen were beginning to do so. In March 1935, a year and more before the confrontation on the riverbank, he had adopted a more direct approach, which would seem to indicate that he was already aware that there were signs, in his own words, of 'a recrudescence of purism'. In an article in *The Salmon and Trout Magazine* he discussed the part played by Halford in establishing the purist code, and what he perceived to be the flaws in his thinking. It signalled a further deterioration in his attitude towards Halford. Clearly the influence of the man was still strong. Halford, in short, was in a sense still alive, and another attempt must be made to put purism down.

Shortly after writing this article he discovered some correspondence on the subject which had begun in an unlikely place. On 19 March there appeared in the columns of *The Times* an angling article describing the plight of an ultra-dry-fly purist, who was forced to abandon the siege of a trout because it was feeding beneath the surface. Skues intervened in a letter pouring scorn on such a proceeding: hammering a nymphing trout with dry flies would not work and would merely add to its education. It was, he wrote, 'unjustified by the purists' or by any other standard'. He had been warning of the folly of this practice for at least two decades, and was probably annoyed to find how little impression his advice had produced. A correspondence ensued which lasted for six weeks, in a national newspaper unused to material of this sort. Norman McCaskie joined in to praise the work of Skues, and pointed out that, in earlier times, the purists had accused the crude wet-fly men of spoiling sport and of over-educating the fish in the river. Now the purists could legitimately be accused of doing the same thing by the inappropriate use of the dry fly. Mr Skues, who had already led a successful rebellion against dry-fly tyranny, had thereby carried the war into the enemy camp. McCaskie also wrote that Skues had been the first to emphasize that the majority of the food of a trout was taken underwater. This was not true: ironically Halford had, in fact, been the first to mention this, a fact which Skues, with some amusement, could not resist pointing out.

Another correspondent, Sir Francis Lindley of Alresford, put forward an argument which was to appear again in the debate of 1938, namely that there were only a certain number of good fish in a stretch of river and it would be a pity to catch them by methods which were less enjoyable than the dry fly. Skues replied – his fourth letter – pointing out that there was no question of one style prevailing over another: both were valid in different conditions. He also questioned the assumption that the dry fly could claim to provide a superior form of enjoyment, and praised 'the subtle fascination of responding to the trout taking the nymph under water ... which those who have not mastered the method do not realize'.

The other participants in the *Times* correspondence never really addressed the issue of the admissibility of the nymph in the chalk stream, and wasted their letters in irrelevant reminiscence about the caution of trout. No purist emerged to attack the nymph method. But it was enough to raise awareness and to indicate that differences of opinion existed. Some of Skues' earlier-acquired confidence may therefore have been shaken by this muttering of distant thunder, even before the fatal encounter with Simonds. For years he had been encouraged by the rising tide of enthusiasm for the nymph. Many leading anglers – R.B. Marston, William Senior and Sheringham (who had invented the phrase 'exact wet-fly fishing' to describe the new art) – had shown their support in the journals. In 1921 Marston had written, in a review of *The Way of a Trout with a Fly*, that the practice of nymph fishing had 'achieved a deserved popularity'. Now the period of peace and apparent acceptance was coming to an end, and the concerns of a number of individuals who had privately never been happy about the new doctrine were coming together. The news of the Simonds/Skues encounter must have reached the Flyfishers' Club soon afterwards, and thence permeated into the wider world of chalk-stream angling. The correspondence in *The Times* in 1935 had been inconclusive, but the pamphlet war that began in the latter part of 1936 was much more to the point.

The growing uneasiness in the 1930s about the place of the nymph on the chalk stream needs examining. What brought it about, and why did it arise at that time instead of much earlier? It is customary nowadays to regard the purist point of view as wrong-headed. In the long term they were bound to lose the argument, or at least the major part of it. As for the culmination of the dispute, the debate of 1938, it has been held up as an enduring example of witless fatuity, and the opponents of the nymph have been seen at best as obstructive club bores out of touch with progress and at worst as malevolent enemies of a lonely genius.

Perhaps this oversimplified modern view, in which there is a good deal of hindsight, needs some considering. At least we owe to the purists the courtesy of giving their arguments a fair examination.

There was one class of angler that ought to be mentioned, if only to identify them before taking them away from the argument. These were the men who simply preferred the dry fly as offering the supreme delight of fishing, or perhaps were unable to master Skues' nymph method, particularly the subtle response to the quiet underwater take. But for many others there was more at stake and for them it included a moral ingredient.

For many anglers, and not necessarily purists, there were two main ingredients of good behaviour on the river. One concerned the relationship between angler and fish, the other between angler and angler.

The trout, for all its caution and instinct for self-preservation, can easily be caught by methods generally frowned upon as too deadly, or even simply illegal. What was generally regarded as reasonable restraint in fishing practice was developed over the years to create a fair contest between man and fish. New methods would naturally be scrutinized to see if they were fair and sportsmanlike. For some, the sunk nymph was felt to be rather near the borderline. Halford had recognized that the dry Gold Ribbed Hare's Ear bore a resemblance to the hatching nymph, and used it for many years until overcome by ultra-purism towards the end of his fishing career. He had also developed a pattern for the pupa of the grannom, but he intended it to be fished dry. There is evidence to show that, in later years, some anglers, such as Anthony Buxton and Sir Francis Lindley, felt their consciences to be clear if they fished a floating nymph, something which could be regarded as a sort of honorary dry fly. In 1932 Walter Barrett, an extremely successful angler on the Kennet, pleaded this particular form of defence, when he captured two difficult fish that had defeated the other rods. Using a half-floating Mayfly nymph of his own design he caught these two fish in half an hour. His host thought that the new pattern ought to be banned: 'It's too deadly.' Barrett insisted that his hybrid pattern was a dry fly, because the stumpy wings at the front of the fly were visible and only the tail (representing the shuck) sank beneath the surface. His justification was accepted.

This sort of logic-chopping looks a little quaint to us in the twenty-first century, but there was a good deal of it in the 1930s, as men sought for guidelines that they could regard as acceptable. Some felt that if the artificial nymph was just beneath the surface it was marginally acceptable. But the really deep nymph, especially if loaded with lead was, in the view of many anglers, nothing but a poacher's engine.

Moral considerations were also deemed to be important in the behaviour of one rod to another. An over-active angler restlessly pacing the bank and busily offering sunk flies to any visible fish, or even into every possible holding place, was likely to be unpopular. These ideas were not invented by Halford, but he was a powerful influence in establishing the etiquette of the river. For his followers the familiar elements of the fishing day – the leisurely beginning at the fishing hut, the waiting until the hatch began – were all part of the stately punctilio of the chalk stream, an accepted etiquette as well as something familiar and reassuring. This pattern persisted for decades after Halford's death, and can still be observed today. For some years after the Second World War the members of the Wilton Club enjoyed a remarkable standard of fishing for wild trout of a high average weight, some of them up to 5 and 6lb in weight. An angler who knew the old hands of the 1950s remembers that one seldom saw them actually fishing. They waited, sometimes for hours, until the finely-judged optimum moment arrived and the cautious trout became negotiable.

The timing of the revolt against the nymph is also interesting. As we have seen, the appearance of Skues' first book in 1910 did not immediately produce the storm of opposition that he had expected. There was a certain amount of discontent, but it was not expressed openly and for some years there existed a subterranean grumbling. It was not until the

1930s that the purists decided that at last they had some arguments to deploy. By then the use of the nymph had become widespread, and it was common knowledge that many anglers were practising a debased form, using lures and often fishing downstream. Dr H.B. McCaskie recorded seeing an angler catching a limit bag in two hours on a Derbyshire river, fishing a large wet fly downstream, 'quite frankly when he thought that nobody was looking'. In some parts of Derbyshire the nymph was forbidden and in others it was regarded with disfavour, in McCaskie's words, 'in view of the rainbow's suicidal addiction to any form of subaqueous lure'.

There may be a clue here to the question of timing. By this period the systematic stocking of chalk streams had become the general rule and the stew-bred fish, especially if newly released, had become easy targets. Hills noticed that the fish at Houghton, once thought to be catchable only with discreet tiny dry patterns, were by 1935 appreciative of much larger flies. Stocking was, in fact, having a coarsening effect on trout behaviour and on fishing methods. This was a matter of concern for owners and fishery managers, for it involved an impact on restocking costs. Fish were more likely to be caught by sunk flies, and the amount of fishing time each day was increased. Keeping to the dry fly at least slowed things down and cost the owner less. The complaints multiplied. Those guilty of 'fishing the water' were suspected of pricking and frightening fish and of catching the undersized. And tackle dealers were marketing a range of peculiar inventions under the name of nymphs, later described by Skues as 'monstrosities and absurdities' which had no place on chalk streams.

There may have been another and more subtle reason for explaining the purist point of view. The period between the wars was one of accelerated and violent social change. For many it seemed a menacing and crazy era, and among some people there was felt to be a need to hold onto old customs and familiar certainties. Perhaps the attempt to preserve the more traditional standards of chalk-stream behaviour was affected by such feelings.

The incremental effect of these concerns and anxieties, some genuine, others misplaced, began to come to a head in 1936. In the winter 1936 issue of the *Journal* there appeared 'An Open Letter' by a writer using the pen name of A.F. Loater. He wrote that, having been carefully educated by his father, a clergyman and 'a rigid purist of the cult', he regarded a nymph in the same category as a maggot or a worm, and wondered if there was any way of curbing the spread of the sunk fly practice, 'or is the country too corrupt and wet-bug ridden!' He gave an account of his own attempt to fish a 'nymph', guiltily entered into in the interests of research. This device was not described, save that it was weighted with a ballast of fuse wire. It was hurled at random into a hatch hole and a trout of 3lb was caught. So, by his own account, the writer had only made one trial, and it bore no resemblance at all to the Skues nymph method. Dr Barton, at that time one of the editors of the *Journal,* replied to this foolish article with a piece entitled 'The Ethics of Fishing the Nymph', accusing the writer of adopting 'the dialect of the soap box', and of missing the point if he imagined that such a lure could be described as a nymph. If such crude practices were to spread then it would discredit genuine nymph fishing – 'a very fascinating and scientific addition to our pleasure'. Skues also joined in the fight, for so it was becoming, with a letter over the signature of A.N. Other, an addition to his long list of pseudonyms. In this letter he appraised and dismissed every point made by A.F. Loater.

A.F. Loater may have written an ill-informed and opinionated letter, but it was enough to set off a war of words, which grew until it eventually led to the debate of February 1938. In the summer issue of the *Journal* there appeared three articles and a letter by Skues (using another new pseudonym, viz. A.Y.Z.), an irrelevant letter by a humorist calling himself P. Rawn and an article by Mottram, in which he discussed the logic which might be supposed to govern the ethical rules of chalk-stream fishing. The matter was also referred to in the editorial, in which Mottram was described as 'a hardshell dry fly purist' (probably written by Barton or by 'Tup' Wauton).

Once the floodgates had been opened, letters and articles (in which the ominous word 'ethics' occurred fairly often) followed briskly in the *Journal*, which lasted until the climax of the debate.

The appearance of Dr Mottram in the field had changed the pattern of the controversy. Adopting Dr Barton's title he intervened in the *Journal* in the summer of 1937 with an article 'The Ethics of Fishing the Nymph'. This rather heavy-handed piece included an attempt to identify an ethical standard whereby the use of the nymph might be condemned. Pursuing what he regarded as a logical course – and, incidentally, echoing the 1935 letter of Sir Francis Lindley mentioned earlier – he argued that a trout caught by such means is of less value because it has been caught by an inferior method. It should have been caught with a dry fly, which would have afforded more sport and therefore more enjoyment. This rather ludicrous argument – reminiscent of the philosopher Jeremy Bentham's famous attempt to measure human happiness by way of his 'felicific calculus' – involved assuming that fishing the dry fly is necessarily always more enjoyable. Into this argument was built the assumption that all fly-fishermen would estimate enjoyment in the same way. But enjoyment, as Skues had often pointed out, was a matter of opinion. In support of the idea that nymph fishing was a cruder technique, Mottram argued that it was simply easier, because drag was no threat to its success, adding 'If I wish to give a novice or duffer his best chance of catching a trout in a chalk stream, I remove his dry fly, soap his cast and tie on a nymph.' (It was a pity that he did not tell his readers if the trout in question were stew-bred or not.) For good measure he added that trout were often pricked with the nymph, or caught and returned, which would disincline them to feed at the surface.

The Mottram turnabout has fascinated anglers ever since, for these ideas represented a far cry from the ideas he had developed years earlier, and had included in his much-admired book *Fly-Fishing: Some New Arts and Mysteries* (1915). In a chapter called 'Flies of the Future' he explored problems of colour, form, transparency, buoyancy and the effects of light – all matters which were exercising the mind of Skues at that time. For a time Mottram was a sunk-fly rebel and his broad liberal approach in designing patterns such as the Fry Fly, the Alevin Fly and patterns to imitate shrimps, water boatmen, caddis, the larvae of dragonflies, stoneflies, water beetles and even small crayfish would have alarmed the purists of that time. Telling readers in 1915 that there was nothing wrong in fishing a sunk fly downstream must have confirmed their suspicions. He added that he had no time for the theory that the sunk fly caused chalk-stream trout to become bad risers. That might have been true of the older crude style of fishing the wet fly but 'against the modern school this objection cannot be raised'. The chapter 'Nymphs and Bulgers', the most forward-looking section of his book, introduced the reader to the difference between the behaviour of the active fish chasing free-swimming nymphs, and that of the fish quietly taking the nymphs rising to hatch (see Chapter 7).

For two decades Mottram held to these beliefs and, as late as 1935, in an article in the *Journal* called 'Simple Flies' he was still advocating opinions likely to chill the purist soul, for example: 'the leaded nymph is far more attractive than the unleaded'. And he was still, at that date, trying to improve on nymph design, in particular by teasing out the fibres of dubbing to produce the effect of movement. Mottram would, therefore, have appeared on the face of it to be an obvious ally of Skues in the 1938 debate. But at some date between 1935 and the summer of 1937 he had entirely retreated from his heterodox position and had defected to the ranks of the purists, thus providing another of the problems of angling history for posterity to ponder. In the debate of 1938 he appeared as a convert to the purist ranks, but trailing the embarrassing lumber of his book of 1915 and a number of articles approving of the artificial nymph. To the audience on that evening he must have seemed to be an inappropriate running-mate for Sir Joseph Ball in the debate.

The warfare of 1937 continued, and several more shots were fired in the autumn *Journal*. The editorial noted that 'Dr Mottram seems to have stepped on a wasps' nest as judged by the quantity of correspondence received as a result of his article.' The now-familiar title 'The Ethics of Fishing the Nymph' was used again by Skues as he grappled again with his opponent. He had read the article 'with a certain degree of amusement' and could not resist reminding Mottram of his noticeably non-purist credentials in the past. He then quoted this striking trumpet call from Mottram's book of 1915: 'I believe the day is not far distant when the dry-fly fisherman may have to give up or share his throne with another', and added three paragraphs of his excellent argument (dating from 1915) in favour of the sunk fly. Skues ended dryly: 'He has changed his opinion. Well, why not?', and proceeded with a demolition job of several pages. Other members joined in, including Skues' American friend Eugene Connett, and the tone of the argument became even more overheated. Another contributor accused Mottram of being guilty of a 'depressing thesis' and of 'spiritual kinship with the Pharisee'. His attempt at arriving at an estimate of an angler's happiness was derided as metaphysical nonsense, and the purists were begged to confine themselves to their own practices and to leave other mortals alone.

Mottram was not at all abashed by these attacks. Using yet again the overworked 'Ethics' title, he wrote another piece in the winter 1937 number of the *Journal*, in which he blandly admitted that he had indeed changed his view, because many years of experience with the nymph had convinced him 'that the sport of fly-fishing is being harmed by its improper use'.

In the same issue appeared the most extraordinary of all the contributions. The pamphlet war must have led to heated discussions at the Flyfishers' Club and a general feeling that the controversy ought to be thoroughly aired in a debate. Such an idea had never been suggested in the Club's history. As a result there appeared in the same number the most surprising contribution of all, in the form of an article by Skues entitled 'Halford and the Nymph'. This was intended, in his own words, 'to give the Club Members matter to ponder on, to look up and verify, and to chew over' before the debate. It was probably the most aggressive and ill-tempered piece he had ever written (see Appendix 7). It included a list of nine ingredients of Halford's doctrine: at the end of each appeared the words 'HE WAS WRONG'. The constant repetition of these words in capitals is striking: it was as if Skues was shouting in print. At the end of this warlike tirade he threw down his gage like an old-time knight: 'Now what is your answer?'

The style and content of this article did not show Skues at his best. There was not much sign of his usual skilful footwork here. Exasperation had got the better of him, and for once his tactical sense had deserted him. Rather than taking a positive line by setting out the case for his own practice, he had chosen to single out a number of detailed points derived from Halford's writings. These included the frequently rehearsed argument over the inertness or activity of the ascending nymph, about which readers may have felt that they had heard enough. By setting down what he considered to be this devastating list Skues had merely enlarged the target to receive the missiles of any potential adversary. How much simpler it would have been for Skues to brush aside that particular argument and to point out that, whether or not there was movement in the natural, his artificial nymphs were nevertheless regarded by the most important individual in the matter, the trout, as sufficiently lifelike to be taken. H.D. Turing, the editor of the *Journal of the Salmon and Trout Association*, wrote that, in his view, what Halford said about these matters was of no importance.

It was not surprising that Skues' discussion document, in which he had so unwisely shown his hand, would be taken as a challenge. The acceptance was not long in coming, and a formidable champion stepped forward to take a leading part on behalf of the purists.

Sir Joseph Ball (1885–1961) has not so far been discussed in detail in these pages. As with Simonds, here was a heavyweight, a distinguished man with a confident and, indeed, somewhat overbearing public manner, and therefore a serious adversary with whom to cope. His career had been impressive, but much of it had developed in areas obscure to the general public. It has never been easy for investigative journalists to get hold of a clear picture of this man. His experience in his working life had made him secretive, so interviews were not encouraged, and any unwanted intrusions into his privacy were often followed by threats of actions at law. This need not mean that he had an unusually thin skin; men involved in the world of secrets commonly develop an official reticence of manner.

As a young man Ball had worked for Scotland Yard before the Great War, and was called to the Bar at Gray's Inn in 1913. In 1915 he joined MI5, later becoming head of B Branch. Christopher Andrew, the historian of the British Secret Service, regarded Ball as one of the most able officers of MI5. Away from official life his chief relaxations were angling and shooting, and in 1920 he joined the Flyfishers' Club. After Halford's death he had befriended his son Ernest, and from May 1918 his name began to appear in the record-book of the Halford family fishery at Mottisfont on the Test. When Ernest gave up Mottisfont and migrated further upstream to the fishery at Newton Stacey, Ball continued to be a guest. In view of the complaints of the purists that the use of the nymph resulted in inadvertently catching small trout it is amusing to find in the record that, although using the driest of dry flies, he was unable to avoid catching undersized fish – one day at the end of May 1925 Ball caught thirteen trout, eight of which had to be returned as undersized – and on a day in 1928 at Bransbury Common he returned seven. He was fascinated by Halford's doctrine, and acquired from Ernest a quantity of his father's papers, including scrapbooks containing cuttings of all Halford's articles in *The Field*. These seem to have made a deep impression on him. But, unlike Halford, his tastes were wide-ranging. In the early 1920s he contributed a series of pieces over the signature of 'March Brown' in *The Daily Mail*, describing his exploits with salmon, pike, perch and grayling, as well as bass and pollack at sea. His own papers indicate that he was planning to combine them into a book, although this plan was never carried out.

In 1926 Ball left MI5, being dissatisfied with his career prospects, and in 1927 was recruited by Viscount Davidson into the Conservative Research Department at its office in Old Queen Street. Here his experience in undercover operations was useful, and he was soon getting valuable information by covert means from the headquarters of the Labour Party. Davidson and his colleagues would have been quite satisfied that these somewhat unscrupulous activities were justifiable. Many elements of the Left in Britain at that time had leanings towards communism, and were therefore considered to be a danger to national security. The fear of revolution in Britain was very real in the inter-war years, particularly after the General Strike of 1926, and this would have soothed any twinges of conscience about spying on the opposition.

In the 1930s Ball began to work for Neville Chamberlain, and became a close friend as well as a colleague. Chamberlain had been fishing for salmon since 1914. He now began to learn much more about trout fishing from Ball, becoming a welcome guest at his house on the Test at Kimbridge. In 1936 Ball, having been known for years as Major George Joseph Ball, was appointed KBE and was henceforth known as Sir Joseph Ball. When, in the following year, Chamberlain succeeded Stanley Baldwin as Prime Minister, Ball, who was already by now head of the Conservative Party organization, was appointed chief policy adviser to the Cabinet. Although almost unknown to the general public he was closely involved in the secret diplomacy of the next two disastrous years.

Chamberlain now believed that keeping the peace in Europe was the main object of his political life. For some time he followed a line of rapprochement with Italy, hoping that Mussolini could be persuaded to restrain Hitler's ambitions. His contacts with Count Grandi, the Italian ambassador in London, of which the general public were kept in ignorance, were all arranged by Ball. It is not surprising that one leading historian of the period referred to him as 'the ubiquitous Sir Joseph Ball', adding: 'Whenever one looks into the more shadowy aspects of Chamberlain's personal actions, Ball is there.' It is easy enough nowadays, with the convenience of hindsight, to dismiss as doomed from the start the attempt to use Italy to drive a wedge between the Berlin/Rome Axis, and to pour contempt and scorn upon the appeasers and their peace-at-any-price views. Appeasement has been much criticized since, but fears of another world war made it popular at the time with the majority of the British public. As for the talks with Grandi by way of Ball's 'secret channel' (as it was known), the Foreign Secretary Anthony Eden was not permitted to know much about them. Chamberlain liked to conduct his own foreign policy, and was aware that Eden did not agree with him about befriending Mussolini. There had been several other disagreements between them, and by early February 1938 a cabinet crisis was developing. It ended with Eden's resignation on 20 February.

Meanwhile the Flyfishers' Club was in the throes of its own crisis. The Club had always been a friendly and convivial one, and there is nothing in its earlier records to indicate that there had ever been much in the way of noisy argument and conflict. But in the winter of 1937–8 the atmosphere was deteriorating, although the familiar courtesies of a gentleman's club would still have been observed. The committee hoped that a debate on the nymph question might clear the air a little, and fixed the event for Thursday 10 February, to take place after the usual weekly dinner.

Sir Joseph Ball, who was playing an important part in grave events in a more public sphere, must have been one of the most preoccupied men in London, but he nevertheless found time to prepare for the nymph debate. It is an indication of how seriously he took the role of unofficial prosecutor on behalf of the purists, with all the work it involved. Perhaps, for him, it was a form of relaxation. By 10 February he had researched the background of his case by reading all the relevant parts of Halford's printed output – itself a mammoth task – had consulted several experts and had composed his brief. This still survives in his papers, a densely packed typescript of seventeen pages. He was still settling the final form at the last moment. He had been corresponding with the entomologist F.T.K. Pentelow, asking for more information about the ascending nymph. Pentelow's reply (see Appendix 8), which arrived on the morning of the debate, must have gladdened his heart, for it confirmed the information he had already received from Mosely, that the nymph in its upward journey to hatch was not inert and helpless, but active. He incorporated the information from Pentelow into his brief, wrote 'Final Version' on it, and awaited the evening. The image of a powerful man, helping and advising his chief on matters to do with the peace of Europe and turning to deal with the behaviour of maturing ephemeropterans, is certainly an intriguing one.

Ball had also busied himself in another area. It looks from the printed account of the debate as if he had persuaded Dr Mottram to speak, and had settled with him a boundary line between their contributions. Ball was to lead the main attack, and Mottram would produce a much shorter presentation, merely dealing with the danger of the nymph enthusiasts hooking undersized fish. Martin Mosely probably gave a great deal of technical advice, but declined to participate directly.

It is difficult to imagine Skues busily networking and arranging for allies in the same way. He had always preferred to work alone, and would have regarded politicking behind the scenes as indelicate and ungentlemanly. Letters calling for support to Dr Barton, Eric Taverner, 'Tup' Wauton, John Evans and several other possible candidates might have helped to make up a defence team. Whether or not he did cautiously approach any friends in the hope of their support we cannot know, but there was a notable absence of them on the night.

On Thursday 10 February 1938 members of the Flyfishers' Club finished their dinner with the customary port and entered upon the serious business of the evening. What followed has always been difficult to define and estimate. A record of sorts has survived and was included in the spring 1938 number of the *Journal* (see Overfield 1977) but it is incomplete, and only gives a bald account of the major contributions. The task of assembling a version of the proceedings cannot have been easy. The two editors, Barton and Norman Heath, probably pounced on the speakers at the end of the meeting in order to get their material, but in some cases they were unsuccessful. Those who spoke from prepared versions handed them over, or perhaps promised a tidied-up copy by the end of the week. Others had simply extemporized and had nothing substantial in the way of a written version to hand over. John Waller Hills was a practised speaker in public, having been a Member of Parliament and a Privy Councillor. He may have had a few headings written on the back of a menu card but would have felt no need of a full text. His speech does not therefore exist in the printed version, and we have to make do with the editors' brief summary of eight lines. This is a pity, for he was one of the two warmest supporters of Skues.

It is details such as this which give the record of the debate an unbalanced feeling, and one regrets that arrangements were not made to have a shorthand writer unobtrusively present. This was, after all, a common device with the Club. Exactly a week after the debate the Annual Dinner took place, the account of which included a verbatim record of all the speeches. None of these contained any matter of lasting significance when compared with the debate of the previous Thursday. Perhaps those organizing the debate were afraid of making the occasion appear too formal and serious, as if it were a business meeting rather than what they hoped would be a relaxed gathering of a normally friendly body of members. We do not even know who was present, apart from the main participants. The modern custom of passing round a sheet to be signed would have been thought inappropriate then. Were Simonds and Bostock there? Was Martin Mosely, or was he merely content to provide ammunition for Joseph Ball in the days leading up to 10 February? If Mosely was present it would have been a curious experience for him, for he had co-operated with Halford in 1908 and 1909 in the secret experiments with nymphs at Mottisfont, which he had tied for Halford.

It would be possible to know who might have been present, and also to get a better idea of what happened, if a few useful diaries and letters had survived. A perceptive piece of writing could have recreated for us the mood and atmosphere of the evening. Excellent descriptions have come down to us about some of the great controversies of the past, such as the famous clash over Darwin's theory at the meeting of the British Association for the Advancement of Science in Oxford in 1860, when Huxley demolished Bishop Wilberforce. The nymph debate must have been strikingly dramatic, at times uncomfortably so, but it was an important, indeed a unique event in the annals of the Club, and apart from the imperfect record in the *Journal* no one has described it for us.

It may even be fairly asked whether the event can be described as a debate in any formal sense. The chairman, Strachan Bennion, was hardly mentioned and seems to have run the proceedings with a light hand. No formal motion or proposition was announced at the beginning. There is no record of Skues having been asked to come back to respond to any of the various points raised, nor was there any mention of a summing up at the end of the evening, or the taking of a vote. What has usually been called a debate more resembled in this case a rather loosely organized general discussion or seminar, dominated by the attack by Joseph Ball. His paper occupied one half of the time of the proceedings, while the other ten named participants were huddled into the remaining half.

The event began fairly gently with a cheerful speech by the distinguished neurologist Dr F.M.R. Walshe. He was a strong supporter of the use of the artificial nymph, and was a successful after-dinner speaker. At the Club's Annual Dinner in 1935 he had gone out of his way to pay a lengthy and affectionate tribute to Skues and his work, calling him 'a genius ... still happily amongst us', a description which had produced applause. Now, three years later, he was still a warm supporter. He identified many of the contradictions of the purist point of view so effectively within a few minutes of the beginning of the debate that one wonders if some purists who had intended to take part quickly changed their minds. The campaign of the dry-fly supporters against the nymph was a 'solemn and pompous business', 'the nymph has justified its use in chalk stream fishing', and, of Skues, 'whoever is not convinced by his arguments is not amenable to reason, and is the timid slave of outworn convention'. These and other forceful remarks seemed at first to be a good start for the Skues party.

It is likely that Dr Barton persuaded Walshe to open the proceedings. As someone closely involved in the organizing of the evening he may have felt unable to participate directly, but he was anxious to support Skues and to protect him from undue distress. As a medical man he knew quite well what an ordeal the evening was likely to be for his old friend. Skues was going to be attacked in his own club, his refuge from the outside world and a place of friendship and trust. For forty-five years it had been his second home – now it was going to become a threatening arena. Perhaps Walshe could help – he was a close colleague of Barton at University College Hospital and an ideal person to persuade into opening the discussion and defusing tension.

Skues was next called upon to contribute and read what, at first, must have seemed a well-reasoned paper. He began by defining the practice of nymph fishing in fairly narrow terms, i.e. presenting to a fish visibly feeding beneath the surface the best match of its natural food. The use of the marrow scoop would improve one's diagnosis of the type of nymph being taken. This was an unexceptionable beginning.

Skues then moved on to an aggressive examination of the part played by Halford in establishing the purist habit on the chalk stream, and thereby made a capital error. It should be remembered that Skues was now in his eightieth year. His sense of proportion and the dexterity in the disputes of his younger years had, to some extent, left him. Instead of expanding on the positive theme of the beauty and effectiveness of the art, he set himself to demolish the arguments advanced by Halford to show that the artificial nymph must necessarily be useless. In so doing he was returning to some of the material in his challenge-article in the *Journal*. It was an interesting example of the enormous influence that Halford still had over the chalk-stream mind a quarter of a century after his death. This inevitably led Skues on to strike at what he believed to be Halford's major error, namely the activity or otherwise of the ascending mature nymph. It may be that most members of the audience had heard or read more than enough of this hardy annual by then. In any case, this was a matter in which Skues himself had gone astray rather than Halford. His mistakes were threefold. In the first instance, entomologists at the time (and indeed ever since that date) have pointed out that the nymph comes to the surface with a good deal of activity, though with short periods of rest, only becoming inert in the last second or so before eclosion. Secondly, attacking someone long dead may have aroused some disapproval in his audience. Finally and most obviously of all, it was a curious move to be engaging in a theoretical argument that had already been settled in practice by many years of success of nymph fishing.

This latter part of Skues' presentation was the first disaster of the evening. Instead of concentrating on commending his own practice, he spent too much time attacking an ancient enemy. Eight years later Skues defended his mode of attack in a letter. He still held to his belief of 1938 that demolishing the pronouncements of Halford was vital to his case. Halford had established purism, the opposition speakers at the debate had all relied on Halford and, as he put it, 'he was my most prominent and emphatic enemy'. This was a good defence in retrospect, but in 1938 his tactic must have left a rather negative impression upon his audience. Demonstration would have been better than remonstration. Raising such points of view in the debate, and in the curtain-raiser article in the *Journal* in the winter of 1937, which had attracted the notice of Joseph Ball, merely made his position vulnerable. To claim in this article that 'if Dry-Fly Purism is founded on a number of mistakes, misobservations and misunderstandings on the part of Halford, then Dry-Fly Purism has got to go' was perhaps a little too aggressive. A battering ram frontal assault does tend to arouse opposition. There are times when what military men call 'the strategy of the indirect approach' might be more politic and effective.

As soon as Joseph Ball rose to speak the main attack developed. The atmosphere in the room must have changed entirely. What had begun in an amusing after-dinner manner changed abruptly into an accusatorial confrontation. Ball traversed all the points made by Skues in his article in the *Journal* and rebutted or attempted to rebut them all. In some cases he was successful. As Skues had insisted on the necessary inertness of the ascending nymph, Ball made it one of his main points of assault. For this he decided to rely on passages of Dr Mottram's intriguing book *Fly-Fishing: Some New Arts and Mysteries* (1915). However, he quoted one passage, in which the nymphs were described as coming quietly downstream and rising slowly to the surface, and reinforced it with another passage referring to 'rapid vibrations of the tail' and 'the peculiar undulations of the abdomen'. This was a piece of sharp practice for, as he must have known, Mottram had been careful to differentiate between two distinct types of underwater behaviour. The first passage referred to trout taking nymphs rising to hatch, described by Mottram as 'dimpling', and the second to trout taking nymphs swarming over weed beds, or bulging. These latter are certainly extremely active. He then returned to more reliable ground and supported his claim by quotations from Pentelow's letter and from recent conversations with Martin Mosely.

This minute unpicking of Skues' interpretation of Halford's doctrine, which continues for over six pages in Ball's printed notes, would not have been necessary at all, but for the fact that, in his article in the *Journal*, Skues had used the influence of Halford as a major part of his case. Skues must have been thunderstruck. He had not expected to be the victim of a case so minutely argued. But Ball had not finished. Having set up his defence of the Halford position he enlarged his approach and turned to what he considered to be the deleterious effects of nymph fishing. He argued that fishermen employing the dry fly used only a small part of the river in a day, approached a rising fish with caution and making a discreet withdrawal after it had been caught or had refused the fly, having been careful not to frighten other fish in the area. The nymph fisherman, however, 'casts upstream and wet and, unless he is both ultra-pure and ultra-clever, he casts to fish that are not taking nymphs at all'. On the lower Test, where the water is deep, he would not be able to see the fish. In his efforts to peer into the water he would approach too closely and spread alarm throughout the underwater world. He would wander around too much, covering the same stretch more than once, fish at a venture and prick many fish. Ball claimed to know of 'one magnificent dry-fly water' (not named), which had been ruined by treatment of this sort. Skues had gathered from a conversation with C. Ernest Pain, author of *Fifty Years on the Test*, that the artificial nymph was in common use on the Test from source to mouth. Ball impatiently rejected this, citing an impressive list of Test fisheries where it was banned. And anyway, he concluded, why not imitate the shrimp, the snail and the caddis larva?

Perhaps Ball began to be a little sorry for his rival, who may have begun to look increasingly forlorn during this diatribe, for at the end of his presentation he referred to him as 'my old friend Mr Skues'.

Ball was followed by Dr James Mottram, the dark horse of chalk-stream literature. His address was short and, after his forceful part in the war of correspondence, something of an anticlimax, being confined entirely to the theory that the use of the nymph led to the catching of undersized trout. This point was supported by a speech (one of those unfortunately not reported *in extenso*) of Hedley Norris.

As the evening progressed the tide of battle went one way then another. It has been suggested by some authors that the weight of opinion went against Skues and even that his opponents were almost unanimously against him, so that he lost the argument. A close reading of what was actually said shows that the position was a little more complicated.

Four members were dead against the practice: Ball, Mottram, Norris and Sheriffs. The first two were damaging critics, whereas the views of the third and fourth were flimsy and carried little weight. Norris admitted that he had made only one trial of the nymph, and a man who could say, as did Sheriffs: 'I have been fishing the nymph since 1868 – we called them wet flies then' must have had very little idea about nymph fishing.

Two were warm supporters: Walshe and Hills. Hills was a well-known supporter of Skues, with frequent opportunities to admire his skills when he fished with him at Houghton and Abbots Barton. He was fascinated by the nymph, and had been a practitioner since July 1914. In 1930 he had written about Skues in terms of unstinted admiration in the second (extended) edition of *A Summer on the Test*, and in that engaging book *My Sporting Life* (1936) he called Skues 'a great man', adding: 'He showed fishermen much which was plain for us to see had we not been too stupid and opinionated to see it.' Nymph fishing was 'not only legitimate fly-fishing, but fly-fishing of a high order, harder than the floating fly'. No doubt these sentiments were also present in his speech, which sadly we have only in summary.

The remaining members of whose participation a record has survived took up varying positions. It is not quite true to say that the weight of opinion was against Skues. There remained four more speakers: Phelps, Marling, Myers and Peck. The first two were uneasy about the nymph but had reservations in favour. They were not for or against it, but somewhere in the middle. Their view was that the nymph would be acceptable if everyone could be relied upon to fish it in the manner of Skues. Major T.T. Phelps emphasized the discourtesy point. A crude and over-generous interpretation of nymph fishing was bad for fellow anglers and for the fishery. Marling agreed; Myers and R.D. Peck were rather more against. Myers thought that legitimate nymph fishing was allowable in a private and trustworthy context, although if he had his own fishery he would bar it. Ralph Peck, author of *Fly Fishing for Duffers* (1934), made it clear that he admired Skues, but thought that the nymph was not appropriate for heavily stocked waters in the south, where trout were easily caught with sunk flies. It should be reserved for 'virgin waters'.

At the end of this extraordinary evening many members probably left the Club wondering who had won. As for Skues, he must have gone away wishing that he had been able to do his cause more justice, by a more forceful and effective presentation. Posterity has come to the same conclusion. How satisfying it would have been, we feel, if he had fallen in wrath upon his detractors like an avenging archangel and scattered them all in flight. The sympathy in later days has always been with Skues. This has led to a slightly inaccurate view of the event. Whether they were right or wrong, his opponents considered that they had a legitimate point of view, and the suggestion sometimes voiced that they were motivated by malice is not sustainable: enough is known about the majority of the speakers in the debate to acquit them of that. And it seems as if the other members of the Club, who probably had no inkling in advance of the nature of Joseph Ball's contribution, were left with a feeling of sympathy and embarrassment.

As the dust settled, Dr Barton saw himself as the peacemaker. He wrote in the editorial of the spring 1938 *Journal* that 'the subject was argued with the friendliest contention, but it was evidently a matter on which opinions were sharply divided', adding firmly: 'However, the matter has been threshed out and we feel inclined to leave it at that, nor to encourage any further correspondence on the subject.' At the annual dinner a week after the debate the President, in his speech, made a kindly reference to 'Skues' perfect imitations of a minute nymph'.

Skues realized that the best move now would be to press on with finishing his book on nymph fishing, which he had been writing since 1937. He published a holding letter in the spring number of the *Journal*, referring to 'Sir Joseph Ball's brilliant address', and mentioning his forthcoming book, which he hoped to complete 'if time be granted to me by destiny', in order to expose 'the fallacies underlying his entire argument', adding: 'I write this to make it clear to members that I accept neither his arguments nor his conclusions.' In the same number there appeared an unrepentant letter from Ball, ironically anticipating what Skues might have further to say, and adding by way of concession 'that it would be unfair to expect members to read any further arguments about nymph fishing for some time to come'.

In 1938 Skues secured from a man called Reyersbach some fishing on the River Nadder in Wiltshire for the next three years, sharing with four other rods, in order to dilute his constant appearances during his last season at Abbots Barton. Reyersbach was an absentee landlord living in Barnet, and probably regarded the fishing rights, which he leased from the Pembroke Estate, as a sort of investment. The fishery began on the western edge of Wilton and extended through the village of Burcombe and upstream as far as Barford St Martin, a distance of about two miles.

At Wilton the Nadder may, in a settled period of summer weather, look very like another of the clear chalk streams of the south, with a healthy growth of water crowfoot. A period of heavy rain will soon dispel this illusion. The geological map of the upper part of the river shows a complicated tangle of different limestones and the greensand of the Cretaceous. There is also a good deal of the infamous gault clay, good for making bricks but not popular with anglers. Consequently the Nadder can rise quickly and will colour like the streams of Devon and the Welsh border. Prolonged wet weather will cause it to come up by several feet, flooding the surrounding meadows and even sometimes bearing downstream the timbers of a shattered henhouse or the corpse of a drowned sheep. Skues was several times defeated in his attempts to entertain fishing guests by an inundation of thick water.

The geology affects the fishing in other ways. The upper end of the Nadder is more acid in character, but as it flows eastwards towards Salisbury the benevolent influence of the chalk begins to assert itself and it becomes a more fertile stream with a good potential for sport. It does not, however, reach the level of alkalinity of a pure chalk stream. There were other drawbacks. In late spring the abundant growth of weed quickly choked up the watercourse. This problem became more serious during the war, owing to lack of labour for weed-cutting. Skues soon discovered that the grayling and coarse fish outnumbered the trout. Up-winged flies were much less abundant than on the Itchen, and the fish were more catholic in their diet. An autopsy would show a wide variety of items: shrimps, caddis in their cases, small fish and terrestrial insects such as crane flies, gnats, caterpillars and beetles. Nymphs were not numerous.

As often happens on mixed fisheries of this sort there were large trout if one could find them, but catching them needed a different approach: the delicate tactics of Abbots Barton were not likely to work. There were rumours of fish of 5lb or more, which may have been entirely possible, although there seem not to be any surviving records. In the years after the war several wild fish between 5 and 8lb were caught in the area above Wilton. Skues never really got on terms with these trout. In 1941 he rose and missed a fish that he believed to have been at least 4lb. His largest from the Nadder is mentioned in Chapter 13. Skues only made use of it on three weekends.

On one of these weekends in 1938 Dr Barton was a guest, and the account in his diary can give us some idea of what sort of a domestic life Skues might expect in the next few years. He had selected as his base camp the Nadder Vale Hotel, a fairly unappealing specimen of a small pre-war establishment. Barton at once discovered that it was worse than any of the assorted substandard hotels with which Skues had experimented in the past, and everyone else who stayed with him agreed. It is perhaps needless to add that Skues was, as usual, quite indifferent to – perhaps unaware of – the shortcomings of the place; in fact he thought it was ideal, its main advantage being that one could walk down to the river in two minutes. Barton recorded in his diary that its attempts to seem up-market were far too ostentatious for a small place like Wilton. There was a porter in a dirty uniform, a waiter in a long-tailed dress coat and a dinner menu in French. What Barton termed 'a beastly dinner' followed, inadequate as to quality and quantity. He went to bed hungry. The following day he caught a number of grayling and was confronted with another appalling dinner in the evening. He was served with an object described on the menu as a sole: Barton called it 'a flagrant dab'. The next day, burdened by his heavy camera, he accompanied Skues to the middle part of the fishery. It was on that day that the picture was taken of Skues on the bridge over the hatch in the village of Burcombe, which later appeared in Barton's *An Album of the Chalk Streams* (1946). It began to rain but, as usual, Skues paid no attention to the weather and fished on. Barton had been planning to stay until the morning of Monday, but decided at this point to leave, as he 'could not stick the hotel'.

Apart from these raids into Wiltshire, Skues was on the Itchen as often as he could manage, determined to make the most of his last season. Skues' fifty-sixth and last season at Abbots Barton in 1938 was again remarkable for the small number of fish caught and for their large average size. He later said to several friends that his withdrawal from the syndicate was triggered by a feeling of embarrassment because of their disapproval of nymph fishing. It may have been so, but he treated his promise to Simonds in 1936 as if it only applied to the remainder of that season, reverting to nymph practices in 1937 and stubbornly continuing them throughout 1938. Embarrassment seems, therefore, not to have troubled him much.

He killed a number of fish, eighteen of which were over 2lb. Nymphs accounted for all fish except two. He continued to the end to invite his friends as rod-sharing guests, even though his fellow members had done their best to discourage too much of this. At the end of August he took his last sorrowful leave of Abbots Barton. He wrote later to Edward Boies that, in justice, he had to admit that Simonds had never actually insisted that he resign from the syndicate. Boies wrote thus of his sympathy and anger over the treatment of his friend:

> If your friend Gaven [sic] Somebody or other has been making any more uncalled for comments and suggestions will you do me the favour to present my compliments to him and tell him that you understand from me in the United States that he is considered to be a S.O.B. If he doesn't understand the somewhat crude and pointed language I can elucidate.

Skues did not pass on this specimen of American straight talking. He wanted no recriminations to follow the trouble in the syndicate or the debate at the Flyfishers' Club. He wrote to Boies: 'I am glad you did not tackle Mottram. The controversy is getting embittered enough.'

In a letter written after his brother's death, Charles Skues wrote that the jealousy of the other members of the syndicate eventually made things very unpleasant for him, but he thought there might have been another good reason for leaving Abbots Barton:

> That length of the Itchen is not a very safe one for an old man. There are several places crossed only by a single plank with no handrail and with deep mud below. The banks too are slippery and treacherous in places and he had twice fallen into deep water and found great difficulty in clambering back onto the bank.

One reason for the dangerous nature of the banks was that repair work of banks was usually carried out with chalk from the nearest quarry. Once the surface of a repaired section had consolidated it could become as slippery as soap in wet weather. On one occasion Skues slid into water eight feet deep and floated down for some distance, anxiously pursued by Norman McCaskie, who was at last able to reach out a landing net and draw him to the bank. Skues wrote: 'I am not a strong swimmer, but I never felt in the least danger.'

Skues spent the autumn and winter of 1938–9 finishing work on the book that was intended finally to state his case for the nymph and destroy the arguments of his opponents, particularly those of Sir Joseph Ball. Once again there is a curious similarity with Halford. The life's work of each man was called into question at the latter end of his life, and each felt that he had to go into print to justify it. The writing of this book must have involved a great effort for a man of over eighty, and he was probably getting a little tired of polemics. Some years later a correspondent marvelled at the mental exertion needed for such a project. Skues replied: 'The energy to write Nymph Fishing was generated largely by resentment at having to give up my Itchen because of dry fly Purism.' Also, he had never sat down to write a planned and structured book of this sort. His former works in hard covers had all been edited collections of his earlier journalism.

His approach was, for the most part, cautious. He was determined to provide no opportunities for attacks by his enemies, and in Chapter III there were several important attempts at getting the central terms absolutely correct. These definitions were much more restricted than in his earlier writings. Artificial nymphs should closely resemble their natural counterparts. The only creature in nature entitled to be called a nymph was the mature larval stage of members of the ephemeroptera. Other forms of invertebrate underwater life were therefore excluded. He ignored the fact that he had named a number of other creatures as candidates for artificial nymphs in *Minor Tactics*, and that in an article in 1924 he had suggested that some aspiring fly-dresser from the younger generation might devise a pattern for the caddis pupa. As for the fanciful lures which were to be found in tackle shops and catalogues – the Bloody Butcher, the Professor and similar inventions – these were to be scorned and rejected by the honest angler. Such lures had no resemblance to anything in nature, and the use of them would only hand a weapon to the 'dry fly fanatics' who wished to 're-establish the rigid and exclusive despotism of the dry fly'. Even wet flies with full-sized instead of short hackles were to be rejected. This had the effect of consigning to oblivion all the winged and hackled wet flies mentioned in *Minor Tactics*, the use of which he had long abandoned. As for tactics, he made it clear that fishing a nymph at random, something which he had frequently done himself, was also not permissible: 'The only legitimate method of nymph fishing and the true sporting method is to cast to the individual selected subaqueously feeding fish.'

Thus, by narrowly prescribing the limits of the art in a way that might be acceptable to most anglers, he hoped to ward off any further aggression. But even these precautions were open to attack.

The rest of the book gave advice on equipment, technique and fly-dressing, with a section on points to use in argument with a purist. But the longest chapter is devoted to yet another attack on Halford. Skues would, no doubt, have defended himself by saying that purism was responsible for the trouble and Halford was responsible for purism, but some of his readers were probably becoming weary of these endless criticisms. Charles Skues later wrote that he felt that his brother's feelings towards Halford became obsessional over the years, and C.F. Walker wrote some years later that Skues had too much of 'a bee in his bonnet', and that 'he had never really forgiven Halford for what appears to have been their last conversation in the Flyfishers' Club'. Mottram also received some critical attention in the book.

The reviews were generally friendly. In *Salmon and Trout Magazine* the editor H.D. Turing welcomed 'the first text book on the subject', adding: 'Many men – editors at all events – will breathe something of a sigh of relief.' He had always been an advocate of the common-sense approach to the subject, and thought that there was little to choose between a Skues nymph and an artificial representing a spent spinner flush with the surface or even below it, yet still called a dry fly. E.V. Connett in *The Anglers' Club Bulletin* thought it 'a good book for Americans to read, as the prevalent idea of nymph fishing in this country is very different from that of the inventor of this important form of fishing'. *The Fishing Gazette* sounded a different and more cautious note. The reaction of the purists was not against nymph fishing 'as preached and practised by Mr Skues, but rather at those who used the term to describe a practice which was really "a disguised and less skilful form of wet-fly fishing"'. To practise the art properly was a demanding technique and rather beyond the abilities of many anglers. *The Sunday Times* carried a notice from Eric Taverner, author of *Trout Fishing from All Angles* (1929) and other books. Taverner had always been an enthusiast for the correct use of the nymph. His review was a paean of praise: Skues' work in reintroducing the wet fly to the chalk streams 'already occupies a place of honour in angling literature'. However, 'there has lately been a strong movement to discredit the use of the nymph on what are erroneously called "dry-fly waters"'. In Taverner's opinion the appearance of the book was therefore timely. It was 'a triumphant exposition of reason, fairness, and the fruits of thirty years' experience.... No thoughtful angler will be without it. No dry-fly purist ought to be.' Sir Joseph Ball cut out Taverner's review and kept it for his scrapbook, but the surviving evidence from his papers indicates that he did not respond.

It was common knowledge that *Nymph Fishing* was going to be, at least in part, a defence of Skues' work and an answer to the case presented at the debate the year before. Certain enemies had been waiting for the appearance of the book in the shops, and the heavy step of Sir Joseph Ball was soon heard. He had got hold of a pre-publication copy of *Nymph Fishing*, and his archive contains a typescript of a damaging review that he had written before the end of February 1939. He took particular note of the fact that, for obvious reasons of caution, Skues had narrowed his definitions, so that dragging nymphs, fishing in 'likely places' and the use of lures and fancy flies should all be avoided. He then pounced on these passages: 'He has now apparently become the purist of the nymph fishermen, but he was not always so rigid in his "purism".' He quoted passages from *Minor Tactics* in which Skues had described catching trout 'with the wet fly fished into likely places without seeing a single rise', and referred, not without scorn, to Skues' use years earlier of wet flies with wings, which were obviously not close copies of ephemeropteran nymphs. He also fastened upon another passage, which Skues probably wished he had never written, describing the use of shrimps, caddis and even maggots, a practice that Skues had soon abandoned, in his own words 'conscience-stricken'. Ball must have regretted not consulting *Minor Tactics* a year earlier in preparing for the debate. If he had done so, the assault on that memorable evening would have been even more damaging. It was a lucky escape for Skues.

Returning to the main argument, Ball held to his point that 'persistent nymph fishing tends to render the trout of our chalk streams inordinately shy and uncatchable, and eventually therefore, to ruin the water on which it is practised'. He ended on a more kindly note, writing that Skues was always an interesting writer, and that his book should be read by all chalk-stream anglers.

It may be that Ball subsequently retreated to a more even-handed view. In an introduction to a later edition of Hills' *A Summer on the Test* in 1946 he asserted his right to stick to the dry fly on his own fishery and conceded that if a neighbour wished to use the nymph elsewhere 'who am I to say him "Nay"?' His obituary in the *Flyfishers' Journal* in 1961 lamented that his part in the 1938 debate had earned him the reputation of being an extreme purist: the writer added 'which he certainly was not' (perhaps an odd judgement). Two years later Desmond Berry wrote the obituary for Neville Bostock in the *Journal*, admitting that to the end 'he abhorred the nymph' and that 'if he was a purist at least he stuck to his principles and abhorred the spinner and the nymph'.

A few months later another familiar figure entered the fray. Skues had been expecting this new attack. In May 1939 he wrote to Edward Boies: 'Martin E. Mosely, the eminent entomologist, is very averse to my views on Nymph Fishing, and I understand that he is proposing to pulverize them (and me) in the Salmon and Trout Magazine.' Mosely's attack appeared in the June issue of the magazine. It consisted largely of a long discussion of the behaviour of the natural nymph, including yet another return to the hardy annual of the inertia or activity of the ascending nymph. Perhaps the most striking part was the final paragraph:

If 'Seaforth and Soforth' should complain that I have been unduly severe in my criticism of his methods and patterns, has he been more merciful in the continuous attacks that he has been making for nearly twenty years on the writings and reputation of Halford who, unhappily, is no longer with us to answer them for himself?

Skues answered these points in his usual meticulous way, and pointed out that identifying someone's mistakes was not improper simply because they were dead. How else would progress ever be possible? But it was the end of a friendship. For years Skues, John Evans and Mosely had kept up an amicable correspondence on matters of mutual interest. There were to be no more letters from Mosely beginning with 'My Dear Skues'. George Monkhouse, whose relations with Skues are considered in the next chapter, went to the Natural History Museum to meet Mosely in 1943, and got into an argument with him about the colour of insects. He gave Skues a report about the interview. The atmosphere deteriorated when Monkhouse brought up the subject of nymphs. Mosely replied that 'he was not in the least interested in nymphs and that anybody who fished the nymph was in his opinion a bad thing'. Skues replied: 'Mosely is a very decent chap, but like Halford he has become an "authority" and must not be questioned.'

No more assailants stepped forward in 1939 to criticize *Nymph Fishing for Chalk Stream Trout*. By the end of the trout season of 1939 everyone had other problems to consider.

13

The End of the Season

IN 1939 SKUES settled as philosophically as he could to fishing a
stream which was by no means the equal of the Itchen. If he had any
rosy expectations about the Nadder at Wilton, the brief experience
of the previous year would have dispelled them. And so began the
increasingly sad course of Skues' last years, of exile from his Eden at
Abbots Barton, of weekends in Wiltshire, followed in 1940 by a retreat
from wartime London to a more permanent settlement at the Wilton
hotel and of slow decline and encroaching infirmity. In 1939 solicitors
practising in Britain received a circular from the Law Society inviting
them to give particulars of themselves to show how they could help the
war effort. Skues replied that he was eighty-one years of age, thinking of
retiring soon, had two damaged wrists, one damaged knee, one badly
damaged shoulder and fallen arches in both feet. He seems not to have
heard from the Law Society again. With his usual stoical courage he
coped well with his life, generally without descending to futile complaints
about his lot. But in the last three or four years of his life he admitted to
close friends that he was finding loneliness difficult to endure.

The fishing of the 1939 season began well enough. On the Burcombe
fishery his custom in the morning was to make his way down the slope
behind the hotel to the lower end of the fishery, where an iron lattice-
work bridge crossed the river. Here he would examine the spiders' webs
for data about the current fly life. Ahead of him were two miles of water,
including six hatch pools. It was in one of these interesting pools that
Skues caught his largest Nadder trout (3lb 3oz), an adventure he related
to Edward Boies, to Tup Wauton and to other correspondents. He had
observed the fish during several weekends in July 1939. This patriarch of
the pool had with him several smaller attendants. One by one Skues
captured these, including a two-pounder. The big one refused Sedge Flies,
an Alder and several nymphs. Eventually it fell to a shrimp pattern with

a body of mixed green and yellow seal's fur ribbed with gold, a small olive hackle point at the tail and a largish hackle drawn under the belly to suggest the legs of the natural.

In spite of these and some other successes the fishing was slow. Summer fishing on the Itchen could be interesting, whereas on the Nadder it fell away noticeably after mid-June, at least during the day. Evening fishing could be profitable, but Skues' eyesight had deteriorated too far for fishing, as he phrased it, in 'owl light'. There were a small number of larger trout, a good many undersized and a great lack of medium fish of the sort that should provide the entertainment of the average fishing day. At times he was driven to concentrate on the grayling, of which there were great numbers: during two weekends in 1939 he captured eighty. In 1942 he wrote to a friend: 'I do not like grayling in a trout water, though I would rather fish for grayling than not fish.' By the end of the season of 1939 he had written to Wauton: 'The Nadder has been a great disappointment to me.'

On 10 May 1940 the so-called 'phoney war' came to an abrupt end with the massive German attack westward. Events after this moved with alarming speed. After Dunkirk and the fall of France, Skues believed that a German invasion of Britain would soon follow: many of his countrymen had similar thoughts. He acted quickly to withdraw from his house in Croydon. In the spring of that year the Skues household included his sister Mary, who had kept house for him for many years, and his brother Frederick, who had come to live with him. There were also his two surviving sisters, Minnie and Elsie, living nearby. Frederick had returned from South Africa a sick man, and the burden of caring for him had fallen entirely upon Mary, who was worn out and in need of rest and recovery. He died on 27 May, which simplified the problem for Skues. He dispatched his three sisters to a safer place away from London and negotiated an arrangement to live at the Nadder Vale Hotel, at least for the time being. He then began to empty his house of a large part of his possessions. The main part of his angling library was moved to a storeroom in Wilton, the future access to which turned out to be far from easy. A few items of furniture went to his room at the hotel, and the remainder was left for the time being in his Croydon house, the rent of which had been paid up to Christmas 1940.

A great deal of sorting and destruction of his papers now took place. Much material that nowadays would be thought priceless disappeared for ever at this time, including many thousands of letters. Skues' habit of writing to any contributor with interesting ideas in *The Field* and *The Fishing Gazette* had begun in the late 1880s, and by 1940 he had amassed an enormous archive of letters from most of the well-known anglers in that period and from many other enthusiasts. Over fifty names of his correspondents can be identified today: there must have been many more. The loss of letters, either totally or in part, from H.S. Hall, George Holland, R.B. Marston, Irwin Cox, Martin Mosely, Colonel Harding, H.T. Sheringham and a host of others is particularly sad, for they would have cast much light on an important period of development in British angling history. Skues also organized the shredding of the manuscripts of his four books. He regarded them as being of no value once publication had taken place. He would have been mystified at the high prices they would nowadays realize in the auction room.

The process of sorting and destruction, which had to be carried on at great speed, would have been stressful and exhausting at Skues' time of life. There must have been a certain amount of chaos and confusion, which would have irked the soul of such a tidy-minded man, and later he was not able to be quite sure what had or had not disappeared. In particular the correspondence of Colonel Harding, whose work he had so much admired, was later found to have vanished. In 1947 he wrote to George Monkhouse: 'I imagine it was destroyed when my house at Croydon was broken up in 1940.'

On 14 June, having given notice to quit at Christmas his dwelling house of nearly fifty years, Skues completed the arrangements for retiring from the practice in Essex Street, and left for Wilton. His correspondents would no longer receive typed letters on the handsome notepaper, still carrying the heading of Powell, Skues and Graham Smith, seventeen years after the retirement of Powell. Instead they would now have to cope with Skues' handwriting, once elegant and pleasing, but which was now becoming impenetrable. His hands had begun to acquire a tremor, and his way of dealing with this was to write in a script which became increasingly small. The recipients of these letters must have needed a magnifying glass at hand, and the skills of a cryptographer. Some of them, such as George Monkhouse, began to type out a fair copy for their own use, especially of some passages they felt to be particularly significant.

In early July Skues wrote to Edward Boies from the Nadder Vale Hotel:

I have settled in here for the present to see what Adolf makes of his promised invasion of this country. If all goes well I go back in early autumn for a few days either to sell or to store my furniture and later to decide what to do about a new home pending my translation to the Hotel Necropolis at which we all eventually put up.

He began almost at once to feel isolated and cut off from the mainstream of life and the familiar company at the Flyfishers' Club. Keeping in touch by letter now became even more important. In the same letter to Boies can be heard the voice of a lonely exile, as he asks him to greet friends at the Anglers' Club of New York, mentioning La Branche, Eugene Connett, Franklin B. Lord, Allan Bradley, H.A. Ingraham and Richard Carley Hunt, also Otto von Kienbusch, 'though I have never actually met him' .

It had been Skues' plan to lodge at the hotel and to search the country around for a cottage with accessible fishing nearby. Eventually he abandoned the fruitless search and was forced to sit out the war in Wilton, condemned to live in a place described by his sympathetic friend Douglas Goodbody as 'his lonely unsuitable hotel'. The unappetising cuisine so bitterly commented upon by Dr Barton in 1938 (and later by other guests) became much worse as a result of wartime conditions. In fact the general standard of comfort in the place was poor. There was no heating in Skues' bed-sitting room, so that tying flies in winter was difficult and his handwriting became even more indecipherable. If he wanted warmth he had to go downstairs to the lounge. Goodbody did allow that 'they looked after him as well, with his simple tastes, as he would have wished'. The landlady, Mrs Prynne, was said to have been fond of him and 'thought that he was no trouble'. Skues, however, felt that he had to be wary of her. If friends wished to visit for a weekend he would advise them to give plenty of notice, adding: 'I have a fidgety landlady.' Her husband seems to have been a less attractive character. When the keeper carried Skues' large hatch-hole trout back to the hotel Prynne, without consultation, took it into Salisbury and sold it for 5s 6d. When his wife died in 1948 he decided to close the hotel in order to convert the place into flats, and compelled Skues, then aged ninety, to leave at short notice. Unsurprisingly, Dr Barton and some other guests took a violent dislike to Prynne.

In the summer of 1940 air activity in the skies over England became alarming and spectacular. The official instruction was to take cover when the sirens sounded, but this was often ignored, at least outside towns and cities. On one occasion the guests and the Prynne family, including the children, came out into the garden to watch a Spitfire bringing down an enemy aeroplane, which crashed near the Nadder at Dinton. Skues wrote to Edward Boies: 'Aeroplanes make their weird droning music over the Nadder valley (a very pretty one) at all hours of the day and night, and Fritz has dropped some of his H.E. bombs not so far away.'

In the autumn the Germans turned their attention to London. Skues' plan to return to Croydon to deal with the remainder of his furniture became more difficult to carry out when a bomb exploded near his house. He wrote to a correspondent on 10 October: 'I heard yesterday that my front door had been blown in, all my windows shattered and most of my ceiling down.' None of his fishing treasures were affected, but a large part of his fly-dressing materials were lost in the hasty removal operation to Wilton and were never recovered.

Four days after the near miss of Skues' house in Croydon the Flyfishers' Club was badly damaged. The Club had come to 36 Piccadilly in 1907, after several decades of restless wandering. By 1940 the length of the tenure was a record in the Club's history; a record which still stands today. An account of that alarming night appeared in the next number of the *Journal*. There were only two members present at the time. One of them was Charles Giveen, the President, who was to play a decisive role in saving the premises from destruction. The two men had just settled to a quiet dinner together when a bomb fell on the rectory of St James's Church on the other side of Piccadilly. The windows came in on them and, in the wry deadpan words of the account in the *Journal*, 'the President's wine glass was upset'. The domestic staff recovered quickly and began to serve the next course, but a quarter of an hour later a shower of incendiaries fell on the area. Giveen and George the steward went to the top floor and together carried a stray incendiary in a sand bucket to the street, otherwise the building would have been gutted, and the historic treasures of the Club lost. But the danger was not over. The adjacent shop on the corner of Swallow Street was now on fire, and a brisk wind was driving the flames across the road to threaten the Club. The window frames and curtains began to take fire and Giveen quickly organized a hosepipe which was fixed to a bathroom tap. With some timely help from two passing soldiers this small team of people spent several exhausting hours running from one fire to another on different floors.

It ought to be placed on record that some members lunched at the Club the day after the raid. Though much shattered, with a tarpaulin over the remains of the roof and with a wooden post holding up the ceiling of the dining room, it limped on for several months, with members, in a show of defiance, calling in for lunch and dinner. From the window could be seen on the other side of Piccadilly the dreary sight of St James's Church, familiar to members as the burial place of Charles Cotton, with the spire and most of the roof destroyed. The final blow fell in April 1941, when a land mine exploded on the traffic island nearby in the middle of Piccadilly. The Club building was declared unsafe; four days of access were allowed for removing everything, and the offer of shelter by the Garrick Club was gratefully accepted.

Skues wrote to Edward Boies in America of his sadness that they would never see the inside of 36 Piccadilly again. For Skues it had been a haven and a place close to his heart. He had played a major part in getting the premises in 1907 and dealing with the legal side of the tenancy, and his brother Charles and C.F. Cook had worked hard to build up the Club to a membership of 600 by the 1930s. There must have been a host of memories of Thursday night dinners and of the rummage sales of rods and tackle presided over by Charles, a natural showman who enjoyed his role as auctioneer. Boies had always been grateful for the good offices of Skues in arranging honorary membership for him.

For Skues, other problems were pressing upon his life. In 1940 a programme of destructive dredging began on the Nadder. In November 1940 he paid a visit to Dr Barton's close colleague Sir Frederic Still at his house at Lower Bemerton and was shocked to see that the bed of the Nadder nearby was being torn up by machines. Skues reported to Douglas Goodbody that this was only the beginning. The plan was to move up the valley, towards Wilton and beyond, in order to convert the river into a tank trap in readiness for resisting the German armoured columns. Within a short time the precious gravel bed of the river was scooped out and piled in unsightly heaps along the banks, and many sections were straightened and canalized. The effect on the ecology of the river was ruinous. The cranes and bulldozers moved up into Wilton Park, and then into the Burcombe fishery above. Dredging also began on the Wylye nearby. Although the threat of invasion faded, the vandalizing of the rivers continued, now driven by the needs of wartime agriculture. Land drainage of water meadows formerly intended for rearing cattle and sheep would, it was hoped, make arable farming more profitable. It was naturally impossible for fishing interests to complain about a policy designed to help deal with the problem of feeding the nation in wartime, but for Skues it was a sinister portent of the events of the next two years and a disaster for his plans of a tranquil retirement of fishing.

In 1941 he joined the Bemerton Club below the parkland of Wilton House, which had been run by his friend Dr Arthur Holmes until his death in 1935. His idea was to provide himself with a reserve of fishing opportunities if the action slackened upstream at Burcombe. In former years it had acquired a good reputation, and in the years after the war it recovered. The Nadder and the Wylye met there, and below the junction the combined stream used to produce a better pattern of fly life than the Nadder above. It was bad luck for Skues that his experience of these two fisheries above and below Wilton coincided with a low point in the history of this valley. By the summer of 1941 both of the two fisheries available to him were in sad decline, and his correspondence with friends continued for several years to contain fulminations about 'that damned Catchment Board'.

Troubles now began to multiply in Skues' life with the relentless purpose of a Greek tragedy. Towards the end of 1941 he learned from a chance remark of Penny, the keeper for the Burcombe reach, that Reyersbach, the absentee landlord, was surrendering his lease of the fishery from Lord Pembroke. Early in 1942 a new landlord arrived on the scene with a completed syndicate, in the list of which there was no room for the name of Skues. No longer would it be possible for him to leave the hotel and walk down to the river to fish. His fall-back reach at Bemerton was a mile and a half away: a visit involved a bus journey and a walk to the upstream boundary of the fishery at Fourteen Hatches. A further drawback was that membership gave him only thirty days fishing a year out of a possible 153, a meagre total in his view. Also, the season in the Bemerton Club ran from the beginning of May.

Although he had been (as usual) thinking since 1939 that each season would be his last, he was surprised to find a new energy as April arrived. His mind turned to other possibilities that he had considered before, such as the River Ebble, another of the interesting tributaries of the Avon. But the Ebble, though derived from pure chalk, is a miniature brook and the trout, though numerous, are not of great size. In such a small stream a great deal of creeping and crawling was called for and, as Skues wrote, 'I am not a good bush fighter'. He decided that he felt reasonably settled where he was. At his age the idea of searching for fresh accommodation was too daunting. In January 1942 he wrote to Boies:

I do not want to give up this neighbourhood. The country is beautiful, the air suits me, the people are kindly and I have a small circle of pleasant friends and between visiting, reading, correspondence and fishing I have not had a moment of boredom since my retirement.

His thoughts turned also to the large fish that he had never succeeded in catching at Burcombe:

I have kept fit enough to be rather aggrieved that I am precluded from another season on the water.... One particular reason for wanting to renew my rod on this water is that I know of one particular big trout, certainly 5 lbs, maybe 6lbs, with a small string of satellites down to 2½ lbs.

So 1942 became a turning point for Skues. Now restricted to one badly damaged fishery – in his own words 'a grisly canal' – he fished with diminishing returns and more difficulties. Bemerton was not even safe for a man of eighty-four years, and the sloping banks of piled-up gravel spoil left by the dredgers were good places for accidents. On one visit he fell down three times. By the end of September his correspondence carried lamentations about the most disappointing season for years. 1943 was even worse. In July he wrote to Edward Boies that he was finding a full day out more and more tiring, especially clambering over the steeply inclined gravel spoil.

Meanwhile, wartime conditions left their mark on the angling world. It was realized that, for many people, days on a river provided a beneficial escape from stress, and the Flyfishers' Club urged members to provide fishing opportunities to people on leave from the armed forces or otherwise involved in war work. Skues was anxious to help and was able to entertain a few fishermen, but he may have been a little embarrassed at only having a rather inferior angling experience to offer. There was also discussion in the angling press about the possibilities of freshwater fish as food, as had happened in the previous war. Poaching increased greatly and efforts to stop army and air force personnel from bombing likely places with grenades were not pursued with much energy. By the end of the war men from a nearby aerodrome had succeeded in removing nearly all the fish from the Anton, a major tributary of the Test.

In the shops there was a fishing tackle famine and gut casts were being sold at bizarre prices. Some bold spirits were beginning to get their hands on DuPont nylon from America. Skues was uncertain about it, having had difficulty with the knotting: 'It is so infernally slippery.' German bombs wrecked Hardy's shop in Pall Mall. Messeena's premises in Clapton were also destroyed, but the firm quickly moved away from London and established itself at Leamington. Fly-dressers everywhere learned with relief that most of their plumage had survived.

Apart from fishing and tying flies for himself and friends, an important element of Skues' comfort and well-being in retirement was his almost daily correspondence with friends and acquaintances. He would continue to pursue the Nadder grayling until the end of November, but deteriorating weather would force him to a life spent mainly indoors. At this time, connecting with his correspondents would become especially valuable to him. C.F. Walker discovered a letter he wrote when he was eighty-nine containing the words: 'I sat down this morning with a list of twenty one letters, including yours, to answer. I have done six up to lunch and this is the seventh.'

The correspondents of his last years can be divided into several categories. The old friends such as 'Tup' Wauton, Edward Boies, Lamorna Birch, Edwin Barton and Norman McCaskie continued to write to him to exchange views and to pass the time of day, or just out of old habit and affection. New acquaintances appeared, such as C.E. Sykes and Douglas Goodbody, in which the element of friendship predominated, and others from whose correspondence subjects of real interest emerged, such as Frank Sawyer and James Leisenring. The letters have survived of three new and particularly prolific correspondents: Tom Eastham, George Monkhouse and Paul Barbotin. These men were anxious to get to know Skues as a source of knowledge and experience from whom they could learn. Some men might have resented the torrents of enquiry of this sort, involving much time-consuming attention from him, but Skues welcomed anything that could fill the long hours. Besides, he had always been ready to be helpful, and rather liked the idea of being appealed to.

Eastham was a successful barrister, a bencher of Lincoln's Inn, Recorder of Oldham from 1924, and from 1936 to 1944 Senior Official Referee of the Supreme Court. As an angler, however, he confessed to being still a learner and eager for any help. He began to write to Skues in 1942, and may have been surprised at his readiness to open a correspondence. When, eventually, he came to Wilton to pay a visit, Skues, who had met him only once, did not at first recognize him. But in the latter part of his life Skues found relationships carried on by letter rather easier than by direct contact. His hearing loss made conversation difficult, and by the time the war was over his vision was seriously impaired. But those who could decipher his handwriting could perceive an undiminished intellect at work. He was happy to play Piscator to an angler keen to learn, but he issued his usual brusque warning about being called an authority. He may have been startled by a robust reply from Eastham: 'You must not object to being looked up to as an authority. Your great experience and writings put you in that category.' For once Skues avoided an argument upon this point, but explained that much of his advice would be deemed inappropriate or even condemned by some anglers. His own practice had, for many years, followed a personal and eccentric course and was not likely to be transferable: 'I am the last person who should lay down the law on the equipment of a fly-fisher.' As a result, much of his advice was allusive and general rather than particular.

There is also much interesting detail in this correspondence about Skues' own fly-dressing habits. He never tied dun patterns with single wings, although this was the method followed by the great Hassam. Single wings, he believed, were too fragile and quickly became shredded in use: the double wing would keep its shape for much longer. How much of these details Eastham could have absorbed is not clear. He was after all still learning, whereas the ideas and methods of Skues had always been addressed to more advanced scholars. To underline the importance of the nymph, Skues advised Eastham to look at the illustration in *Nymph Fishing* of the contents of a trout's stomach, with its overwhelming proportion of subaqueous food forms. This would have struck a chord, for Eastham had originally intended to follow a career in medicine and had practised as a qualified doctor before crossing over to the law. He appreciated the importance of post-mortem examinations, observing: 'The post-mortem often reveals the doctors' mistakes and it explodes many theories.'

George Monkhouse was a correspondent of a very different stamp. He comes across in his letters as a man of enormous drive, accustomed to achieving goals by persistence, sometimes at the expense of politeness and tact. He was a director of the Kodak camera company, and an enthusiast for motor racing, about which he had written and illustrated two books. Some years later he became President of the Mercedes Benz Club. There could hardly have been a greater contrast between this energetic extrovert and a man twice his age whom he was approaching for help in developing his skills and knowledge in fly-fishing. It seems doubtful if Monkhouse had many original ideas but he was adept at picking them up from other anglers and synthesizing them. It is quite likely that, earlier in his life, Skues would have quietly detached himself from such a curious relationship, but persistence on one side and politeness on the other caused it to become established and to last for years.

Monkhouse had first written to Skues in November 1939, in the cautious style of an admirer: 'I hope you will forgive my audacity in writing to you.' He then praised Skues' writings ('your literary efforts' – perhaps an unfortunate description). He added: 'I would very much like the honour of meeting you.' His main purpose was to discuss a project to write a fishing book in collaboration with a friend, the emphasis to be on using good photographic illustrations. As an expert on photography he felt able to say that the pictures in most fishing books were of little value. He also treated Skues to a short homily of advice:

> Being a wizard at the game yourself it is probably difficult for you to realize that a large proportion of your soliloquies on the subject fall on waste ground to the tyro, and it is only when one has graduated from the duffer stage that one begins to really appreciate the terrific amount of information contained on almost every page of your books.

Skues may have found this familiar and boisterous letter rather jarring. He responded with his usual courtesy but without much warmth or encouragement. He explained that the suggested meeting would not be practicable: he now lived far from London and anyway had no useful ideas about photography. He also wrote reprovingly that he was 'by no means a wizard at the sport': one needed to have started at the age of fourteen rather than twenty-one, as he had. And yet this correspondence persisted for ten years and 433 letters, driven on by the persistence of Monkhouse, and by Skues' need for contact with keen players bursting with subjects to discuss. After some time Skues confided to Dr Barton and Paul Barbotin that there was something about Monkhouse that he did not quite care for. He managed to fend off several more attempts at a visit and it was two years before this came about. He wrote to Douglas Goodbody in September 1941: 'A man named Monkhouse who has been writing to me long fishing letters for the past year or so is volunteering a visit here, to try the Nadder and to talk fly fishing. I don't know him and am doubtful whether I shall like him.'

In spite of an obvious wish to keep him at arm's length, Skues made no attempt to extricate himself from this situation and their correspondence threw up many interesting topics. The two men remained locked in a specialized dialogue in which the outside world and the horrors of war were ignored. For Skues it was another element in his search for an antidote to loneliness. The motives of Monkhouse were more complex. He had progressed far enough in his own career as an angler to be aware of the large number of intriguing problems waiting to be solved, or at least examined, and he bombarded Skues with calls for help and detailed advice. Fly patterns fascinated him. He had not been able to buy any nymphs tied to the Skues recipes – where should he go? Skues at once warned him off Farlows, with whom he had recently had a bruising argument. He advised him to apply to T.J. McHale of Ballymacool in Co. Donegal, a professional who had the best understanding of his ideas about patterns. Roger Woolley and Tommy Hanna he regarded as the next best in the field.

In 1940 Monkhouse made his first attempts at fly-tying, and the enquiries increased. Eventually, a year later, he felt he needed more direct assistance. Would Skues look at his efforts and advise? Skues wrote a helpful but cautious reply:

By all means send me specimens of your fly tying. I may be able to tell you what, if anything, is wrong with them, but it will be less easy to make clear what ought to have been done to get the desired effect. My observation of all books on fly tying is that the writers omit to tell a number of minute details which in practice they would do as a matter of course, but the learner, not having the knowledge either omits or goes wrong about, and though I do my best to avoid that failing I cannot guarantee that I shall always do so.

The correspondence immediately dives into a mutual search for excellence. By his persistence Monkhouse had succeeded in establishing a consultancy with the best person available. He had been eagerly buying up plumage wherever he could find it, including two necks from Farlows, with all the small feathers still intact, for 5s each, a fairly scorching price for 1941. In early October he began a letter with the words 'I am afraid that I am now going to start being rather a nuisance, but I hope you won't think so.' Enclosed were twenty-four numbered hackles. How should each be named and for what flies would each be used? 'I am particularly anxious to find out exactly what you term Honey Dun, Rusty Dun, and Brassy Dun as mentioned in the various dressings given in your books.' Monkhouse had asked the same question of the well-known firm of Messeena, who were too cautious to commit themselves. They immediately recommended the obvious leader in the field: 'Mr Skues knows the exact shades ... [he] is a genius.' Skues may have sighed a little at coping with this new budget of work – 'You have given me rather an undertaking' – but as usual the interest of the task overtook him and he patiently responded with a detailed appraisal (see Appendix 9), adding 'Messeena is absurd in writing of me as a genius. I try to apply a modicum of common sense.'

At the end of November Monkhouse sent 'a few flies' (in fact twenty-three) of his own tying, asking Skues 'to put me on the right road'. He received a three-page letter of comments on his patterns, not many of which Skues felt able to praise, although he did add a consoling judgement at the end, to the effect that Monkhouse was on the right lines as to handiwork and that the criticism referred mainly to choice of materials. Monkhouse tried again in February 1942 and received a higher marking ('creditable progress'), although each individual fly attracted some fine-tuning remarks. These two exercises provide an excellent example of Skues' deep knowledge and a concern for detail carried as far as could be.

In April 1942 Monkhouse unveiled another scheme. He planned to collect together examples of all Skues' dressings as set forth in his writings. By the middle of the month he was able to send a list for comments. Skues, who had hitherto been patient and forbearing, responded a little despairingly to this relentless pressure for help: 'You have given me a whale of a job. I do not feel that I can tackle it competently without access to my books and the back numbers of the F.F.C. Journal. Even with them it would take hours to do it competently.'

By July Monkhouse was asking Skues for samples of his own tyings, but Skues was becoming evasive and merely sent some of George Holland's patterns that must have been tied many years earlier. Monkhouse, not to be put off, supplied a list of eleven flies, copies of which (tied by Skues) would be very welcome. Many men might have brought down the guillotine upon the connection with such an exacting and tactless correspondent. When Monkhouse enlarged his project to make up a bound book of Skues' tyings and invited him to write something appropriate to add to it and to add his signature Skues very firmly declined.

Their relationship faltered again on several occasions in a particularly sensitive area. Monkhouse was not content merely to be an attentive pupil. As a scientist and a director of a camera company he knew that on one subject at least he was better informed than Skues. Having been advised by him in 1940 to read Colonel Harding's book *The Flyfisher and the Trout's Point of View* he wrote:

> I certainly think there are some arguable points regarding his statements on the colour vision of trout and also on general optical principles ... I am referring to the collective views of various experts in our Research Laboratory regarding such matters as colour, because I do think that he has either slipped up in one or two places or expressed himself very badly.

Not knowing that Harding had died in August 1935, Monkhouse wrote that he intended discussing these points with him. Skues replied: 'I wish you could discuss the matter with him direct, but to my great and lasting regret, it would be necessary that you should address your criticism to c/o St. Peter.'

Monkhouse returned to the subject several times in the next four years, pointing out that 'all experiments regarding the trout's window have been conducted with the observer's eye in air and not in water'. He added further criticisms of Harding and Dr Francis Ward, whose ingenious observation tank had been seen by Skues thirty years earlier. This long-running attack must have caused Skues some personal distress, but he remained stubbornly loyal to his late friend. In 1946 he wrote to Eastham that he still thought that Harding had produced the most important book on the subject: to the end of his life he was still referring to 'Colonel Harding's great book'.

Monkhouse was a tireless collector of angling books, the number of which had, by May 1943, risen to 200. He was anxious to add to his library Skues' de luxe copies of Halford, *Dry-Fly Entomology* (1897) and Edmonds and Lee, *Brook and River Trouting* (1916). He received no encouragement: Skues had discovered from the report of a sale at Sotheby's in 1943 that a copy of the latter book had recently been sold for £32. Not long afterwards a collector advertised in *The Times* offering the same sum for a copy. This aroused the interest of Skues, who was beginning to think of selling his books, and he began to regret promising the Flyfishers' Club the first choice of having as a gift any of his angling books of which they did not already possess a copy. His aim was to disperse his personal property at the most advantageous figure possible, partly to avoid leaving behind too many problems for his personal representatives to handle, and also to pass on a reasonable amount of money to his brother Charles and his family.

Monkhouse's interest in *Brook and River Trouting* was unsurprising. For collectors it is one of the most sought-after rarities. Only fifty copies of the de luxe edition were printed, with thirty-eight artificial North Country fly patterns in sunken mounts and the materials to make them, after the fashion of Aldam's famous book. Skues later revealed to Monkhouse ('it must be in *strict* confidence while either of them lives') the curious explanation of how he had acquired such an expensive book. Lee had approached Skues when the volume was in preparation to ask advice about the standard of the tying of the flies. The flies turned out to be exquisitely tied, but he had been startled by the manuscript:

> I found their English so appallingly illiterate that, because their patterns were so good and their practical advice so sound, I took a heap of trouble to make them rewrite the text, often several times over until I could pass it. I would not let them use my wording. It had to be their own, but passable.

By the summer of 1943, the weight of the years was bearing down on Skues. He had not been to London since 1940, and after 1942 had given up the annual pilgrimage to watch the Winchester v. Eton cricket match. The visit of the previous year had been a melancholy failure: no Old Wykehamists of his vintage were there. No doubt he had outlived most of them. Fishing was becoming increasingly tiring. In the previous year he had told Monkhouse that he did not feel equal to his invitation to fish at Twyford: 'I used to weigh 14 stone in my birthday suit. I now weigh 10 stone 3lbs in my summer rig.' Already, in 1943, he was telling his friends that he was thinking of giving up fishing. In May 1944 he had some success, catching nine trout on a No. 1 Whitchurch. Seven were returned, no doubt undersized. But he was forced to give up at midday, too tired to continue. He wrote to Eastham: 'It looks like my last season.' When he moved into the Nadder Vale Hotel in 1940 he had been able to walk into

Salisbury and back, a round trip of eight miles: this would not now be a possible feat.

The war dragged on. Victory seemed to be coming nearer, but the enemy was still capable of springing some unpleasant surprises. Skues reported to Boies that Dr Barton's house in Putney had been repeatedly shaken by the nearby explosions of the German V1s (Skues called them 'Hitler's bomb planes' or 'robot bombs'). Charles Skues was so alarmed that he moved his family away from Beckenham to a safe haven in Dorset, and the two unmarried Skues sisters, who had returned to London after the invasion scare of 1940, decamped to the safer refuge of Worcester.

None of these dangers affected Skues in his Wiltshire retreat, but 1944 was the last year in which his fishing was attended by any success. Monkhouse reported to Barton, whose acquaintance he had made, that Skues was definitely ageing, and that it was an effort for him to write. Barton, in reply, thought that it would be hard for Skues to give up fishing: 'He will have nothing to do but sit and doze in that beastly hotel … his writing is getting all but illegible.' He added that he did not expect to see Skues again. Monkhouse made a number of prints of the portrait photographs made by Barton and rejected by Skues in 1927. They planned to hold them in readiness for distribution among his friends after his death, which they thought could not be far off. In fact they were both wrong: Skues was to live for another five years.

Early in 1945 he was in a confident mood. In March he began his usual pre-season training and was soon able to manage a two-mile walk in the morning. Later in the month an episode of lumbago slowed him down, but he recovered and tried to make the best of the season. But because of the poor state of the river and of his own health the last season of his angling life came to nothing. Seventeen visits to Bemerton produced no sizeable trout at all and only a few small grayling. Eastham asked if he had given up fly-dressing. Skues replied sadly:

Fly dressing has practically given me up as my hands have become so shaky this year as to render good winging almost impossible.... I fear too that I must give up fishing, as recently I have been troubled with fits of giddiness, and if one should overtake me on one of those treacherous banks engineered by the Catchment Board or when wading and I should fall in the water I should not get up again.

In the autumn he was forced to accept defeat. He resigned from the Bemerton Club and began to adjust himself to a new pattern of life. This must have been a hard task. For sixty years his passions in life had been making flies and using flies. Now he could do neither. In December he wrote to Tom Eastham: 'I must confine my sporting activities to reading and writing', and courageously set about making the most of his remaining time. In 1928, in a piece called 'Go Softly' in the *Journal*, he had quoted a saying of George Herbert, the seventeenth-century poet and parish priest of St Andrews at Lower Bemerton: 'He begins to die who quits his desires.' This could not be applied to Skues in the last years of his life. His days were full and his correspondence increased. So also did his writing. A few years earlier he had said that he did not feel that he had anything new or worthwhile to impart to fellow anglers, but his articles and letters continued to appear in the journals until the summer of 1948. He wrote to his brother Charles that giving up fishing had not been as distressing as he had expected: 'I have not found it too bad. There are compensations.' But he must have regretted the loss of the company of so many old friends. In October 1945 he wrote mournfully to Douglas Goodbody: 'I wish I were dining at the F.F.C. tonight.'

During the winter of 1945/6 Skues began to organize the sale of his angling library. He had been giving away books to friends as long ago as 1942, and had spent some time compiling a list of what remained (see Appendix 10). He renewed his offer as a gift to the Flyfishers' Club of all back numbers of the *Journal* and copies of anything on the list that they did not already have. Encouraged by this, the Club accepted over a hundred books, including some scarce items. The list took a long time to prepare and must have been a wearisome business. The Wilton book store had been sold some time earlier and his books had been moved further away. Skues now had to take a bus into Salisbury and to sit in a cheerless, unheated place to compare current prices from catalogues. The highest prices asked were £6 for the 1913 de luxe edition of Ronalds, £5 for Aldam's *Quaint Treatise* and the same price for seventy-one numbers of *The Salmon and Trout Magazine*. In a separate list, which seems not to have survived, were the surviving bundles of letters.

Upon learning of the book list, Monkhouse at once again became deeply interested. In May 1946 he wrote eagerly asking for sight of it. And so began an extraordinary dialogue about prices, comic enough in retrospect, but irritating for Skues and frustrating for Monkhouse. The

man of business, accustomed to getting his own way in a deal, was up
against the solid resistance of an old-fashioned Victorian gentleman who
was concerned about the protocol of personal relations and of what used
to be called 'the fitness of things'. Selling books directly to friends was, he
decided, too embarrassing to contemplate. The neutral ground of the
auction room would therefore be the best course: 'I want to take advantage
of the present extravagant prices in the interests of my residuary legatee.
So you will understand why I prefer to deal with strangers.' Monkhouse
was not so easily discouraged, and reopened the matter of Edmonds and
Lee, which he had been clamouring to buy in 1943, adding that he would
also like to have copies of Bowlker, Best and Gervase Markham. Could
he not drive down to Wilton and see Skues' collection? Skues replied
irritably: 'As regards your suggested visit you do not appear to have
appreciated the reasons which make me prefer to deal with a stranger.'
But even plain speaking was lost on this stubborn correspondent. He
assured Skues that he quite appreciated his reasons, 'but even this cannot
destroy my very strong desire to own at least one of the better books
from your library'. Skues replied briskly that he had 'quite decided' to
auction his books. His friends could then bid for them without feeling
that any advantage had been taken of them. As for visiting, the hotel was
full up.

In 1946 Skues began to change his mind, having discovered that the
custom of the better auction houses was to make up lots composed of
several books. He then corresponded with the London bookshops of
Quaritch, Maggs, Sotheran and Francis Edwards but got little encouragement. Eventually he circulated his list in the Flyfishers' Club, the Anglers'
Club of New York and in the fishing world as widely as he could, and
steeled himself to the task of selling his books by degrees and dealing
directly with anyone who might come forward. Monkhouse was, of
course, the first to do so, and he reopened the matter of *Brook and River
Trouting*. He had rightly estimated this as the most valuable, or at least
the most costly, of Skues' book. Monkhouse was an experienced negoti-
ator but he was dealing with an equal. Skues invited him to make an
offer. Having played hard for this prize Monkhouse drew back a little
and offered £20. Skues wanted more and would not budge. After a year
of intermittent pressure Monkhouse learned in March 1947 that it had
been sold elsewhere for £25.

In June 1946 the American collector Otto von Kienbusch began to
buy from the list. He also wished to have the de luxe copy of *Brook and*

River Trouting, at that date still unsold, but Skues raised an objection on quite another ground. He told Kienbusch that he regarded him as a friend, and would therefore feel unable to ask such a large sum for the book. Kienbusch assured him that there need be no embarrassment, and that he would be happy to pay any reasonable sum, but for Skues it was out of the question. As compensation for the disappointment, he offered the surviving letters of Louis Bouglé as a free gift: 'It will be satisfaction enough to know that they are preserved ... I have the strongest objection to putting a price on or to receiving payment for letters which were written to me in pure friendship.' In the same unselfish spirit he had given the Theodore Gordon letters to the Anglers' Club of New York in 1929. Years later Kienbusch quarrelled with the Anglers' Club, which had looked forward to the bequest of his angling materials, and gifted the Bouglé letters to the library of the University of Princeton. He also gave to Princeton other examples of Skues' generosity: the Theodore Gordon letters, the Austin letters, one of the copies of Skues' memoir 'Trivialities' and items of Skues memorabilia, including the school badge from his scholar's gown embroidered with the medieval motto of Winchester College, 'Manners Makyth Man'.

In addition to books, other useful items were dispersed to good homes at this time. For some time Skues kept his beloved 1905 Leonard rod, even though he was not now using it. At length and no doubt with a pang, he passed it on to his brother Charles. He sold two more 10ft Leonards dating from 1903 and 1904 (when they had cost £7 each) for £17 10s and £15 respectively. His fly-tying materials were divided up and given without payment to several friends in the Flyfishers' Club. Most of the remaining Bartleet 7362 hooks went to Neville Bostock at the rate of 4s a hundred, and the balance to Monkhouse, who had been asking for them for some time. Skues' method was, in the main, to give things to friends and to ask for money from people not regarded as friends, in which latter category were Bostock and Monkhouse.

The news of the effect of wartime conditions upon Abbots Barton was depressing for Skues. The condition of the fishery had held up fairly well in the early part of the war, but at the end of 1941 the syndicate closed down, and the fishing reverted to the riparian owners. John Barrow Simonds continued to manage the meadows for his father, Colonel Barrow Simonds, and Mullins the keeper was kept on to do what he could, which was not much in the conditions of wartime. Gone were the days when a team of casual workers could be gathered together for a major piece of work on the river. The family continued to use the water in a desultory way, and allowed friends to fish from time to time. Skues had his last fishing there as a guest of the Barrow Simonds family in July 1942, after watching the Eton v. Winchester cricket match the previous day. Very few fish showed, in spite of a good hatch of pale wateries, and he caught nothing.

By 1943 Abbots Barton was deteriorating. As far as is known, Skues never saw it again, which was a good thing. Signs of neglect were everywhere. No weed-cutting was done, mud began to accumulate, poaching was rife and pike overran the fishery. For a time Monkhouse and his partner, a well-known building contractor called Drewery, toyed with the idea of taking it. They had given up the lease of the Twyford fishery, which had become infested with pike, and were renting the Kingsworthy stretch of the Itchen. This extended from the bridge at Easton down to the top of Abbots Barton, so the idea of acquiring at least a part of the fishery immediately downstream naturally followed. Dr Barton wrote to him in July 1943:

I am interested in your bidding for old Skues' water. It used to be good, but the cost of making it worth anything now will be great. I am not very fond of it. It is very ugly, fish are few, and it needs so much keepering. Don't give a big price for it. 'Crab' it well before bargaining.

This initiative did not prosper. Their examination of the place must have caused alarm rather than confidence. They were wise to draw back from negotiation. By the end of the war enormous mudbanks had formed, in places reaching the surface, causing flooding on the meadows. The Catchment Board applied the usual remedy of drastic dredging. In September 1947 Skues wrote sadly to Edward Boies of the deplorable condition of his once-beloved fishery: 'It will take five years to restore it.' In the closing months of 1947 Monkhouse tried again, hoping to get together a group of interested riparian owners from the valley of the Itchen to put up money for restoration. Skues brightened at the news: 'I shall never see it in its pristine glory – but it will be a comfort to know that it will be in hands that are doing their best to restore it.' But there seems to have been little enthusiasm for the Monkhouse scheme and it faded away. It was not until the Piscatorial Society leased the fishing in the 1950s that matters began to improve.

Skues' post-war existence continued to be enlivened by an extensive correspondence. In November 1945 he wrote to Richard Carley Hunt:

I have lately had an enthusiastic letter from an American angler and fly dresser James Leisenring, with his book on tying American wet flies. He also sent me a shoal of his patterns, which looked, in the lightness and delicacy of their dressing, far more like some of our North Country patterns than any American patterns I have seen.

James Leisenring is an important figure in the history of American fly-fishing. His intriguing book, *The Art of Tying the Wet Fly*, has ideas in it which echo or complement those of Skues. He had previously written him an admiring letter (now lost) after reading *Nymph Fishing*. Skues had responded with a gift of some samples of his nymphs. Leisenring's method in fly-dressing was to be sparing with the hackle – one turn or at most two – and to use dubbing for producing a translucent effect, rather than silk or quill. These techniques would have made an immediate appeal to Skues, whose criticism of the over-liberal use of materials in shop-tied patterns appeared frequently in his conversation and letters to the press.

In 1947 Skues received from Leisenring a letter containing a long account (thirteen pages) of a fishing day on the Little LeHigh river, a master class arranged to convince an incredulous friend, who had said 'I am not fishing nymphs any more – they are no good', of the virtues of the method. It worked well. Five trout were caught. The highlights of the day were twofold: a fish of 23½in, and a sceptic humbled and converted. The big trout refused the Skues imitation of a spring medium olive which had been the undoing of the other fish, but was caught with 'a small Greenwell's Glory as tyed [sic] by my friend Skues, which I said I knew was good medicine for such a big and contrary trout'.

It is a pity not to know more of the connection between Skues and Leisenring. There were other letters, one of which described a long-ago meeting between Leisenring and Theodore Gordon, which have disappeared in the unfortunate liquidation of so much of Skues' papers. Skues wrote to Monkhouse: 'He appears to have adopted me as a special personal friend, and writes me at great length about his fishing. He is a queer profane old bird and at times not too choice in his language, but I should hate to hurt his feelings.'

One of the last anglers, if not the last, to open a correspondence with Skues appeared out of the blue on 21 May 1947. Paul Barbotin was a keen and accomplished French angler with some points of resemblance to Louis Bouglé. In his working life he was the sales director of Kodak in France and therefore knowledgeable about trout vision, a curious parallel with Monkhouse. In a letter from the rue de Boulainvilliers in Paris he introduced himself in a polite and apologetic style as an unknown newcomer. He need not have worried: Skues was delighted to get to know another enthusiast, and their correspondence continued, sometimes on a daily basis, until August 1949. And it was to Barbotin that Skues wrote on the day before his death what must have been his last letter.

In his first letter, which ran to twelve pages of excellent English, Barbotin explained his need for help. He possessed copies of *Minor Tactics* and *The Way of a Trout with a Fly*, from which he claimed to have derived 'most of my deepest joys in fishing; for I am indebted only to you if I have developed any proficiency in the gentle art.... You taught me the importance of "hands", of delicacy, the use of the light line and of the priceless light rod.'

He was now anxious to acquire a copy of *Sidelines, Sidelights and Reflections*. This was, of course, a pretext to set up a connection with a famous master of the craft. Skues would have been well aware of this. He responded cautiously to the flattery, thanking Barbotin for his 'kind, if somewhat super-lyrical letter'. In fact a good deal of this letter must have interested him, dealing as it did with the post-war angling scene in France. The Germans had dynamited many rivers, the post-war food shortage had caused the price of trout to increase everywhere, and streams were emptied of fish. Barbotin's house in Brittany was damaged during a German counter-attack in 1944, his mother only just escaped with her life and much of his angling library was destroyed. For some time after the war many streams were not worth visiting and he complained that war profiteers had secured much of the best fishing on the Normandy chalk streams. In most places the threadline reel reigned supreme. Alexander Wanless was not popular with Barbotin; since 1934 500,000 fixed-spool reels had been sold in France. The excellent streams of the Pyrenees were infested with hordes of maggot fishermen. Few Frenchmen bothered about the artificial fly and of these not many knew how to make flies. Charles Ritz and Tony Burnand were trying to improve matters with their magazine *Au Bord de l'Eau*, but they were forced by commercial pressures to provide copy for the threadline anglers.

If the French angling culture at this time was really like this, Barbotin must have felt isolated. To be able to set up a relationship with Skues must have been a piece of luck, and together they began to share their knowledge of artificial and natural flies. The mention by Barbotin of the occurrence of the soldier beetle on French streams reminded Skues of his own attempts to imitate the beetle forty years earlier, and they immediately began to compare patterns and generally indulge in the minute examination of detail in the manner so dear to anglers. Skues spent the next six days searching the meadows by the Nadder for soldier beetles.

A feature of Skues in this correspondence was a certain degree of loosening of some of his earlier inhibitions. It was as if he felt that he had reached the age when he saw no reason to be cautious any more in expressing disapproval of people, whether alive or dead, and his letters began to show a critical and somewhat testy tendency. Barbotin mentioned having acquired a copy of *The Science of Dry Fly Fishing* (1906), by Fred Shaw, once a fairly well-known casting instructor. Skues was instantly dismissive: Shaw was 'an ignorant vulgarian. He could write of a hatch of "blue quills".' Other well-known names were cut down to size. J.W. Dunne's flies, at least the shop-tied versions, were 'a complete dud'; J.W. Hills' *A History of Fly Fishing for Trout* was 'not entirely reliable' (unfortunately true); E.M. Tod was a fine angler but 'a tedious old egotist'; the author W. Earl Hodgson was

> rather a brilliant man, but I regarded him as intellectually dishonest and unsound.... He made a deplorable mess of an edition of Stewart's *Practical Angler*, published by Black. The illustrations of flies were quite unlike Stewart's and he did not realize that the Mayfly of Stewart was not an Ephemera but a Stonefly.

And of course, three decades and more after his death, his ancient adversary was singled out:

> Halford was a very able man, spoilt by the adulation won for him by his first and second books and got to think himself infallible and to resent any criticism ....There can be no doubt that Halford made a mess of the Ramsbury length of the Kennett [sic] in the four years he ran it and his friends knew it. Yet he had the impudence to publish *Making a Fishery* and to let it go into a second edition.

A much more serious problem arose later that summer. Barbotin reported that a French edition of Skues' book *Nymph Fishing* was being prepared. The translator, Colonel Ogareff, was a well-known figure in French angling circles and the first person, so he claimed, to have advocated nymph fishing in France. In 1947 he was a salesman with St Hubert, a gun and fishing tackle shop in Paris. Skues' interest soon turned to alarm. It would, he thought, require a good linguist to do justice to the original. Barbotin approached Ogareff, who admitted that he was having difficulty in achieving a satisfactory rendering into French of 'your concise and very idiomatic English', but did not provide a proof, alleging a paper shortage in France. Skues was particularly anxious about finding a good way to translate 'bulging', a term which he believed was not used accurately in England. If Ogareff had been prepared to co-operate with Skues and Barbotin, a great deal of heartache could have been avoided, but he preferred to press on with his translating without any delays. Eventually his version appeared without any help from them. Apart from the definition of bulging Skues later discovered that the text was full of 'incompetent misunderstandings'. This sort of thing was gall and wormwood for a man who had always striven hard for accuracy. He wrote: 'My text and its quotations are in careful, precise English and I think they deserve better treatment', although he was pleased to find himself acknowledged in the preface as '*le grand maître anglais*'.

Skues' agitated pursuit of the translator and publisher of *Nymph Fishing* was suspended (though not for long) by another crisis in his life. At the end of April 1948 his landlady died, and her husband decided to convert the Nadder Vale Hotel into two flats. This involved ejecting his guest of eight years with, in Skues' words, 'uncomfortably short notice'. Now approaching ninety and too old to argue, he was once more cut loose from his moorings and was lucky to find temporary accommodation nearby in Victoria Road, Wilton. When contractors arrived a few days later to move his belongings it was found that Prynne had shifted them, no doubt to begin conversion and decoration, and that several items were missing. For Skues the experience of quitting his refuge must have been a sorry and graceless business.

Fortunately his stay was not of long duration, and towards the end of August 1948 he took his leave of Wilton. Charles Skues met him at Waterloo Station and carried him off to his house in Beckenham. Here Skues was able to settle for a few days of rest while the family made ready the house they had organized for him nearby at 23 Kelsey Park Road. He wrote with justifiable pride to Barbotin: 'I found the journey of the 27 August rather exhausting but my brother's doctor who overhauled me next day said I was a wonder.'

Skues was soon established in a comfortable house and some of his loneliness must have been left behind in Wilton. He began a programme of short daily walks as far as Kelsey Park and the tiny stream flowing out of the nearby ponds. He wrote to Tom Eastham in December: 'I am in pleasant lodgings with a very pleasant and attractive young Irish lady and a most obliging maid.' Charles and his family lived in Copers Cope Road, Beckenham, a short walk away, and so were able to call in to enquire after his welfare. Sunday lunch with the family became a fixture, and Monkhouse, who had imagined that Skues in Beckenham might be more approachable than in Wiltshire, was told that Fridays, Saturdays and Sundays were reserved for visits to or from his family. It seems a pity that they had not intervened to bring him back to London at the end of the war.

He resumed his reading, tending now towards authors who formerly had not held much interest for him, such as Roderick Haig-Brown. In general, books for Skues had been the means of discovering yet more ideas and techniques which would advance the art of fishing. He now discovered a taste for light, undemanding prose. He even continued writing, and was still contributing to *Angling* in 1948. His last great effort was to provide a long introduction for Norman McCaskie's book, *Fishing: My Life's Hobby.* McCaskie had died in 1944, leaving a manuscript with his publisher and a request that Skues write an introduction for the book. Post-war conditions in publishing had delayed its appearance, and it was not until March 1949 that Skues got down to work. His introduction was not completed until June. The book was mainly concerned with McCaskie's experiences in Scotland. There is a chapter on nymph fishing, a practice which had little appeal for him and which he never really mastered: one wonders why it was included. There is also a chapter on grayling on the Itchen at Winchester, but he is curiously unwilling to mention names. Skues was referred to as 'my host', and the fishery is cryptically introduced as A.B. The man he had known since 1910 is nowhere mentioned by name. Skues paid no attention to this and used most of his own contribution to discuss Abbots Barton and some of his own exploits. The main part of the book is largely ignored, which gives the introduction a slightly comic bias. Eleven pages long, it was nevertheless a remarkable achievement for a man of Skues' advanced age.

A sustained barrage of letters about the French translation continued long after it had been published. Barbotin's attempt to place a note of rectification in *Au Bord de l'Eau* produced the wrong effect. Tony Burnand published parts of Barbotin's private letter to him, which gave an entirely opposite version of the true meaning of 'bulging'. For the first time in their correspondence Skues lost his temper: this was 'a *gross blunder* and looks like yours and *must be repudiated and corrected* ... Last night I took hours to get to sleep through cursing this mishap.' At this point Barbotin may have become a little weary of his role as unofficial agent for Skues' vendetta in France and wished himself well out of it. It is to his credit that he made no move to extricate himself. Skues admitted that the copyright was not his, and that 'my complaint is merely of injury to my prestige'. He continued to press for an apology at large and wrote: 'I would like to take Tony Burnand through the French edition and to bring home to him the outrage which he has done to me and its deliberate character.' At last, in November 1948, Barbotin was able to report that *Au Bord de l'Eau* had published a full acknowledgement of their blunder.

Close on the tail of this success the problem announced itself again in a new form. Skues wrote to Barbotin on 9 June that A&C Black had revealed that work had begun on a French translation of *The Way of a Trout with a Fly*, 'which I always feel has been my best book', and that they were proposing to pass the proofs. Deeply shocked, he wrote to point out that this afforded him no protection at all, and that they had shown little interest in the liberties taken in the translation of *Nymph Fishing*. The publisher immediately retracted and agreed to send the proofs to him. All that was needful was to get the co-operation of the French translator, Dr Pierre Barbellion. Skues' alarm was increased on discovering that Barbellion was an expert on threadline fishing but knew little of fly-fishing.

The letter of 9 June was the last to Barbotin to have been written in Skues' own hand. He took to his bed and continued to bombard Barbotin, A&C Black, Barbellion and the French publisher with angry letters dictated to the nurse who was now looking after him. For Skues was now mortally ill, though unaware of the fact. He was physically weak and barely able to add his signature to a letter but there was no decline in his intellect. Twenty-two well-considered letters followed, most of them on the subject of the French translation. To simplify a complicated story, no progress was made, in spite of all his efforts. Barbellion and the French publisher, no doubt alarmed at entering upon a course which might lead to serious delays, continued to be unhelpful. Charles Skues was acutely aware of his brother's distress, and wrote at length to Barbotin, hoping to find some way of easing his distress, but without result. Unfortunately, Skues did not live to know that Dr Barbellion agreed to collaborate with Barbotin in 1950, and together they discovered and put right many errors.

It is a relief to learn that small scraps of encouragement came Skues' way at this last difficult time. Sir Grimwood Mears wrote to congratulate him on the publication of the fourth English edition of *The Way of a Trout with a Fly*: 'It will be being read three hundred years from now – indeed as long as trout exist and men exist to fish for them, and read with delight.' And only a fortnight before his death Skues wrote to Barbotin: 'I am re-reading *Minor Tactics of a* [sic] *Chalk Stream* and finding it most amusing. It seems incredible that *Minor Tactics* and *The Way of a Trout with a Fly* could be from the same pen.'

Skues continued his dogged but unsuccessful fight to the end of his life. His last letter was sent to Barbotin on 8 August, complaining that he had received no further news from A&C Black, and promising to write again 'when I feel less tired'. He died shortly after nine o'clock in the evening of 9 August 1949, a few days short of his ninety-first birthday.

Tributes to Skues appeared in the angling press and in several daily papers. In *The Sunday Times* Maurice Wiggin referred to 'the engaging modesty' of his writings, and thought that 'the stubborn purists who regard nymph fishing as little better than "chuck and chance it" are, I think, becoming fewer every year'. Grimwood Mears, who had known him since they first fished the Kennet together in 1895, wrote in *The Fishing Gazette*: 'He had a great number of friends who had a warm regard and admiration for him and an immense outer circle of friends and admirers who knew him by his writings only.' In a long and warm tribute in *Au Bord de l'Eau* Paul Barbotin wrote: '*Jusqu'au dernier instant, il conserva sa lucidité et sa vivacité d'esprit.*'

The most heartfelt of many tributes came from Dr Barton, his closest friend:

> It is with more than formal regret that we have to record the passing of Mr G.E.M. Skues, for in his departure we recognise the loss of the last of the great authorities in our art.... Personally he was a most lovable man, tolerant, generous and unselfish. He hated deception either in his business or in conversation, and was the soul of honour in all his dealings.... And so we wave goodbye to him, we who knew him intimately; and we return to the present with something of a lump in our throats for the loss of a staunch friend and a great angler.

Skues' cremation was only attended by a small number of angling friends and relatives. His will, signed in September 1948, was short and to the point. Apart from two small legacies to his surviving sisters, Minnie and Elsie, his property passed to his brother Charles. The net value of the estate was £13,735. The will also directed that his ashes should be scattered at Abbots Barton, 'preferably in the tussocky paddock on the East bank of the main river adjoining the clump of trees near the Winchester Gas Works'. This part of the river is a short distance upstream from the scene of Skues' ever-to-be-remembered triumphs with the B.W.O. in the summer of 1916. Donald Overfield discovered many years later that it had been William Mullins, the keeper at Abbots Barton, who had, in the winter of 1949, carried out this last office for Skues, who had been for him a friend of many years.

Skues had also left certain private directions which were not included in the will. Some years earlier he had prepared a list of his services to angling (reproduced in Overfield (1977) pp. 272–3) and requested Dr Barton to publish this in the *Journal*. His brother Charles was directed to arrange the publication, not less than two years after his death, of his reminiscences. These were published in 1951 as *Itchen Memories*, illustrated by Alex Jardine, whose office was in the same building in Chancery Lane as Charles Skues' architectural practice. This interesting collection was somewhat marred by a staggering number of typographical errors: over fifty have been identified. There seems to have been no one on the staff of the publisher with a knowledge of angling and its terms, and the task of interpreting Skues' handwriting was given to an unfortunate typist, who no doubt did her best. A corrected version, edited by Roy Darlington, appeared in 1999, and the book retains its popularity as a portrait of a vanished age.

At the beginning of the book Skues had added 'Posthumous Preface: To Join the Brimming River', which reiterated his hope that 'each angler should produce his own patterns from nature', instead of relying on inferior representations from the tackle dealers, something for which he had been striving for many years. The Preface ends:

'For myself, by the time, when, if ever, these pages reach the public, my bolt will have been shot and I shall have no more to communicate to my brothers of the fly rod ...

Well there it is. *Ave atque vale.*'

Appendix 1

Original document was a holographic manuscript on copybook paper.
Copied by Alfred Miller.
Some editing and correction by author.

FOR TOMORROW WE DIE

A Mayfly Idyll

G.E.M. Skues
Hyrst View, Campden Road,
South Croydon

> Come fill the Cup, and in the fire of Spring
> Your Winter Garment of Repentance fling
> The Bird of Time has but a little way
> To flutter – and the Bird is on the wing.

> Omar Khayyam

Sunday by the Kennet. Acres beyond acres of water meadow, golden with buttercup, flanked with noble slopes peopled with copse and open timber. The sun already sloping toward afternoon.

I lay on my face deep in grasses, my coat powdered with the mustard-hued pollen of buttercups. Round me grew great horse-daisies and spikes of ragged robin. The broken edges of the river, over which I peered, were fringed and clothed with meadowsweet, and in the low ledges where the bank shelved slowly to the water the yellow iris flaunted gaily, and the sword-pointed flags round her whinny, [and?] wicker [sic] in the playful breeze.

It was the lushest, the most beautiful of green valleys, the fullest in all England of a riotous yet orderly profusion of life.

From the coppice on the hill came the full-mouthed chorus of the mated birds, the sedge warbler chittered in the reeds, in the long grass I heard the corncrakes calling to each other their monotonous crek-crek, while overhead the larks shouted in sheer impotent happiness. Fitfully the peewit flapped up from below the skyline and quested restless about with petulant cry. The cuckoo called his challenge now and again across the meadows and a great heron flapped solemnly downwind towards the upper reaches of the river. For a while the skreeling of the swifts was hushed. The swallows and the martens sped low over the grasses in their hawking. The May bushes abuzz with the tossing black bodies of the hawthorn fly, the coch-y-bonddu beetle sprawled in the grass, and brown and green-winged dragonflies with bodies of peacock blue hurtled round in search of prey.

Overhead the sun beat strongly from a heaven without a cloud. The orangetip butterfly flickered from flower to flower and now and then a little Yellow May dun rose from the stream and drifted slowly down the wind. Everywhere the little Brown Alder was engaged in her busy trot. Later on, the resting Mayflies would get up from the herbage and dance their queer ecstatic madrigal in the air to the sound of pan-pipes, inaudible to other ears than theirs, and the rustle of their whirring wings would keep time to the music. Now as they hang, the chaffinches hovering daintily over the grass-heads pick them neatly and make off to the nest in the hedgerows.

I have lain so long the black-headed bunting in the clump of meadowsweet heeds me not. She has four hungry little maws to feed, and has grown bold to disregard me.

On the opposite bank a weasel scampers along in hot pursuit of a rat. Presently from among the reeds yonder comes a pitiful little squeal and then weasel number 2 comes galloping along *ventre a terre* to share in the savoury meal.

All this evidence of riotous life oppresses me. Yesterday was a red letter day in my life as an angler. Coming down from London and getting onto the water soon after four o'clock, I filled my creel to overflowing with three and a half brace of the most stalwart trout it was ever my luck to encounter, crawling into my little wayside inn at 8.30 laden with two-and-twenty honest pounds of fish ranging from 4lb 9oz to 2lb 7oz. For a while contentment reigned, and I went to sleep in a peace which a good conscience could not give.

But today the lust of slaughter inscrutably innate in every bosom may not be gratified and, as I lie here prone, watching the dace taking down minute insects with a tiny dimple, or the more ponderous rush of a chub as he plunges on his quarry, inaction and reaction have their way, and leave me prey to that inexplicable passion of melancholic loneliness which makes and keeps so many of us anglers. What induced me to come down companionless for my two or three days with the Mayfly, I know not. I only know that I felt the loneliest of God's creatures.

Fear and horror and helplessness were strong upon me. All this marvellous fecundity of flower and bird and beast, all this carnival of battle and murder, and death, more riotous even than life! I felt thrust aside, impotent to interfere, helpless to prevent, helpless to take a part in the game. Sick at heart at the remorseless multitudinous slaughter that was nature's unmitagable [sic] law. In what way was I more worthy to endure than these lives that were taken in such arrogant profusion, yet lose themselves so simply and bravely in the span allotted to them? Indeed, in the vast record of eternity the rings that widen on the surface of the river of life when I go under will be effaced well-nigh as soon as theirs. And withal, I felt, as I watched the strong hurtling current of the river and felt it ripple through my fingers, that life was ebbing, ebbing, ebbing at frightful speed and leaving nothing, nothing in my grasp.

As I turned over my well-thumbed little volume of Omar Khayyam, I found that poet of seven hundred years agone had been through all the same. I read:

When you and I behind the Veil are past
Oh what a long time the world shall last
Which of our Coming and Departure heeds
As the Sea's self should heed a pebble cast.

A moment's halt, a momentary taste
Of being, from the Well amid the Waste
And lo the phantom caravan has reached
The nothing it set out from – Oh make haste!

Into the Universe, the Why not knowing
Nor Whence, like water willy-nilly flowing,
And out of it, like Wind along the Waste
I know now Whither, willy-nilly blowing.

We are no more than a moving row
Of Magic Shadow Shapes that come and go
Round with the Sun's illumined Lantern, held
In Midnight by the Master of the Show.

Just helpless pieces of the game He plays
Here on the chequer-board of Nights and Days
Hither and thither moves, and checks or slays
And one by back in the Closet lays.

So rapt was I in my reverie that I did not turn as I heard the *frou-frou* of a petticoat moving through the grass near to me as some woman came along picking here a flower and there another, and indeed I was inclined to resent the interruption.

She had not seen me till nearly on me.

"I beg your pardon," she said. "Oh, is it you?"

I sat up and looked at her. It was Kate Anson. I leapt to my feet.

"And you too," I answered, "for the matter of that."

She laughed cheerfully. "What brings you here?" she said.

For answer I bent down and pulled from a drooping grass stalk a drowsy, pendent Green Drake, taking him by his folded wings, and held him up to her.

"That?" she said.

"And this," said I, holding up to her one of my straw-bodied patterns that had been so deadly yesterday.

"Oh, I know that," she said. "Mayfly. So you're fishing. Is that meant for an imitation of the live one? It is not a bit like. But it's very pretty. Do you catch trout with it? I want to see a trout caught."

"I am going to try again tomorrow afternoon. Today, I am waiting till the afternoon rise comes on, to see where the big trout lie. But they will not move for another hour. And so I was ----". I held up my little volume and closed it and slipped it into my side pocket.

"Let me show you where the flowers hide," I said, and led her away across the meadow to where the little winding, nestling, sequestered Elbourne babbles down to the Kennet. I showed her the moorhen's nest, and the kingfisher speeding like an arrow through the shadows. We inspected the nurseries of willow wren and chiff-chaff, garden warbler and reed sparrow, and left them undisturbed, and we filled her basket with a royal posy.

"You know all these country things," she said presently. "How came you to when you live in London?"

"The country is my home," I said. "I am banished to London – a life sentence with an occasional ticket of leave for a day or two."

"Why?"

"Oh, for my sins I suppose," said I.

"Oh, your sins," said she. "You are always talking about your sins. What is it sits so heavy on your conscience?"

"I should like to confess to you," said I, "and obtain absolution – if only I knew what my offences were. I sometimes suspect you know more about them than I do."

"I!!!?" said she.

In truth, though I had met her a bare dozen times, I had exchanged but few words with her. Often we passed without a word, sometimes without recognition on her part, sometimes with recognition grudgingly, as it seemed to me, accorded. And always when we met there seemed to be some constraint, some gulf between us, that prevented me from knowing her better, as I wished to. To others her smile was kind and ready. From me – it seemed that I must have given her some offence – that smile was withheld. And it troubled me more than such a trifle should.

"Haven't I sinned against you, offended you in some way?" I said. "You give me that impression always. And I don't pretend to like it. Won't you tell me what I've done?"

"Nothing; indeed nothing," she said.

"Then why ----" I did not know how to put what I had to say without giving offence again. "There's no truth in the notion then?"

"Not a word," she said.

"Sure?"

"Sure."

"And we are friends?"

"Yes."

"Shake hands on that!"

We shook hands cordially, looking for the first time frankly into one another's eyes, I, with an emotion which surprised me, over an incident comparatively so trivial.

The incident placed us quite suddenly on a footing of shy newborn intimacy on which we had never stood before.

"Well, then," I said cheerfully, "since you have forgiven my offences – "

"I've told you I don't remember any."

"Forgiven and forgotten. And most people who forgive and forget only forget that they have forgiven."

"Why won't you believe what I say?"

[*Following two paragraphs cancelled in original with vertical pencil line*]

"I know," I said, "something of the divine compassion of kind women that will make them say a thing that is not, rather than hurt a fellow creature."

"You must have had a great deal of experience."

"In five-and-thirty years there is room for much that requires forgiveness."

"You have had no forgiveness from me."

"Then why – why is everything so different since – since you –"

"Are we not going too fast?" she inquired demurely. The remark was irrelevant. We were walking at a snail's pace.

"Does it distress you?" I said, falling in with her humour. "We are friends?"

"I think that would be better," she said gravely.

"Or we might stop where we are – for a while. I am very happy where we are. Are you?" She did not answer.

"You don't want to turn back yet, do you?"

"N-n-o-o," she said doubtfully.

"Yet there is no standing still in this world. One presses on, always imagining the future will be happier than the past. Do you think tomorrow will be happier than today?"

"No – not tomorrow," she exclaimed half involuntarily.

"Next week, then – or next month? Next year?"

"That would give more time for things to change, wouldn't it!"

"But we are not going back, are we?"

"Not by the way we came."

"Do you know where we are going to?" I asked with a certain amount of trepidation.

"I don't know where you are taking me. 'I am a stranger in these parts'," she quoted.

We turned the corner of the coppice, and were right upon the lych gate of the little rustic church. There was my answer. Sounds of hymn music floated from within.

"Shall we go in?" I said, holding out my hand.

"Yes," said she and put hers in mine, and we went in together.

The service had begun and we crept in on tiptoe and took our seats side by side in a little high pew, sharing a mouldy, much-thumbed Book of Common Prayer.

The brief service was soon over and the sermon began. And the vicar took for his text, as well as I can remember, "This is the message that ye have heard from the beginning, that ye love one another."

I did not dare look at her; the works of the world seemed to have stopped for an instant as my hand slipped down to where hers nestled in the folds of her gown, and my little finger linked into hers. She did not withdraw it. I hardly breathed, but I was conscious of the muslin of her bosom rising and falling. Presently I slid my hand under hers and took the whole of hers in mine. She gave me back my clasp; and there we sat through the sermon hand in hand, palm to palm with interlacing fingers, so that each could feel the throbbing of the other's heart.

What the old vicar said I know not, except that he concluded, in the words of the text: "This is the message that ye have heard from the beginning, that ye love one another."

We moved out silently and did not speak until the little village congregation had dispersed.

"From the beginning, Kate," I said.

"Yes, but I never guessed it till today."

"Nor I."

· · · · · · · ·

And now, as I stand upon the bridge watching the Grey and Black Drakes dancing in the dying sunbeams, I can sum up their philosophy, and mine for the moment, in another quatrain of old Omar:

> Ah, fill the Cup; what boots it to repeat
> How Time is slipping underneath our feet
> Unborn Tomorrow and dead Yesterday –
> Why fret about them if Today be sweet?

Appendix 2

Obituary of Harry McClelland

Marston wrote under the heading 'The Late Mr Harry McClelland' in *The Fishing Gazette* on 23 July 1898: 'I had a long and pleasant correspondence with "Athenian", and always found him most courteous, and ready to fall in with suggestions. His articles were eagerly looked for by all who take more than a superficial interest in fly dressing, and certainly deserve the very high praise given them by "Val Conson", than whom there is no better judge living, and I cannot do better than to reproduce his note here.'

Death of "Athenian"

Dear Marston, –You have doubtless heard from the family of the contributor who wrote over the singularly appropriate name of "Athenian" the announcement of his death. It was only in correspondence, both private and in your columns, that I had to do with him; but I should like to say this, that in him the art of fly dressing has lost, at a very early age, probably the most prolific, ingenious, and inventive intellect of the century. He was always eager to hear and to tell some new thing, and the new thing he told was nearly always of his own discovery. In controversy he was always a fair and courteous opponent, and as a correspondent he was generous to a degree in his communication of what he thought would interest or help.

Thus, though I never had the pleasure of meeting him, his early death touches me with a sense of personal loss, in which you, I feel sure, will share, and I should like, as one of the many readers of *The Fishing Gazette* who has had the benefit of perusing his singularly clear and exhaustive contributions, to testify, through your columns, to those he leaves behind him how warmly we appreciated him and how sincerely we deplore his loss. – Very truly yours

VAL CONSON

Appendix 3

Skues' First Statement of Sunk Fly Practice

From the *Journal of the Flyfishers' Club,* Vol. 20, No. 77 (spring 1931)

A Resurrection

A very few weeks before his death my attention was called by H.T. Sheringham to the following little article which appeared in the "Field" in December 1899, as being the first public statement of the modern theory of wet-fly fishing on chalk streams which was afterwards embodied in book form in Minor Tactics of the Chalkstream, and in that connection he described it as of historical interest. Instead, therefore, of leaving it to be dug out by some serious student years hence from the files of the "Field" or to remain there buried in perpetuity, I have felt encouraged by Sheringham's interest to seek for the article the more permanent publicity afforded by its republication (with the goodwill of the present proprietors of the "Field") in the columns of the JOURNAL.

A Wet Fly Suggestion

It is the bitter complaint of the dry-fly man that the trout are taking more and more, as each succeeding year goes by, to the vicious and reprehensible practice of bulging, or feeding on the nymphs about to hatch. On many wet-fly rivers where trout are taken freely with the fly, it is the rarest thing to see the surface broken by a rise. On others the rise is an almost imperceptible breaking of the surface, not by the fish's neb, but by the swirl he makes in seizing his prey under the surface. In each of these cases, the trout is taking nymphae, at or under the surface, on their way to hatch out, yet the wet-fly angler does not despair; on the contrary, he reaps his harvest from these bulging fish.

What is the moral for the dry-fly man? What but this: when your fish are bulging, give it to them wet. It is not suggested that the dry-fly man should so far derogate from his natural dignity as to rake the water down stream. On the contrary, let him deliver his fly to the trout with the same precision as if he were floating his fly, and with the same absence of drag. The pace of the river will help him less than it does on wet-fly rivers, and he will catch fewer fish; but if he uses his tackle aright, he should have a far better chance of making a basket than if he stuck stolidly and stupidly to the dry-fly. He is faced with the difficulty that, though it be easy enough to imitate the floating dun in its imago or sub-imago stages, the nymphae to be imitated are with difficulty procurable.

Let us again go back to school to our wet-fly masters. It will be found that on the Border rivers a fly known as Greenwell's Glory is a great stand-by. It is made with wings of hen blackbird, waxed yellow silk ribbed with fine gold wire and a coch-y-bondhu hackle. Vary the wing from dark blackbird to pale starling, the body from dark dirty olive to pale yellow or cream, and the hackle from coch-y-bondhu to pale ginger or honey dun, and you get a great range of duns. Let the wings be split and the dressing be light, and let the flies be tied on gut with double cipher irons. In years gone by, anglers used to get good baskets on Itchen and Test with the wet-fly. They will have to come back to it again. Some day they will learn to combine a judicious admixture of wet-fly science and dry-fly art, and then ---

Then will be the time for some new development. In the meanwhile, why not? I speak as a dry-fly man.

Seaforth and Soforth

G.E.M.S

Appendix 4

From R.S. Austin's Original Note of Tup's Indispensable

Notes 1900. –

In the latter part of April I found the Badger Hackle on a 00 hook killed well, and at the same time, and also earlier in the month, an Olive Dun, with peacock quill body and gold tip, hackle blue cock's olive dyed, and goose wing's was fancied. Following on the Badger, at the beginning of May, fish took well two duns, the Dirty Dun and the Yellow Dun, dressed buzz on a 00 hook. On the 15th May the Black Gnat made its appearance, and I killed with two patterns of that fly, one, winged, with body 3 or 4 turns of Magpie herl, very slender starling wings, and a dark blue cock's hackle, and the other tied buzz with body of two strands of Turkey tail feather, fairly mottled, with white and brown, on coloured silk.

Hooks for both no.000. After that hackled Olive Quill and the Pale Summer Midge killed well up till about 8th June, when a preference was shown for the Red Spinner, dressed with full yellow silk buzz on a 00 hook (Pennells) with Blue Hackle of a lightish colour and freckled thickly with gold, body of a mixture of ram's wool, cream colour seal's fur, lemon spaniel's fur and a few pinches of crimson mohair. The first evening I used this fly I got six fish weighing 4¾ lbs. in the pool at the top of the Kag, biggest fish 1 lb 7 oz. The next night I had four weighing 5 lbs. biggest fish 3 lbs ½ oz and another night about 2½ lbs.

The Red Spinner spoken above has been christened "Tup's Indispensable" by Mr Skues who has had good sport with it on various streams. Since 1900 I have used this fly a good deal and I think it is about the best that can be put up early in the year say from the middle of April till towards the end of June. After June I have found another spinner do better, a spinner with a sooty blue hackle, and a body more pronounced in colour. One of dull red mohair ribbed with gold twist.

Appendix 5

Letter from Edward Mills to Paul Barbotin

ESTABLISHED 1822

CABLE ADDRESS
ARTMILL, NEW YORK

WILLIAM MILLS & SON INC.

SOLE AGENTS FOR
H. L. LEONARD
CELEBRATED SPLIT BAMBOO
RODS

FISHING TACKLE

P. O. BOX 538
CHURCH STREET ANNEX

21 PARK PLACE
NEW YORK 8, N. Y.

TELEPHONE BARCLAY 7-6579

August 27th, 1952

Mr. Paul Barbotin,
26 Avenue de Neuilly,
Neuilly-sur-Seine,
FRANCE

Dear Sir

We have yours of August 12th and take pleasure in sending you one of our catalogs under separate cover.

The writer remembers very plainly the Rods which he had in London in 1904 and 1905 and which Mr. Skues had. We still make this model which is the No.51DF you will find on the top of Page 5 of the catalog. If you wish an extra large handle we can make it that way. We did this for Mr. Skues. The regular handle now is 6 inches long, moderately shaped. The Cork is 3/4 in. diameter at the top end by the bamboo and 3 in. back the diameter is 1-1/16 in. and 4½ in. back 7/8 in. and at the reelseat it is 1-1/16 in. in diameter. It is not the "Wells" handle like we used to make for Mr. Skues. The regular style Rods we have in stock and can supply them promptly – with the "Wells" handle it would take about three weeks.

If you are coming to United States we shall be glad to have you stop in and see us.

Yours truly

WM MILLS & SON INC. EJM:EG

Edward Mills

airmail

Appendix 6

Letter from Skues to Tommy Hanna

POWELL, SKUES & GRAHAM SMITH
JAMES POWELL
G.E.M. SKUES
GRAHAM SMITH

TELEPHONE: CENTRAL { 2444/2445}

TELEGRAPHIC ADDRESS:
"SKUESOWEL", ESTRAND, LONDON

34, ESSEX STREET,
STRAND, LONDON, W.C.2.

19th May, 1933.

Dear Sir,

I have become the possessor of a copy of your "Fly Fishing in Ireland" and have read it with exceptional interest, and I hope you will forgive a few comments. I am glad to see that you put nymph-fishing in the forefront of your exposition. Its importance is only just beginning to be realised and up to the present mine has been rather the voice of one crying in the Wilderness. I am unable, however, to accept all you say on the subject. I do not, for instance, agree that at the times when they are coming to the surface to hatch they must be active. In the sand, in the mud, among weeds, gravel and rocks, while they are growing up they are no doubt extremely active; but my observation (backed by Dr. Mottram's) is that at the stage when they are about to burst their sheaths and emerge they are almost inert and comatose, tossed about more or less at the mercy of the current.

As regards colour I consider that it is more essential that one's artificial nymph should be a good representation of the natural nymph than that one's floater should be a good representation of the hatched dun. The natural outline and colours of the nymph are not obscured by refraction or in any other way.

I am a little puzzled by what you say in the last paragraph on p.16 about the use of the hackles of snipe, grouse and partridge. I do not think I could find in either of these birds a hackle small enough and short enough in the fibre to resemble the short legs of the natural nymph. The smallest brown partridge hackle requires a No.2 hook, and then it does not represent a nymph. I hope you don't lend yourself to the absurdities of Mr Bridgett who calls large flies, with hackles longer than the hook, nymphs.

In using the nymph I do best when casting up my own bank and across to the other bank. I don't oil my cast to such a short distance of the nymph as 9 inches. I find that when fishing across that produces surface drag. I usually leave two feet unoiled.

Again, I don't believe that one ever has a nymph anything like two feet below the surface. I doubt whether if there be a moderate current it ever sinks over six inches.

My observation as to fish coming short is that it is generally the wrong fly. I recall in particular one evening in May when the trout were rising to spinners. I put on a Tup dressed to represent a spinner and got false rise after false rise, but as soon as I changed to my little rusty spinner the fish took soundly and I killed three nice trout before the rise was over. If I had begun with that pattern I might have had five or six brace.

P.44. Why "hollow bodies of the Ephemeridae"?

P.44. I don't think there is anything new in Dunne's clipping away the V under the hackle. I cannot remember where I read it before.

P.45. I don't understand your saying that the point of the hook points upwards. Even if it did I think the suck with which the fish absorbs the fly is quite vigorous enough to overcome the difficulty of hooking.

P.45. I find a dragging dun always scares my fish, but a dragging sedge is a different proposition.

Apropos of the bubble following a rise my view is that the air is sucked in with the floating fly and expelled with the water taken in at the same time through the gills.

I am inclined to think that you make too much (p.49) of the difficulty of sipping in a floating artificial fly. At the same time I am with you in disliking an overdressed fly. But my little red sedge with a body hackle and six turns of front hackle is an admirable hooker, and the fish take it down greedily and easily.

On p.56 you class Tup's Indispensable as a fly bearing no close resemblance to the natural. I remember one April snatching at what I took to be a pale watery spinner in the air and hooking myself soundly in the hand with my Tup's Indispensable.

As regards Pope's Nondescript I doubt whether trout see the gold in that (or in gold ribbed Hare's Ear) as we do. I expect it looks olive to them.

I agree cordially with what you say on p.78 about flies, but I don't agree that Greenwell's or Tups are fancy flies. They are what I call general flies. They can represent several natural flies.

On pp.86 and 87 you say that the fibres of an artificial nymph should point forward. Why? I always dress mine to slope well back, and my nymphs are very successful, being dressed with the model before me floating in a baby plate. You say the same thing about wet flies (p.87).

The last three lines of the penultimate paragraph on p.87 seem to require correction in your next edition.

P.89. Last paragraph but one. Don't you ever wind the silk through the turns of hackle? It makes a very sound tie.

I am not greatly attracted by the Vice depicted opposite p.97. I like the jaws filed away so that one can get the tips of one's fingers down to the work.

I cordially agree with you (p.98) that nymphs are very badly tied by professionals. I could give glaring examples from high class firms.

What part of pheasant-tail do you use for nymphs' wing cases? Surely not the ruddy feather. I find that the teeth of the fish cut pheasant tail very readily. I always tie in my hackle <u>first</u> by the stalk. The stalk helps to taper the fly or nymph, and latterly I have given up any serious effort to produce wing cases.

I don't follow your second paragraph on p.105. May I see a sample fly?

P.114. Branchiae. There are some herls which are quills with a furry edge, and represent branchiae very nicely. The goose primaries do so quite nicely. I never used clipped hackles for this purpose. I must try.

<u>Horns</u>. The natural nymph has no apparent horns, and I fail to see the need for them. Legs are a different matter, but you do not mention these.

<u>B.W.O. Nymph</u>. The legs and whisks of the natural insect are freckled like a partridge hackle, but closer.

You seem to make many of your bodies smooth with floss silk, if that is what you mean by "base colour", in spite of your remarks about branchiae. You could dub a body and rib it with floss to get the effect of branchiae.

In your nymph dressings why do you divide your named half dozen from the unnamed dozen – putting the latter into a new chapter?

What is balloon rubber? Is it from tyres, or from toy balloons?

No.1 looks to me quite a fancy fly. So do several of the rest. Do you never use a blue upright body, with or without a silver wire rib, with pad of hare's ear for thorax and a black henny cock's hackle for legs?

Why no sizes or shapes of hooks? I regard an appropriate shaped hook as an essential part of a nymph. Pennells down eyed snecks, 15,16 and 17 and Pryce Tannatts down eyed round bend Nos. 1 and 2 (the latter seldom) seem to me the best shape for sizeable nymphs; but for very small nymphs B.7362 Bartleets. Are not all your dry and wet flies fancy patterns? Why three hackles on the dry flies? Why no sedge patterns and no patterns of perlidae?

Please forgive this bombardment. I wish I had seen your book in M.S. so that you could have made some of the matters of my enquiry clearer. You refer to me so frequently in your text that folks may not give you the credit to which you are entitled for your own ingenuity and for your personal experience. I saw recently an advertisement by Allcocks of a new series of patterns. Are these yours?

Yours faithfully,
G.E.M. Skues

Thomas J. Hanna, Esq.,
Stonard Street,
Moneymore,
Co. Derry,
N. Ireland.

Appendix 7

Extract from the *Journal of the Flyfishers' Club,* Vol. XXVI, No. 104 (winter 1937–8)

HALFORD AND THE NYMPH

This paper is going to be rank blasphemy. The name of F. M. H. is going to be taken in vain --- or is it *not* in vain?

This is written in order to give Club Members matter to ponder on, to look up and verify and to chew over, in preparation for the forthcoming February debate on "Nymph Fishing on Chalk Streams."

My first proposition is that, but for Halford, there would have been no Dry-fly Purism.

My second is that, if Dry-fly Purism is founded on a number of mistakes, misobservations and misunderstandings on the part of Halford, then Dry-fly Purism has got to go.

My third proposition is that it *is* so founded.

By this I do not mean that all F. M. H.'s teaching has to go. What he taught about fishing the floating fly to trout which are taking floating natural flies on the surface stands. It was great work. It is what he said about fishing the wet fly and the nymph to trout feeding subaqueously that has got to go.

If you doubt me, listen to this, every word of which can be substantiated as regards Halford's doctrine from his writings, and as regards my comments thereon from my own practice and experience and from that of others who have ventured to think and experiment for themselves.

Miscon- ceptions	I.	He would not believe that wet fly or nymph could be cast to a feeding fish in position as exactly as a dry fly: and that if that fish were feeding under water a suitable wet pattern was likely to be taken and a floating fly unlikely. HE WAS WRONG.
Misobser- vation	II.	He thought all wet-fly fishing on chalk streams was "fishing the water": searching it with a dragging fly or flies.

HE WAS WRONG.

Miscon- ceptions	III.	He thought that trout that took wet fly (or nymph) were

        (1) Often unsizeable;

        (2) Often pricked and scared.

HE WAS WRONG.

Misobser- vation	IV.	He did not believe nymphs could be successfully imitated to take fish, because he thought the mature nymph about to hatch was active and its motions could not be imitated. HE WAS WRONG.

The mature nymph floating up to hatch is practically inert.

Misobser- vation	V.	He did not realise that fish feeding subaqueously under banks and elsewhere near the surface were generally taking mature inert nymphs. HE WAS WRONG.
Miscon- ceptions	VI.	He did not believe that such fish could be fished to with wet fly or nymph without flogging great lengths of water to the detriment of other anglers and the fish. HE WAS WRONG.
Mistake	VII.	He thought that while the dry fly might take trout in still weather and clear water, the wet fly could not do so (except, perhaps, on rare happening days). HE WAS WRONG.
Mistake	VIII.	He thought that only small fish could be taken with wet fly and nymph. HE WAS WRONG.
	IX.	If he had been right, it would have been unethical to fish the wet fly on chalk streams, but . . . . HE WAS WRONG, and each error and misapprehension led to others.

I say he was wrong because

1. for over a quarter of a century I have been freely taking subaqueously feeding trout in position with wet fly and
2. for nearly as long with nymph.

(3) My Itchen trout often nymph for hours.

(4) They take a correct pattern of nymph

(5) In clear water and in bright and still weather.

(6) Often I do not cover 100 yards during the trout's feeding time.

(7) Trout taking nymphs are generally soundly hooked.

(8) Most of my biggest fish have been caught on nymph and wet fly.

I claim for nymph-fishing in chalk streams

(1) that it does not interfere with dry-fly fishing when the dry fly is appropriate.

(2) That it enables the angler to get feeding fish in position when they are feeding on nymph and neglecting the hatched-out fly, when the dry fly is not only inappropriate, but definitely wrong; and thus

(3) it enlarges the opportunities of the chalk stream fisher.

(4) That it is a difficult and delicate art well worthy of study and practice.

Now what is your answer?

Appendix 8

Letter from F.T.K. Pentelow to Sir Joseph Ball
Original was a holographic manuscript

MINISTRY OF AGRICULTURE AND FISHERIES

Fisheries Research Station
ALRESFORD
Hampshire
9/ii/38

Dear Sir

Dr. Butcher passed on to me your enquiry about the activity of nymphs about to emerge and he tells me you would like an answer this evening. I am afraid, however, that as I returned only this morning this will be too late unless the post office excels itself.

The nymph when it comes to the surface to hatch is reasonably active. It wriggles and swims and comes up actively, i.e. it does not rise passively by the agency of gas or anything of that kind. My impression is, however, that at this stage the nymphs are less active or perhaps I should say, more ponderous in their movements, than when they are younger.

When once the nymph has reached the place it has chosen for its emergence it does remain apparently passive until the moult is complete. There is of course a good deal of movement during a moult, but it does not result in the movement of the insect as a whole.

Butcher also tells me you would like some data on trout stomachs from the Itchen. I will look up what I have and send it to you later. Please excuse the haste of this letter but the only chance of your getting it tonight lies in catching this morning's post.

Yours faithfully

F.T.K. Pentelow

Appendix 9

1. *Iron Blue Duns.*
   Wings cut. The natural fly has pale legs with red feet and pale practically white whisks.

2. *Iron Blue Nymph.*
   (1) What is the hackle. (2) Quite nice.
   In both cases I should not have darkened the tying silk showing at tail so much.

3. *Female Iron Blue Spinner.*
   (1) Spent pattern too long in wings. (2) Hackled patterns.
   Hackle perhaps rather light. In both cases the winding of the silk through the hackle shows and slightly mars the precision of the winding of the hackle.

4. *Pope's Green Nondescript.*
   The colour of the body is not that of the standard pattern. The green has too much blue in it. The hackle and whisks should be a much lighter red. The gold ribbing should be of flat tinsel. Wings none too happy. Surely not starling.

5. *Red Quill.*
   The quill is not what is usually so termed, which is from Peacock eyed feather stripped of flue. Taper of No.1. rather thick at tail. No reason why the fly should not kill excellently.

6. *Red Spinner.*
   Should kill quite well. Whisks of No.1. rather long. Silk shows through winding of hackle on both.

7. *Lunn's Particular.*
   Wings a bit long, also freckled. The standard pattern has plain wings. Whisks slightly long.

8. *Pheasant Tail.*
    No. 1. Hackle unduly pale. No. 2. Alright – a little more rust in the hackle desirable.

9. *Rusty Spinner.*
    Not either of my patterns but should kill as ordinary red spinner. My patterns more red ant colour.

10. *Large Greenwell.*
    Body so thin it does not look as if it contained the stalk of the hackle. Hackle over long and with a rather ungainly gap on the underneath.

11. *Orange Quill.*
    Wings wrongside foremost. Hackle rather dark. Quill peacock instead of Condor.

12. *Large Dark Olive.*
    I recommend a stouter gold wire for body. Body does not look as if it contained stalk of hackle to assist taper. Hackle much too pale in No.1. and too dark in No. 2. Wings of No.2. wrong way on.

13. *Medium Olive.*
    Hackle rather light. Wings in both cases wrong way on.

14. *Pale Watery Dun.*
    Would be excellent if wings put in the right way on.

15. *Olive nymph*
    (1) Hackle should match body. (4) ?what insect? No.2. best of the four.

16. *Hare's Ear.*
    Wings in wrong way and cut. Otherwise O.K. The gold of the ordinary Goldribbed Hare's Ear is flat.

17. *Mayfly Nymph.*
    Not much like the natural. See illustrations in Halford.

18. *B.W.O. Nymph.*
    If meant for "Occasionally it" not a bit like. The body should be short and tubby, the hackle hens, dark blue and fuller.

19. *Pale Watery Spinner.*
Bodies unspinner like.

20. *Grannom.*
Larger than natural. Wings cut and broken. Hackle would be better for a freckle in it.

21. *March Brown Male.*
As tying apart from representation the best. With whisks removed might kill as a sedge.

22. *March Brown Female.*
Body much too thin. Dubbing required.

23. *Orange Partridge.*
Both good but different types. Body of No.1. a bit long. No.2. best.

It will be seen from the above observations that criticism is more often addressed to the composition than to the handiwork. That shows that the dresser has the root of the matter in him and that with practice and observation of the natural insects and with study of the effects obtainable with materials he should now improve beyond knowledge.

G. E. M. S.
26.XI.41.

Note: Names of flies in the original document are handwritten.

Appendix 10

Skues' Catalogue of Books for Sale 1945–6

(As found – no editing)

Year Published	Title	Author	Purchased from	£	s	d
1886	Floating Flies and how to Dress Them	Halford	Gilbert	1.	1.	0.
1897	Dry Fly Entomology	Halford	"	1.	1.	0.
1903	An Angler's Autobiography	Halford	Marks		12.	6.
1889	Dry Fly Fishing in Theory and Practice	Halford	Edwards	1.	1.	0.
1910	Modern Development of the Dry Fly	Halford	Gilbert	1.	5.	0.
1913	The Dry-Fly Man's Handbook	Halford	"	1.	2.	6.
1921	A History of Fly Fishing for Trout	Hills	"		7.	6.
1934	River Keeper	Hills	Marks		10.	0.
1930	A Summer on the Test	Hills	Marks		10.	6.
1936	My Sporting Life	Hills	Foyles		4.	0.
1932	The Golden River	Hills	"		2.	0.
1914	Minor Tactics of the Chalk Stream (Autographed by the author)	Skues	Edwards		10.	6.
1932	Sidelines, Sidelights and Reflections (Autographed by the author)	Skues	Gilbert		12.	6.
1928	The Way of a Trout with a Fly (Autographed by the author)	Skues	"		7.	6.
1939	Nymph Fishing for Chalk Stream Trout (Autographed by the author)	Skues	Hardy		7.	6.
1898	Old Flies in New Dresses	Walker	Gilbert		12.	6.
1929	Where the Bright Waters Meet	Plunket-Greene	Marks		6.	0.
1932	Trout Flies	Courtney-Williams	Gilbert		10.	0.
1936	About Fishing	Hartman	"		7.	6.
1936	Trout Heresy	Allan	Edwards		6.	6.
1916	Brook and River Trouting	Edmonds-Lee	Marks		18.	0.
1939	Fly Tying for Trout	Taverner	Gilbert		5.	0.
1934	Fifty Years on the Test	Pain	"		5.	6.

Year Published	Title	Author	Purchased from	Price for Sale £	s	d
1921	The Natural Trout Fly and its Imitation	West	"	1.	10.	0.
1930	Fly Fishing (de luxe edition)	Grey	Edwards	2.	2.	0.
1937	The Compleat Angler	Walton				
1904	Fishing (Country Life 2 vols)		"		10.	0.
1911	Diary of A Test Fisherman	Durnford	"		6.	0.
1938	Modern Trout Fishing	Platts				
1886	North Country Flies	Pritt	Marks	1.	1.	0.
1897	The Book of the Dry Fly	Dewar	Gilbert		15.	0.
1924	Sunshine and the Dry Fly	Dunne	"		5.	0.
1933	Fly Fishing in Ireland	Hanna				
n.d.	Fly Rods and Fly Tackle	Wells	Edwards		2.	0.
1908	Dry Fly Fishing for Trout and Grayling	Englefield	Gilbert		6.	6.
1932	Fly Dressing	Bernard	"		7.	6.
1861	Halcyon	Wade	Marks		3.	6.
1880	A Book on Angling	Francis	Gilbert		10.	6.
1847	Handbook of Angling	Ephemera	Marks		6.	0.
1904	Trout Fishing	Hodgson	Gilbert		8.	6
1906	Dry Fly in Fast Water	Le Branche	Marks		12.	6.
1920	Lines in Pleasant Places	Senior	"		5.	0.
1915	Fly Fishing: Some New Arts and Mysteries	Mottram	"		5.	0.
1909	The South Country Trout Streams	Dewar	Foyles		1.	6.
1851	Fly Fishing	Pulman	Gilbert		2.	0.
1936	Fly Fishers' Guide to Aquatic Flies	Bainbridge	Edwards		5.	0.
1905	Practical Angler	Stewart	Marks		5.	0.
1822- 1908	Chronicles of the Houghton Fishing Club	Maxwell	Gilbert	1.	0.	0.
1908- 1932	Chronicles of the Houghton Fishing Club	Page	Marks		17.	6.
1938	Trout Flies	Kingfisher				
1821	Northern Memoirs	Franck	"		15.	0.
1883	Bibliotheca Piscatoria (A.N. Gilbey's copy)	Westwood	"		10.	0. 6.
1921	Fishing from Earliest Times	Radcliffe	"		12.	6.
1919	Animal Life Underwater	Ward	Edwards		7.	0.

Year Published	Title	Author	Purchased from	Price for Sale £	s	d
1912	Marvels of Fish Life	Ward	Marks		5.	0.
1901	Grayling Fishing	Rolt	Foyles		2.	0.
1921	Dry Fly Fisherman's Entomology	Moseley	Gilbert	2.	2.	0.
1930	Troutfishers' Entomology	Wauton	Marks	1.	1.	0.
1939	How to tie Flies	McClelland	"		5.	0.
1855	Fly Making (Coloured plates)	Blacker	"	1.	10.	0.
1864	River Angling	Younger	"		8.	6.
1863	Art of Trout Fishing on Rapid Streams (Westwood's copy)	Cutcliffe	"		16.	0.
1862	List of Angling Flies	Theakston	"		8.	6.
1888	British Angling Flies	Theakston	"		3.	6.
1936	Chalk Streams and Water Meadows	Barton	Gilbert		2.	6.
1935	Fly Fishers' Club (Library Catalogue)		Edwards		5.	0.
1884-1934	Fly Fishers' Club (Book of)		"		7.	0.
1918-1932	Fly Fishers' Club (Journal Vols. IV – XXI)					
1906	The Science of Dry Fly Fishing	Shaw	"		8.	0.
1920	Trout Fishing Memories and Morals	Sherringham	"		5.	0.
1921	The Flyfisher and Trouts Point of View	Harding	"		7.	6.
1911	A Scottish Flyfisher	Leitch	Gilbert		4.	6.
1921	Some Piscatorial Problems Idly Considered	Lamond	Edwards		3.	0.
1936	Keeping and Fishing	Peart	"		5.	0.
1892	By Hook or by Crook	Sandeman	Foyle		8.	0.
1888	The Book of the All-round Angler	Bickerdyke	Marks		6.	6.
1906	Fishing for Pleasure and Catching it	Marston	"		3.	6.
1893	Practical Fly Fishing (Keith Rollo's copy)	Beever	"		3.	6.
1880	Practical Fly Fisher (Keith Rollo's copy)	Jackson	"		3.	6.
1840	Fly Fishers' Guide	Bainbridge	"		5.	0.
1847	Trout Flies of Devon and Cornwall	Soltau	Edwards		2.	0.

Year Published	Title	Author	Purchased from	Price for Sale £	s	d
1879	Fly Tying	Ogden	Marks		4.	6.
1932	Modern Trout Fly Dressing	Woolley	Farlow		5.	0.
1862	Fly Fishers' Entomology	Ronalds	Gilbert		7.	6.
1913	Fly Fishers' Entomology (de luxe 2 vols)	Ronalds	Marks	6.	0.	0.
1876	A Quaint Treatise on "Flees, and the Art ..."	Aldam	"	5.	0.	0.
1918	Fresh Water Biology	Ward-Whipple	Edwards		7.	0.
1910	Tales of Fishes	Zane-Grey			3.	6.
1927	Tales of Swordfish and Tuna	Zane-Grey				
1930	Sea Angling Fishes of the Cape	Biden				
1937	Giant Fishes, Whales & Dolphins	Norman-Fraser				
1928	The Pike Fisher	Spence				
1924	The Life History of the Salmon	Hutton	Edwards		12.	0.
1895	The Salmon Fly	Kelson	"		15.	0.
1910	Salmon Sea Trout and the Freshwater Fish	Malloch	"		10.	0.
1933	The Art of Salmon Fishing	Jock Scott	Marks		9.	0.
n.d.	How to Dress Salmon flies	Pryce-Tannatt	Edwards		3.	0.
1919	How to tie Salmon Flies	Hale	Marks		7.	6.
1867	The Poultry Book		Foyles		7.	6.
1822	The Art of Angling	Best	"		1.	0.
1886	The Scientific Angler	Foster	"		1.	6.
1908	Trout Waters	Armistead	"		2.	0.
1928	Fireside Fishing	Courtney-Williams	"		2.	0.
1895	Grayling and How to Catch Them	Walbran	"		1.	0.
1800	Angling in all its Branches	Tayler	Dobell		4.	6.
1886	Red Palmer on Fly Fishing	Tayler	"		2.	0.
1839	British Angler's Manual	Hofland	"		4.	6.
1927	The Pleasures of Princes together with the Experienced Angler (1622)	Gervase Markham & Robert Venables	Edwards "		15.	0.
1929	Trout Fishing from all Angles	Tavener			10.	0.
1919	Golden Days	Romilly Fedden	Smith		2.	6.
1911	Chalkstream and Moorland	Russell	"		2.	6.
1825	Anglers Guide	Salter	"		2.	6.
1821	The Modern Fisher	Mackintosh	"		3.	6.

Year Published	Title	Author	Purchased from	Price for Sale		
				£	s	d
1726	The Gentleman Angler	Smith	"		4.	6.
1854	Art of Angling	Bowlker	"		1.	0.
1903	The Game Fowl	Proud	"			6.
1801	Art of Angling	Brookes	Edwards		12.	0.
1689	Angler's Vade Mecum	Chetham	Marks		15.	0.
1880	A Treatise of Fishing with an Angle (facsimile of original 1496)	Juliana Berners	Spencer		8.	0.
1885	Ditto (Bibliotheca Curiosa) edited by "Piscator"		"		4.	0.
1883	Ditto edited by T. Satchell		"		4.	0.
1854	The Anglers Guide	Martin	"		4.	0.
1847	The Anglers Companion	Stoddart	"		15.	0.
1852	The Anglers Assistant	Carpenter	"		4.	6.
1903	Wet Fly Fishing	Tod	"		2.	0.
1925	Secrets of the Salmon	Hewitt	"		4.	0.
1892	How to tie Salmon Flies	Hale	"		12.	6.
1886	Floating Flies and How to Dress them. (Large paper edition)	Halford	"		1.	0
1885	Salmon & Trout Fishing (Large paper edition)	Pennell	Marks			
1938	Cock Fighting and Game Fowl	Atkinson	Miles		16.	0.
1934	Fly Fishing for Duffers	Peck	Foyles		2.	0.
1932	Angling in East Africa	Hately & Copley	"		3.	0.
1924	Tales of Southern Rivers	Zane-Grey	"		1.	6.
1895	A Mixed Bag	Red Spinner	"		2.	6.
1923	The Angler in South Africa	Bennion	"		2.	0.
1866	The Anglers Instructor	Bailey	"		1.	6.
1927	Fisherman's Knots & Wrinkles	Hunter	"		1.	6.
1922	A Troutfisher in South Africa	Kingfisher	"		3.	0.
1923	Angling Adventures of an Artist	Shirley-Fox	Foyles		2.	6.
1856	Catalogue of Angling Books	Russel-Smith	Edwards		6.	0.
1895	Making a Fishery	Halford	"		5.	0.
1827	Experienced Angler (Gosden)	Venables	"	1.	5.	0.
1942	Going Fishing	Farson				

Year Published	Title	Author	Purchased from	Price for Sale		
				£	s	d
1818	Angler's Vade Mecum	Carroll	Quaritch	1.	0.	0.
1880	Anglers Notebook					
1888	" "				7.	0.
1915	Clear Waters	Bradley	Edwards		10.	0.
1864	Fishermans' Magazine Vol. I	Pennell	Miles			
1865	Fishermans' Magazine Vol. II	Pennell	"		3.	6.
1888	The Book of the Grayling	Pritt	Hatchards		7.	0.
1931	The Book of the Fly Rod	Sheringham-Moore	"	1.	10.	0.
1930	The Anglers Anthology	Austin	"		1.	6.
1929	Travel Diary of an Angler	Van Dyke	"		7.	6.
1928	Certain Experiments concerning Fish and Fruit	John Taverner 1600	"		6.	0.
1883–1888	A Revisional Monograph of Recent Ephemeridae	Eaton	Quaritch	3.	10.	0.
1795	The Young Anglers' Pocket Companion (1st Edition)	Cole	Jeffery		7.	6.
1899	Fishermans' Luck	Van Dyke	"		4.	6.
1891	Fly Fishing and Fly Making	Keene	"		2.	6.
1864	The American Anglers' Book	Norris	"		8.	6.
1883	The Angler and the Loop Rod	Webster	"		2.	6.
1911	An Angler at Large	Caine	"		3.	6.
1908	Life, Scenery & Sport in Hampshire	Dewar	"		7.	6.
1873	Flies and Fly Fishing	Dick	"		2.	6.
1870	Anglers Garland (also 1871 edition)	Pearson	"		4.	6.
1912	Wings and Hackle	Hill	"		5.	0.
	Angling Dodges	Lowth	"		2.	6.
1854	The Book of the Axe	Pulman	"		5.	0.
1924	Fly Fishing in Northern Streams	Keith Rollo	"		1.	0.
1931	The Art of Fly Fishing	Keith Rollo	"		4.	6.
1874	By Lake and River	Francis	"		3.	6.
	The Anglers Complete Guide	Little	"		2.	0.
1920	An Anglers' Garland	Parker	"		2.	6.
1907	Salmon Fishing	Hardy	"		4.	6.
1896	An Anglers Basket	Pritt	"		2.	0.

Year Published	Title	Author	Purchased from	Price for Sale £	s	d
1912	Practical Dry Fly Fishing	Gill	"		2.	6.
1884	Fly Fishing	Hamilton	"		3.	6.
1929	Fishermans' Log	Ashley-Dodd	"		4.	6.
1901	Amateur Fish Culture	Walker	"		1.	0.
1898	The Rainbow Trout	Walker	"		1.	0.
1890?	Fishing Catalogue	Cummins	"		1.	0.
n.d.	The Gentleman Angler	–				
1817	The North Country Angler	–	"		2.	6.
	Plates from Ronalds' Entomology (probably for Sheringham edition)	–	"		10.	0.
1925	The Fellowship of Anglers	Hutchinson	Edwards		8.	0.
1860	Stray Notes on Fishing	Simeon	"		7.	0.
1836	Anglers Rambles	Jesse	"		7.	0.
1845	Fly Fishers Textbook	South	"		15.	0.
1882	1001 Books on Angling (Catalogue)	Sabin	"		10.	0.
1924	Books on Angling (Catalogue)	Silson Browne	–			
1921	Fly Fishers' Ephemeridae	Wauton	–			
1656	The Universal Angler containing the 5th edition of Walton, the 1st of Cotton and the 4th of Venables, damaged but in original binding and Containing H.T. Sheringham's bookplate.	Walton	Jeffery		15.	0.
1898	Days and Nights of Salmon Fishing	Scrope	Edwards		10.	0.
1913	The Game Fishes of the World	Holder	"		15.	0.
1931	Fishermen's Angles	Chalmers	"		15.	0.
1913	Fishing at Home and Abroad	Maxwell	"	2.	0.	0.
1936	River management	Coster	"		13.	0.
1821	Anglers' Companion	Price	"		10.	0.
1801	Practical Observations on River Trout	Short	"		10.	0.
1854	Fish and Fishing in Scotland	Knox	"		3.	0.
1811	{The Secrets of Angling, together with	Lauson	"	1.	4.	0.
1809	{Vanier on Fishing (trans)	Dunerobe	"			
1819	The Art of Fishing	Charleton	"		18.	0.
1911	An Anglers' Lines (Autographed copy)	Price	"		5.	0.

Year Published	Title	Author	Purchased from	Price for Sale £	s	d
1865	Secrets of Angling	Moffat	"		7.	6.
1927	Fish, Fishing and Fishermen	Caine	"		7.	6.
1895	Angling Travels in Norway	Sandeman	Thin		5.	0.
1902	Where to Catch Fish on the East Coast of Florida	Gregg	"		3.	6.
1851	Fly Fishing in Salt and Fresh Water	Anon.	"		4.	0.
1913	The Salmon Rivers of Scotland	Grimble	"		5.	0.
1923	Salmon and Other Things	Nicoll	"		2.	0.
1934	Tunny Fishing for Beginners	Taylor	"		2.	0.
1924	Salmon and the Dry Fly	La Branche	Foyle		4.	0.
1935	American Big Game Fishing	Connett	"		6.	0.
1931	Surtees on Fishing	Tidy				
1939	Modern Salmon Fishing	Bridges				
1936	Letters to a Salmon Fisher's Sons	Chaytor				
1808	Angler's Vade Mecum	Williamson	Edwards	1.	5.	0.
1902	The Speckled Brook Trout	Rhead	Brown		5.	0.
1862/5	Fishes of the British Islands (4 Vols)	Couch		1.	10.	0.
1879	British Fresh Water Fish (2 Vols)	Houghton		1.	10.	0.
19 . .	Salmon and Trout Magazine Nos. 35 – 106			5.	0.	0.
1880–1894	Anglers' Evenings (3 Vols)	–			15.	0.
1865	Trichoptera Britannica	McLachlan	Quaritch	1.	5.	0.
1924	Fly and Bait Casting	Hughes	Brown		3.	6.
1898	Angling	Blakey	"		6.	0.
1852	Coquet-Dale Fishing Songs	A North Country Angler	"		8.	6.
1886	The American Salmon Fisherman	Wells	"		3.	6.
n.d.	Spinning up to Date	Jock Scott	–		12.	6.
1944	Running Water	Barton	Presentation copy			
1929	Fifty Years with the Rod	Stirling	Edwards		15.	0.
1938	Fifty Years Angling	Adams	"		15.	0.
1937	Fishing Round the World	McCormick	"		12.	6.
1892	My Favourite Flies	Marbury	Marks	2.	15.	0.

Year Published	Title	Author	Purchased from	Price for Sale £	s	d
1898	Trout Fishing	Granby	Wetherhead		6.	0.
1829	Salmonia	Davy	"		12.	6.
1870	Modern Practical Angler	Pennell	"		8.	6.
1835	Piscatorial Reminiscences (and Gleanings)	Anon.	"		12.	0.
1918	Catalogue of Angling Book Plates		"		4.	6.
1857	The Anglers Guide	Young	"		2.	0.
1886	Les Oiseaux d'Eau ou Nageurs	O. Des Murs	"		8.	6.
1851	The Erne and its Legend	Newland	Sawyers	1.	1.	0.
1883	Fishing with the Fly	Orvis	Truslove		8.	6.
1860	The Fishing Rod	Glenfin	"		3.	6.
1898	The Salmon	Gathorne Hardy	"		6.	0.
1849	Alphabet of Angling	Rennie	"		3.	6.
1898	Salmon and Seatrout	Maxwell	"		7.	6.
1930	Rod Fishing for Salmon	Hutton	"		7.	6.
1940	Fly Tying	Burrard	"		7.	6.
1740	The British Angler	Williamson	Marks	3.	0.	0.

Appendix 11

Letter from G.E.M. Skues to R.B. Marston
Original was a holographic manuscript

10. III. 1914
Hyrst View
Campden Road
S. Croydon

Dear Marston

Messrs. A & C Black tell me there is now no objection to mention being made of the fact that Minor Tactics is just about to enter on a new Edition. It is just 4 years since it first appeared. It brought me many pleasant things but one very sincere regret, and that is that, though I hoped and believed I had done all that man could to avoid giving offence, yet to one friend of many years standing the book was a cause of a, to me, incomprehensible bitterness. I had hoped that time and the sense of the drift of opinion around him would have brought reconciliation. But now he has passed beyond the opportunity of that. I never ceased to have a cordial kindness for him and it is a sincere sorrow to me that for the last four years of his life our relations should have been clouded. I owe him gratitude not only for his work for angling, but for many kindnesses, not least being the putting of me up for the F.F.C

K R.

Sincerely yours

G E M Skues

Bibliography –
Sources and Printed Works

Sources for the Skues story are numerous. Even after the destruction of much of his correspondence when he quit London in 1940 there still remains a substantial amount of letters and papers, scattered in many places in Britain and abroad. These are crucial for an understanding of the process of his work and achievement, of his fishing and of the research that became a continuous part of it. They also contain many clues, sometimes subtle and unexpected, of the man behind the angler. They help, therefore, to fill the gap consequent upon the absence of diaries. We know from Skues' own admission that he made several attempts to keep an angling diary but could never keep it up. It is obvious that he kept a record from time to time, perhaps fleeting and informal, of his results on the river, otherwise the precision of the weights of fish caught and mentioned in his articles and books would not have been possible. The phrase 'my notes show' occurs in various places in his writings.

It is not known if he kept a personal diary, but from what is known of Skues and his character it cannot be surprising if it did not survive. In common with many reticent people Skues was not going to let anyone into his private world, whether in his lifetime or in posterity. He would have approved of the resolve of Henry James, who once observed: 'My sole wish is to frustrate as utterly as possible the post mortem exploiter.'

Primary Sources

I have examined nearly two thousand letters in manuscript, some in public depositories and others in private hands, the important ones of which include correspondence from or to Major John Evans, Robert Austin, Louis Bouglé, Edward Boies, Sir Tom Eastham, Dr Edwin Barton, Douglas Goodbody, Tommy Hanna, Paul Barbotin and – most prolific of all – George Monkhouse (729 letters). There is a second category of letters which, though important, exist in small quantities only, by or to

Frank Sawyer, Sir Joseph Ball, Charles Skues and a number of American anglers: Dr Warren Coleman, E. Baird Foster, Franklin B. Lord, Richard Carly Hunt, L.K. Moreshead, Otto von Kienbusch and James Leisenring.

At one time there would have been far more letters stored in Skues' house in Croydon. I have identified thirty-four collections that have been destroyed or have apparently been lost. In particular we would be much better informed if the letters and papers had survived relating to W.D. Coggeshall, G.M.L. La Branche, Irwin Cox, H.S. Hall, Col. E.W. Harding, H.T. Sheringham, Martin Mosely and W.H. Lawrie. Most significant of all might have been correspondence passing between Skues and Halford.

Other manuscript papers include the records of Skues' career at Winchester College, the twelve surviving volumes (two are lost) of Skues' commonplace books entitled 'Notions', the angling diary of Dr Norman McCaskie, the seventeen diaries kept by Dr Barton between 1922 and 1938 and a small sample of the papers of Sir Joseph Ball.

Skues' memoir 'Trivialities of a Long Life' exists in several typescripts, with some minor differences between them. It is a rambling, somewhat shapeless document, taken up and added to at different times over a period of years. After his death his brother tried to sort it out with a view to publication but eventually gave up in despair. It is probably not publishable, but it contains some interesting detail.

Printed Sources

At different times several devoted angling historians have worked hard to put the achievement of Skues before the public. In 1947 John McDonald published *The Complete Fly Fisherman,* an edition of the papers and letters of Theodore Gordon. It included ninety valuable letters from Gordon to Skues. McDonald admired Gordon's style and wrote: 'It is doubtful whether fly fishing thought has been more finely drawn anywhere in angling literature.' C.F. Walker worked on several collections of Skues' letters (mostly in private hands), and in 1956 produced *The Angling Letters of G.E.M. Skues.* As Skues had only died seven years earlier the letters were carefully edited to remove anything of a private and personal nature and to confine the text to fishing matters only. In 1977 Donald Overfield edited seventy-three articles and thirty letters written by Skues in the *Journal of the Flyfishers' Club.* This was a valuable piece of work, introducing many readers to material not readily available, although the above figures represent only a small fraction of Skues' output. In 1998 Kenneth Robson published edited extracts from Skues' books, carefully choosing those that threw light on the novelty and originality of his ideas. More recently Paul Schullery has collected a number of stimulating extracts from *The Way of a Trout with a Fly*. Walker and Overfield included some background information about Skues' life, and Robson a good deal. Skues' own selection of his past journalism was published in 1931 under the title of *Sidelines, Sidelights and Reflections*.

Apart from the above collections there are many of Skues' articles to be found in the old files of *The Fishing Gazette, The Field, The Salmon and Trout Magazine, The Bulletin of the Anglers' Club of New York*, and *Angling*.

Published Works

Published in London unless otherwise stated.

Andrew, Christopher, *Secret Service: The Making of the British Intelligence Community* (1985)

Bergman, Ray, *Trout* (New York 1943)

Carey, H.E., *One River* (1952)

Chetham, James, *The Angler's Vade Mecum* (1681)

Clarke, Brian and Goddard, John, *The Trout and the Fly* (1980)

Colvin, Ian, *The Chamberlain Cabinet* (1971)

Cutliffe, H.C., *The Art of Trout Fishing in Rapid Streams* (1883)

Dewar, G.A.B., *The Book of the Dry Fly* (1897)

Dilke, Christopher, *Dr Moberley's Mint-Mark* (1965)

Durnford, Richard, *The Diary of a Test Fisherman 1809 to 1819*, ed. H. Nicoll (1911)

Eaton, A.E., *Revisional Monograph of Recent Ephemeridae or Mayflies* (1883–1888)

Edmonds, H.H. and Lee, N.N., *Brook and River Trouting* (1916)

Firth, J.D'E., *Winchester* (1936)

Fuchser, L.R., *Neville Chamberlain and Appeasement* (1982)

Gathorne-Hardy, J., *The Public School Phenomenon* (1977)

Goddard, John, *Trout Fly Recognition* (1966)

Halford, F.M., *Floating Flies and How to Dress Them* (1886)

— *Dry-Fly Fishing in Theory and Practice* (1889)

Hanna, Thomas, *Fly Fishing in Ireland* (1933)

Harding, E.W., *The Flyfisher and the Trout's Point of View* (1931)

Harris, J.R., *An Angler's Entomology* (1952)

Hayter, Tony, *F.M. Halford and the Dry-Fly Revolution* (2002)

Hewitt, E.R., *A Trout and Salmon Fisherman for Seventy-five Years* (New York, 1948)

Hills, J.W., *A History of Fly Fishing for Trout* (1921)

— *A Summer on the Test* (2nd edn 1930)

— *My Sporting Life* (1936)

Honey, J.R. de S., *Tom Brown's Universe* (1977)

Lawrie, W.H., *The Book of the Rough Stream Nymph* (1947)

Leach, Arthur F., *A History of Winchester College* (1890)

Leisenring, James and Hidy, Vernon, *The Art of Tying the Wet Fly and Fishing the Flymph* (New York, 1971)

Mack, Edward C., *Public Schools and British Opinion since 1860* (1941)

McCaskie, Norman, *Fishing: My Life's Hobby* (1950)

McDonald, John, *The Complete Fly Fisherman* (New York 1947)

Mosely, Martin E., *The Dry-Fly Fisherman's Entomology* (1921)

Mottram, J.C., *Thoughts on Angling* (1948)

— *Fly Fishing: Some New Arts and Mysteries* (1915)

Newsome, David, *Godliness and Good Learning* (1961)

Oman, Sir Charles, *Memories of Victorian Oxford* (1941)

Overfield, T. Donald, *Famous Flies and their Originators* (1972)

— *The Way of a Man with a Trout* (1977)

— *50 Favourite Nymphs* (1978)

Phelps, T.T., *Fishing Dreams* (1949)

Ridding, Lady Laura, *George Ridding: Schoolmaster and Bishop* (1908)

Robson, Kenneth, *The Essential G.E.M. Skues* (1998)

Sawyer, Frank, *Nymphs and the Trout* (1958)

Schullery, Paul, *American Fly Fishing: A History* (New York, 1987)

Stewart, W.C., *The Practical Angler* (1857)

Tod, E.M., *Wet-Fly Fishing Treated Methodically* (1903)

Walker, C.F., *The Angling Letters of G.E.M. Skues* (1956)

Williams, A. Courtney, *A Dictionary of Trout Flies* (1949)

Index